WEDDING PLANNING AND MANAGEMENT

CONSULTANCY FOR DIVERSE CLIENTS

SECOND EDITION

MAGGIE DANIELS
AND CARRIE LOVELESS

Routledge
Taylor & Francis Group

LONDON AND NEW YORK

First edition published 2007
by Elsevier Inc.

Second edition published 2014
by Routledge
2 Park Square, Milton Park, Abingdon, Oxon OX14 4RN

and by Routledge
711 Third Avenue, New York, NY 10017

Routledge is an imprint of the Taylor & Francis Group, an informa business

British Library Cataloguing in Publication Data
A catalogue record for this book is available from the British Library

Library of Congress Cataloging in Publication Data
Daniels, Maggie
  Wedding planning and management: consultancy for diverse clients/
  Maggie Daniels and Carrie Loveless. – 2nd edition.
    pages cm
  Includes bibliographical references and index.
  1. Wedding supplies and services industry. 2. Wedding supplies and services
  industry–Management. 3. Weddings–Planning. 4. Consultants. I. Loveless,
  Carrie. II. Title.
  HD9999.W372D36 2013
  392.5068–dc23
  2013016881

ISBN: 978-0-415-64444-0 (hbk)
ISBN: 978-0-415-64445-7 (pbk)
ISBN: 978-0-203-07953-9 (ebk)

Typeset in Univers and Classic Roman Standard
by Florence Production Ltd, Stoodleigh, Devon, UK

Printed in Canada

For those who help to create
a happily ever after!

CONTENTS

ILLUSTRATIONS

FIGURES

TABLES

Accompanying online resources for both students and lecturers are available at: www. routledge.com/cw/daniels. Here you will find an extensive bank of support materials including customizable power point slides, links to further reading, links to relevant videos, video lectures per chapter, sample exam questions and sample costings, timelines and business proposals.

CASE STUDIES

ABOUT THE AUTHORS

MAGGIE DANIELS

Dr. Maggie Daniels (*MaggieDaniels.com*) is an Associate Professor and the Academic Program Coordinator for the Tourism and Events Management program at George Mason University (GMU). She has taught a wide variety of undergraduate courses over the past 20 years, including wedding planning as well as areas such as finance, events management, tourism planning, statistics, communication and research methods. In 2008, Maggie was named one of *Modern Bride*'s 25 Trendsetters along with icons such as Oscar de la Renta and Tiffany & Co. A recipient of the 2012 GMU Teaching Excellence Award, Maggie is a believer in experiential learning. She received her BA from Miami University of Ohio, her MA from the University of Georgia and her PhD from Clemson University.

Maggie has conducted extensive fieldwork-based research and has a combination of over 100 published papers, book chapters, professional presentations and technical reports to her credit. She partners with agencies in the Washington DC metropolitan area to assist them with event and tourism implementation and evaluation. Just a few of the media outlets that have featured her wedding and tourism expertise include *ABC Nightline News*, MSNBC, NPR, United Press International, *Fox 45 News*, *The Washington Post*, the *DC Examiner*, Washingtonian.com, the WallStreetJournal.com and SmartMoney.com. Maggie enjoys running, swimming, reading and traveling with her husband, Matt, and their son, Josh.

CARRIE LOVELESS

Carrie Loveless is the owner of Carried Away Events (*CarriedAwayEvents.com*), a wedding planning and events management company. She has more than 20 years' experience managing corporate and social events ranging from large trade shows to intimate weddings. She has been a guest lecturer at the Rhode Island School of Design and adjunct professor at George Mason University teaching Wedding Planning and Management. Ms. Loveless received a BA in English Literature from Chestnut Hill College and an MBA in Marketing from George Mason University. She studied interior decorating and design at the Corcoran College of Art and Design in Washington DC and the Rhode Island School of Design in Providence, and floral arranging at the Judith Blacklock Flower School in London and U. Goto Florist in Tokyo.

Ms. Loveless is a national spokesperson and Chairman of the Board of Directors for WomenHeart, the national coalition for women with heart disease. A heart attack survivor herself, Ms. Loveless received her spokesperson training at the WomenHeart Science and Leadership Symposium at the Mayo Clinic in the fall of 2008. When she is not planning events and reminding women that heart disease is their number-one health risk, she enjoys traveling and living around the world with her husband Bruce, a Rear Admiral in the US Navy, and their Wheaten Terrier, Dunkin.

ABOUT THE PHOTOGRAPHER

Rodney Bailey of Wedding Photojournalism by Rodney Bailey (*RodneyBailey.com*) is a photojournalist in the purest sense. He does not manipulate his surroundings, orchestrate his subjects or distract from the moments he is capturing. He has documented weddings for 22 years using this unobtrusive (and now trendy) approach and is one of the most sought-after wedding photographers in Washington DC. He has also worked in destinations such as Bermuda, Paris and Rome. Rodney's work has been featured in many of today's top bridal magazines including *Modern Bride*, *The Knot*, *"I Do" for Brides*, *Grace Ormonde Wedding Style*, *Engaged*, *Elegant Bride* and *Wedding Dresses*.

Rodney is also commissioned for corporate, fashion and commercial photography projects, though weddings still remain his passion. He has captured images for the Library of Congress, *Vogue* and Disney, as well as Oprah Winfrey and *O Magazine*. Rodney has been voted the top photojournalist in the *Washingtonian Magazine* for 14 consecutive years and is featured in *Grace Ormonde Wedding Style Magazine* as one of the top five photographers in Washington DC. During his down time, Rodney can still be found behind the camera; however, his subjects are sharks and sea life as he is an avid scuba diver and underwater photographer.

PREFACE

The first edition of this book was written to fill a void in wedding planning literature. When searching for a textbook for the wedding planning class at George Mason University, we found an array of books that targeted specific areas, but no single one had the breadth we sought. Specifically, we were looking for a book that covered four vital areas: first, the reader would need a strong foundation in the cultural, historical, social and political influences on weddings and marriage; second, the book had to include all of the specifics essential to the practice of planning weddings; third, the text should provide a clear overview of what it takes to start a wedding consulting business; and finally, the book had to be visually appealing in order to fuel the imagination of every reader. This comprehensive book did not exist, and we were faced with having our students purchase multiple texts or writing a book that brought all of these areas together. We chose the latter and the result was *Wedding Planning and Management: consultancy for diverse clients*.

Six years later, we find the landscape of weddings and marriage has altered dramatically. The question is not "What has changed?" but, instead, "What hasn't?!" Most seismic has been the shift in public opinion toward broad acceptance of same-sex marriage, leading to landmark legislative change. Simultaneously, the average age of marital onset continues to rise, as has the percentage of interfaith and intercultural marriages. Today's couples are diverse and their wants, needs and expectations for their weddings are sophisticated.

Another significant change since we first wrote the book pertains to the explosion of technology and related social media outlets. Smartphones and tablets have entered the mainstream, affecting how and with whom we do business. Wedding clients demand communication immediacy, and businesses that cannot respond are left behind.

Lastly, economic upheaval, combined with the fact that couples are more frequently footing the entire bill for their weddings, has resulted in more mindful spending habits. While the days of bling and conspicuous consumption are not completely forgotten, today's couples are returning to their roots and incorporating more casual elements in their weddings, such as DIY décor, comfort food, suits instead of tuxes and games such as cornhole rather than expensive entertainment at their receptions.

We sincerely hope that the second edition of *Wedding Planning and Management: consultancy for diverse clients* challenges and inspires you. Whether you are a student taking a wedding planning class, a bride planning her own wedding, a vendor working in the industry or an entrepreneur preparing to start your own consulting business, the ideas, case studies and images within this text are designed to spark both your curiosity and creativity.

Maggie Daniels and Carrie Loveless
March 2013

ACKNOWLEDGMENTS

The Beatles famously sang, "I get by with a little help from my friends . . ." With apologies to the songwriting team of Lennon and McCartney, we would like to say, "We get by with a *lot* of help from our friends." It is true. The second edition of *Wedding Planning and Management: consultancy for diverse clients* would not have come to life without the help of many good friends and colleagues.

Writing an exceptional book about wedding planning is like planning an exceptional wedding; you surround yourself with the best in the business and give them a forum to showcase their expertise. This is precisely what we have accomplished.

First and foremost, we would like to acknowledge and thank Rodney Bailey (*RodneyBailey.com*), Washington DC's best wedding photojournalist, for providing us with the stunning images found throughout the book. Our writing comes to life through the lens of his camera. Rodney's creative genius complements our narrative, allowing you to understand and visualize the roles of the consultant and many other wedding vendors.

In addition to Rodney, we owe a tremendous debt of gratitude to the many industry professionals and university scholars from around the world who contributed their words of wisdom and humorous anecdotes. Special thanks to the members of the Association of Wedding Professionals (*WeddingProfessionals.org*) who rallied around this project, as well as the many academic contributors who learned about the text through the *TRINET* and *SPRENET* listservs and hopped on board to share their international experiences. The names of these valuable colleagues are recorded throughout the book.

The students, faculty and staff at George Mason University have been tremendous sources of support for this project. In particular, our students' enthusiasm for this class from day one has been heart-warming. We remember all of you who signed up the first time the Wedding Planning and Management course was offered, in the spring of 2005. The class filled up on the first day of registration, so we opened a second section and it filled up just as quickly. We will never forget the student who, upon learning that there was not another seat available in the class, didn't miss a beat and said, "Well, I can bring my own chair!" How fabulous it is for us to have your ongoing excitement, innovation and even your foibles (Will we ever get you to spell stationery with *-ERY*?!) to draw upon.

A special shout out to Lindsey Reeves. Her diligence as a proofreader and editor has greatly minimized the number of errors you will find in the text – any remaining ones are our fault entirely! Marielle Barrow kindly assisted us by tracking down many of the numerous sources that are cited in the text. Thanks also to Emma Travis, Pippa Mullins, Emily Davies and the design staff at Taylor & Francis, for believing in this project and keeping us on track. We recognize that it is the rare textbook that has over 150 color images included, and greatly appreciate that you advocated on our behalf.

We would like to thank our friends and family members who kept us laughing and motivated throughout the project. Maggie could not have done it without the constant calls of support from her sister, Mary Gamberale, as well as girl-power sessions with Page Adgani, stress breaks with running partners, Ceil Boyle and Kris Richmond, and sanity checks with swim buddies at Cub Run. Margaret Cartier, Cynthia Morath, Sheri Masich and Jessi Godoy of our Moms' group provided laughs, playdates and excellent wine. Her mom and dad, Peggy and John Daniels, as well as siblings Janet Daniels, Jack Daniels and Gibby Bittman, have shown her the value of family. Maggie's husband, Matt Michel, listened tirelessly as she discussed content, and their wonderful son, Josh, provided all of the best hugs.

Carrie would like to thank her family and friends for their help and support with this project, particularly her mother and father, Judy and Walt Wosicki, her brother and his family, David, Yao, Walter and Samantha Wosicki, her sister and her family, Kimberly, Ashley and Michael Davis, and, of course, her husband and their dog, Bruce and Dunkin Loveless. Here's to Betsy Hannah, Toni Lipe and Nancy Smith for your encouragement and support throughout the writing process.

And last, but certainly not least, a special thanks goes to Earl Grey and the rest of the Twinings family, without whose contributions this book would not have been possible.

CHAPTER 1

Wedding consulting as a growth occupation. Titles and packages. Roles of the wedding consultant. The organization of this book. References

CHAPTER 2

Cultural hegemony and socialization for marriage. Mate selection: who decides? Wedding customs. References

CHAPTER 3

The quest for perfection and impulse buying. Invented traditions. Celebrity influences. Planning eco-weddings. References

CHAPTER 4

Female workforce dynamics. The missing male. Cohabitation. Divorce. Same-sex marriage. Intercultural and interfaith marriages. References

CHAPTER 5

Visiting friends and relatives travel. Honeymoon travel. Destination weddings. References

FOUNDATIONS

The beautiful traditions that you see each time you witness or plan a wedding are influenced by culture, religion, history, the media, family and politics. Thus, it is essential that you explore these dynamics to become an informed consultant with an appreciation of and sensitivity to the diverse needs of your clients.

Chapter 1 begins with an overview of the role and scope of wedding consultancy by highlighting information that explains why careers dealing with the business of weddings have grown substantially over the past 50 years. This chapter also introduces the multitude of roles held by wedding planners and previews the main features found throughout the text. Chapter 2 details how culture and religion influence marriage socialization, mate selection and wedding customs, with attention given to historical and modern hegemony. Chapter 3 explores consumerism and influence of the media on wedding planning purchase decisions. Chapter 4 reviews significant trends that are resulting in a changing family dynamic. Specifically, this chapter tracks the evolving definition of family by considering workforce changes, cohabitation, divorce, same-sex marriage and the blending of religious and cultural wedding traditions. Chapter 5 reflects on the contribution of weddings to local economic development through tourism, with attention given to guest travel, honeymoon travel and destination weddings.

The information provided in this section is designed to establish a context for the rest of the book. The material allows you to approach the practice of weddings with an understanding of where and how many traditions and beliefs about matrimony originated. The perspective gained by reading Section 1 will give you added sensitivity and confidence as you step into the business of wedding planning.

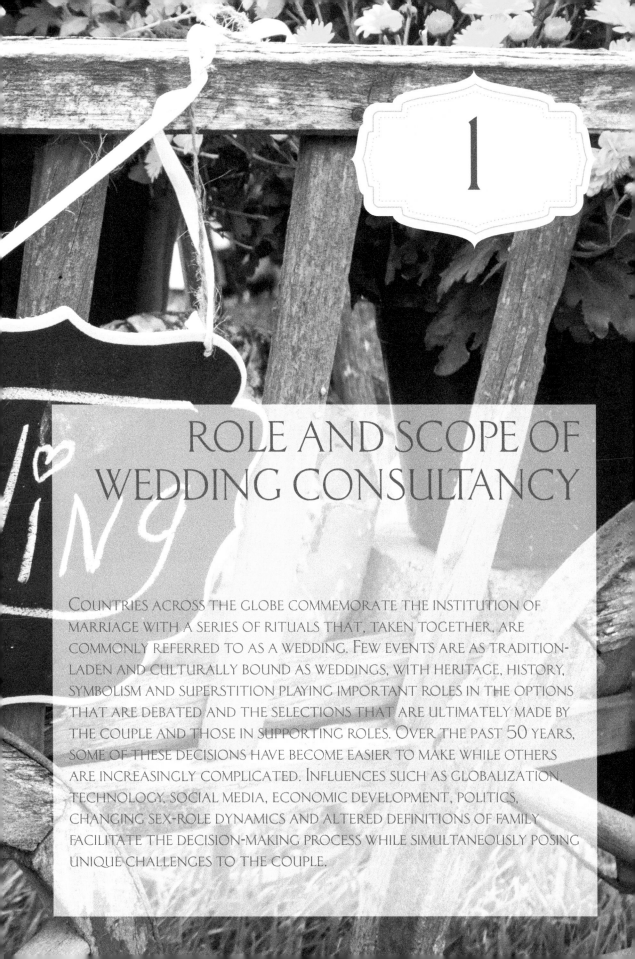

1

ROLE AND SCOPE OF WEDDING CONSULTANCY

COUNTRIES ACROSS THE GLOBE COMMEMORATE THE INSTITUTION OF MARRIAGE WITH A SERIES OF RITUALS THAT, TAKEN TOGETHER, ARE COMMONLY REFERRED TO AS A WEDDING. FEW EVENTS ARE AS TRADITION-LADEN AND CULTURALLY BOUND AS WEDDINGS, WITH HERITAGE, HISTORY, SYMBOLISM AND SUPERSTITION PLAYING IMPORTANT ROLES IN THE OPTIONS THAT ARE DEBATED AND THE SELECTIONS THAT ARE ULTIMATELY MADE BY THE COUPLE AND THOSE IN SUPPORTING ROLES. OVER THE PAST 50 YEARS, SOME OF THESE DECISIONS HAVE BECOME EASIER TO MAKE WHILE OTHERS ARE INCREASINGLY COMPLICATED. INFLUENCES SUCH AS GLOBALIZATION, TECHNOLOGY, SOCIAL MEDIA, ECONOMIC DEVELOPMENT, POLITICS, CHANGING SEX-ROLE DYNAMICS AND ALTERED DEFINITIONS OF FAMILY FACILITATE THE DECISION-MAKING PROCESS WHILE SIMULTANEOUSLY POSING UNIQUE CHALLENGES TO THE COUPLE.

Enter the wedding consultant. A spin-off of the larger discipline of events management, the wedding consultant acts as a liaison between clients and their chosen vendors. The goals of this introductory chapter are to highlight why this cutting-edge field of study represents a growth occupation; present the titles used and packages commonly offered by wedding consultants; delineate typical consultant roles; and offer an overview of the entirety of the text.

WEDDING CONSULTING AS A GROWTH OCCUPATION

There are four significant reasons why, globally, there is an increasing demand for trained professionals within this occupation. First is the fact that women's educational attainment and participation in the global workforce continues to rise. As will be detailed in Chapter 4, women across the globe are advancing their educations and putting those skills to use. For example, in the United States, the percentage of women in the workforce with a college degree has increased dramatically, from 11.2 per cent in 1970 to 36.4 per cent in 2010 (US Bureau of Labor Statistics 2011). When considering workforce share, in 1950, 30 per cent of those in the workforce were female and 70 per cent male; by 2010, women made up to 46.7 per cent of the workforce, a percentage that will stay fairly stable with a projection of 47 per cent by 2020 (Toossi 2012).

As a result, couples are marrying later, with the median age of first marriage increasing from approximately 20 (female) and 23 (male) in 1950 to 27 (female) and 29 (male) in 2011 (US Census Bureau 2011). Perhaps even more telling are the findings that 29.7 per cent of women and 39.1 per cent of men in the age range of 30–34 have never married, choosing to stay single or cohabitate (US Census Bureau 2012). In 1970, only 6 per cent of women in the age range of 30–34 had never married (US Census Bureau 2005). The bottom line is that more women are well educated and in the workforce, and therefore have less time but more disposable income to hire a wedding consultant to sweat the details so that they can have a dream wedding with minimal stress.

Second, interracial and intercultural marriages have increased dramatically, with younger and better-educated couples more likely to intermarry than older, less educated individuals. A study by the Pew Research Center illustrated that the percentage of spouses who were of different race or ethnicity more than doubled between 1980 (6.7 per cent) and 2010 (15 per cent) (Wang 2012). Wedding consultants can help successfully blend different ethnic traditions and rituals into the ceremony and reception.

Third, weddings entail significant financial output on what are often first-time purchase decisions that are emotionally laden and fraught with external pressures from family members, friends, colleagues and the media. As will be discussed in Chapter 7, wedding budgets vary dramatically based on geographic location and the global economy, but the average wedding hovers around $26,000 (The Wedding Report 2012). With close to 2.1 million weddings taking place on an annual

PHOTO 1.2 WEDDING CONSULTANTS HELP COUPLES BLEND DIFFERENT ETHNIC TRADITIONS.

SOURCE: WWW.RODNEYBAILEY.COM

basis (National Vital Statistics System 2012), the broader wedding market in the United States is worth $54.6 billion dollars annually. Couples are increasingly footing the wedding bill, with 36 per cent of couples paying for the wedding entirely themselves (The American Wedding Study 2012). A wedding consultant brings experience to the process, often saving couples money based on the knowledge and logic they bring into the process. Finally, international acceptance of divorce has led to a global increase in second marriages; accordingly, second marriages are a common occurrence. Wedding consultants can assist in making arrangements that support blended families. These trends clarify why more and more couples are hiring a wedding consultant.

TITLES AND PACKAGES

An individual entering the wedding business from a planning perspective has many titles from which to choose. Some of the more common include: wedding consultant, wedding planner, bridal consultant, wedding designer, wedding coordinator and wedding director. While all of these titles may be equally marketable, the terms wedding consultant and wedding planner will be primarily used in this text for the sake of consistency. Simultaneously, the word "you" will be used throughout the text to get you in the mindset of thinking like a wedding consultant. Irrespective of the title, a wedding consultant fulfills a number of identifiable tasks, which vary based on the package their clients select.

Consultant packages generally come in three types: comprehensive packages, partial packages and day-of packages. Consultants often also provide individualized *à la carte* or *ad hoc* services. For marketing purposes, most planners devise clever names for these packages and the services will vary somewhat; however, the nature of the three types is offered as a means of differentiation. For a *comprehensive package*, the consultant's involvement begins early in the planning process and extends until and often beyond the wedding day. Because of the time commitment and the variety of services performed, this is the most expensive type of package. With a comprehensive package, the consultant offers initial and ongoing assistance with areas including but not necessarily limited to: vision determination and overall design; budgeting, purchasing and payments; timelines, site layout and organization; vendor selection, negotiation and contracts; guest lists and mailings; legal issues such as the marriage license; and on-site implementation of the rehearsal, ceremony and reception, while acting as a liaison between the clients, the vendors and the guests. Specifics in each of these service areas will be offered throughout this text. In some comprehensive contracts, the clients have either no time or no desire to make vendor visits, and will literally hand over a credit card and entrust the consultant to make decisions on their behalf. More commonly, the consultant accompanies the couple on vendor visits, offering insight and advice along the way. Some planners will only accept comprehensive packages, as they want to be involved with every step of the planning process to ensure an outcome that matches their reputation and meets the expectations of their clients. When starting your business, however, you will most likely want to diversify your services.

Partial packages occur when clients have already initiated the planning process. Partial packages are often tiered in price based on the number of vendors that have already been selected and expectations in terms of vendor visits. With a partial package, clients generally already have a sense of their theme and are comfortable handling some of the details on their own, but have gotten stuck along the way in terms of pinpointing and selecting the appropriate service providers for their vision and budget. A wedding consultant can offer invaluable advice to the couple that does not have the time to comparison or quality shop. The assumption is that the consultant will make vendor suggestions and assist with setting up appointments, but not necessarily accompany the clients on all of the visits, as this is often the most time-consuming aspect of the planning process. As the expectation in terms of vendor visits increases, the price of the partial package should also increase. It is important that these details are specified in the contract, as discussed in Chapter 22. Partial packages should include timeline and site layout assistance, as well as on-site implementation of the rehearsal, ceremony and reception.

Day-of packages have become increasingly common and are designed for clients who have completed the planning process on their own, yet desire assistance and coordination during the rehearsal, ceremony and reception. The term "day-of" is a misnomer, in that it is essential for the

PHOTO 1.3 WITH COMPREHENSIVE PACKAGES, NO DETAIL IS TOO SMALL.

SOURCE: WWW.RODNEYBAILEY.COM

consultant to be involved prior to the wedding day if the oversight is to go smoothly. "Month-of" is more appropriate, because this is the minimum amount of time that a consultant should be involved, even if on a limited basis, to become familiar with the couple and obtain the necessary information to make the day flow. Specifically, the consultant will need a list of all vendors who will assist in the preparation and implementation of the wedding day timeline. It is imperative that the consultant touch base with each vendor and confirm the agreed-upon services. Further, the day-of consultant must prepare a site layout and timeline if these materials are not provided. These organizational materials will ensure that the consultant can be the primary point of contact during the rehearsal, ceremony and reception so that the couple can enjoy themselves without constant interruptions. The drawback of this type of package is that, if less-than-ideal vendor decisions have been made by the couple, the consultant will end up troubleshooting more than in cases where consultant-informed decisions were made. Generally, wedding consultants have a variety of trusted and established vendors that they can recommend. These relationships greatly facilitate the day-of process. Therefore, in cases where the consultant has not been involved in the vendor selection process, it is critical to obtain the vendor list as soon as possible. By touching base with each of the selected vendors in advance and confirming all arrangements, the consultant can more readily mitigate problems that may arise on the wedding day. See *Consultant in Action*, Case 1.1 for an example of a day-of consultant challenge.

CONSULTANT IN ACTION, CASE 1.1

A THORNY SITUATION

You have contracted with a couple for day-of services. They are being very conscientious with their funds, with several DIY elements. During the initial interview, the bride mentioned that she will be purchasing fresh-cut roses in bulk from a wholesale company, and she would like you to arrange the roses for their centerpieces. You are just starting your business and anxious to please, so you agree to design the centerpieces without asking for additional details beyond verifying that they will be providing the vases. Their August wedding is being held on the grounds of a quaint inn, and when you arrive several hours before the ceremony you see that the flowers have arrived in boxes that have been placed outside on the patio by a staff member, along with twenty 10-inch vases that were dropped off by the bride's mother. You open one of the boxes and quickly realize that the prickly thorns have not been stripped, which would not be a problem except for the fact that the stems are far too long for the vases. Luckily you have scissors and a knife with you, but after working on the first two vases your hands are bleeding, you are sweating profusely and you have over 200 quickly wilting roses left to arrange.

WHAT DO YOU DO?

PHOTO 1.4 CONSULTANTS ORGANIZE DAY-OF ACTIVITIES SO THE COUPLE CAN HAVE
A STRESS-FREE WEDDING DAY.

SOURCE: WWW.RODNEYBAILEY.COM

In addition to packages, many consultants offer *à la carte* or *ad hoc services* on a for-fee basis. While this may entail just about anything that pertains to the wedding process, some of the more common added services include: addressing, stuffing and mailing stationery elements (i.e., save-the-date, invitations, announcements, thank-you notes); monitoring the guest list; planning engagement parties, showers and post-wedding events such as day-after luncheons and honeymoons; gift selection, purchases and delivery (such as guest baskets at hotels); and preparing seating charts.

As a consultant, it is important that you carefully delineate the services that go with each package type as well as which services are considered add-ons. As will be discussed in the third section of this text, you need to be business savvy if you wish to stay in business.

ROLES OF THE WEDDING CONSULTANT

The wedding consultant will fulfill a variety of roles throughout the planning and implementation of any wedding. The nature of the package will influence those roles, as the comprehensive package will allow the consultant to become more fully integrated in the lives of the couple and their families, whether desirable or not! For any given couple, seven common roles the consultant may take on include service provider, decision-maker, organizer, artistic designer, confidant, mediator and friend.

First and foremost, never forget that the consultant is in a business relationship with the couple. As a service provider, you have specific obligations to fulfill and must maintain the highest standards of professionalism. These obligations extend beyond your clients and also include the chosen vendors. While you are often advocating and negotiating on behalf of your clients, your business depends on whether you also treat the wedding service providers fairly and respectfully. The third section of this text is devoted to establishing and building a sustainable business.

While the business relationship is paramount, other roles will emerge, some related to the nature of the business and others due to human nature. The consultant will often become the decision-maker by default. In particular, for those couples who select a comprehensive wedding package and want minimal involvement, the consultant will consistently make choices on behalf of the clients. In cases such as these, it is still important to give the couple the sense that they were involved in the final decisions. Even limited participation provides a feeling of ownership and accountability. Importantly, and to be explained more fully later in the text, as the consultant, you should never sign any contract on behalf of the couple, nor should you sign your own name to any vendor contract.

A third role you will take on as a wedding consultant is that of organizer. As the couple's consultant, the assumption is that any person involved in a given wedding can turn to you for direction. Timelines, checklists and itineraries are crucial to maintain a sense of order and clarity amidst all the confusion that can arise. A key facet of organization is time management. The wedding consultant must be able to prioritize the tasks that need to be completed and when each must occur. Having a comprehensive calendar for each wedding and written agendas for each meeting will help keep both you and the couple on task.

Your fourth role will be that of artistic designer. Many individuals get into the business of wedding planning because they have inherent good taste and a sense of flair that friends and family

PHOTO 1.5 MANY CONSULTANTS ARE HIRED FOR THEIR DESIGN EXPERTISE.

SOURCE: WWW.RODNEYBAILEY.COM

members have commented on throughout their lives. These traits lend themselves to helping couples bring their visions to life. Consultants must be careful, though, to not over-impose their views if that is not what the couple wants. Generally, however, a wedding consultant is hired in part because the couple wants artistic design advice as related to items such as stationery essentials, floral décor, linens and other decorative elements.

Few weddings are stress free, and the fifth role that a consultant often acquires is that of confidant. If you are involved from the onset, it is likely that clients and family members involved in the planning process will turn to you in moments of anxiety, pressure and strain. The line between business and interpersonal interactions blur as trust develops, and skilled communicators have a business advantage in that they have a repertoire of skills to sensitively assist clients in handling periods of emotional stress (Hargie 2011). You may quickly become the sounding board of choice and, as discussed more in Chapter 22, it is important to hone your listening skills and avoid giving advice when dealing with sensitive topics.

Should the stress of wedding planning move beyond the individual level, the consultant often acts as mediator, a sixth role. Mediators are not problem solvers per se, instead, they respond to conflict-laden situations by encouraging reflective dialogue through honest communication, constructive listening and empathic recognition (Stains 2012). As a mediator, the wedding consultant can help disputing parties by creating a forum where each gets to speak and listen, allowing for a depth of conversation that establishes insight so that those in conflict can work together to clearly define the problem, seek alternative and creative solutions and ultimately implement an agreed-upon strategy (Picard and Jull 2011). Many wedding planners form vendor relationships with marriage and family counselors, whom they can recommend to clients that are facing significant relational crises.

Finally, the relationship between the couple and the wedding consultant may evolve to the point of friendship. In many cases, consultants start their businesses by working with friends and family members. Because consultants depend on referrals, often friends will suggest your services to other friends, and your business grows from there. Importantly, you do not have to befriend your clients to have a successful business. Sooner or later, you will have a client whom you do not like at all, which does not mean you cannot have a successful working relationship. Friendship should be viewed as a natural outcome of some client–provider interactions rather than a forced business necessity. By the same token, the wedding vendors that you work with consistently over time may bridge the gap between colleague and friend.

THE ORGANIZATION OF THIS BOOK

This book is presented in three main sections: Foundations, Practice and Building Your Business. Section I is comprised of the first five chapters and delves into the foundations of weddings, including the cultural, historical, mediated, political and social factors that influence our widely held beliefs, values and preferences pertaining to weddings. Section II, which includes the middle 14 chapters, is devoted to practice, and concentrates on the services and associated vendors with whom the couple and consultant will interact. The growth in numerous industry sectors can be attributed to income derived from the business of weddings. Consultant checklists are found at the end of each of these chapters. Section III contains the final five chapters and concentrates on the steps needed to establish your wedding planning business.

Throughout the text, you will find four different types of case studies to complement the chapter material, entitled *Consultant in Action*, *Culture Corner*, *Vendor Spotlight* and *Research Roundtable*. First, *Consultant in Action* cases pose management situations based on scenarios that actual wedding planners or vendors have faced. You are challenged to think about how you would contend with the issues raised in each of these cases. Second, *Culture Corner* cases highlight unique and blended traditions, customs and practices from weddings around the globe. Third, *Vendor Spotlight* segments present tips of the trade as offered by top wedding vendors. Finally, each *Research Roundtable* includes a summary of an academic study that pertains to weddings and wedding planning.

Whether you are a student interested in becoming a wedding consultant, an already practicing wedding or events specialist, a vendor who provides wedding services or you are in the process of planning your own wedding, this book offers the information and tools necessary to successfully engage in the business of weddings. Our focus on diversity broadens the meaning and applicability of the principles, while the case studies and photojournalism bring the concepts to life.

REFERENCES

Hargie, O. (2011) *Skilled Interpersonal Communication: research, theory and practice*, 5th edn, New York: Routledge.

National Vital Statistics System (2012) 'National marriage and divorce rate trends', Centers for Disease Control and Prevention, Online. Available HTTP: <http://www.cdc.gov/nchs/nvss/marriage_divorce_tables.htm> (accessed 12 January 2013).

Picard, C. and Jull, M. (2011) 'Learning through deepening conversations: a key strategy of insight mediation', *Conflict Resolution Quarterly*, 29: 151–176.

Stains, R.R., Jr. (2012) 'Reflection for connection: deepening dialogue through reflective processes', *Conflict Resolution Quarterly*, 30: 33–51.

The American Wedding Study (2012) 'Brides', Online. Available HTTP: <http://candieanderson.com/2012/06/interview-2012-bridal-trends-with-brides-magazines-vice-president-and-publisher-michelle-myers.html> (accessed 11 January 2013).

The Wedding Report (2012) 'Wedding statistics, industry reports and wedding trends', Online. Available HTTP: <http://www.theweddingreport.com/> (accessed 10 January 2013).

Toossi, M. (2012) 'Labor force projections to 2020: a more slowly growing workforce', US Bureau of Labor Statistics, Online. Available HTTP: <http://www.bls.gov/opub/mlr/2012/01/art3full.pdf> (accessed 10 January 2013).

US Bureau of Labor Statistics (2011) 'Educational attainment of women in the labor force, 1970–2010', Online. Available HTTP: <http://www.bls.gov/opub/ted/2011/ted_20111229.htm> (accessed 23 January 2013).

US Census Bureau (2005) 'Number, timing, and duration of marriages and divorces: 2001', Current Population Reports, Household Economic Studies, Report Number P70-97.

—— (2011) 'Estimated median age at first marriage, by sex: 1890 to the present', Current Population Survey, March and Annual Social and Economic Supplements, Online. Available HTTP: <http://www.census.gov/population/soc demo/hh-fam/ms2.xls> (accessed 21 September 2012).

—— (2012) 'America's families and living arrangements: 2012', Online. Available HTTP: <http://www.census.gov/ hhes/families/data/cps2012.html> (accessed 10 January 2013).

Wang, W. (2012) 'The rise of intermarriage: rates, characteristics vary by race and gender', Pew Research Center, Online. Available HTTP: <http://www.pewsocialtrends.org/2012/02/16/the-rise-of-intermarriage/?src=prc-headline> (accessed 1 February 2013).

REVIEW

1. Name and describe a minimum of two reasons why the percentage of couples who rely on the services of a wedding consultant is increasing.

2. Name and differentiate three common types of wedding packages.

3. Name and describe four of the seven roles that are commonly held by wedding consultants.

TERMINOLOGY

- *À la carte* / *ad hoc* wedding services

- Comprehensive wedding package

- Day-of wedding package

- Mediation

- Partial wedding package

Photo 2.1 Weddings allow couples to blend their cultural traditions.

Source: www.RodneyBailey.com

2

WEDDINGS AND CULTURE

When considering the historical meaning and ongoing development of weddings, cultural traditions, underpinned by religion, have played a dominant role in how societies conceptualize, implement and realize the married state of being. For clients who closely identify with their heritage and/or have deep spiritual beliefs, the social implications will be very influential to the planning process and the associated rituals often comprise the most cherished moments of the wedding.

The goal of this chapter is not to cover the wedding-related influences of every unique human culture and subculture, as it would take a library of texts to complete such a task. Instead, the primary purpose is to consider how an individual's cultural background can shape how she or he thinks about weddings and marriage. As a consultant, you are urged to expand your knowledge by carefully interviewing each couple with whom you work to help them pinpoint the unique elements that will highlight their cultural identities. The blending of traditions that occurs in intercultural and interfaith marriages is discussed in more depth in Chapter 4. Further, specific attention is given to a wide variety of unique customs that accompany weddings in the *Culture Corner* cases throughout the text.

Cultural and religious wedding customs are embedded in history; however, at times, this context evolves to the point where the underlying meaning is lost. In other cases, the historical implications of a certain tradition may be seen as best forgotten; yet, it is through this exploration of the past that a depth of understanding of one's background can be reached. Weddings offer a unique opportunity to examine the nature and purpose of marriage norms through a cultural lens. As such, four points will frame this chapter: 1) cultural hegemony and socialization for marriage; 2) mate selection; 3) wedding customs; and 4) changes in identity due to marriage. As you will discover, each of these areas is bound by both geography and heritage.

CULTURAL HEGEMONY AND SOCIALIZATION FOR MARRIAGE

WHAT IS HEGEMONY?

The foundations of marriage are rooted in history and cultural hegemony. While there is widespread support for considering the historical past and how it influences modern weddings, the concept of hegemony is a contested term and there is debate regarding the hegemonic influences on weddings. *Hegemony*, in its most generic form, is related to terms such as authority, domination, subjugation, order and control. More specifically, definitions of cultural hegemony focus on how power is used, and potentially abused. The creation of cultural hegemony is dependent on a wide acceptance of its legitimacy in the form of social norms, values and belief structures that lead to social order and consent formation (Condit 1994; Prys and Robel 2011). Hegemony, at its worst, involves socially prescribed exclusion and violence. When considering the roots of marriage and weddings, there is significant evidence that hegemonic standards existed. These standards of order, power and control maintain influence in many cultures today.

HISTORY AND MARITAL HEGEMONY

Historically, marriage put women at a sexual and economic disadvantage. Marriage facilitated sexual cooperation by "transferring to a husband the right for sexual control over his wife" (Smith

2004: 491). The transfer of sexual power to the male had inherent risks; for example, "until the mid-nineteenth century in England, a husband was legally permitted to use physical violence to secure the conjugal services of his wife. Alternatively, a wife could be jailed or confined in the matrimonial home for refusing marital rights" (Smith 2004: 491). Further, historically, a woman's property was lost upon matrimony; thus, making her financially dependent on her husband and solidifying his dominance (Will 1999).

Under such a threat of dominance, why did women desire to marry? Researchers suggest that women were set up, so to speak, with societal messages of romantic love as a desirable outcome, while glossing over the fact that they were participating in their own oppression, allowing the interests of the powerful to be maintained (Wilding 2003).

Importantly, marital hegemony was not and is not limited to women. Many historic weddings are worthy of analysis because they took place in an environment hostile to unions. For example, Will examined slave marriages in the antebellum South and explains that, "the Southern legal system never recognized slave marriages on the grounds that property could not enter into a legal contract" (1999: 100). Some slave owners forbade their slaves to wed, some disdainfully allowed the proceedings to take place and others approved the unions because they felt marriage strengthened the slaves' ties to the plantation, in essence, supporting the hegemony. In rare cases, the owners allowed for Big House weddings, which took place in the plantation home with the support and assistance of the masters. The primary risk associated with marriage was that masters could sell one slave while maintaining the other. Regardless, the importance of the ceremonies and the commitment that was evidenced in slave marriages was apparent because, "to slaves, wedding ceremonies and receptions legitimized their personal relationships to the extent possible within the slave system" (Will 1999: 113).

Similarly, *miscegenation* laws, defined as statutes prohibiting interracial marriage, existed in the United States for over 300 years (Pascoe 2004). The first miscegenation law was passed in the colony of Maryland in 1664 and, by the Civil War, similar laws were passed through much of the south and mid-west and were continuing to move west (Pascoe 2004). Civil rights groups began to openly challenge the laws in the 1920s, and in 1967 the United States Supreme Court declared all remaining state miscegenation laws unconstitutional in the landmark case *Loving v. Virginia* (US Supreme Court 1967). *Culture Corner*, Case 2.1 summarizes the historic civil rights case. Fast-forward over 40 years to 2009, when Justice of the Peace Keith Bardwell who, "through his unabashed and unswerving devotion to racism" (King 2009), refused to marry an interracial couple. The public outcry, coupled with a federal discrimination lawsuit, resulted in Bardwell's resignation (CNN 2009).

MODERN MARITAL HEGEMONY

While the case of Keith Bardwell illustrates that many hegemonic principles of marriage are widely condemned, the fact remains that controlling practices supported by the social order are still practiced today. A compelling example pertains to child wedding ceremonies.

CULTURE CORNER, CASE 2.1

MILDRED JETER AND RICHARD LOVING

Mildred Jeter and Richard Loving did not see themselves as civil rights activists. Instead, they were childhood sweethearts who happened to be African American (Jeter) and Caucasian (Loving). When the Virginia couple returned from their Washington DC wedding to set up their new home, the police were called. "Caroline County Sheriff R. Garnett Brooks rousted them from their bed at 2 a.m. in July 1958 and told them the District's marriage certificate was no good in Virginia. He took them to jail and charged them with unlawful cohabitation. They pleaded guilty, and Caroline County Circuit Court Judge Leon M. Bazile sentenced them to a year's imprisonment, to be suspended if they left the state for the next 25 years" (Sullivan 2008: A01). They moved to DC, but were arrested again five years later for traveling together. This time, they fought back. Working with an attorney from the American Civil Liberties Union, the case went to the US Supreme Court, which on June 12, 1967 unanimously declared: "There can be no doubt that restricting the freedom to marry solely because of racial classifications violates the central meaning of the Equal Protection Clause" (in Sullivan 2008: A01). The Lovings, who lived a modest, quiet life and never viewed themselves as pioneers, achieved their goal to move back to their hometown in Virginia.

SOURCE: NEWBECK (2004); SULLIVAN (2008)

The problem of child wedding ceremonies has commanded international attention. Although widely denounced and often performed illegally, child wedding ceremonies are still an accepted practice in many developing countries, fueled by poverty, illiteracy and food shortages (Raghavan 2012). *Girls not Brides: The Global Partnership to End Child Marriage* (2012) estimates that, annually, 14 million girls under the age of 18 are married. While child marriage is a global problem, UNICEF (2012) findings indicate that the five countries with the highest rates of child marriage are Niger, Chad, Mali, Bangladesh and Guinea. In Niger, 75 per cent of girls marry before the age of 18 and nearly half before the age of 15 (UNICEF 2012). Raghavan notes that "struggling parents might marry off their daughters even earlier for the dowries they fetch, including animals and cash, to help the families survive" (2012: A1). A study by Nasrin (2011) indicates that the persistence of dowry exchanges in rural areas of Bangladesh, in spite of laws against these practices, has resulted in an ongoing subordination and disempowerment of women. "In many poor countries, girls are viewed as commodities, used as currency or to settle debts. In some cases, men 'reserve' especially young girls to marry them later as a way to unite families and communities" (Raghavan 2012: A11).

Archbishop Desmond Tutu, who is a Nobel Peace Prize-winning human rights activist, has joined the *Girls not Brides* initiative to assist in the campaign to end child marriage by 2030. During an interview, Tutu explained that the tradition arises from not only the economic benefits from dowries and having one less mouth to feed, but also fears of young, unmarried women being common targets of rape; therefore, child marriage is seen as a way to protect a girl's virtue (Rein 2012). Child brides are typically forced to leave school, therefore limiting their options and creating a cycle of poverty. Further, they are propelled into a sexual relationship and childbearing, with emotional and physical consequences: "The statistics are that girls who give birth when they are under 15 are five times more likely to die giving birth than girls of 19 and over. And their children are 60 times more likely to die before their first birthday" (Rein 2012: C3). Child marriage has been denounced as a form of slavery, and organizations around the globe are working together to end this hegemonic practice.

In most developed countries, hegemonic practices in relationship to marriage have abated or are being openly challenged. For instance, same-sex marriages, which will be discussed in detail in Chapter 4, are an illustration of a civil rights movement with significant political momentum. Yet, in spite of significant progress, social expectations in relationship to weddings and marriage still abound. Domestic relationships have evolved; yet, the work–family struggle (as discussed more in Chapter 4) is still higher for women. Moreover, for those who elect not to marry or simply never find "the one," there remains a social stigma. The married state is viewed as the social norm for adults and those who do not participate, but wish to, may feel excluded from certain social contexts because of their singleness and may suffer from depressive symptoms, in particular as the gap between their desired age of marriage and their current age widens (Carlson 2012; McCarthy 2012). Even in a world where cohabitation has become a commonplace replacement for marriage (Liu and Reczek 2012), a dominant ideology of marital expectations continues, as

> the expectation of a woman to marry (a man) and do so in a wedding with the costly pageantry associated with it, . . . has become so inculcated into everyday practices and values regarding social life that we do not even question them.
>
> (Engstrom and Semic 2003: 149)

The assumption embedded in a lifetime of media messages is that a lavish wedding becomes "*the* life goal for women" (Engstrom 2008: 61). While progress has been made, a hegemonic standard remains intact.

Returning to the definition of hegemony, having a social norm that dictates a marital state is not necessarily a negative thing, as many significant benefits related to income, child rearing, physical health, psychological well-being, social ties and longevity have been correlated with a joint household (Kuperberg 2012; Liu and Reczek 2012; Musick and Bumpass 2012). However, this standard gets muddied by redefined racial and gender discrimination, resulting in a "messy" hegemony that is often harder to pinpoint but results in "contradictory, conflicted, and ambiguous relationships" (Coontz 2000: 290). As will be discussed in detail in Chapter 4, the evolution of the family has presented positive changes accompanied by new challenges for couples considering marriage.

MATE SELECTION: WHO DECIDES?

MATE SELECTION BY CAPTURE OR ARRANGEMENT

Human mate selection may or may not include the input of those who are getting married. Mate selection by capture and by arrangement are two approaches where at least one party has little say in the matter. The idea of a woman being abducted into marriage seems antiquated and is generally relegated to discussions of ancient customs (see Ingoldsby 1995). However, this form of mate selection still exists in some areas, most notably in the country of Kyrgyzstan, located in Central Asia, where the practice of nonconsensual bridal abduction or kidnapping is the beginning of approximately 12,000 marriages annually (Radio Free Europe 2012). This illegal and often violent custom is known as *ala kachuu* or "grab and run" and is often chosen so men will not have to pay a bridal price or because they wish to prove their manliness (Smith 2005: A1). Once girls have reached their teen years, they often suffer from anxiety and the fear of abduction, as cases generally involve hysterical women screaming for freedom and being denied food, drink and sleep while they are cajoled to accept the groom (Lom 2004). While most women eventually submit and often are ultimately content, cases of rape and suicide exist (Sadiq 2004). This common occurrence, while a largely taboo topic in Kyrgyzstan, gained worldwide attention when academic Petr Lom filmed a graphic documentary on the subject that was broadcast on PBS (Lom 2004). In 2012, Kyrgyzstan lawmakers passed a bill to increase the maximum jail terms for bridal kidnapping from three to ten years (Radio Free Europe 2012).

A second form of mate selection, marriage by arrangement, was historically enacted for economic reasons, to preserve bloodlines or to advance political agendas. However, this form of mate selection is still common in countries such as Japan and India. For example, wedding-related details documented in a Cable News Network (CNN) report included the finding that government officials from India indicate that 95 per cent of marriages are arranged, with supporters noting that arranged marriages come with the automatic support of the family, and that religious, social and financial backgrounds are similar thus contributing to a very low divorce rate (Udas 2012). While *ad hoc* evidence suggests that most couples have a say in these "arranged" marriages, cases of couples having little to no input are still common. For instance, the CNN report highlights the marriage of Priyanka and Aditya Anand, who met the first time with their families for a dinner and the next day agreed to marry. Priyanka is working on her MBA and Aditya is a Wall Street trader. Both are global citizens and have travelled widely, but felt that, when it came to marriage, it would be decided based on cultural traditions. Priyanka explains that you grow up knowing that you have to be open to the idea of arranged marriage, the marriages mostly work out and that ultimately those selected can reject the match. This issue of choice is relevant, as it does not always apply. The same CNN report indicates that, in rural areas, girls are seldom given any say and often feel forced into the arrangement.

MATE SELECTION BY CHOICE: THERE IS AN APP FOR THAT!

If mate selection is not externally determined, individuals are left to their own devices to select a suitable partner. Even in these cases, social, biological, chemical and anthropological cues will influence selection. Just a few of the determinants that have been studied include cultural/religious similarity, social mobility, educational background, occupational equivalence, personality, physical attractiveness and pheromones.

For instance, anthropological researcher Helen Fisher (2004) describes how four neurotransmitters (i.e., chemicals that send messages to the brain) impact the likelihood that we fall in love. She explains that high levels of dopamine, associated with reward and pleasure, increase the susceptibility of falling in love. Norepinephrine, a stimulant related to stress, is linked to the elation and general feelings of craziness associated with falling in love. Serotonin, which creates feelings of calm, lowers in the early stages of love, explaining the anxiety associated with new romance. Finally, oxytocin influences feelings of trust and bonding, thereby creating feelings of attachment when released. Fisher's research illustrates how the balance of these compounds can influence if and when individuals fall in love.

While an understanding of how our brain is wired for love is all well and good, it does not necessarily help you get a date. In modern times, we are increasingly relying on the mobile dating market, where "smartphones and apps are just the shiny new tools in the age-old quest for love. . . . Globally, the mobile dating market is expected to be worth $2.3 billion by 2016, up from $1 billion in 2011, according to Juniper Research" (Jayakumar 2012: G1). Dating apps can target general audiences or a distinct segment, such as seniors or single parents, and each app touts the specialized features that make it better than the competition. Most dating app users note that they would prefer to meet someone without the use of technology and many express privacy concerns or worry about catfishing (i.e., an online relationship with someone who has presented a false identity), in particular when linking their profiles to their social network; yet, mobile dating services offer a valuable means for meeting new people in a world progressively on the go (Jayakumar 2012).

Technology improvements, in general, have been linked to isolation and social fragmentation; as such, individuals seeking a mate may be "increasingly on their own in changing societies, yet empowered with proliferating social media and personalized communication technologies" (Bennett 2012: 21). Undergraduate students generally note that their social opportunities are broad enough that they do not need to rely on dating services. However, once in the workforce, ready access to potential dating partners may be minimized, making mobile options more useful.

PHOTO 2.2 HUMAN MATE SELECTION HAPPENS IN A VARIETY OF WAYS.

SOURCE: WWW.RODNEYBAILEY.COM

In terms of relational development, technology again plays a role. Texting and social media outlets such as Facebook have both enhanced and hampered the dating scene. The explosion of texting, tweeting and posting on Facebook has been accompanied by a rapid decline of telephone conversations, in particular for the 18–24 age bracket (Shapira 2010). *Research Roundtable*, Case 2.2 summarizes how undergraduates taking our wedding planning class at George Mason University view the impact of texting on dating relationships.

Combining technology and anthropology, Fisher's work suggests that, once you meet someone who interests you, the ways to increase the likelihood that the person will fall for you include: 1) discovering the activities that are very pleasurable and rewarding to the person and participating in them, and/or 2) introducing the person to novel activities that are physically or cognitively stimulating. Both of these approaches are likely to increase levels of dopamine and norepinephrine, thus priming the person's brain circuitry to send messages indicating the desire to spend more time with you (Newman 2012).

Yet another way we seek a mate is by considering the selections of others. *Mate-choice copying* is an imitation phenomenon initially studied in animals that suggests that a female may seek an already chosen male because the fact that he has already been selected indicates his suitability

RESEARCH ROUNDTABLE, CASE 2.2

TEXTING AND DATING

Purpose: To determine undergraduate students' perceptions of the influence of texting on dating relationships.

Methods: Undergraduate students enrolled in an online wedding planning course were asked to respond to the following questions, using a blog format:

- How many text messages do you send a week?

- How many phone calls do you make a week?

- How has texting influenced modern dating relationships?

Results: The responses from students from three semesters of classes were analyzed. The number of texts sent per week ranged from 200 to 600, while the number of calls made per week ranged from 1 to 40. Thematic analysis illustrated relational concerns specific to: misinterpretation of content and emotions; decreased conversational confidence/competence; arguments based on different beliefs regarding the frequency of texting needed or allowable response time; faster relational fatigue due to non-stop communication; and insecurity/jealousy based on knowledge of a partner's texting patterns with others.

Conclusion: While undergraduate students appreciate the efficiency and practicality of texting, they indicate that texting increases the complexity of interpreting emotional meaning, often leading to relational discord.

as a mate (Uller and Johansson 2003). In a study of female undergraduates having introductory conversations with two men in a research setting, the women found the man who was wearing a wedding ring to be equally desirable as a man who was not wearing one, as indicated by willingness to have dinner, engage in sex and start a serious relationship (Uller and Johansson 2003). The perception of commitment did not appear to decrease the interest in the ostensibly married male subject. Chances are that you know someone who always seems to be attracted to someone who is taken, or perhaps has been unfaithful during a relationship, or is known to "steal" the significant others of friends. The inherent desirability of those who are already involved in a relationship is a factor that appears to influence human behavior as well.

RESEARCH ROUNDTABLE, CASE 2.3

MATE SELECTION IN KISUMU, KENYA

Purpose: To determine how individuals in Kisumu, Kenya search for a suitable spouse. Do specific characteristics relate to the outcome of the relationship?

Methods: Respondents, ages 18–24, provided detailed information about each of their romantic and sexual partnerships over the last ten years. A total of 1,365 relationships were analyzed based on relationship outcome (ended, ongoing dating, engagement or marriage).

Results: Motivations for entering relationships included liking the individual's personality, being in love, physical attraction, wanting sex, receiving money/gifts, wanting a partner and wanting to find a spouse. The most common reason cited for ending a relationship was sexual infidelity. Those who started a relationship with the intent to find a partner were significantly more likely to marry than those whose motivation was based on physical attraction. Pregnancies were common due to inconsistent condom use while dating, with close to half of the 214 pregnancies reported occurring prior to marriage.

Conclusion: While sexual exclusivity is highly valued when choosing a life partner, concurrent partnerships are common. HIV prevention messages that promote abstinence appear to be going unheeded.

SOURCE: CLARK *ET AL.* (2010)

In sub-Saharan Africa, the AIDS epidemic has complicated the mate selection process. The process through which mate selection occurs in Kisumu, the third largest city in Kenya, is summarized in *Research Roundtable*, Case 2.3.

WEDDING CUSTOMS

Cultural customs related to weddings occur before, during and after the wedding day itself. Festivities prior to the wedding start with the proposal and then often focus on gifts that will assist the new couple in setting up their joint household. Dowry and bride price practices are still common in some countries, as illustrated in *Culture Corner*, Case 2.4. Other countries use wedding customs to celebrate their heritage, as demonstrated in *Culture Corner*, Case 2.5.

The Westernized wedding shower, also commonly referred to as the bridal shower, is an anticipated pre-wedding ritual that was historically conceived as an offshoot of dowry practices to prepare brides for marriage. Legend has it that bridal showers originated in Holland. According to Clark, a young woman wanted to marry a poor Dutch miller whose generous nature had led him to give all of his possessions away to those in need, "so that when the time came to marry, he had nothing left to offer his prospective bride" (2000: 7). The girl's father, fearing that the miller would not be able to adequately provide for his daughter, forbade the marriage and refused to provide a dowry. Out of appreciation for the miller's longstanding kindness, the community came together and showered the girl with household items so that she could marry the miller (Clark 2000). Adaptations of this account are in the folklore of many countries. In the United States, most women marrying for the first time have bridal showers regardless of their financial status. These events are often held a month or so before the wedding, involve food and sometimes games, are hosted by either a family member or close friend and focus on opening gifts from the guests that have been requested by the bride through her registry.

Men are included in wedding showers to varying extents. In some cases, the groom is the only male and may make a late entrance, primarily to thank the guests. Occasionally, the shower is planned for the groom and the bride is not present. Increasingly, couples opt for a co-ed shower, which includes female and male guests. Montemurro (2005) found that, in comparison with traditional bridal showers, co-ed showers are more likely to take place at night, involve alcohol, have less emphasis on gift opening, follow a neutral or masculine theme (e.g., lawn tools) and the groom-to-be often takes on the role of comedian to maintain his sense of masculinity and heterosexuality. Gift giving as associated with showers and weddings is discussed more in Chapter 18.

Many wedding customs reflect the religious or cultural affiliation of the bride and/or groom, as will be discussed in cases throughout this book. Although religion remains a dominant influence for most weddings, an individual's spiritual identity is not always directly attached with a traditional religious group. Religiosity has decreased over the years, with 20 per cent of all US adults and 33 per cent of adults under the age of 30 indicating no specific affiliation (Boorstein 2012; Diener *et al.* 2011).

While religious ties have lessened, cultural bonds remain strong. For example, the Mehndi (henna) ceremony is a much-anticipated tradition for brides from India as well as their female family members and friends. This custom is described in *Culture Corner*, Case 2.6.

Wedding rituals vary from modest proceedings that involve only the necessitated rites to lavish, lengthy affairs. Amish couples, at one end, usually marry on a Tuesday or a Thursday in autumn with a simple ceremony that stresses dignity and devotion, followed by a bountiful feast prepared by and for the community (Clark 2010; Wagner 2011). On the other end of the spectrum are the

CULTURE CORNER, CASE 2.4

A TRADITIONAL SETSWANA WEDDING

Botswana is an African country located in the southern African region. Its people are referred to as Batswana and the culture is called Setswana. The marriage is governed by set customs and rituals. The traditional Setswana wedding/marriage process starts off with the boy informing his mother and father that he has found "*sego sa metsi*," a lady he is interested in marrying. The terminology here implies someone who will take responsibility for household chores and important among this is fetching water (Metsi). The traditional wedding is a relationship between two families: the family of the bride and the groom as well as their extended families. The father of the groom does not play an active role in negotiations that follow. Instead, he delegates the negotiation process to his younger brother (Rrangwane) and his wife's brother (Malome). The first process is called "*go bona lelwapa*," a background check on the girl to ensure that she comes from a "good home." If the background check is positive, feedback is disseminated to the two families and a meeting made up of the boy's extended family is convened. The aim of the meeting is to inform the elders of the maternal and paternal families that the boy has "*found a flower that has caught his eye* (a wife)." It is during this meeting that a date is set to formally approach the girl's family and inform them of their intention to marry their daughter. The meeting is also used to negotiate "Bogadi" dowry for the girl. The delegation from the boy's family is composed of the boy's father, his father's sister "Rakgadi", and the initial two men who visited the girl's family (Rrangwane and Malome). A second meeting will then be arranged depending on the response of the girl's family. This second meeting is to pay "Bogadi" and hold a traditional wedding ceremony.

Bogadi is generally eight young cows. The Bogadi is shared to show the importance of the extended family in the bringing up of the girl. The beneficiaries to Bogadi include the girl's father, her father's sister "Rakgadi," her mother's younger sister "Mmangwane" and "Malome." The traditional wedding takes place the day the cattle are brought to the in-laws. It is very important that cattle are paid early in the morning before sunrise. They have to be driven to the chief's kraal to legalize the marriage and also to ensure that, if there are any problems in the future, the chief and other villagers will bear witness that the marriage actually took place and the man paid the required bride price. Once the cattle have been handed over to the girl's family, the other members of the extended families are formally introduced.

CASE SUBMITTED BY HARETSEBE MANWA

CULTURE CORNER, CASE 2.5

MACANESE WEDDINGS

The 450-year-plus history of the Portuguese administration in the tiny city of Macau, China, has created a unique mixed race of Eurasians, of mostly Chinese and Portuguese ancestries. The Macanese people live life with their own unique traditions, food and language; hence very different from the majority, who are Chinese, and many other minority groups who call Macau home. In part due to the dying culture of the Macanese, and partly because of the fashion, the Macanese people have no real opportunity to celebrate their heritage, except during life events like baptism, marriages, funerals, and certain festivals such as Christmas and Catholic feast days. Social events gather people and are important to communities; therefore, weddings are considered to be very important occasions and appointments on the calendars of Macanese people. The Macanese calendar of events and traditions are structured around the Catholic Church; the celebration of holy matrimony is not an exception. A typical Macanese wedding is only distantly similar to a Chinese one for this reason, and has a lot of Portuguese influence instead.

The Macanese couple adopts the practice of bachelor and bachelorette parties known as *despedida de solteiro* (farewell of single status). For the groom, this is typically organized by the groom's best friends or wedding godfather. The witnesses of Macanese weddings, usually a male and female friend or relative, are considered to be the godparents of the new couple, which may not necessarily be the same as their respective baptism godparents. Unlike the majority of grooms in Macau, who are of Chinese descent, Macanese grooms do not meet their brides until at the wedding venue, which is always in a parish church. Depending on the couple, if both are Catholics, the wedding ceremony is conducted in full with a complete service, whereas, if only one of the couple is a Catholic, the ceremony is simply a religious blessing of their matrimony. The law in Macau allows marriages to be registered either in churches or officially designated conservatories. Therefore, it is interesting to note that many Chinese couples, particularly brides, opt to become a Catholic for a typical dream wedding of walking down the aisle in a church setting.

Many Chinese weddings are scheduled in the late morning or early afternoon, leaving ample time in the day to carry out other traditional rituals until the wedding banquet in the evening. Macanese weddings are typically scheduled early in the afternoon, followed by a luncheon or *cha gordo* (fat afternoon tea) instead of an extravagant banquet. Depending on budget and the social circle of the newlyweds, this catered gathering can happen anywhere from their own homes to a hotel ballroom, a local restaurant to more exotic venues such as a theatre dining room. In the old days when professional wedding planners, florists and decorators were unavailable, most decorations for the wedding venues were done by family members or friends. These include ample homemade dolls in bridal dresses for guests to take home, wedding rum cakes wrapped in a folded cake lace paper, and handmade paper flowers with a coconut base. It is also worth noting that the use of coconut is by no means accidental because many older Macanese people related the linkage of the Macanese to Chinese ancestry; the sound of coconut in Cantonese, *yeh chi*, rhymes with the words 'grandfather' and 'son', hence the auspicious symbol of parenthood, the next stage of life.

Case submitted by Ubaldino Couto

Photo 2.3 Many wedding customs reflect the cultural background of the bride or groom.

Source: www.RodneyBailey.com

weddings of the elite class, celebrities and royal families, where the festivities can cost millions of dollars and span several days.

The extent to which a person's identity shifts upon entering the marital state also has cultural influences. Symbolic indicators of marriage send the message to the community at large that a person's marital status has changed. In many countries, some symbols of the marital state remain primarily within the female domain, for instance, the changing of the family name. With more women entering the workforce and delaying marriage, those opting for alternatives to a complete change of name have increased, in part because they may not want to lose their professional identity. Therefore, a woman may choose to hyphenate her last name or simply keep her maiden name rather than changing her surname to that of her husband's.

The social convention of wearing a wedding ring is another symbolic indicator of marriage. In most cultures, traditionally only the woman was given a wedding ring, but now a double ring ceremony is commonplace in many countries. The role of the media in the transition from a single to double ring ceremony will be detailed in Chapter 3. The *Claddagh* ring, made up of heart, hands and crown, is an excellent cultural example of symbolic change in relational status as well as a timeless symbol of enduring love used in traditional Irish weddings (Royal Claddagh 2013). When it is worn on the right hand with the crown and heart facing out, the ring tells that the wearer's heart is yet to be

CULTURE CORNER, CASE 2.6

THE MEHNDI CEREMONY

One distinct tradition that most Indian brides love, much as one loves her veil, is Mehndi. Mehndi is henna, which is applied in intricate designs (stencils) that are temporary and provide décor for the hands, arms and top of the feet. The ornate designs are applied by expert beauticians who are sought for their talent in applying the henna, which initially begins like a clay paint and then hardens. Lemon juice is applied or lemons are rubbed to the arms and feet to keep the color or prolong it. The Mehndi is an important occasion for the bridal party, close girlfriends, sisters and other female relatives. Particularly exciting for the bride is that, though stencils are used for the patterns, no two henna applications are alike because it is tradition to hide the groom's name within the grand design. Centuries ago, if the groom could not find his name, the marriage could not be consummated!

CASE SUBMITTED BY NEHA SHAH

PHOTO 2.4 THE WEDDING RING IS A SYMBOL OF MARRIAGE.

SOURCE: WWW.RODNEYBAILEY.COM

won; on the right hand facing in, one is under loves spell; whereas when worn on the left hand, with the crown and heart facing inwards, it signifies the marital state and that love has been requited (Royal Claddagh 2013).

REFERENCES

Bennett, W.L. (2012) 'The personalization of politics: political identity, social media, and changing patterns of participation', *The ANNALS of the American Academy of Political and Social Science*, 644: 20–39.

Boorstein, M. (9 October 2012) 'Study: 20% list religion as "none," but many still believe', *The Washington Post*, A1, A9.

Carlson, D.L. (2012) 'Deviations from desired age at marriage: mental health differences across marital status', *Journal of Marriage and Family*, 74: 743–758.

Clark, B. (2000) *Bridal Showers*, Carpinteria, CA: Wilshire Publications.

Clark, M.S. (2010) *A Pocket Guide to Amish Life*, Eugene, OR: Harvest House Publishers.

Clark, S., Kabiru, C. and Mathur, R. (2010) 'Relationship transitions among youth in urban Kenya', *Journal of Marriage and Family*, 72: 73–88.

CNN International Edition (4 November 2009) 'Louisiana justice who refused interracial marriage resigns', Online. Available HTTP: <http://edition.cnn.com/2009/US/11/03/louisiana.interracial.marriage/> (accessed 12 December 2012).

Condit, C.M. (1994) 'Hegemony in a mass-mediated society: concordance about reproductive technologies', *Critical Studies in Mass Communication*, 11: 205–230.

Coontz, S. (2000) 'Historical perspectives on family studies', *Journal of Family and Marriage*, 62: 283–297.

Couto, U. (2013) 'Macanese weddings'. E-mail (31 January 2013).

Diener, E., Tay, L. and Myers, D.G. (2011) 'The religion paradox: if religion makes people happy, why are so many dropping out?', *Journal of Personality and Social Psychology*, 101: 1278–1290.

Engstrom, E. (2008) 'Unraveling the knot: political economy and cultural hegemony in wedding media', *Journal of Communication Inquiry*, 32: 60–82.

Engstrom, E. and Semic, B. (2003) 'Portrayal of religion in reality TV programming: hegemony and the contemporary American wedding', *Journal of Media and Religion*, 2: 145–163.

Fisher, H. (2004) *Why We Love: the nature and chemistry of romantic love*, New York: Owl Books.

Girls not Brides (2012) 'About child marriage', Online. Available HTTP: <http://www.girlsnotbrides.org/> (accessed 26 February 2013).

Ingoldsby, B.B. (1995) 'Mate selection and marriage', in B.B. Ingoldsby and S. Smith (eds) *Families in Multicultural Perspective*, New York: Guilford Press.

Jayakumar, A. (19 August 2012) 'Finding love on the run: the fast rise of mobile dating apps', *The Washington Post*, G1, G6.

King, C. (20 October 2009) 'Post partisan', *The Washington Post*, Online. Available HTTP: <http://articles.washington post.com/2009-10-20/opinions/36918796_1_keith-bardwell-tangipahoa-parish-s-8th-ward-fox-news> (accessed 10 January 2013).

Kuperberg, A. (2012) 'Reassessing differences in work and income in cohabitation and marriage', *Journal of Marriage and Family*, 74: 688–707.

Liu, H. and Reczek, C. (2012) 'Cohabitation and U.S. adult mortality: an examination by gender and race', *Journal of Family and Marriage*, 74: 794–811.

Lom, P. (2004) 'The kidnapped bride: the story', *PBS Frontline World*, Online. Available HTTP: <http://www.pbs.org/frontlineworld/stories/kyrgyzstan/thestory.html> (accessed 12 August 2012).

McCarthy, E. (12 February 2012) 'Some people never find the love of their lives. And live to tell about it', *Washington Post Magazine*, 10–19.

Manwa, H. (2013) 'A traditional Setswana wedding'. E-mail (13 March 2013).

Montemurro, B. (2005) 'Add men, don't stir: reproducing traditional gender roles in modern wedding showers', *Journal of Contemporary Ethnography*, 34: 6–35.

Musick, K. and Bumpass, L. (2012) 'Reexamining the case for marriage: union formation and changes in well-being', *Journal of Marriage and Family*, 74: 1–18.

Nasrin, S. (2011) 'Crime or custom?: motivations behind dowry practice in rural Bangladesh', *Indian Journal of Gender Studies*, 18: 27–50.

Newbeck, P. (2004) *Virginia Hasn't Always Been for Lovers: interracial marriage bans and the case of Richard and Mildred Loving*, Carbondale: Southern Illinois University Press.

Newman, J. (12 February 2012) 'The science of love', *Parade*, 8–10, 15.

Pascoe, P. (2004) 'Why the ugly rhetoric against gay marriage is familiar to this historian of miscegenation', *History News Network*, Online. Available HTTP: <http://hnn.us/articles/4708.html> (accessed 23 March 2013).

Prys, M. and Robel, S. (2011) 'Hegemony, not empire', *Journal of International Relations and Development*, 14: 247–279.

Radio Free Europe (18 October 2012) 'Kyrgyz lawmakers vote to toughen law on bride kidnapping', Online. Available HTTP: <http://www.rferl.org/content/kyrgyzstsan-lawmakers-pass-tougher-law-on-bride-kidnapping/24743556.html> (accessed 18 December 2012).

Raghavan, S. (10 July 2012) 'Will hunger crisis fuel child marriages?', *The Washington Post*, A1, A11.

Rein, L. (11 October 2012) 'Targeting child marriage', *The Washington Post*, C3.

Royal Claddagh (2013) 'Claddagh symbolism', Online. Available HTTP: <http://www.claddagh.com/howtowear.asp> (accessed 8 January 2013).

Sadiq, S. (2004) 'Interview with Petr Lom: marriage by abduction', *PBS Frontline World*, Online. Available HTTP: <http://www.pbs.org/frontlineworld/stories/kyrgyzstan/lom.html> (accessed 3 October 2012).

Shah, N. (2013) 'Cultural traditions for Indian weddings'. E-mail (2 January 2013).

Shapira, I. (8 August 2010) 'For millennials, love is never asking them to call you back; texting generation doesn't share boomers' taste for talk', *The Washington Post*, A01.

Smith, C.S. (30 April 2005) 'Abduction, often violent, a Kyrgyz wedding rite', *The New York Times*, A1.

Smith, I. (2004) 'The foundations of marriage: are they crumbling?', *International Journal of Social Economics*, 31: 487–500.

Sullivan, P. (6 May 2008) 'Quiet Va. wife ended interracial marriage ban', *The Washington Post*, Online. Available HTTP: <http://articles.washingtonpost.com/2008-05-06/news/36898886_1_interracial-marriage-ban-white-couple-black-woman> (accessed 4 September 2012).

Udas, S. (30 May 2012) 'Arranged marriage is not forced marriage', *CNN*, Online. Available HTTP: <http://thecnnfreedomproject.blogs.cnn.com/2012/05/30/arranged-marriage-is-not-forced-marriage/> (accessed 18 September 2012).

Uller, T. and Johansson, C. (2003) 'Human mate choice and the wedding ring effect: are married men more attractive?', *Human Nature*, 14: 267–276.

UNICEF (2012) 'UNICEF supports efforts to eradicate child marriage in Niger', Online. Available HTTP: <http://www.unicef.org/infobycountry/niger_65336.html> (accessed 17 November 2012).

US Supreme Court (1967) *Loving v. Virginia*, 388 US 1.

Wagner, I. (2011) *Growing Up Amish: a memoir*, Carol Stream, Il: Tyndale House Publishers.

Wilding, R. (2003) 'Romantic love and "getting married": narratives of the wedding in and out of cinema texts', *Journal of Sociology*, 39: 373–389.

Will, T.E. (1999) 'Weddings on contested grounds: slave marriage in the antebellum South', *The Historian*, 62: 99–119.

REVIEW

1. Define hegemony and give examples of historic and modern marital hegemonic practices.

2. Explain the phenomenon of mate-choice copying and discuss why you think it does or does not apply to human mate selection.

3. Should you decide to marry one day, do you think you will change your name?

4. Read *Research Roundtable*, Case 2.2. Do the results reflect your own experiences? Explain.

TERMINOLOGY

- Bride kidnapping
- Bride price
- Catfishing
- Claddagh ring
- Courtship
- Dowry
- Hegemony
- Mate-choice copying
- Miscegenation laws
- Neurotransmitters

PHOTO 3.1 WEDDINGS ALLOW COUPLES TO FEEL LIKE CELEBRITIES.

SOURCE: WWW.RODNEYBAILEY.COM

3

CONSUMERISM
AND THE MEDIATED
CONSTRUCTION OF
WEDDINGS

CONSUMERISM SUGGESTS THAT AN EVER-EXPANDING PURCHASE OF GOODS IS ADVANTAGEOUS TO AN ECONOMY. THE CONSUMPTIVE MENTALITY THAT GRABS HOLD OF MANY COUPLES DURING THE WEDDING PLANNING PROCESS HAS BEEN A COMMON SUBJECT OF CRITIQUE, WITH SELF-ABSORBED BRIDEZILLAS AND GROOM-MONSTERS ACTING AS EASY TARGETS FOR THOSE WHO SENSE THAT THE COMMERCIALIZATION OF WEDDINGS IS OVERTAKING THE SANCTITY OF MARRIAGE VOWS. BRIDEZILLA HAS BECOME A MAINSTREAM TERM, SO MUCH THAT "WOMEN'S ENTERTAINMENT" TELEVISION CREATED THE POPULAR SHOW *BRIDEZILLAS* TO SHOWCASE HOW AND WHY SOME WOMEN TURN THEIR NUPTIALS INTO A NIGHTMARE FOR ALL INVOLVED.

While all forms of media encourage consumerism, the explosion of online retail opportunities and social media have added a tremendous amount of fuel to the fire. Websites and apps associated with *The Knot*, *WeddingWire*, *The Wedding Channel*, *Brides* and *InStyle Weddings* are just a few of the countless media outlets devoted to weddings and wedding planning, while companion resources such as Facebook, Twitter and Pinterest offer forums to share ideas.

The abundance of information available on the internet can overwhelm a prospective bride and groom. While some suggest that the proliferation of material available on websites negates the need for a wedding consultant, quite the opposite is true. A wedding consultant can help the couple sort through the information and determine what is relevant. Further, the consultant's firsthand knowledge of local vendors will help the couple to not get misled or sidetracked by the inundation of paid advertising on these sites.

Most couples, understandably, use their engaged status as an excuse to throw caution to the wind in light of consumptive patterns. However, with increasing global attention being given to financial instability and environmental concerns, some couples are embracing a conservationist mentality in relationship to their planning. The goal of this chapter is to analyze consumerism and the accompanying media influences that are evident in many facets of wedding planning by considering: 1) the quest for perfection and impulse buying; 2) invented traditions; 3) celebrity weddings; and 4) planning eco-weddings.

The quest for perfection and impulse buying

Weddings have become a year-round and then some shopping spree, with preparations taking an average of 16 months (US Census Bureau 2011). The pressure and emotions inherent in ritual-related consumption can stress both personal finances and relationships, in particular if those involved are not in agreement on some purchases. The urge to splurge is driven by the quest for the perfect wedding. This perfectionism has ballooned into a wedding obsession craze that has become an international contagion (Horyn 2004; Ourahmoune and Özçağlar-Toulouse 2012). From an early age, many women fantasize about their dream wedding, with ubiquitous fairy tales such as "Cinderella," "Snow White" and "Beauty and the Beast" feeding young imaginations that translate into adult purchase decisions (Otnes and Pleck 2003). The lavish wedding allows for a temporary escape from a world of imperfection, as "the magic invoked by a performative spectacle and symbolic objects becomes a key means of generating a rite of passage through a public display of success" (Clarke 2005: 350).

Documented critique regarding the heightened pressures associated with weddings as a form of pageantry can be traced back to the late 1800s. In his critique of the leisure class, Veblen (1899) coined the phrase *conspicuous consumption*, asserting that, beyond the recreation and conviviality needs fulfilled through private festivities, these events operate to ostentatiously showcase the superiority of the host:

PHOTO 3.2 LITTLE GIRLS DREAM OF HAVING A FAIRY TALE WEDDING.

SOURCE: WWW.RODNEYBAILEY.COM

Conspicuous consumption of valuable goods is a means of reputability to the gentleman of leisure. As wealth accumulates on his hands, his own unaided effort will not avail to sufficiently put his opulence in evidence by this method. The aid of friends and competitors is therefore brought in by resorting to the giving of valuable presents and expensive feasts and entertainments.

(1899: 64–65)

The conspicuous consumption phenomenon is as robust now as it was in the 1800s. For example, Ourahmoune and Özçağlar-Toulouse (2012) analyzed the role of wedding fashion as related to social status in Algeria, summarized in *Research Roundtable*, Case 3.1. Similarly, Nguyen and Belk (2012) explore the role of wedding ritual consumption as a sign of social change in Vietnam, as reviewed in *Research Roundtable*, Case 3.2.

Consumer passion often leads to impulse buying, which occurs when a consumer experiences a sudden, unplanned and powerful urge to buy something immediately. Impulse buying is accompanied by a roller coaster of emotional states prior to, during and after the purchase (Xiao and Nicholson 2013). For instance, a newly engaged woman is likely to be feeling excited

RESEARCH ROUNDTABLE, CASE 3.1

WEDDING FASHION AND SOCIAL STATUS IN THE KABYLE SUBCULTURE OF ALGERIA

Purpose: The goal of the study was to analyze how women communicate about their wedding fashion choices to project their social identities.

Methods: One of the authors attended 17 Kabyle weddings and documented descriptive data generated from informal conversations, interviews and photographs. Intercultural weddings were common, with many of the weddings involving a Kabyle individual marrying someone of Arab, French or Chaoui descent. The analysis focused on the outfits worn by the brides of the 17 weddings.

Results: "During wedding ceremonies, Algerian brides traditionally wear up to seven outfits" (Ourahmoune and Özçağlar-Toulouse 2012: 86); however, only recently have external cultures influenced fashion selections for Kabyle weddings. Kabyle brides were either noted as being "inside," thus adhering to Kabyle fashion as inspired by French couture, or "outside," with the inclusion of exotic, Arabic aesthetics.

Conclusion: Fashion is used as a form of control to reproduce and stabilize an existing social order by mirroring the family position in the community and providing signals of success.

SOURCE: OURAHMOUNE AND ÖZÇAĞLAR-TOULOUSE (2012)

RESEARCH ROUNDTABLE, CASE 3.2

WEDDING RITUAL CONSUMPTION AND SOCIAL CHANGE IN VIETNAM

Purpose: The purpose of this study is to examine how traditional wedding rituals have changed as a result of the renovation and modernization of Vietnam's global market.

Methods: Qualitative observations were made at wedding business sites, wedding ceremonies and receptions in Ho Chi Minh City. Interviews were conducted with couples, their parents and wedding vendors both before and after the associated weddings. Historical context was employed to shed light on the extent of change in consumptive patterns.

Results: Prior to social reform that integrated Vietnam into the world economy, consumptive practices were frowned upon by the government and weddings were very simple affairs, where even the affluent "rarely dared to openly demonstrate their status" (Nguyen and Belk 2012: 111–112). As a result of the dramatic political and economic changes in the country, "Weddings have become the means for Vietnamese consumers to display their status. Affluent consumers can spend billions of Vietnamese Dong (hundreds of thousands dollars) for a wedding" (Nguyen and Belk 2012: 112).

Conclusion: While Vietnamese consumers increasingly use Westernized weddings as a means of showcasing their status or to temporarily emulate a desired lifestyle, a tension remains between those pursuing modernity and those who seek to preserve national identity through the revitalization of traditional cultural rituals.

SOURCE: NGUYEN AND BELK (2012)

and self-indulgent. She goes out shopping with friends just for fun, with no intention of buying anything. She enters a bridal boutique and notices a designer dress on the clearance rack that is completely impractical, non-returnable and way out of her price range, but gorgeous. Her heart races just looking at it; she is feeling exhilarated and stressed at the same time. With her friends egging her on, she tries it on and then throws caution to the wind and buys the dress. Later that evening, she begins to experience self-doubt and dreads telling her fiancé about the purchase.

Trying the dress on again, she thinks it makes her look ridiculous. She regrets the decision and blames her friends for pushing her.

The ubiquitous, 24-7 nature of online shopping often results in e-impulse buying. *E-atmospherics* are defined as "socially constructed marketing imageries" where momentum cues are combined with functional content and design elements to encourage online purchase behavior (Kervenoael *et al.* 2009: 320). Because tactile experiences are lost with online retail transactions, the compensation must go beyond functional convenience to address social engagement and psychological empowerment (Kervenoael *et al.* 2009: 320). While praised for convenience, price and accessibility, researchers who analyze online wedding retail sites have also critiqued the directives, norms and roles embedded within online content (Engstrom 2008; White 2011).

Just as emotionally complicated as impulse buying is when a good or service is desperately desired yet completely out of reach in terms of finances, as the inability to purchase within a wedding context has been associated with disappointment, regret and anger (Nguyen and Belk 2012). As a wedding consultant, you are likely to see friendships and family relationships become strained due to the emotional and financial ups and downs that occur during the planning process. In general, those who relate the acquisition of material goods to success and a positive self-identity are more likely to be impulse buyers; however, it is not uncommon for the typically restrained individual to become a consumptive powerhouse during life-altering events such as a wedding, where social acceptance of materialism is high (Xiao and Nicholson 2013).

INVENTED TRADITIONS

Many wedding items that are generally viewed as absolute necessities are a result of invented traditions. The progressive advent of print, film, television, computers and social media has greatly expanded the ability to structure, create and recreate the meaning of weddings as well as the manner in which these events take place. Some wedding traditions are so taken for granted that couples seldom stop to question their origins. *Media framing* involves the ability of a media presentation to define a situation and includes the psychological processes that persuade us to buy into the definition (Nabi and Moyer-Guse 2013). In the case of weddings, mass communication operates to frame specific views or traditions to the extent that they become so expected and dominant that people accept them without notice and seldom pause to reflect upon their geneses. Three commonly accepted Western wedding traditions with invented roots that were largely framed by the media are the diamond engagement ring, the double ring ceremony and the white wedding gown.

The fact that "the American diamond engagement ring sector is a keystone to the worldwide natural diamond market" (Fram and Baron 2004: 340) is solely due to very successful marketing initiatives. The royal beginning of the story occurred when Archduke Maximilian of Austria reportedly gave Mary of Burgundy the first diamond engagement ring in 1477. However, diamonds as the stone of choice did not become a preferred option until much later.

PHOTO 3.3 THE DIAMOND ENGAGEMENT RING IS AN INVENTED TRADITION.

SOURCE: WWW.RODNEYBAILEY.COM

The legal precursor of the modern engagement ring was the Breach of Promise Action. Brinig (1990) explains that, from the mid-1800s to the early 1900s, this action entitled a woman whose fiancé had broken off the engagement to sue him for economic damages as well as personal damages for embarrassment, humiliation and loss of other marriage opportunities. Most women who sought such damages had also lost their virginity, as a woman was supposed to remain chaste until the time of engagement but it was common for intimacy to occur during the engagement period. Thus, Breach of Promise Action lawsuits where intimacy had occurred resulted in damages more substantial than in cases where it had not. By the 1940s, Breach of Promise Action lawsuits became known as "legally sanctioned blackmail" (Brinig 1990: 205). While largely abolished by the 1970s, this law still exists in some jurisdictions.

While the Breach of Promise Action dissipated, the sale of diamonds began to take off, made possible by the discovery of the South African diamond mines during the 1870s and 1880s, which emerged as supplies in India and Brazil were diminishing (Ingraham 1999). De Beers Group was formed in 1888 to protect diamond mine investors. In its early years, De Beers produced over 90 per cent of the world's diamonds and thus completely controlled pricing (Fram and Baron 2004). De Beers continues to have the "largest diamond resource and reserve position in the world" (De Beers Group 2012).

Before the Depression, diamond rings were available but not an essential element of engagement (Brinig 1990). National advertising for them was largely thought of as vulgar. During the Depression, supply exceeded demand as new diamond sources were discovered. Diamonds were stockpiled so there would not be a perceived glut. To stimulate the market, De Beers formed an alliance with a prominent New York advertising agency, N. W. Ayer. In 1939, the famous "A Diamond is Forever" slogan, combined with diamonds being worn by Hollywood stars, energized this invented tradition (Howard 2003). De Beers also popularized the "Two Months' Salary" tradition to suggest how much a man should pay for the engagement ring. By the end of World War II, the diamond engagement ring had become the ring of choice in America and, by 1965, 80 per cent of couples chose the diamond engagement ring (in Brinig 1990). More recently, researchers have studied whether gender roles and love styles influence attitudes toward diamond engagement rings, as summarized in *Research Roundtable*, Case 3.3.

With the ongoing popularity and value of the diamond engagement ring, it has been suggested that the psychological attachment to and financial investment in the diamond engagement ring has allowed it to supplant the safety net of the Breach of Promise Action (Brinig 1990). However, this legal antecedent resurfaced in 2008 with a widely publicized lawsuit. Specifically, a jury awarded RoseMary Shell $150,000 in damages when her fiancé called off their wedding, based on the fact that she had left a high-paying job in order to move to where he lived once they were engaged (Gurr 2008). Thus, the diamond engagement ring may be viewed as necessary, but perhaps not of sufficient value to offset the economic and psychological damages that occur when an engagement comes to an end.

An equally invented tradition with historic roots similar to the diamond engagement ring is the double ring ceremony, as explained by Howard (2003). The impetus for the double ring ceremony was the failed campaign for a male engagement ring. During the late 1800s, the growth of mail order catalogs and large department stores put the jewelry retailers at risk, so they searched for new customs to broaden the market. "In 1926, manufacturers and retail jewelers launched a major campaign to popularize the custom of male engagement or betrothal rings" (Howard 2003: 838). Jewelers had to counteract widespread beliefs that jewelry was a female domain and that "engagement was something that happened to women" (Howard 2003: 840). Despite concerted marketing efforts, the campaign failed.

By the late 1920s, jewelers changed tactics and began focusing on the male wedding band rather than the male engagement ring. Prior to this time, wedding bands for men were not a common Western tradition, as a ring was only given to a bride by the groom, and not the opposite (Kanarek and Lehman 2013). The success of the groom's ring was sealed in the 1940s, when "wedding consumption became a patriotic act" (Howard 2003: 847) during World War II. Images of soldiers wearing wedding bands were used to illustrate emotional bonds of commitment from afar. After the war, when marriage rates soared, the groom's ring became a symbol of the masculine ability to support a wife and children.

Interestingly, this invented tradition affected the Church, as the popularity of the double ring ceremony led to the transformation of the religious legislation, as the wording of the ring blessing

RESEARCH ROUNDTABLE, CASE 3.3

GENDER ROLES, LOVE STYLES AND ATTITUDES

TOWARD ENGAGEMENT RINGS

Purpose: To determine: 1) if women view the diamond engagement ring as more important than men do; 2) if those who value traditional gender roles rate the diamond engagement ring as more important than those who value egalitarian roles; and 3) to determine if those who have romantic love styles rate the diamond engagement ring as more important than those with practical love styles.

Methods: As part of a larger study, 112 male college students and 193 female college students completed questionnaire items specific to engagement ring attitudes, social roles and love styles.

Results: No significant differences were found in comparing men and women based on their ratings of the importance of a diamond engagement ring. Further, no differences were found based on love style; those with a pragmatic love style viewed the diamond engagement ring as equally important as those with a romantic love style did. However, those who scored higher on traditional gender roles also scored higher on wanting an expensive ring and the expectation that the ring be a diamond.

Conclusion: "Stereotypical gender role attitudes are manifested in expectations related to commitment indicators such as engagement rings" (Ogletree 2010: 75).

SOURCE: OGLETREE (2010)

had to be changed from singular to plural. The double ring ceremony has been viewed as an indication of an egalitarian wedding ceremony, as the bride and groom become symbolically and verbally betrothed to one another with the exchange, rather than the bride only being betrothed to the groom (Kanarek and Lehman 2013).

A third, created Western tradition is that of the white wedding gown. Prior to 1840, the common color was red or another bright color. Queen Victoria's marriage to Albert of Saxe in 1840 changed this tradition when she wore what was considered a flamboyant white gown (McCoy 2001). This statement of class and style was immediately copied by the wealthy and the tradition spread. The white dress had nothing to do with being virtuous at the time; instead, it was an overt sign of being able to afford a gown that you would likely never wear again, as cleaning techniques were not sophisticated. During the Depression, simple white dresses were chosen that could be dyed and worn again or brides just wore the best dress they owned. After World War II, royalty and movie stars were seen wearing extravagant white gowns and the tradition was set.

The white wedding gown remains the norm in Western weddings and is often adopted as one of multiple gowns worn during weddings in Eastern cultures. However, a measure of backlash has been documented, with some Eastern brides eschewing the white gown in favor of a range of garments specific to their unique cultures, while Western women may lament the lack of alternatives to the white dress (Thomas and Peters 2011). Wedding gowns will be discussed in more detail in Chapter 10.

CELEBRITY INFLUENCES

Celebrities have always captured the attention of the media, with their weddings of particular interest. From the wedding dress of classic movie star Grace Kelly to the 18-carat sapphire and diamond ring worn first by Diana Spencer, Princess of Wales and now by Kate Middleton, Duchess of Cambridge, the design choices of celebrities are sure to be discussed and mimicked by their fans. Security measures employed by celebrities during their weddings to protect their privacy are extreme, which simply heightens the intrigue of the event as well as the public's desire to learn the specifics of the ceremony and reception.

Media outlets disseminate the details of celebrity weddings and retail outlets hasten to offer knock-offs of items chosen by the rich and famous. The power of the stars to set trends and/or make political statements has been illustrated by: 1) non-traditional engagement rings such as emeralds, sapphires and rubies; 2) gowns that experiment with vibrant color; 3) having different gowns for the ceremony and reception; 4) the incorporation of dark flowers in bridal bouquets; and 5) involving animals in the ceremony. When celebrities are used in retail advertising, their persuasive capacity is linked to the viewer's desired self-concept. A study conducted by Choi and Rifon found that "when a consumer perceives a celebrity endorser as possessing an image close to his or her ideal self-image, the consumer is likely to rate the ad as more favorable and report greater purchase intentions" (2012: 647). Celebrity weddings also bring attention to changing social trends, including the mainstream nature of intercultural weddings, same-sex marriages and having children before marrying.

Celebrity weddings have increased the exposure and status of wedding planners. The over-the-top events orchestrated by planners for stars generate tremendous press, often making them celebrities in their own right based on their famous clients. Celebrity planners go on to write books, create wedding packages for famous resorts, create their own lines of retail goods and star in reality television shows. By stretching themselves too far, however, the primary goal of this career path may get muddied for celebrity planners. Lawsuits against celebrity planners and counter-suits against the clients have resulted in significant media attention, with cases related to not showing up or neglecting to fulfill contract obligations.

PHOTO 3.4 CELEBRITIES INFLUENCE WEDDING TRENDS.

SOURCE: WWW.RODNEYBAILEY.COM

Celebrities do not have to actually get married to influence wedding trends, as fans are equally fascinated by their fictional weddings. Modern filmgoers are captivated by how romance, weddings and marriage are portrayed in cinematic texts, whether portrayed comically or through drama. A review of the "100 Greatest Movie Weddings," selected by *Us* magazine (2012), showcases the designer dress selections for brides and bridesmaids, eco-friendly choices, cultural traditions, wedding destinations and all of the trappings of fairy tale weddings that are, quite frequently, balanced by a healthy dose of humor based on planning and implementation mishaps. Just a few of the favorites listed include *Enchanted*, *Jumping the Broom*, *Bride Wars*, *The Twilight Saga: Breaking Dawn – Part 1*, *The Five-Year Engagement*, *Monsoon Wedding*, *Bridesmaids*, *Mirror Mirror*, *Wedding Crashers* and *Your Highness*. While the primary goal of these films may be to entertain, they also act as a valuable marketing channel that can inform wedding purchase decisions.

In some cultures, local celebrities are directly involved in wedding traditions. In Jordan, for example, the tradition of *el-jaha* has evolved to selecting prestigious leaders, as detailed in *Culture Corner*, Case 3.4.

CULTURE CORNER, CASE 3.4

WEDDING TRADITIONS IN JORDAN: *EL-JAHA*

The tradition of *el-jaha* was and still is one of the main pillars in Jordanian weddings. Originally, but less nowadays, parents choose the bride for their son, and far in the past the groom did not see the face of his bride until the first night of their marriage, called *el-dukhla* in Arabic. However, over time and as a result of openness in social relations, education and work, where women and men meet and see each other nearly every day, the main role of parents in marriage decisions diminished. Consequently, the role transferred to the groom and the bride themselves, with their parents becoming involved in a later stage to realize this dream.

The *jaha*, in a Jordanian context, is simply defined as a group of men from the groom's side who go to the bride's family to ask for their consent to the marriage. Generally, the *jaha* is composed of the groom's family, relatives and friends; the number increases or decreases depending on the social, economic and political status of both families. Every *jaha* has a head who is accompanied by the members of the *jaha*. Recently, a new trend has developed in Jordan pertaining to prestige, where a celebrity or dignitary such as a prime minister, a minister, a member of the parliament, a head of a tribe or any famous personality in the society is invited by the groom's family to work as the head of the *jaha*. The head of the *jaha* is the one who formally demands the consent of the bride's guardian such as her father, if he is alive, or her eldest brother or eldest uncle.

The process begins when one of the bride's brothers, normally the eldest, offers Arabic coffee to the guests, starting from the head of the *jaha*. The head of the *jaha* takes the cup of coffee and puts it down on the floor; then, the guardian of bride says, "Drink your coffee and the thing you are demanding will be fulfilled, God willing!" Then the head of the *jaha* and the rest of the people drink their coffee. Next, the head of the *jaha* stands up and greets the people and reads something from the Holy Quran and from the Prophet's Hadith that encourages people to get married. He then turns to the guardian of the bride and asks him to agree on the marriage between the bride and the groom. If there is a pre-agreement on the groom, the guardian replies directly by saying "Yes" and welcoming the *jaha* and the groom's family. When the groom and the groom's family are not known to the bride's family, the guardian will ask for a grace period to get the consent of the bride and then to investigate the social, moral and economic status of the groom and his family. The grace period generally lasts between one week and one month, after which the guardian calls the head of the *jaha* or the groom's father to relay his decision. The decision can be either "Yes" or "No." In rare cases, no decision is made. In Jordan, this is known as "No news is bad news" as opposed to what is common in Western countries, where "No news is good news."

CASE SUBMITTED BY SALEM HARAHSHEH AND RAFA HADDAD

PLANNING ECO-WEDDINGS

While many couples embrace the consumptive mentality when planning their weddings, others reject it; yet, they still may wish to celebrate their transition to marriage. Eco-weddings, also known as "green" weddings, are anti-consumptive, conservationist and stress global awareness in intent. Conservationist ideas can be found on all the major online wedding sites, while other online resources and books such as *The Green Bride Guide*, *Eco-Chic Weddings* and *Green Wedding* are specifically devoted to sustainable wedding practices.

The extreme anti-consumptive approach is participating in a mass or collective wedding. This approach has become popular over the past decade in Islamic countries such as Iran, Jordan, Pakistan and Yemen where government institutions organize public events for those who otherwise would not be able to afford lavish wedding ceremonies that can be financially crippling (Cordier 2010). Government and religious organizations in Asian countries such as China, India and South Korea have also organized collective weddings where hundreds or even thousands of couples are simultaneously married (BBC News 2012; NBC News 2009).

A second, common means to reduce consumption is to forego certain traditions. For example, cross-cultural couples are able to use their differences as an excuse to avoid some of the materialistic mandates of their individual cultures. Couples who wish to release their guests from the burden

PHOTO 3.5 CONSERVATIONIST ELEMENTS ARE FOUND IN MANY WEDDINGS.

SOURCE: WWW.RODNEYBAILEY.COM

of wedding gifts will make a request for no gifts in their invitations or ask that, in lieu of gifts, guests make a contribution to a charity if they feel the need to commemorate the occasion. For example, couples can register with organizations that allow guests to give funds that result in the donation of food, water, livestock, educational support or healthcare in least-developed countries, such as Angola, Bangladesh and Rwanda, as designated by the United Nations (2013).

The do-it-yourself (DIY) couple can (if motivated, inspired and willing to put in the effort) cut back on consumptive practices by making their own stationery items, centerpieces, bouquets, decorative items, food, favors and more. Couples can ask friends to mix music, act as photographer or videographer, assist with hair and makeup and complete many of the other tasks that are often typically done by wedding vendors. While couples may realize significant savings with DIY components, the trade-offs are time and stress, in particular when taking on tasks with which they have little to no prior experience. Further, the outcome may not have a desired professional look and personal liability increases dramatically if something goes wrong. When a DIY undertaking goes haywire, it may end up being more expensive than if a trained vendor had been hired to complete the task. When considering DIY components, it is advisable to tell clients to only take on areas of planning that are well within their comfort zone.

Some anti-consumptive choices are not necessarily cost-effective, but are practiced for ethical or conservationist reasons or to promote one's local community. A simple wedding practice that most couples can consider pertains to the selection of favors. Rather than purchasing a favor that guests are unlikely to ever use, couples can select "consumable" favors, ideally produced organically and in their local community, such as fruit, seeds, flower bulbs, chocolate, honey, candles or soap. Alternatively, there are a myriad of not-for-profit companies that sell functional retail items made by artisans residing in impoverished areas, the proceeds from which go back to support these communities. Selections from the online catalogs made available by these organizations can act as favors or wedding party gifts. Favors and gifts are discussed in detail in Chapter 18.

Other mindful practices might include using stationery elements made from recycled paper or foregoing paper altogether and sending e-invitations, renting rather than purchasing dresses and tuxes for the bridal party, using an organic caterer and making sure the selected reception venue recycles materials that are commonly used such as glass bottles and aluminum cans. Floral décor can be recycled at local hospitals or nursing homes as an offering to patients who may not have ongoing family support. Couples can also select a not-for-profit venue, such as a museum or historic plantation, where the venue fees go to support the mission of the property. For example, many sites that are listed on the National Trust for Historic Preservation have opened their doors to weddings. The related fees are used to maintain the buildings, gardens and grounds that allow for gorgeous, timeless settings.

Ethical practices may also apply to the selection of engagement and wedding rings. For example, the *Kimberley Process Certification Scheme* is a global system of scrutiny that requires rough diamonds to be accompanied by a certificate of origin to assure that they are conflict free, where *conflict diamonds* are those whose proceeds are used by rebel groups to fund wars against legitimate governments (Kimberley Process 2013). Organizations such as Amnesty International (2012) advocate for even stricter legislation that would require corporations to disclose detailed sourcing practices related to diamonds, gold and other minerals, based not only on a history of armed conflict, but also related to worker exploitation, child labor practices and environmental harms that have been associated with these goods (Brilliant Earth 2013).

Finally, while just about every item selected for a wedding can be eco-friendly in nature, the most effective way to decrease the carbon footprint of a wedding is to invite fewer guests, as airline travel emissions, car emissions and energy use in hotel rooms comprise the bulk of a wedding's carbon footprint (TerraPass 2013). When coupled with food selections and the recycling practices associated with the wedding, it is easy to recognize the carbon footprint difference between 50 guests and 200 guests, in particular if most of them are from out of town.

Couples who identify with eco-friendly practices yet do not want to have to pick and choose between family members when planning one of the most important days of their lives may elect to participate in a carbon-offset program, where donations are used to fund forest conservation and reforestation projects (The Nature Conservancy 2013). The projects are designed to reduce the impact of climate change and protect natural habitats; therefore, a contribution allows a couple to "retire" the carbon offsets associated with their wedding (The Nature Conservancy 2013).

REFERENCES

Amnesty International (2012) 'Amnesty International to defend conflict minerals reporting requirements from attacks by corporate groups', Online. Available HTTP: <http://www.amnestyusa.org/news/press-releases/amnesty-international-to-defend-conflict-minerals-reporting-requirements-from-attacks-by-corporate-g> (accessed 18 January 2013).

BBC News (2012) 'In pictures: mass wedding in India "prostitute village"', Online. Available HTTP: <http://www.bbc.co.uk/news/world-asia-india-17336512> (accessed 1 January 2013).

Brilliant Earth (2013) 'Defining "beyond conflict free"', Online. Available HTTP: <http://www.brilliantearth.com/conflict-free-diamond-definition/> (accessed 5 February 2013).

Brinig, M.F. (1990) 'Rings and promises', *Journal of Law, Economics, & Organization*, 6: 203–215.

Choi, S.M. and Rifon, N.J. (2012) 'It is a match: the impact of congruence between celebrity image and consumer ideal self on endorsement effectiveness, 2012', *Psychology and Marketing*, 29: 639–650.

Clarke, A. (2005) 'The globalization of feminine consumption', *Current Anthropology*, 46: 349–351.

Cordier, B.D. (2010) 'On the thin line between good intentions and creating tensions: a view on gender programmes in Muslim contexts and the (potential) position of Islamic aid organisations', *The European Journal of Development Research*, 22: 234–251.

De Beers Group (2012) 'Our approach', Online. Available HTTP: <http://www.debeersgroup.com/en/About-Us/Our-approach/> (accessed 17 January 2013).

Engstrom, E. (2008) 'Unraveling the knot: political economy and cultural hegemony in wedding media', *Journal of Communication Inquiry*, 32: 60–82.

Fram, E.H. and Baron, R. (2004) 'Are natural diamond engagement rings forever?', *International Journal of Retail & Distribution Management*, 32: 340–345.

Gurr, S. (27 July 2008) 'Jury awards jilted bride $150,000: ex-fiancé found in breach of contract', *Gainesville Times*, Online. Available HTTP: <http://www.gainesvilletimes.com/archives/7296/> (accessed 17 December 2012).

Harahsheh, S. and Haddad, R. (2013) 'Wedding traditions in Jordan'. E-mail (15 February 2013).

Horyn, C. (6 June 2004) 'Recipe for the new perfect wedding: a $5,000 cake and hold the simplicity', *The New York Times*, A32.

Howard, V. (2003) 'A "real man's" ring: gender and invention of tradition', *Journal of Social History*, 36: 837–857.

Ingraham, C. (1999) *White Weddings: romancing heterosexuality in popular culture*, New York: Routledge.

Kanarek, J. and Lehman, M. (2013) 'Assigning integration: a framework for intellectual, personal, and professional development in seminary courses', *Teaching Theology and Religion*, 16: 18–32.

Kervenoael, R., Aykac, D.S.O. and Palmer, M. (2009) 'Online social capital: understanding e-impulse buying in practice', *Journal of Retailing and Consumer Services*, 16: 320–328.

Kimberley Process (2013) 'How does the Kimberley Process work?', Online. Available HTTP: <http://www.kimberleyprocess.com/web/kimberley-process/kp-basics> (accessed 19 January 2013).

McCoy, D. (2001) *The World's Most Unforgettable Weddings: love, lust, money and madness*, New York: Citadel Press.

Nabi, R.L. and Moyer-Guse, E. (2013) 'The psychology underlying media-based persuasion', in K.E. Dill (ed.) *The Oxford Handbook of Media Psychology*, Oxford: Oxford University Press.

NBC News (2009) 'Big wedding: 20,000 gather for mass nuptials', Online. Available HTTP: <http://www.nbcnews.com/id/33296507/ns/world_news-world_faith/t/big-wedding-gather-mass-nuptials/> (accessed 9 December 2012).

Nguyen, T.T. and Belk, R. (2012) 'Vietnamese weddings: from Marx to market', *Journal of Macromarketing*, 32: 109–120.

Ogletree, S.M. (2010) 'With this ring, I thee wed: relating gender roles and love styles to attitudes towards engagement rings and weddings', *Gender Issues*, 27: 67–77.

Otnes, C. and Pleck, E. (2003) *Cinderella Dreams: the allure of the lavish wedding*, Berkeley: University of California Press.

Ourahmoune, N. and Özçağlar-Toulouse, N. (2012) 'Exogamous weddings and fashion in a rising consumer culture: Kabyle minority dynamics of structure and agency', *Marketing Theory*, 12: 81–99.

TerraPass (2013) 'Wedding carbon footprint calculator', Online. Available HTTP: <http://www.terrapass.com/wedding-carbon-footprint-calculator/> (accessed 2 February 2013).

The Nature Conservancy (2013) 'What's my carbon footprint?', Online. Available HTTP: <http://www.nature.org/greenliving/carboncalculator/index.htm> (accessed 2 February 2013).

Thomas, J.B. and Peters, C.O. (2011) 'Which dress do you like?: exploring brides' online communities', *Journal of Global Fashion Marketing*, 2: 148–160.

United Nations (2013) 'Least developed countries', Online. Available HTTP: <http://www.unohrlls.org/en/ldc/25/> (accessed 8 January 2013).

US Census Bureau (2011) 'Number, timing, and duration of marriages and divorces: 2009', Current Population Reports, Report Number P70-125, Online. Available HTTP: <http://www.census.gov/prod/2011pubs/p70-125.pdf> (accessed 1 January 2013).

Us Editors (2012) *100 Greatest Movie Weddings*, New York: Us Weekly LLC.

Veblen, T. (1992) *The Theory of the Leisure Class*, New Brunswick, NJ: Transaction Publishers; reprinted with new introduction, original published (1899) New York: The Macmillan Company.

White, M. (2011) 'Engaged with eBay: how heterosexual unions and traditional gender roles are rendered by the site and members', *Feminist Media Studies*, 11: 303–319.

Xiao, S.H. and Nicholson, M. (2013) 'A multidisciplinary cognitive behavioural framework of impulse buying: a systematic review of the literature', *International Journal of Management Reviews*, 15: 333–356.

REVIEW

1. What is a Breach of Promise Action?

2. Explain how the diamond engagement ring, the double ring ceremony and the white wedding dress became invented traditions.

3. Were you surprised by the research finding that there were no differences in the importance ratings of the diamond engagement ring when comparing men and women? Why or why not?

4. What are three recent trends that have emerged because of celebrity influences?

5. What is your favorite wedding movie? Why?

6. What is your favorite wedding-based reality TV show? Why?

7. Explain what impulse buying is and why it is so common in the context of weddings.

8. If an engagement comes to an end, should a woman keep her diamond engagement ring? Why or why not?

9. What are three ways to add anti-consumptive wedding practices?

TERMINOLOGY

- Breach of Promise Action

- Carbon footprint

- Carbon offsets

- Commercialization

- Conflict-free diamonds

- Conspicuous consumption

- Consumerism

- De Beers

- E-atmospherics

- Eco-weddings

- Impulse buying

- Kimberley Process Certification Scheme

- Mary of Burgundy

- Media framing

- Perfectionism

- Queen Victoria

- Sustainability

THE CHANGING FAMILY, POLITICS AND LAW

Expanding parameters of what constitutes "family" and the evolving expectations of each member therein have led to considerable political and legal upheaval. The past five decades have evidenced an extraordinary shift in cultural norms concerning education, marriage and child bearing. Factors such as the availability of effective birth control, the entry of more women into the workforce and the increasing acceptability of cohabitation, divorce and childbearing out of wedlock have resulted in decreasing social pressure to get and stay married. Six trends that will be reviewed in this chapter, each with underlying implications for weddings and wedding planning include: 1) female workforce dynamics; 2) the missing male; 3) cohabitation; 4) divorce; 5) same-sex marriage; and 6) intercultural and interfaith marriages.

FEMALE WORKFORCE DYNAMICS

Women's educational attainment and career opportunities have improved dramatically in the past five decades (US Bureau of Labor Statistics 2012). In the United States, the percentage of college-educated women in the workforce went from 11.2 per cent in 1970 to 36.4 per cent in 2010 (US Bureau of Labor Statistics 2011). Perhaps even more telling is that fact that, in 1970, 33.5 per cent of women in the workforce had less than a high school education, compared with just 6.8 per cent in 2010 (US Bureau of Labor Statistics 2011).

These findings are not unique to the United States or other Western countries, with well-educated, career-oriented women entering the workforce in record numbers in regions and countries such as Hong Kong, Egypt, Singapore and Japan. In some cases, however, educational attainment and career placement do not coincide. For example, in Saudi Arabia, there is a "rising generation of young Saudi women caught between a government spending billions to educate and employ them, and a deeply conservative religious society that fiercely resists women in the workplace" (Sullivan 2012: A01). The unemployment rate for women who wish to work is nearly five times that of men, and 40 per cent of the unemployed women have college degrees (Sullivan 2012). Thus, while Saudi Arabia has made great strides in terms of funding women's education, with record numbers seeking undergraduate and graduate degrees either in domestic or foreign universities, these young women are becoming increasingly frustrated with the inability to put their skills to work (Sullivan 2012).

International data offer a sense of the overall growth in female labor force participation. Table 4.1 offers a summary of data from 1980 and 2009, comparing a sampling of 10 countries based on women in the workforce. While all indicate that participation has increased, in some cases, the rise is more dramatic than others.

For working women who elect to marry, significant work–family coping issues often result, in particular in countries that tend to be gender stereotyped in terms of roles and/or where childcare is prohibitively expensive. Thus, women with career expectations are putting off marriage or opting out completely. In Japan, for example, a collision of traditionalism and liberalism has led to a demographic collapse, with women opting out of marriage and childbearing due to disinterest in upholding the patriarchal expectations of duty customarily associated with marriage (Eberstadt 2012). The situation is dire, with a birthrate that has been well below population replacement rate for over 40 years, leading to a demographic imbalance that is heavily weighted to the elderly, and what would seem to be an inconceivable median (i.e., most common) age of 55 projected by the year 2040 (Eberstadt 2012). While childbearing has decreased dramatically, pet ownership has skyrocketed as an outlet for affection. The flight from marriage, combined with a culture where giving birth out of wedlock is stigmatized, is so extreme in this culture that relatives are few and far between, leading to spikes in loneliness and depression as well as increased demand for rental "relatives" (for celebrations where requisite kin are needed), as well as therapeutic babyloids (robotic babies), humanoids (robotic adults) and robotic pets (Eberstadt 2012).

PHOTO 4.2 HIGHLY EDUCATED WOMEN OFTEN DELAY MARRIAGE.

SOURCE: WWW.RODNEYBAILEY.COM

TABLE 4.1 FEMALE LABOR FORCE RATES BY COUNTRY

Country	1980	2009
Australia	52.5	71.4
France	54.0	66.1
Greece	33.0	55.0
Japan	54.8	68.5
South Korea	46.1	58.3
Mexico	34.0	47.0
Netherlands	35.5	74.2
Switzerland	54.3	82.8
United Kingdom	58.2	70.4
United States	59.5	70.2

SOURCE: US CENSUS BUREAU, INTERNATIONAL STATISTICS (2012)

THE MISSING MALE

A second factor that is influencing changing family dynamics is the diminishing role of males in many households. Starting in the 1970s, women's enrollment in institutions of higher education slowly but surely caught up with and then passed men's. In an arena where men once dominated, the distinctions are now startlingly clear, as indicated by a report issued by the National Center for Education Statistics:

> In 2010, as in every year since 1980, a lower percentage of male than female 18 to 24-year-olds were enrolled either in college or graduate school (39 vs. 47 percent). This pattern was also observed for Whites (43 vs. 51 percent), Blacks (31 vs. 43 percent), Hispanics (26 vs. 36 percent), American Indians (24 vs. 33 percent), and persons of two or more races (40 vs. 49 percent).
>
> (2012: v)

While record numbers of Americans are completing college degrees, university campus administrators are increasingly concerned about a shortage of men who are enrolling in or completing college in comparison with women, with researchers indicating reasons such as women having higher grades and fewer expulsions; thus, greater access and, subsequently, more persistence once they are in college, as men are more likely to drop out (National Center for Education Statistics 2012; Williams 2010; US Bureau of Labor Statistics 2011).

Education trends have a direct impact on wedding and marriage statistics, as expectations to marry are "linked not only to one's own school and work-related experiences but also to those of a partner" (Barr and Simons 2012: 726). In terms of meeting a mate, women are finding it harder to date on college campuses due to a relative shortage of men (Williams 2010). Individuals who are college educated are far more likely to be married than those with less education (Pew Research Center 2010). Additionally, individuals without college degrees are more likely to be involved in criminal activities and incarcerated as a result (Shelden 2011). Further, there is evidence "that a college degree has a protective effect against divorce among all races" (Science Daily 2011).

The missing male is leading to a breakdown of family structure, a problem that is most severe in low-income communities, where a cycle of poverty and crime results in single-parent households and a shortage of marriageable males. "In 2010, some 21 percent of children under age 18 were living in poverty, and the poverty rate for children living with a female parent with no spouse present was 44 percent" (National Center for Education Statistics 2012). Intervention that stresses educational attainment is the key to breaking a cycle that impairs career, economic and marriage prospects.

COHABITATION

A third trend that has led to changing family dynamics is the increasingly commonplace nature of cohabitation. In Western countries, rates of cohabitation have increased dramatically since the 1970s. In England and Wales, for example, it is estimated that, by 2033, the percentage of the adult population that is married will decline to 42 per cent; simultaneously, of those adults who are cohabiting, 87 per cent of them will have never been married (Office of National Statistics 2010). Combined, these statistics indicate a trend where marriage is on the decline and cohabitation before or in place of marriage is expected. While cohabiting couples may aspire to marry, attitude surveys in Great Britain suggest that couples often delay marriage based on concerns over observed rises in unemployment and the cost of housing (Ward 2011). Further, the proportion of births occurring outside of marriage in Great Britain increased from approximately 10 per cent in 1970 to 45 per cent in 2011 (The Center for Social Justice 2011), so couples will often defer marriage longer than they wait to start a family. In the United States, rates of cohabitation are also on the rise. An analysis conducted by the National Center for Marriage and Family Research (2010) found that, when assessing women aged 19–44, 58 per cent indicated that they had lived with an opposite-sex unmarried partner at some point, up from 33 per cent among a comparable group in 1987. Premarital cohabitation has been consistently linked to the delay of first marriage for both women and men, and research indicates that cohabitation decreases the likelihood of a first marriage reaching the 20th anniversary mark; however, the association between cohabitation and marital instability is weakening over time and is less apparent for younger generations, most likely due to changing attitudes and expectations regarding marriage (Copen *et al.* 2012). Similar to the findings in Great Britain, having children outside of marriage is "the new normal. After steadily rising for five decades, the share of children born to unmarried women has crossed a threshold: more than half of births to American women under 30 occur outside marriage" (DeParle and Tavernise 2012: A1). Other examples of countries with high rates of cohabitation include France and Sweden, where cohabitation is seen as an alternative, rather than a precursor, to marriage (Raymo *et al.* 2009).

Cohabitation is not limited to young adults. For adults over the age of 50, rates of cohabitation doubled between 2000 and 2010 (Brown *et al.* 2012). Older adults are drawn to cohabitation over marriage for reasons such as: 1) they are past the point of childbearing; 2) they do not wish to pool finances in such a way that would jeopardize their individual wealth; and 3) they may not wish to be tied down to a caregiving burden that often accompanies marriage during the later stages of life (Brown *et al.* 2012).

In Asian countries, the rates are significantly lower, yet still on the rise. For instance, in Japan, the percentage of single women who had ever cohabited went from an estimated 3 per cent to 14 per cent in less than a decade; however, the percentage of births to unmarried parents remains negligible (Raymo *et al.* 2009). Other countries with low rates of cohabitation include Italy, Mexico, Poland and Spain (Raymo *et al.* 2009).

While the social acceptability of cohabitation is on the rise, unmarried couples have historically been at financial and legal risk. From an economic perspective, college-educated cohabiters were found to have a similar household income to married couples, but cohabiters without college degrees had a significantly lower household income than married couples without college degrees (Fry and Cohn 2011). The distinction is based on the fact that cohabiters without college degrees are much more likely to have children in the household than college-educated cohabiters (Fry and Cohn 2011). When considering the legal ramifications, unmarried partners do not have the same tax advantages, entitlement to assets, medical benefits or right to financial support as married couples.

DIVORCE

Divorce trends also vary significantly by country and are strongly influenced by divorce legislation. In the United States, divorce rates increased sharply between 1970 and 1975, as *no-fault divorce* laws were introduced and it became easier to obtain a divorce. Prior to this legislative change, there had to be evidence of "fault," such as cruelty, adultery, abandonment or imprisonment for a divorce to be granted (Grossman 2004). This made it extremely difficult for couples who had simply fallen out of love or gone in separate directions to be granted a divorce. Prior to the 1970s, cases of *collusive adultery*, where infidelity had not truly taken place but the couple would set up a fake adultery so that they could divorce, became notorious and created confusion and anxiety, as couples were essentially forced to lie in court to obtain a divorce (Grossman 2004). Once no-fault divorce laws were enacted, divorce rates spiked, but then evened out once the new legislation stabilized and have remained relatively flat since. For instance, 70.2 per cent of couples in first marriages where the wedding took place in the early 1960s stayed together for a minimum of 20 years (US Census Bureau 2011). With the adoption of no-fault legislation, the percentage of couples who reached their 20th anniversary dipped to 58.7 per cent and has remained fairly stable ever since (US Census Bureau 2011).

Similarly, in Taiwan, a legislative amendment of the Civil Code in 1996 that was intended to protect married women also facilitated divorce and has caused an increase in the divorce rate (Hsing 2003). In historically ultra-conservative Chile, a shifting cultural landscape resulted in the legalization of divorce in 2004 after a five-year debate (Reel 2005). Similarly, divorce was banned in Malta from 1964 until 2011, when a referendum passed in a closely contested race, with 53 per cent of the voters supporting divorce legislation (Abend 2011). Prior to this change, couples who wished to part ways had to either divorce in another country, separate (but be legally unable to remarry) or petition for an annulment (Abend 2011).

Almost as restrictive was China, where divorce was once nearly unheard of, to the extent that couples even needed permission from their employers to divorce (Fan 2007). Now, however, the divorce rate in China has skyrocketed, in particular in fast-paced cities such as Shanghai where divorce rates are eight times higher than they were in 1980, with explanations for the rise including changes in divorce laws, openness to Western ideas, decreased pressure from family members to stay together, increasing independence of women and a lower tolerance of the rampant mistress culture (Fan 2007; Eimer 2011). The Chinese government became so concerned about the rising tide of divorce that a law was instituted to make divorce less attractive to women, where residential property would no longer be seen as jointly owned and divided evenly upon divorce; instead, it would remain with the owner, which is almost always the husband (Eimer 2011). In a country where men dominate in terms of household earnings, under this law, women are afforded no financial protection upon divorce unless they are registered as co-owners of the property, a stipulation that many women are now requiring of their fiancés (Eimer 2011).

Islamic women seeking a divorce are limited by the provision that talaq (i.e., divorce) "can be invoked only by a husband, unless he grants his wife the same right" (Castaneda 2008: B2) thus denying women due process. This divorce tradition has been challenged in international courts that declare talaq contrary to "constitutional provisions providing equal rights to men and women" (Castaneda 2008: B2).

The Philippines and Vatican City remain the only locales where divorce is banned (Conde 2011). In the Philippines, divorce became prohibited in 1949 and has remained so despite repeated attempts by government proponents to legalize divorce (Conde 2011). Generally speaking, countries that are culturally conservative, such as India, have a very high percentage of Catholic citizens, such as Mexico and Malta, and/or have particularly restrictive laws, such as Italy, have lower divorce rates.

As divorce has become more commonplace, so too have second marriages. With an estimated 30 per cent of first marriages ending before the 10th anniversary and over 40 per cent ending before the 20th anniversary (US Census Bureau 2011), planners who can sensitively handle the needs of couples where the bride, groom or both are entering their second marriage are in demand. *Consultant in Action*, Case Study 4.1 illustrates how sensitive issues may arise during second marriages. First marriages that end in divorce last a median of eight years, and half of those who remarry after a first divorce do so within four years (US Census Bureau 2011). As such, many couples are blending families when they remarry, which poses unique challenges to the wedding consultant. Divorce rates for second marriages are not statistically different from those of first marriages.

SAME-SEX MARRIAGE

While becoming a more mainstream issue on a yearly basis, same-sex marriage remains a controversial topic in many countries. Opinion, policy and legislation vary dramatically, with change evidenced continually but inconsistently, as some political entities grow more open, while others make statements and pass laws to limit the rights of same-sex partners.

As of this writing, 13 US states (California, Connecticut, Delaware, Iowa, Maine, Maryland, Massachusetts, Minnesota, New Hampshire, New York, Rhode Island, Vermont and Washington) as well as the District of Columbia have legalized same-sex marriage. Same-sex marriage affords

CONSULTANT IN ACTION, CASE 4.1

THE TOAST

You are working with a couple, Ben and Hazel. It is Hazel's first marriage and Ben's second. The ceremony went beautifully and the guests are now enjoying the reception, dancing the night away after a delicious sit-down dinner. On schedule, you prepare to round up the best man, Sid, and maid of honor for toasts before the cake is cut. You find Sid, quite inebriated, hanging out by the bar. When the DJ announces the best man's toast, Sid grabs the microphone and begins as follows: "Marriage is really, really difficult. This is Ben's second wedding and I am divorced, too. Ben and his first wife just didn't try hard enough to stay together and my marriage was awful." Sid goes on to talk about how second marriages fail all the time, too. The bride is clearly in distress and it seems like Sid is going to ramble for quite some time.

WHAT DO YOU DO?

couples the same rights, benefits and responsibilities as heterosexual couples. Civil union statutes, often a precursor to same-sex marriage legislation, allow for legal recognition of same-sex couples as well as benefits similar to those granted to married couples (National Conference of State Legislatures 2013a). Civil unions are permissible in Delaware, Hawaii, Illinois, New Jersey and Rhode Island. Domestic-partnership registries, which tend to precede civil unions and are available in California, Nevada and Oregon, allow unmarried same-sex and opposite-sex couples to receive limited rights and benefits, such as those related to property, hospital visitation, health benefits, retirement benefits, inheritance and domestic violence protection (US Bureau of Labor Statistics 2013; National Conference of State Legislatures 2013a). These registries can also be found in local municipalities (i.e., cities and counties) throughout the United States in cases where they do not apply to the whole state.

Although 58 per cent of all Americans and 81 per cent of US adults between the ages of 18 and 29 believe that same-sex marriage should be legal (Fahrenthold and Cohen 2013), much political opposition remains, with over 30 states having laws or constitutional provisions that limit marriage to a man and a woman. This is done by adopting Defense of Marriage Act (DOMA) language that defines marriage as being limited to one man and one woman (National Conference of State Legislatures 2013b). A federal DOMA was enacted in 1996, thus denying same-sex couples access to approximately 1,100 federal laws and benefits that pertain to marriage (Will 2013). Based on

PHOTO 4.3 SAME-SEX MARRIAGE IS GAINING WIDE APPROVAL.

SOURCE: WWW.RODNEYBAILEY.COM

a series of rulings that determined that the federal DOMA was discriminatory, the issue was taken up by the US Supreme Court (Balz 2013a), where justices struck down "a crucial part of the law, making it possible for same-sex couples who are legally married under state law to receive federal benefits" (Balz 2013b: A1).

Internationally, same-sex marriages are legal in Argentina, Belgium, Canada, Iceland, the Netherlands, Norway, Portugal, South Africa, Spain and Sweden, while civil partnerships are recognized in all or part of over a dozen other countries, such as Australia, Brazil, Denmark and the United Kingdom. Those who support same-sex marriage and unions see the issue as one of civil rights discrimination, while opponents contend that same-sex relationships are immoral and undermine marriage and family values (Wagner 2012).

While some argue that same-sex marriage has become commonplace to the point of being practically a nonissue (Dvorak 2013; Marcus 2012), divisiveness and extremism still exist in many jurisdictions around the world. For instance, Hong Kong billionaire Cecil Chao made the international headlines when he offered $65 million to any man who could woo his daughter, Gigi Chao, away from her female partner when he learned of their same-sex wedding ceremony (NBC World News

2012). Same-sex couples assert that, in spite of legal progress, it is the personal evolution that matters most. Writer Jeff Chu eloquently illustrates the point:

> The justices can compel the government to give us tax breaks because we're married. They can't make my relatives add a seat for my husband at the Thanksgiving table. . . . My husband and I have been together eight years, and we've lived together for three. My mom has not visited since 2007. But she's trying her best. Recently she told us that she'd like to visit us this summer. "I thought I would come cook you a dinner, if you want," she said. In this court, that counts as a huge victory.
>
> (2013: A17)

Same-sex commitment ceremonies, whether legal or symbolic, are increasingly taking place all over the world. As a wedding consultant, you will need to determine if this is a niche market you would like to pursue. Most wedding-related vendors are not in the business of turning away clients, and same-sex ceremonies and receptions tend to be as extravagant as those of heterosexual couples. However, if this is not within your comfort zone, you should become familiar with wedding consultants in your area who regularly work with same-sex couples so that you can make referrals as necessary.

INTERCULTURAL AND INTERFAITH MARRIAGES

The changing family, expanding interactions with individuals of diverse ethnicities, increased religious tolerance, widespread access to transportation and the influences of a global economy have led to "demographic changes that are pushing interracial marriage rates to an all-time high in the United States while toppling historical taboos among younger people" (Morello 2012: B1). According to data analysis completed by the Pew Research Center, "about 15% of all new marriages in the United States in 2010 were between spouses of a different race or ethnicity from one another, more than double the share in 1980 (6.7%)" (Wang 2012: 1). However, significant variation was found based on race, where, "among all newlyweds in 2010, 9 per cent of whites, 17 per cent of blacks, 26 per cent of Hispanics and 28 per cent of Asians married out" (Wang 2012: 1). Attitude shift has been dramatic, with the percentage of people saying they would not intermarry decreasing from 67 per cent in 1986 to 6 per cent of whites and 3 per cent of blacks in 2009 (in Morello 2012). These changes are particularly noteworthy, as *miscegenation* laws, defined as statutes prohibiting interracial marriage, existed in the United States for over 300 years (Pascoe 2004).

Progressive attitudes have positively impacted not only larger cultural groups, but also individuals within those groups. For instance, marriage opportunities for individuals with specialized needs have historically been diminished based on lack of understanding of and support for their romantic interests: "In the past, stigmas against people with intellectual impairments led to forced sterilization and laws prohibiting them from marriage" (McCarthy 2013: 13). The wedding story of Shelley and Bill, as beautifully told by writer Ellen McCarthy (2013) and summarized in *Culture Corner*, Case 4.2, illustrates that, with assistance, individuals with disabilities can form loving relationships.

Interfaith marriage remains complicated in many countries. In Lebanon, for example, a civil marriage with no religious contract is a near impossibility, forcing couples who wish to marry yet maintain different religious beliefs to travel out of the country for their wedding, most typically to Cyprus, which is the closest country that allows for civil marriage (Dabbagh 2013; Cambanis 2013). The marriage certificate can then be brought back to Lebanon and recorded (Dabbagh 2013). However, even once the marriage is recorded, the wife is still subject to the religious sect of her husband when it comes to inheritance, children, divorce and other legal matters (Dabbagh 2013). Lebanese couples are more frequently pushing back, hoping to act as catalysts for a movement where they can have a "legally recognized personal life outside of the umbrella of religion" (Cambanis 2013).

An understanding of the historic struggles endured by many interracial and interfaith couples sheds light on why the blending of wedding traditions can cause stress and emotional conflict, in particular if different beliefs are ignored, misunderstood or not respected. *Cross-cultural conflict* at the interpersonal level occurs when cultural perspectives regarding values, norms, habits, practices, customs or traditions clash (Moran *et al.* 2011). *Culture Corner*, Case 4.3 presents an exemplar of how cultural conflict can tear apart a family. Conversely, *Culture Corner*, Case 4.4 offers a model of how consultants can assist with blending traditions.

When acting as a consultant for weddings with blended traditions, you will benefit from considering the following suggestions (González 2005; Kim-Jo *et al.* 2010; Moran *et al.* 2011; Nelson and Otnes 2005):

1. Recognize that each person involved in the planning of a wedding will have a unique identity and cultural lens that will influence personality, attitudes and needs. Strive to be sensitive to cultural differences and each person's distinctiveness.

2. Be certain to involve both families in the decision-making process, so that elements of the ceremony and reception do not inadvertently offend the beliefs and traditions of either family. Encourage the couple to communicate openly with one another and their parents to create a supportive environment and so that arrangements do not come as a surprise to anyone.

3. Respect the customs of both families by finding out how the rituals are observed and helping the couple make sure that they are carried out properly. If the ceremony is going to be held at a place of worship, communicate with the individual who will be leading the ceremony to determine the rules and restrictions specific to the religious site.

CULTURE CORNER, CASE 4.2

THE WEDDING OF SHELLEY AND BILL

Shelley and Bill met when he was 12 and she was 15 at a social club. For Bill, it was love at first sight, and the feeling was mutual. However, this was not a typical courtship, as Bill has Down syndrome and Shelley was born with hydrocephalus, meaning excess fluid on her brain that resulted in intellectual impairment. Shelley went to Bill's high school proms, but, after high school, "they moved into assisted living programs in different parts of the county" (McCarthy 2013: 10). Over a decade later, their paths crossed through a cruise planned for individuals with disabilities. They began to date and, when Bill proposed, Shelley said yes. While their parents were skeptical, they were insistent, ultimately going to a relationship therapist who "helped convince their parents that they were ready for marriage" (ibid.: 13). While they chose to have a commitment ceremony rather than a legal marriage, so as to not jeopardize healthcare benefits, "everyone involved considered it an official wedding" (ibid.: 14). Like every couple, they had to get used to living together, and they still require daily assistance; yet, "everyone in their orbit is acutely aware of how much richer their lives are because of each other" (ibid.: 15).

SOURCE: McCARTHY (2013)

CULTURE CORNER, CASE 4.3

A REAL WEDDING STORY FROM JORDAN

The ear sometimes adores before the eye

The story goes back to April 2007 between a Jordanian man who was living in the UK and a Jordanian woman who was working in an establishment in Jordan. One day, he phoned to talk to the head of the establishment and she replied instead. To love a woman from first sight is common everywhere around the globe, but this was not the case of this story, where the groom loved the bride from the first moment he heard her voice on the phone. This is in keeping with a poem in Arabic culture by Bashar bin Burd which says, "The ear sometimes adores before the eye." From the first call, he was attracted to her voice on the phone, and they exchanged their mobile numbers and e-mail addresses. They continued contact every other day and within less than eight months they met for the first time on 18 December 2007 in Amman, the capital of Jordan. They agreed on marriage and she then travelled to meet him in England in February of 2008 to get married on the 13th of that month. He travelled back to Jordan on 22 May 2008 to celebrate her birthday and they spent a one-week honeymoon in Aqaba. She resigned from her job and prepared herself to reunite in England, where they did in August of 2008.

What is interesting in this story is it opposed all wedding traditions in Jordan, where a man or his parents send a *jaha* (see *Culture Corner*, Case 3.4) and the wedding or marriage goes through a defined process. In this story, the groom and the bride took the role of the *jaha*, the guardian and their families. Another interesting issue is the groom is Muslim and the bride comes from a Christian family and love joined them, although they have different religions, different traditions and different social and economic status. He said to her from the beginning, "It is true that we are coming from different cultures, although we come from the same country, Jordan, but we can create our own hybrid culture since we love each other." She got pregnant almost immediately with their first son, who is now 3½ years old. She is now pregnant with their second child; he wants a girl and she wants a boy, but the ultrasound confirmed it is a boy!

The bride's siblings, despite coming from a reputable, highly educated and open-minded family in Jordan, were shocked when they learned about this marriage. They tried by all means to curb this marriage, asking her to abort and divorce her husband and come back to Jordan, but they failed. Now, after four years of marriage, her family boycotted her. Regrettably, the woman's decision to get married is still overwhelmed by traditions in Jordan, both Muslim and Christian families. The bride's family considered this marriage an honor crime, but they forgot that we people are equal in front of God.

CASE SUBMITTED BY RAFA HADDAD AND SALEM HARAHSHEH

CULTURE CORNER, CASE 4.4

MAKING TIME FOR TRADITION

Jennifer and Kevin, a couple of young professionals, are eclectic, in love and respectful in cultural tradition. Jennifer is of Puerto Rican descent and Kevin is African American. Together they planned a celebration that expressed their genuine love for one another through the lens of blending their cultures.

As Alums of the University of Maryland, they hosted the ceremony at Memorial Chapel in the majestic Main Chapel on the campus where they shared many memories. The chapel has very strict requirements for the amount of time that is allowed for the use. The site's popularity, the frequency of chapel services and the limited amount of parking warrant a strict adherence to timeliness. Regulations prohibit receiving lines and other activities that could compromise the timely exit of the wedding group. As the coordinator, it was my responsibility to understand these rules and to help enforce them.

The excitement about this marriage was contagious. Several family members traveled from as far away as Puerto Rico to witness the wedding and to participate in the family traditions. Jennifer's mother shared two traditions that were very important to her – the handmade *Capias* favors that she had been working on for months and a "Blessing of the Bride" ritual that involves the female family members on the wedding day. Though considerate of her mother's wishes, it was clear that these traditions were not as significant to Jennifer. Through a probing conversation, it was uncovered that Jennifer's primary concern was ensuring that the events of the day would happen on time. Her anxiety stemmed from the fact that neither one of the cultures is known for timeliness. We were very clear on the chapel rules. Armed with that information, it was easy to make strategic recommendations that would keep us on time, while honoring the family traditions.

The day started early for the ladies with "girl time" – breakfast, hair, makeup and getting dressed. The siblings, bridesmaids, aunts and cousins gathered at the home of Jennifer's mother for this special time together. Once dressed, the bride was presented to the elders for their approval and then to shower her with blessings. This ritual involves tossing flowers toward the bride until she enters the limousine.

The "Blessing of the Bride" happened with Jennifer's mother orchestrating it in a way that facilitated a timely departure of the limo, which arrived at the chapel right on schedule. The family arrived in time for choice seating. The ceremony started at the stroke of 2:00 p.m. and by 3:30 p.m. you couldn't tell that we had been there. At the reception, each guest received the handmade *Capias* as a keepsake of the wedding.

CASE SUBMITTED BY MARILYN PATTERSON
JOYOUS EVENTS LLC
WEBSITE: *WWW.JOYOUSEVENTS.COM*

4. Discuss the notion of time carefully with the couple. Different cultures have dramatically varying perspectives of the definition of being "on time." For example, if a wedding invitation states the ceremony begins at 3:00 p.m., guests with Latin American backgrounds are likely to define this loosely, as the notion of time is much more elastic than in the US.

5. Consider a neutral site and leader for the ceremony if tensions arise due to religious differences. Alternatively, celebrants of different faiths can be invited to co-celebrate. However, with some religions, co-leaders from different places of worship would not be permitted or the offer could be rejected, so this option should be approached with caution.

6. If conflict occurs due to differences of opinion, recognize that individuals from different cultural backgrounds may display dramatically different conflict-resolution styles (e.g., competing versus avoiding).

7. Appreciate the multilingualism that accompanies many cross-cultural marriages. Translations can be incorporated in stationery elements such as invitations and ceremony programs, readings and toasts can be performed in more than one language and music from both cultures can be played.

8. Ultimately, some couples will not feel comfortable abandoning cultural norms or having a hybrid ritual. In cases where the customs are appreciably different or the extended families live in two different countries, couples may opt for two separate wedding events. This doubling process increases planning time as well as costs, but ensures that the sacred rituals of both cultures are upheld.

Blended traditions add to the uniqueness and beauty of weddings and are reflective of the evolution of society and family. Incorporating elements of dress, food, entertainment and ceremonial traditions that reflect the different backgrounds of the couple enhances the celebration of diversity.

REFERENCES

Abend, L. (1 June 2011) 'Malta says "we do" to legalizing divorce', *Time*, Online. Available HTTP: <http://www.time.com/time/world/article/0,8599,2074721,00.htm> (accessed 1 August 2012).

Balz, D. (27 March 2013a) 'The take: parties scramble to adjust to debate's realities', *The Washington Post*, A1, A7.

—— (27 June 2013b) 'Victories for gay marriage', *The Washington Post*, A1, A8.

Barr, A.B. and Simons, R.L. (2012) 'Marriage expectations among African American couples in early adulthood: a dyadic analysis', *Journal of Family and Marriage*, 74: 726–742.

Brown, S.L., Bulanda, J.R. and Lee, G.R. (2012) 'Transitions into and out of cohabitation in later life', *Journal of Marriage and Family*, 74: 774–793.

Cambanis, T. (10 March 2013) 'The Middle East's fight for civil marriage', *The Boston Globe*, Online. Available HTTP: <http://www.bostonglobe.com/ideas/2013/03/10/the-middle-east-fight-for-civil-marriage/ITkk16DyemRYsw4uCOb2TL/story.html> (accessed 27 March 2013).

Castaneda, R. (8 May 2008) 'Islamic divorce ruled not valid in Maryland', *The Washington Post*, B2.

Chu, J. (27 March 2013) 'Love is the higher law', *The Washington Post*, A17.

Conde, C.H. (17 June 2011) 'Philippines stands all but alone in banning divorce', *The New York Times*, Online. Available HTTP: <http://www.nytimes.com/2011/06/18/world/asia/18iht-philippines18.html> (accessed 11 October 2012).

Copen, C.E., Daniels, K., Vespa, J. and Mosher, W.D. (2012) 'First marriages in the United States: data from the 2006–2010 National Survey of Family Growth', National Health Statistics Reports, 49, Online. Available HTTP: <http://www.cdc.gov/nchs/data/nhsr/nhsr049.pdf> (accessed 23 January 2013).

Dabbagh, N. (2013) 'Interfaith marriage in Lebanon'. E-mail (2 February 2013).

DeParle, J. and Tavernise, S. (18 February 2012) 'Unwed mothers now a majority before age of 30', *The New York Times*, A1.

Dvorak, P. (11 January 2013) 'Exciting, if not surprising, news for same-sex couples', *The Washington Post*, B1, B5.

Eberstadt, N. (2012) 'Japan shrinks', *Wilson Quarterly*, 36: 30–37.

Eimer, D. (30 October 2011) 'China's divorce rule dubbed "law that makes men laugh and women cry"', *Beijing*, Online. Available HTTP: <http://www.telegraph.co.uk/news/worldnews/asia/afghanistan/8857708/Chinas-divorce-rule-dubbed-Law-that-makes-men-laugh-and-women-cry.html> (accessed 24 October 2012).

Fahrenthold, D.A. and Cohen, J. (19 March 2013) 'Record support for gay marriage', *The Washington Post*, A1, A4.

Fan, M. (7 April 2007) 'Chinese slough off old barriers to divorce', *The Washington Post*, A1, A10.

Fry, R. and Cohn, D. (27 June 2011) 'Living together: the economics of cohabitation', Pew Research Center, Online. Available HTTP: <http://www.pewsocialtrends.org/files/2011/06/pew-social-trends-cohabitation-06-2011.pdf> (accessed 20 October 2012).

González, I.C. (23 June 2005) 'Down the aisle, into the melting pot', *The Washington Post*, H1, H5.

Grossman, J. (2004) 'Will New York final adopt true no-fault divorce?: recent proposals to amend the state's archaic divorce law', *FindLaw: Legal News and Commentary*, Online. Available HTTP: <http://writ.lp.findlaw.com/grossman/20041020.html> (accessed 27 March 2013).

Haddad, R. and Harahsheh, S. (2013) 'A real wedding story from Jordan'. E-mail (15 February 2013).

Hsing, Y. (2003) 'Impact of institutional and socioeconomic changes on marital relationship', *International Journal of Social Economics*, 30: 613–618.

Kim-Jo, T., Benet-Martínez, V. and Ozer, D.J. (2010) 'Culture and interpersonal conflict resolution styles: role of acculturation', *Journal of Cross-Cultural Psychology*, 41: 264–269.

McCarthy, E. (10 February 2013) 'When Bill met Shelley', *Washington Post Magazine*, 8–15.

Marcus, R. (31 October 2012) 'The attack issue that never showed up', *The Washington Post*, A21.

Moran, R.T., Harris, P.R. and Moran, S.V. (2011) *Managing Cultural Differences: leadership skills and strategies for working in a global world*, Burlington, MA: Butterworth-Heinemann.

Morello, C. (16 February 2012) 'Interracial marriage rates soar as attitudes change', *The Washington Post*, B1, B5.

National Center for Education Statistics (2012) 'Higher education: gaps in access and persistence study', Online. Available HTTP: <http://nces.ed.gov/pubs2012/2012046.pdf> (accessed 20 March 2013).

National Center for Marriage and Family Research (2010) 'Trends in cohabitation: twenty years of change, 1987–2008', Online. Available HTTP: <http://ncfmr.bgsu.edu/pdf/family_profiles/file87411.pdf> (accessed 23 January 2013).

National Conference of State Legislatures (2013a) 'Civil unions and domestic partnership statutes', Online. Available HTTP: <http://www.ncsl.org/issues-research/human-services/civil-unions-and-domestic-partnership-statutes.aspx> (accessed 9 February 2013).

—— (2013b) 'Defining marriage: defense of marriage acts and same-sex marriage laws', Online. Available HTTP: <http://www.ncsl.org/issues-research/human-services/same-sex-marriage-overview.aspx> (accessed 9 February 2013).

NBC World News (28 September 2012) 'Lesbian heiress Gigi Chao on "loving terms" with father despite $65 million dowry offer', Online. Available HTTP: <http://worldnews.nbcnews.com/_news/2012/09/28/14138419-lesbian-heiress-gigi-chao-on-loving-terms-with-father-despite-65-million-dowry-offer?lite> (accessed 20 January 2013).

Nelson, M.R. and Otnes, C.C. (2005) 'Exploring cross-cultural ambivalence: a netnography of intercultural wedding message boards', *Journal of Business Research*, 58: 89–95.

Office of National Statistics (2010) 'Marital status population projections for England and Wales', Online. Available HTTP: <http://www.ons.gov.uk/ons/rel/npp/marital-status-population-projections-for-england—-wales/2008-based-marital-status-projections/index.html> (accessed 8 October 2012).

Pascoe, P. (2004) 'Why the ugly rhetoric against gay marriage is familiar to this historian of miscegenation', *History News Network*, Online. Available HTTP: <http://hnn.us/articles/4708.html> (accessed 20 March 2013).

Patterson, M. (2013) 'Making time for tradition'. E-mail (14 February 2013).

Pew Research Center (2010) 'Women, men and the new economics of marriage', Online. Available HTTP: <http://www.pewsocialtrends.org/files/2010/11/new-economics-of-marriage.pdf> (accessed 11 January 2013).

Raymo, J.M., Iwasawa, M. and Bumpass L. (2009) 'Cohabitation and family formation in Japan', *Demography*, 46: 785–803.

Reel, M. (10 December 2005) 'Female, agnostic and the next presidente?', *The Washington Post*, A1, A17.

Science Daily (2011) 'First-time divorce rate tied to education, race', Online. Available HTTP: <http://www.sciencedaily.com/releases/2011/11/111103161830.htm> (accessed 2 March 2013).

Shelden, R.G. (1 April 2011) 'Education as crime prevention', Online. Available HTTP: <http://www.cjcj.org/post/juvenile/justice/education/crime/prevention> (accessed 14 July 2012).

Sullivan, K. (13 November 2012) 'Saudi women, educated but jobless', *The Washington Post*, A01.

The Center for Social Justice (2011) 'History and family: setting the records straight. A rebuttal to the British Academy pamphlet *Happy families?*', Online. Available HTTP: <http://www.centreforsocialjustice.org.uk/publications/history-and-family> (accessed 14 July 2012).

US Bureau of Labor Statistics (2011) 'Educational attainment of women in the labor force, 1970–2010', Online. Available HTTP: <http://www.bls.gov/opub/ted/2011/ted_20111229.htm> (accessed 23 January 2013).

—— (2012) 'Labor force', *Occupational Outlook Quarterly*, Online. Available HTTP: <http://www.bls.gov/opub/ooq/2011/winter/art02.pdf> (accessed 22 January 2013).

—— (2013) 'Employee benefits survey', Online. Available HTTP: <http://www.bls.gov/ncs/ebs/> (accessed 22 January 2013).

US Census Bureau (2011) 'Number, timing, and duration of marriages and divorces: 2009', Current Population Reports, Report Number P70-125, Online. Available HTTP: <http://www.census.gov/prod/2011pubs/p70-125.pdf> (accessed 22 January 2013).

US Census Bureau, International Statistics (2012) 'Female labor force participation rates by country: 1980 to 2010', Online. Available HTTP: <http://www.census.gov/compendia/statab/2012/tables/12s1368.pdf> (accessed 22 January 2013).

US Supreme Court (1967) *Loving v. Virginia*, 388 US 1.

Wagner, J. (30 September 2012) 'Maryland to see ad war over same-sex marriage', *The Washington Post*, C1, C6.

Wang, W. (16 February 2012) 'The rise of intermarriage: rates, characteristics vary by race and gender', Pew Research Center, Online. Available HTTP: <http://www.pewsocialtrends.org/files/2012/02/SDT-Intermarriage-II.pdf> (accessed 24 January 2013).

Ward, V. (2011) 'One in six cohabiting as marriage rate declines', *The Telegraph*, Online. Available HTTP: <http://www.telegraph.co.uk/women/sex/divorce/8924245/One-in-six-cohabiting-as-marriage-rate-declines.html> (accessed 15 January 2013).

Will, G.F. (21 March 2013) 'DOMA is an abuse of federalism', *The Washington Post*, A19.

Williams, A. (5 February 2010) 'The new math on campus', *The New York Times*, Online. Available HTTP: <http://www.nytimes.com/2010/02/07/fashion/07campus.html?pagewanted=all> (accessed 23 January 2013).

REVIEW

1. What are some of the outcomes that have resulted from changing female workforce dynamics?

2. Explain the phenomenon of the "missing male" and give two examples of related impacts.

3. Discuss the intersection between cohabitation, education and household income.

4. Give two examples of divorce trends, using different countries.

5. Name five international locations where same-sex marriages are legal.

6. Name three suggestions that consultants should consider when helping plan weddings with blended traditions.

TERMINOLOGY

- Blended traditions

- Civil unions

- Cohabitation

- Collusive adultery

- Commitment ceremonies

- Cross-cultural conflict

- Defense of Marriage Acts

- Domestic-partnership registries

- Miscegenation laws

- No-fault divorce

- Same-sex marriage

PHOTO 5.1 Wedding and honeymoon tourism contributes to local economic development.

SOURCE: WWW.RODNEYBAILEY.COM

TOURISM AND DESTINATION WEDDINGS

Weddings and honeymoons contribute to local economic development in a number of ways. First, couples generally use local goods and services, relying on vendors such as florists, caterers and transportation specialists whose businesses are in close proximity to the wedding and reception. This spending fuels the economy of the community where the wedding is held. Second, weddings involve out-of-town guests who are, in essence, tourists during their stay. Their expenditures on hotels, food and beverage, gasoline and entertainment bring new money into a region, thus enhancing the local economy. Third, most couples will celebrate their newlywed status by taking a honeymoon.

Now the newlyweds are the tourists and their spending at a chosen destination will enhance the livelihood of the local businesses where they are vacationing. This combined outlay of cash is significant, leading to fierce competition to attract engaged and newly married couples. Finally, communities that historically have served as honeymoon spots are now increasingly repackaging their services to also serve as the wedding site, giving rise to the destination wedding. This chapter reviews three areas of economic development through tourism that are particularly relevant to weddings, including: 1) visiting friends and relatives travel; 2) honeymoon travel; and 3) destination weddings.

VISITING FRIENDS AND RELATIVES TRAVEL

Wedding tourism offers an excellent example of visiting friends and relatives (VFR) travel. VFR travel is considered one of the oldest forms of tourism based on the social connections that act as an impetus for leaving one's home (in Backer 2012). The VFR tourist feels at "home," psychologically, while being away, based on the strength of social ties and interactions that shape a home-like experience (Uriely 2010). Importantly, as Pearce explains, it is possible to visit friends and relatives in places that have no "long standing links to the traveler" (2012: 1029). This is particularly relevant for certain wedding guests, such as college friends, who may have never previously been to the chosen destination.

VFR travelers have been segmented into three groups: PVFRs, CVFRs and EVFRs (in Backer 2012). PVFRs are "pure" VFRs, whose primary purpose for travel is to visit friends or relatives and, importantly, the traveler stays in the home of the friend or relative. CVFRs are "commercial" VFRs, who visit the destination specifically to see the friend or relative but stay in a commercial lodging such as a hotel. EVFRs are "exploiting" VFRs in that they stay at the home of the friend or relative but their main agenda is not to visit with their host. Out-of-town wedding guests who fall into the CVFR category contribute most significantly to the destination's economy based on their stay in local accommodations and increased likelihood of eating their meals at area restaurants.

Historically, businesses did not take a keen interest in VFR travel, as many believed that it had little economic value in comparison with other forms of tourism and that it could not be stimulated by marketing efforts (Shani and Uriely 2012). This attitude has changed dramatically, as research has shown that VFR travel accounts for a significant proportion of short-term departures. For example, Backer found that "VFR travel is almost half the size of the total overnight travel market in Australia" (2012: 79). For many destinations, VFR is a principal form of tourism that operates as a means of generating repeat visitation over time.

VFR tourism is more resilient to crisis situations than other forms of travel. In cases of extremist activities, such as the 9/11 terrorist attacks, vacation plans were postponed and business travel suffered significant losses (Blake and Sinclair 2003), as "firms cancelled or postponed conventions, corporate meetings, seminars, and trade shows" (Goodrich 2002: 576). However, couples were still getting married, and relatives and friends were there to support them. The emotional ties inherent to VFR travel allow these trips to take place even when extenuating circumstances arise.

Travel is also subject to disturbances based on weather patterns and economic shifts. Global warming has been linked to extreme heat, drought and heavy downpours as illustrated in a study that reviewed six decades of weather patterns (Hansen *et al.* 2012). Climate change has been linked to catastrophic weather events, but even relatively minor anomalies can wreak havoc on travel schedules, in particular those that deal with air transport. Global economic conditions also influence travel, with recent recessions directly linked to a decrease in both domestic and international travel. Wedding-related expenditures have been found to recover more quickly from

Photo 5.2 Weddings give elderly family members an excuse to travel.

Source: www.RodneyBailey.com

an economic downturn than other types of spending; similarly, VFR travel is less likely to be cancelled in times of widespread fiscal difficulty than business travel (Daniels *et al.* 2012).

In times of peace and crisis, VFR remains one of the most stable forms of tourism (Asiedu 2008) and is likely to become increasingly important as people age, as it strengthens the participants' social lives and lends to their overall happiness (Larsen *et al.* 2007). Weddings give parents, aunts and uncles, grandparents, cousins and siblings an excuse to travel or play host to family members and friends. As families become less centralized, it is often difficult for groups to get together for holiday gatherings; however, weddings provide a motivation to travel. As a wedding consultant, you will eventually assist a couple and/or their guests in making air travel, ground transportation or accommodation arrangements, and you will need to be sensitive to the travel constraints that may affect some of the guests, in particular those who are elderly, have disabilities or are traveling with young children (e.g., Daniels *et al.* 2005; McCarthy 2011).

Wedding-related travel is increasingly occurring before the wedding as well. An extension of the bachelor or bachelorette party, a get-away may be planned with friends as a last salute to singlehood. The premarital stag tour, for example, has become a recent trend for British men, who are drawn to "popular stag destinations in the Czech Republic, Poland, Hungary and Latvia . . . by the promise of cheap alcohol, restaurants and entertainment including abundant night life" (Thurnell-Read 2012: 801).

HONEYMOON TRAVEL

Honeymoon travel, as we know it today, came about as accommodations, services and transportation became formalized in the early 1820s and 1830s (Towner 1985). Prior to this time was the period of the *Grand Tour*, which lasted from 1500 to 1820 (Fridgen 1996). Travel during the Grand Tour period was physically punishing and often dangerous; hence, it was primarily completed by young, male aristocrats for the purposes of education, curiosity, cultural enrichment and career development (Black 2011; Towner 1996).

Transportation enhancements during the industrial age, including travel by stagecoach, ship and train, allowed tourism to become a commercial business and increased opportunities for individuals to travel purely for leisure and pleasure (Weaver and Lawton 2010). Luxury commercial sea tours to destinations across the globe became available by the late 1800s (Fridgen 1996). The emergence of the automobile and airplane, coupled with shorter workweeks, longer vacation times, increased income and decreased family size opened up the door to mass tourism (Weaver and Lawton 2010). Now the honeymoon is an expected and anticipated travel experience that most Westernized couples employ to launch their new life together.

The most popular honeymoon destinations vary from country to country, in part based on geographical proximity but also influenced by destination attributes. For US couples, the top ten "best" honeymoon destinations based on a review by US News and World Report (2013) include

Santorini, Maui, Crete, Kauai, Florence, Venice, Turks and Caicos, Martinique, St. Martin-St. Maarten and Paris. In the United Kingdom, honeymoon hotspots include exclusive resorts found in Turkey, Maldives, Mozambique, Morocco, Cambodia, Ecuador, Bali, Thailand and Italy (Condé Nast UK 2013). As another point of comparison, the most popular honeymoon destinations for Koreans include Thailand, Japan, the United States and France (in Kim and Agrusa 2005).

Irrespective of country of origin, couples appear to be seeking similar attributes in a honeymoon destination. Research supports that destination image, as constructed experientially or through the media, influences travel, with nice (typically warm) weather, exotic atmosphere, outstanding scenery, perceived safety, reasonable travel costs, excellent accommodations, environmental quality and a wide range of activities rated as particularly important (e.g., Castelltort and Mäder 2010; Kim *et al.* 2009; Lee *et al.* 2010; Lee and Lee 2009).

Despite the pervasiveness of honeymoon travel, there are potential associated drawbacks if the vacation is not planned carefully. Weddings tend to be very public occasions, where couples are surrounded by their closest friends and family members who envelop them with support and create a stimulating environment. When newlyweds select a remote, isolated destination for their

PHOTO 5.3 EXOTIC LOCATIONS ARE OFTEN CHOSEN FOR HONEYMOON TRAVEL.

SOURCE: WWW.RODNEYBAILEY.COM

honeymoon, the seclusion may allow the couple to decompress and reconnect, but it may also lead to feelings of loneliness and strain. These feelings are likely to be exacerbated if the honeymoon destination is more to one person's liking than the other's or if there are not enough activities to keep the couple busy. The honeymoon destination selection process can be complicated, and research has shown that over 50 per cent of engaged couples do not reach early consensus on the honeymoon destination; however, in cases of disagreement, the preference of the bride-to-be tends to have greater influence on the final decision (Jang *et al.* 2007).

So, while couples often think that all they will want to do is be alone on their honeymoon, as a consultant you may want to suggest quite the opposite. Kim and Agrusa warn that beach resorts, in particular, need to offer honeymooners programs that allow them to become actively engaged in the novelties of an exotic culture so that they can feel involved with the community rather than experiencing "the inevitable feeling of boredom that comes with a beautiful beach or tropical scenery with nothing else to do except sit in the sun" (2005: 901). Some couples become so disenchanted with their honeymoon that they cut the stay short. They become anxious to return to their social networks, enjoy their new gifts and review photos and video clips from the wedding day. The decision to leave the honeymoon destination early can be a stressful one, as it may be accompanied by feelings of guilt or the sense that the marriage did not start off on the right note. Increasingly, couples are waiting a few days, weeks or even months to take their honeymoon vacations, allowing them to soak up the wedding moments and then pull away at a later date.

As a wedding consultant, you may be asked to assist with honeymoon planning. Rather than simply directing couples to a travel agent or handing them a list of top destinations, help them to carefully consider their activity preferences and, in particular, what they like to do together. Communicate with them openly about the timing of the honeymoon and present different leave-taking scenarios for consideration.

DESTINATION WEDDINGS

The *destination wedding* occurs when a couple decides to hold their wedding in a location where neither one of them resides. Generally, an exotic or popular tourism destination is chosen and the wedding often merges into the honeymoon. The joining of these two events creates what is popularly called the *WeddingMoon*, a term coined by Sandals Resorts (2013), which specializes in Caribbean destination weddings.

Destination weddings are becoming increasingly popular, with an estimated 10 per cent of couples travelling 200 miles or more from their home to get married, and another 28 per cent travel between 50 and 199 miles away (The Wedding Report 2011). Once they step outside their resident jurisdiction, economically they become tourists. For US residents travelling abroad for their weddings, the most popular destinations remain the Caribbean and Europe (The American Wedding Study 2012).

While Caribbean locations such as Antigua, the Bahamas, Jamaica and St. Lucia attract a significant percentage of the US destination wedding business, other major players include Disney (2013), whose "Fairy Tale Weddings" business model includes a variety of packages at different locations and price points; Las Vegas, where "Viva Las Vegas Wedding Chapels" (2013) offer over 30 themed wedding and commitment ceremony packages from which to choose; and Hawaii, which is able to capitalize on its popularity as a honeymoon destination by offering wedding packages (Bardolet and Sheldon 2008). Hawaiian destination weddings are discussed in more detail in *Culture Corner*, Case 5.1.

CULTURE CORNER, CASE 5.1

DESTINATION WEDDINGS IN HAWAII

With its breathtaking scenery, moderate climate, and unique history and culture, Hawaii no doubt is one of the most exotic wedding destinations. According to Hawaii Tourism Authority (HTA 2012), there were approximately 120,000 visitors married in Hawaii in 2011. Approximately 50 per cent of these non-natives came from Japan, while almost 44 per cent were from the US mainland (HTA 2012). There are many reasons why visitors choose to get married in Hawaii and not to wed in their hometown, one of which regards the wedding costs. According to Crocker (2009), destination weddings usually cost less than weddings held close to home, sometimes as much as 40 per cent less. The major reason is that the average wedding party size of destination weddings is approximately one-third of that of hometown weddings (Crocker 2009). Although it may cost less for a couple to hold a destination wedding in Hawaii rather than marrying close to their permanent residence, it does not mean that their guests are spending less than the average visitor. According to HTA (2012), the average per person per day expenditure by air visitors was $180 in 2011, a $10 increase from 2010. Also, the average spending per trip by air visitors was $1,705 in 2011, a 6.9 per cent increase from 2010 (HTA 2012). Research findings suggest that visitors to Hawaii are interested in the culture and desire an authentic tourism experience (Agrusa *et al.* 2010; Li *et al.* 2012). As such, in addition to taking advantage of the comfortable weather and stunning beaches that Hawaii offers, many couples choose to add Hawaiian cultural traditions as part of their weddings, such as Hawaiian ukulele music, hula dancers, an exchange of floral leis, the pouring of colored sands and a lava rock offering (Heiderstadt 2013).

CASE SUBMITTED BY LINFENG "ABRAHAM" LI

Couples choose to have a destination wedding for a number of reasons. They tend to be intimate affairs with only the closest of friends and family members in attendance, as associated travel costs can be considerable. Because of the distance, stressful haggling over guest lists dissipates and reception costs decrease dramatically, which allows for considerable overall savings of money and sanity. With the average guest increasing the wedding bill by $186 (US), couples can accrue significant savings by taking their ceremony on the road (The Wedding Report 2011). Destination weddings are frequently all-inclusive, so the planning process becomes streamlined.

PHOTO 5.4 DESTINATION WEDDINGS ARE INTIMATE AFFAIRS.

SOURCE: WWW.RODNEYBAILEY.COM

Further, couples will not experience the dramatic separation anxiety that can be associated with honeymoons, as many of the guests stay with the couple for an extended vacation. On the other hand, couples who envision a large affair with all of their friends and family members in attendance are likely to be disappointed, and should therefore not seriously consider a destination wedding.

As a consultant, you will eventually have the opportunity to work with couples who elect to have destination weddings. Most likely they will want you to be in attendance to make sure that their events run smoothly. When creating a contract for a destination wedding, be certain that your costs for transportation, lodging and meals are written in as additional expenses that are separate from your base consultant fee. While the destination wedding is a vacation for the couple and their guests, you will be there to work and should be compensated accordingly. Some planners do not accept destination weddings, as they do not like to be taken away from their own families and other clients, while others thoroughly enjoy the challenge and travel.

If you live in an area that is known for destination weddings, such as a beach or mountain resort community, you should be prepared to market your services to visitors who are looking to get married on your home turf. For example, if a couple from North Dakota plans to marry in Moab, Utah, it may be more practical for them to hire a knowledgeable Moab planner rather than paying

Photo 5.5 Local fare can be showcased at destination weddings.

Source: www.RodneyBailey.com

for the travel costs of a consultant from North Dakota. The destination wedding market is yet another avenue through which you can build your business.

REFERENCES

Agrusa, W., Lema, J., Tanner, J., Host, T. and Agrusa, J. (2010) 'Integrating sustainability and Hawaiian culture into the tourism experience of the Hawaiian Islands', *Journal of Tourism and Cultural Heritage*, 8: 247–264.

Asiedu, A.B. (2008) 'Participants' characteristics and economic benefits of visiting friends and relatives (VFR) tourism: an international survey of the literature with implications for Ghana', *International Journal of Tourism Research*, 10: 609–621.

Backer, E. (2012) 'VFR travel: it is underestimated', *Tourism Management*, 33: 74–79.

Bardolet, E. and Sheldon, P.J. (2008) 'Tourism in archipelagos: Hawaii and the Balearics', *Annals of Tourism Research*, 35: 900–923.

Black, J. (2011) 'The British and the grand tour', Reprinted edition by Taylor & Francis e-Library.

Blake, A. and Sinclair, M.T. (2003) 'Tourism crisis management: US response to September 11', *Annals of Tourism Research*, 30: 813–832.

Castelltort, M. and Mäder, G. (2010) 'Press media coverage effects on destinations: a monetary public value (MPV) analysis', *Tourism Management*, 31: 724–738.

Condé Nast UK (2013) 'Hot new honeymoon havens', *Brides UK*, Online. Available HTTP: <http://www.brides magazine.co.uk/planning/general/honeymoon/2012/06/hottest-new-honeymoon-hotels/gallery#!photo11> (accessed 3 February 2013).

Crocker, M. (2009) 'Destination weddings: practical and emotional reasons for choosing Hawaii', *Travel Weekly*, 68: 32–34.

Daniels, M.J., Lee, S. and Cohen, T. (2012) 'The attributes influencing wedding reception venue selection', *Event Management*, 16: 245–258.

Daniels, M.J., Rodgers, E.B.D. and Wiggins, B.P. (2005) '"Travel tales": an interpretive analysis of constraints and negotiations to pleasure travel as experienced by persons with physical disabilities', *Tourism Management*, 26: 919–930.

Disney (2013) 'Disney's fairy tale weddings', Online. Available HTTP: <http://disneyweddings.disney.go.com/weddings> (accessed 5 February 2013).

Fridgen, J.D. (1996) *Dimensions of Tourism*, East Lansing, MI: Educational Institute.

Goodrich, J.N. (2002) 'September 11, 2001 attack on America: a record of the immediate impacts and reactions in the USA travel and tourism industry', *Tourism Management*, 23: 573–580.

Hansen, J.E., Sato, M. and Ruedy, R. (2012) 'Perception of climate change', *Proceedings of the National Academy of Sciences of the United States of America*, 109(37): E2415–E2423.

Hawaii Tourism Authority (HTA) (2012) '2011 annual visitor research report', Online. Available HTTP: <http://www.hawaiitourismauthority.org/research/reports/annual-visitor-research/> (accessed 28 January 2013).

Heiderstadt, D. (2013) 'Hawaiian wedding ceremony: embrace the Aloha spirit with traditional matrimonial elements', Online. Available HTTP: <http://gohawaii.about.com/od/hawaii-wedding-planner/a/hawaiian-wedding-ceremony.htm> (accessed 28 January 2013).

Jang, H., Lee, S., Lee, S. and Hong, S. (2007) 'Expanding the individual choice-sets model to couples' honeymoon destination selection process', *Tourism Management*, 28: 1299–1314.

Kim, S.S. and Agrusa, J. (2005) 'The positioning of overseas honeymoon destinations', *Annals of Tourism Research*, 32: 887–904.

Kim, S.S., McKercher, B. and Lee, H. (2009) 'Tracking tourism destination image perception', *Annals of Tourism Research*, 36: 715–718.

Larsen, J., Urry, J. and Axhausen, K.W. (2007) 'Networks and tourism: mobile social life', *Annals of Tourism Research*, 34: 244–262.

Lee, C., Huang, H. and Chen, W. (2010) 'The determinants of honeymoon destination choice: the case of Taiwan', *Journal of Travel and Tourism Marketing*, 27: 676–693.

Lee, G. and Lee, C. (2009) 'Cross-cultural comparison of the image of Guam perceived by Korean and Japanese leisure travelers: importance–performance analysis', *Tourism Management*, 30: 922–931.

Li, A., Sizoo, S., Lema, J., Tanner, J. and Agrusa, J. (2012) 'Hawaiian culture into the tourism experience on the Hawaiian Islands: the Japanese perspective', *Asian Journal of Tourism and Hospitality Research*, Manuscript submitted for publication.

Li, L. (2013) 'Destination weddings in Hawaii'. E-mail (30 January 2013).

McCarthy, M.J. (2011) 'Improving the United States airline industry's capacity to provide safe and dignified services to travelers with disabilities: focus group findings', *Disability and Rehabilitation*, 33: 2612–2619.

Pearce, P.L. (2012) 'The experience of visiting home and familiar places', *Annals of Tourism Research*, 39: 1024–1047.

Sandals (2013) 'Sandals WeddingMoons', Online. Available HTTP: <http://www.sandals.com/weddingmoons/> (accessed 27 January 2013).

Shani, A. and Uriely, N. (2012) 'VFR tourism: the host experience', *Annals of Tourism Research*, 39: 421–440.

The American Wedding Study (2012) 'Brides', Online. Available HTTP: <http://candieanderson.com/2012/06/interview-2012-bridal-trends-with-brides-magazines-vice-president-and-publisher-michelle-myers.html> (accessed 17 January 2013).

The Wedding Report (2011) 'Wedding statistics, industry reports and wedding trends', Online. Available HTTP: <http://www.theweddingreport.com/> (accessed 27 March 2013).

Thurnell-Read, T. (2012) 'Tourism place and space: British stag tourism in Poland', *Annals of Tourism Research*, 39: 801–819.

Towner, J. (1985) 'The grand tour: a key phase in the history of tourism', *Annals of Tourism Research*, 12: 297–333.

—— (1996) *An Historical Geography of Recreation and Tourism in the Western World 1540–1940*, Chichester, UK: John Wiley & Sons.

Uriely, N. (2010) '"Home" and "away" in VFR tourism', *Annals of Tourism Research*, 37: 854–857.

US News and World Report (2013) 'Best honeymoon destinations', Online. Available HTTP: <http://travel.usnews.com/Rankings/Best_Honeymoon_Destinations/> (accessed 5 February 2013).

Viva Las Vegas Weddings (2013) 'Viva Las Vegas traditional and themed weddings', Online. Available HTTP: <http://www.vivalasvegasweddings.com/> (accessed 5 February 2013).

Weaver, D. and Lawton, L. (2010) *Tourism Management*, Milton, Australia: John Wiley & Sons.

REVIEW

1. Distinguish between PVFRs, CVFRs and EVFRs.

2. Name a minimum of three attributes that most couples look for in a honeymoon destination.

3. What advice would you give to a couple that is considering leaving for their honeymoon directly after their wedding reception?

4. What are the pros and cons of destination weddings?

5. Would you like to plan a destination wedding if it meant being on site with your clients for seven days? Explain why or why not.

TERMINOLOGY

- Destination weddings

- Grand Tour

- VFR tourism (PVFR, CVFR, EVFR)

- WeddingMoon

PRACTICE

HAVING GAINED AN UNDERSTANDING OF THE HISTORICAL, CULTURAL AND SOCIAL UNDERPINNINGS OF WEDDINGS, YOU ARE FULLY PREPARED TO EXPLORE THE PRACTICE OF WEDDING CONSULTING. IN THE FOLLOWING 14 CHAPTERS, YOU ARE GIVEN THE OPPORTUNITY TO EXAMINE THE INDIVIDUAL ELEMENTS THAT TOGETHER LEAD TO THE DESIGN AND IMPLEMENTATION OF WEDDINGS. FROM DETERMINING THE VISION THROUGH ASSESSING THE SATISFACTION LEVEL OF YOUR CLIENTS, SECTION II OF THIS BOOK FOCUSES ON THE FUNDAMENTALS OF PLANNING A WEDDING.

THE CRITICAL STEPS OF DETERMINING THE VISION, BUDGET AND TIMELINE FOR A WEDDING ARE EXPLORED IN CHAPTERS 6, 7 AND 8. CHAPTER 9 OFFERS AN IN-DEPTH DISCUSSION OF FOOD, BEVERAGE AND THE WEDDING CAKE. WEDDING ATTIRE, THE CEREMONY AND FLORAL DÉCOR ARE EXAMINED IN DETAIL IN CHAPTERS 10, 11 AND 12. FROM THERE, YOU WILL LEARN ABOUT THE INTRICACIES OF STATIONERY ELEMENTS, PHOTOGRAPHY AND VIDEOGRAPHY IN CHAPTERS 13 AND 14. MUSIC AND ENTERTAINMENT, FOLLOWED BY RENTALS AND SITE LAYOUT ARE COVERED IN CHAPTERS 15 AND 16. SPECIFICS RELATED TO TRANSPORTATION, FAVORS AND GIFTS ARE HIGHLIGHTED IN CHAPTERS 17 AND 18. THIS SECTION CONCLUDES WITH A DISCUSSION OF WEDDING DAY DETAILS IN CHAPTER 19. AT THE END OF EACH CHAPTER IN THIS SECTION, YOU WILL FIND A CONSULTANT CHECKLIST AND REMINDERS THAT CAN BE USED FOR QUICK REFERENCE. CASE STUDIES ARE INTEGRATED THROUGHOUT TO KEEP YOU THINKING LIKE A CONSULTANT.

AS YOU WILL FIND, BEAUTIFUL WEDDINGS DON'T JUST HAPPEN. THEY ARE THE CULMINATION OF HUNDREDS OF HOURS OF PLANNING AND MANAGEMENT. IN ORDER TO BE A WEDDING CONSULTANT WITH A SUCCESSFUL BUSINESS, YOU MUST BE WELL VERSED IN EACH OF THESE AREAS SO AS TO EFFECTIVELY COMMUNICATE AND COORDINATE WITH YOUR CLIENTS AND VENDORS.

Photo 6.1 A wedding vision is illustrated through elements such as floral décor.

Source: www.RodneyBailey.com

6

DETERMINING THE VISION

A WEDDING VISION IS AN IMAGINATIVE CONCEPTION OF THE EVENT THAT ENCOMPASSES ALL FIVE SENSES: SIGHT, SOUND, SMELL, TASTE AND TOUCH. THE GOAL OF DISCUSSING VISION WITH YOUR CLIENTS IS TO DETERMINE THEIR IDEAL DAY, AND THEN MOVE TO THE PRAGMATICS OF MAKING THAT VISION A REALITY. THE PURPOSE OF THIS CHAPTER IS TO PRESENT THE TOOLS THAT WILL AID YOU AND YOUR CLIENTS IN ESTABLISHING A FOCUSED VISION THAT WILL BE ACCOMPANIED BY THEME, DESTINATION AND SITE SELECTION.

GETTING FOCUSED

When you have an initial consultation with a couple, before you can start on your checklist of things to do, before you can book a venue or hire a photographer, you have to find out a little bit about the couple's vision. In order to meet their expectations, it is your responsibility to figure out what makes them tick and how that can be expressed in their wedding. This should be handled through a series of focused, open-ended questions asked during a client interview, as presented in detail in Chapter 22. You can also ask the primary point of contact, generally the bride, to bring samples of ideas that she likes. Concepts may come from bridal magazines, her Pinterest boards, photos of outings with her fiancé, swatches of fabric or any items that reflect the most important aspects of her life.

It is helpful to meet with the couple, or at least the primary point of contact, in person. While many of the wedding particulars can be handled by e-mail, text or phone conversation, a face-to-face meeting will help you understand the styles and personalities of the individuals, which will typically be translated during their wedding. For example, you can expect different visions from brides who dress in a tailored fashion versus those who wear cutting-edge, fashion-forward clothing versus those who discuss the wicking ability of the latest outdoor hiking gear. Be careful not to overgeneralize based on appearance; rather, use this information in conjunction with other data provided. The bottom line is to gather a breadth of information that you can draw upon when executing a vision.

Most importantly, you have to remember you are not planning your own wedding. You are planning your clients' wedding. So, when they tell you, for example, that they got engaged at a hockey game and want monogrammed hockey pucks for favors, you need to make that happen even if you have never been to a hockey game. When you are trying to uncover your clients' vision, you must actively listen while looking directly at them. Really listen. Don't get overly caught up in taking notes or talking about your experience. Don't say, "When I did a really high-end wedding, they had . . . " or "I had another couple just like you and what they did was . . . ". You are there to learn about the uniqueness of this couple and focus on their desired wedding day.

WEDDING THEMES

In the process of learning about a couple's vision, thematic ideas are likely to emerge. Wedding themes can vary from subtle to dramatic and generally feed into destination and site selection, as well as influencing other elements such as floral décor and favors. A common starting place is a favorite color. A color scheme can be the impetus for the entire framework of a wedding. Consider *Consultant in Action*, Case 6.1 to see the influence of color on wedding planning.

A second thematic category pertains to seasons and holidays. Seasons often coincide with colors, with pastels working best in the spring, bright colors coordinating with summer, muted tones favored in the fall and festive shades and darks working well in the winter. Considering the calendar

PHOTO 6.2 WEDDING THEMES CAN BE MODERN AND FUN.

SOURCE: WWW.RODNEYBAILEY.COM

year, some popular holidays that coincide with wedding themes include Valentine's Day, St. Patrick's Day, Easter, Memorial Day, Fourth of July, Labor Day, Halloween, Thanksgiving, Christmas and New Year's Eve. Tom Lally (2013) of Alexandria Pastry Shop and Catering Company states that one of the most unique cakes he has ever designed was for a Halloween wedding theme where they used black and orange icing and then added fondant cobwebs, spiders and ghosts. Holiday weekends are a prevalent choice because they generally allow guests to have more travel time; however, because of their popularity, prices tend to be higher during these periods. A specific aspect of a season or holiday period can be used to dictate the thematic elements; for instance, a harvest wedding can include a hay wagon, mums, pumpkin centerpieces, a cider-based signature drink and favors such as baskets of pumpkin bread or candied apples.

For those with an appreciation of the past, a wedding theme based on a specific historic period may be appealing. Renaissance and Victorian periods as well as eras such as the Roaring 1920s and the Big Band 1930s and 1940s lend themselves to specific musical genres as well as clothing styles. A related theme involves drawing upon a specific culture or subculture. This may be based on the experiences or heritage of the bride and/or groom or could be based on a particular interest or borrowed culture. For example, a couple may wish to have an Ascot-themed wedding, not based on a British heritage but because of their love of horses. Another couple, equally passionate about

CONSULTANT IN ACTION, CASE 6.1

COLOR COMPOSITION

Your clients both played basketball in college and remain devoted to their respective teams. The bride was a Lady Vol for Tennessee (school colors: white and orange) while the groom was a Gonzaga Bulldog (school colors: blue and white). They have both played in NCAA tournaments and met through mutual basketball friends. They would like a basketball theme, and want to include the colors of both schools. Help them determine how the colors can dictate other elements of the wedding.

1. Month of year:

Jan	Feb	Mar	Apr	May	June
___	___	___	___	___	___

Jul	Aug	Sep	Oct	Nov	Dec
___	___	___	___	___	___

2. Ceremony time of day:

Morning	Afternoon	Evening
_____	_____	_____

3. Reception location:

Hotel	_____
Historic Estate	_____
Inn	_____
Museum	_____
Garden	_____
Resort or Country Club	_____
Destination	_____

4. How the colors can be incorporated into clothing:

_____

5. Two ideas for favors:

_____

_____

6. One other effect:

_____

PHOTO 6.3 A WEDDING THEME CAN BE INSPIRED BY A HOLIDAY.

SOURCE: WWW.RODNEYBAILEY.COM

horses, may opt for a more casual country-western theme. A subcultural theme can even be based on a career; for instance, military weddings have embedded customs and protocol.

Couples with an interest in outdoor activities may decide to have a beach, mountain, garden or park theme. Gazebos, atriums, resorts, national parklands and estates lend themselves to outdoor themes. A related thematic area is comprised of earth and celestial elements, which can be tied into conservationist weddings as well as those using stars, planets, the moon or angelic features. Review *Culture Corner*, Case 6.2 for an example of a wedding theme that was based on the couple's love for the outdoors.

As implied with *Consultant in Action*, Case 6.1, sports allow for a broad array of themes. Whether your clients are participants or fans, a passion for tennis, golf, football, lacrosse, swimming, martial arts, baseball, archery, ping pong, curling, snowboarding, kayaking, surfing, soccer, track or any other sport can translate into a clever theme. Similarly, other recreational or competitive outlets that resonate with your clients can lead to imaginative themes. Activities and hobbies such as chess, robotics, gardening, antiquing, karaoke, camping and painting bring couples together and can lend to a wedding theme.

PHOTO 6.4 SPORTS ENTHUSIASTS INCORPORATE THEIR FAVORITE TEAMS INTO THEIR VISION.

SOURCE: WWW.RODNEYBAILEY.COM

CULTURE CORNER, CASE 6.2

THE WEDDING OF LAURIE AND RANDY: NATIONAL PARKS THEME

The couple: Randy and Laurie met at Isle Royale National Park. National Parks were an integral part of their life, with Randy working as a Park Ranger and Laurie conducting research in the parks. They enjoyed their first Christmas together visiting Saguaro National Park, took their first vacation together in Acadia National Park and spent their first years together visiting the National Park sites in Virginia. So, it was natural to plan their wedding around National Parks.

The planning: The wedding site was Grand Tetons National Park and involved a weekend event. They flew to the site a year early for a wedding planning weekend during which time they met the florist, the manager of Togwotee Mountain Lodge and their cake baker for an outdoor tasting conducted in the shadows of the Tetons. During the visit, the theme of National Parks was broadened to also encompass a "buy local" and sustainable scope. All of the food, entertainment, and accoutrements were purchased locally at Jackson Hole and they even purchased their wedding gift to each other while on the visit: a signed, framed photograph of the Tetons by a local artist.

The wedding weekend: The weekend began with guests arriving at the lodge and each guest receiving a reusable canvas bag stenciled with the mountain scene used in the invitations and filled with food and drink items reflecting the couple's respective lives individually and together. Each guest was treated with cheese from Wisconsin (the groom's home state), chocolates from Michigan (the bride's home state) and wine from Virginia (where the couple were living at the time of the wedding). They added water, crackers and a welcome note that included information about the region.

In lieu of a rehearsal, all guests were treated to a Cowboy Cookout on Friday evening, They opted for this pre-wedding social so friends and family could meet and get to know each other. The Cowboy Cookout included a wagon ride to the locale in the mountains, beer from a local brewery, dinner, music and group dancing.

The wedding occurred the following afternoon, on Summer Solstice, along the Snake River in Grand Teton National Park. A close family friend played classical guitar while sitting under a pine tree along the river and the bridal party walked to the site down a rustic trail to where the guests and groomsmen awaited. The ceremony was performed by a relative.

The reception followed back at the lodge where the dinner featured local wild game, specifically, bison prime rib and elk stew. The following morning, Sunday, many of the guests met in the lodge restaurant for breakfast and several opted to go horseback riding, while others traveled to the nearby Yellowstone National Park. The couple left the following day and honeymooned in Yellowstone National Park.

CASE SUBMITTED BY LAURIE HARMON

A final, broad theme pertains to popular culture, with couples frequently drawing upon books, theatre, television and film to inspire their weddings. Plot lines, time periods, clothing and music associated with historic or modern fiction, such as *Cinderella, Romeo and Juliet, My Fair Lady, Harry Potter, Twilight* and *Downton Abbey*, fuel the imagination. Heidi Kallett (2013), CEO of The Dandelion Patch stationery store, states that the craziest themed invitation she has designed was for a wedding with a Superman theme. She adds that the clients with unique themes are a joy to work with because they tend to be easygoing and fun.

When choosing a theme, it is important to consider the knowledge base of the guests. If the couple wishes to incorporate Scottish elements into the wedding based on the bride's heritage, it will be helpful to explain the significance of the unique features in the wedding program so the cultural experience will not be lost on guests who are not of Scottish descent. Additionally, the comfort level of the guests must be kept in mind. A couple with a country-western theme might like to offer their guests the option of a horseback ride between the wedding and the reception, but they need to offer transportation alternatives for those who might not want to participate in this activity.

DESTINATIONS AND SITES

Wedding destinations and sites can be chosen based on the theme of the wedding. For instance, a *Great Gatsby*-themed wedding could be held at the Great Gatsby Estate located on the Island of Martha's Vineyard, Massachusetts or at the Rosecliff Mansion in Newport, Rhode Island, which was the setting for the film. As another example, a medieval theme can be carried out at Chillon Castle in Switzerland, with a buffet package that includes spit-roast meat, troubadours, jugglers and fire-eaters. For those with an interest in outdoor recreation, local, regional and national parklands often permit weddings and have the necessary facilities available to rent. Further, as discussed in Chapter 5, destination weddings allow many couples to live out their dream themes; for example, packages from Disney Weddings can even include Cinderella's carriage (Disney Weddings 2013).

In many cases, it is not feasible for couples to choose a destination and site based on the wedding theme. Accordingly, the site can be transformed to reflect the theme and/or destination. For example, many couples who desire to have a beach theme do not reside in close proximity to an ocean or lake. However, the theme can still be established through stationery selections, favors, music and other specific elements. Similarly, many couples get engaged while traveling and may want to incorporate elements of those memories in their weddings. For example, a bride and groom who became engaged in Paris at the Eiffel Tower are not likely to return to Paris for their ceremony but they can readily include Parisian elements to incorporate a French flavor in their day.

While the *destination* is the broader geographical area such as a city, the *site* is the specific physical venue as well as the placement within that venue. Many couples elect to have a religious ceremony held in a house of worship followed by a reception at a different location. Alternatively, many sites can accommodate both the ceremony and the reception. For example, most major hotels have multiple function spaces where a wedding and reception can take place, with options such as a courtyard, ballroom or conservatory being quite common. Each of these spaces has a different feel, thus allowing for a wide range of themes. Other common venues that can manage either or both the ceremony and the reception include aquariums, atriums, ballrooms, country clubs, gardens,

PHOTO 6.5 SOME COUPLES HAVE DIFFERENT SITES FOR THEIR WEDDING CEREMONY
AND RECEPTION.

SOURCE: WWW.RODNEYBAILEY.COM

PHOTO 6.6 MANY VENUES CAN ACCOMMODATE BOTH THE CEREMONY AND THE RECEPTION.

SOURCE: WWW.RODNEYBAILEY.COM

historic estates, inns, museums, park facilities, plantations and resorts. Clients may have some specific attributes in mind that will help narrow down the search. Review *Research Roundtable*, Case 6.3 to learn about the attributes that tend to be most important to couples selecting a reception venue.

Occasionally, you will work with a couple who indicates the desire to have their wedding at their own or a family member's home. While this may be done for financial or sentimental reasons,

> many couples are taken aback by how much sweat equity it takes to successfully pull off such an event and how quickly the costs mount when you have to rent everything from the tent to the silverware to portable restrooms.
>
> (ElBoghdady 2010: E1)

Additionally, if outdoor lighting and live music are involved, problems can arise with power outages or noise complaints from neighbors, potentially leading to an untimely shutdown of the event, in particular if the local police show up (ElBoghdady 2010). While a wedding at a personal residence can be beautifully implemented, this site type is generally best suited for intimate gatherings unless the home and the surrounding grounds are of sufficient size to accommodate a larger group.

RESEARCH ROUNDTABLE, CASE 6.3

RECEPTION VENUE SELECTION

Purpose: To examine the variables that influence the decision-making process when couples select a wedding reception venue.

Methods: Study participants, all of whom were newlyweds, were asked to think back to when they booked their reception venue and then rate the importance of 40 reception venue selection variables, indicating on a 5-point scale from "5 = very important" to "1 = very unimportant" the influence of each variable on their decision.

Results: 379 respondents completed the questionnaire, representing over 260 unique properties. The top ten individual attributes that influenced the final venue decision, based on an average response score of those who responded to all 40 items, included: 1) rental costs; 2) location; 3) professionalism of staff; 4) ease of communication; 5) clean bathrooms; 6) length of time venue available; 7) efficiency in returning electronic communication; 8) friendliness of staff; 9) efficiency in returning phone calls; and 10) room capacity.

Conclusion: Five of the top ten attributes were specific to verbal and nonverbal communication. In an age of hyperconnectivity, where texting has largely taken over phone and face-to-face conversation, the results indicate that a personal touch is still needed and desirable in the context of weddings.

SOURCE: DANIELS *ET AL.* (2012)

Many of your clients will not have a clear vision of their day and may rely on you to help construct a theme and then indicate the appropriate destination and site to carry out the theme. When this occurs, you have to offer guidance while allowing your clients to ultimately make the decisions. Taking classes in design and floral décor as well as keeping up with the latest wedding trends will help you hone your creative skills and enable you to assist each couple in determining a unique style.

You should pay particular attention to the following issues when assisting your clients with venue selection: 1) capacity; 2) rental costs and/or cost per person; 3) taxes, service charges and other fees; 4) restrictions and special requirements; and 5) set-up time. First, capacity will dictate whether a given facility is feasible and practical. Many historic homes, garden sanctuaries and smaller museum sites have capacities limited to 150 or fewer persons; therefore, for large weddings, clients are better served with major hotels, which can often handle as many as 3,000 guests. By the same token, a grand ballroom reserved for a 50-person reception would feel cavernous, so a couple planning an intimate wedding should select an equally personal setting.

Second, rental fees will differ significantly from property to property. For some hotels, there are no rental fees and pricing is based per person for food and beverage. In other cases, venues can charge $15,000 or more simply to reserve the space, which buys your clients nothing but the privilege of occupying the site for a certain number of hours, and all other costs are additional.

When calculating costs, it is important to remember the third consideration: taxes, service charges and other fees. For example, if a hotel using a per person structure gives a reception estimate of $100 per person for 150 guests, the immediate assumption might be to budget $15,000. However, this estimate can be misleading if it is exclusive of tax and service charge. If the tax is 7 per cent and the service charge is 18 per cent, that adds an additional 25 per cent to the bill, and the reception actually costs $18,750, which may be out of the budget range for the couple. When showing your clients proposals from three different venues, be sure to compare apples with apples. If one venue is including everything and one is not, the one that is incomplete will look less expensive, so you have to peel away the layers and make sure that the information provided is consistent and complete. Be mindful of other fees such as those pertaining to cake cutting, beverage corkage and overtime.

A fourth consideration when selecting a venue is restrictions and special requirements. Some facilities, such as historic chapels in academic settings, private country clubs and famous cathedrals, are only available to those who belong to the associated communities. While nominal membership fees may be paid to gain access to some such venues, in other cases it is cost-prohibitive or impossible to secure usage privileges. Some venues are only available if the bride, groom or an immediate family member has an established relationship created through ongoing and noteworthy financial contributions.

Special requirements also refer to what can and cannot occur at the given facility. Many historic buildings have policies that are in place to maintain the integrity of the building and its artifacts. Some common wedding elements that may be prohibited because of their ability to stain or cause damage include: red or blush wines, other red liquids such as tomato and cranberry juice, chocolate fountains, candles and flower petals. Other restrictions often apply to the types of rentals that can be used. For instance, some rental chairs may scratch flooring and will therefore be prohibited. Venues with strict guidelines will generally provide a list of accepted vendors with whom they have cultivated a trusting relationship. For venues such as hotels that have their own catering services, you may be required to purchase their food, beverage and even the wedding cake as part of the contract. It is important that you become very familiar with the policies and regulations of wedding sites in your area so you can assist your clients in making informed decisions.

A final consideration to keep in mind when selecting venues is the amount of set-up time available and the cost for that time. Essentially, you need to know when the vendors can move in to prepare for the guests to arrive. This issue can be particularly problematic at popular venues that book back-to-back receptions, which may mean that one ends at 5:00 p.m. and the next starts at 6:00 p.m. This makes the turnaround time very, very tight. Have a candid conversation with the venue manager to determine if the staff can accomplish the following in a one-hour turn: get the previous guests out, get the gifts taken away, vacuum the carpet, turn the room, reconfigure the tables, replace all the linens and clean the bathrooms. Simultaneously, you will need adequate set-up time for the escort card table, floral décor, food, cake, musicians, lighting and other reception elements.

The bottom line is that a short turnaround does not allow for the emergencies, problems and challenges that invariably arise. Generally speaking, you should look for a set-up time of no less than four hours and a break-down of no less than one hour, but preferably longer. If set-up has to be less than four hours, make sure that you have plenty of assistants on hand. With large weddings, it is best to advise your clients to select a venue that only handles one event per day so the stress of set-up and break-down is minimized. With set-up and break-down, you also need to be aware if the venue works with unions, as this will also influence time orientation. Most unions work within the exact specifics of their contracts and can leave if activities do not take place as scheduled.

One way to get an answer to all of the key questions pertaining to a venue is to send out a *request for proposal* (RFP) to the two or three venues under consideration. The RFP details the specific requirements of your client's wedding and asks potential vendors to bid based on the guidelines provided. You will send out the exact same RFP to all of the venues where you ask them to address the same issues. This way, your clients can readily compare information when making a venue decision. Decisions are not based solely on budget competitiveness; additionally, your clients should be assessing the completeness, organization, creativity and feasibility of the proposal. Do not blindly send out RFPs and hope for the best. Instead, you should start with a trusted list of venues and allow your clients to select the one that is the best fit.

REFERENCES

Daniels, M.J., Lee, S. and Cohen, T. (2012) 'The attributes influencing wedding reception venue selection', *Event Management*, 16: 245–258.

Disney Weddings (2013) 'Disney's fairy tale weddings and honeymoons', Online. Available HTTP: <http://www.disneyweddings.com/site/wed/cus/start/index.jsp> (accessed 3 March 2013).

ElBoghdady, D. (9 January 2010) '"I do" right here at home', *The Washington Post*, E1, E3.

Harmon, L. (2013) 'Personal wedding story'. E-mail (20 January 2013).

Kallett, H. (2013) 'Themed wedding stationery'. E-mail interview conducted by Lina Abu-Baker (18 February 2013).

Lally, T. (2013) 'Themed wedding cakes'. E-mail (3 March 2013).

CONSULTANT CHECKLIST AND REMINDERS FOR DETERMINING THE VISION

☐ The theme should resonate with the couple.

☐ Stick to one primary theme and stay consistent in the application of the theme.

☐ Don't overdo a theme, as it can take away from the meaning of the day.

☐ Keep the guests' knowledge base and comfort level in mind.

☐ Keep the budget in mind, as the implementation of some themes can be cost-prohibitive.

☐ Destinations and sites can be chosen based on the wedding theme; alternatively, a venue can be transformed to reflect the theme.

☐ When helping your clients compare venues, be very familiar with the:

1) capacity;

2) rental costs and/or cost per person;

3) taxes, service charges and other fees;

4) restrictions and special requirements; and

5) set-up time.

REVIEW

1. Name three categories of themes and give examples of each category.

2. What are four common venue types where wedding receptions are held?

3. Name five of the top attributes that influence the wedding reception venue selection.

4. What are five considerations to bear in mind when booking a wedding venue?

5. Explain why it is important to keep taxes, service charges and other fees in mind when selecting a wedding venue.

6. Name three restrictions that are common to historic buildings that influence the selection of wedding elements.

TERMINOLOGY

● Destination

● Rental fees

● Request for proposal

● Site

● Vision

● Wedding themes

Photo 7.1 A wedding budget will dictate a couple's venue options.

Source: www.RodneyBailey.com

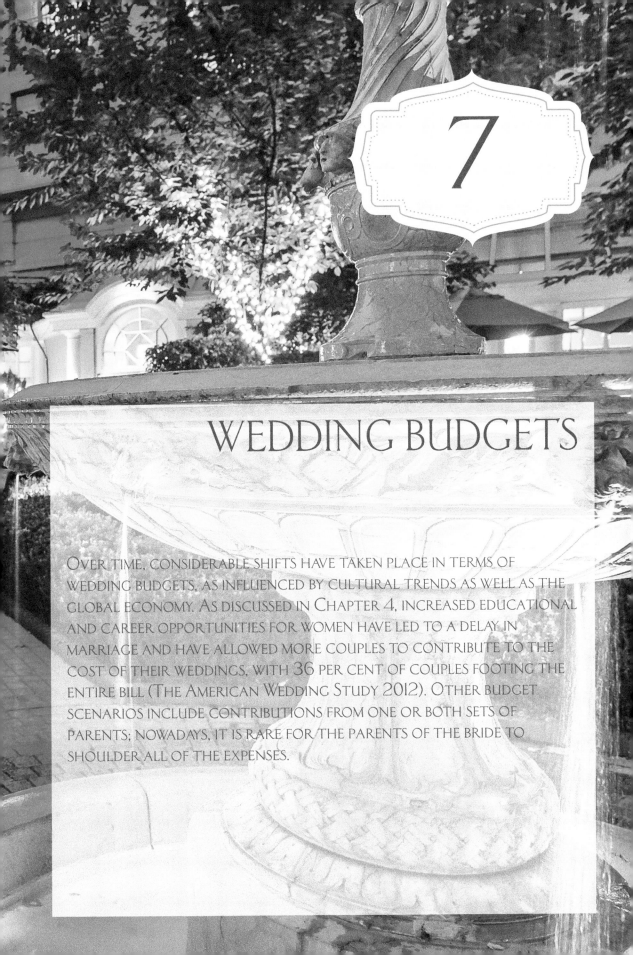

7

WEDDING BUDGETS

Over time, considerable shifts have taken place in terms of wedding budgets, as influenced by cultural trends as well as the global economy. As discussed in Chapter 4, increased educational and career opportunities for women have led to a delay in marriage and have allowed more couples to contribute to the cost of their weddings, with 36 per cent of couples footing the entire bill (The American Wedding Study 2012). Other budget scenarios include contributions from one or both sets of parents; nowadays, it is rare for the parents of the bride to shoulder all of the expenses.

While the average wedding in the United States is estimated to cost approximately $26,000 (The Wedding Report 2012), significant variations exist. For example, weddings held in cities with a low cost of living, such as Ashland (Ohio), Fayetteville (Arkansas) and Harlingen (Texas), tend to range in cost from about $16,000 to $27,000, while weddings in areas with a high cost of living, such as Manhattan (New York), San Francisco (California) and Stamford (Connecticut), have a range that averages between $25,000 and $46,000 (CBS News 2013; Ellin 2012; The Wedding Report 2012). The useful online resource *costofwedding.com* allows you to enter in any zip code to get an estimate of the average budget. This tool will help you get a sense of the expenditure patterns in your target market.

Despite yearly fluctuations based on the global market, the general trajectory of total outlay for weddings is upward. Couples are often caught off-guard by the price tags associated with many wedding items and over 30 per cent of couples in the US go over the budget they originally had in mind (Grossman 2012). Similarly, Chinese culture has seen a drastic increase in wedding spending coupled with the demand for more Western-style weddings (Madden 2013). With over 10 million couples marrying yearly and often holding banquets that go on for days, the wedding market is worth $80 billion a year in China (Madden 2013). In some cultures, weddings involve separate ceremonies for men and women, thus adding to the expense, as highlighted in *Culture Corner*, Case 7.1.

CULTURE CORNER, CASE 7.1

GENDER-SEGREGATED WEDDINGS IN THE SULTANATE OF OMAN

Weddings in Oman are traditional and meticulous affairs. Many rituals and ceremonies have to be observed to get married.

First, the proposal: The groom and his male relatives present themselves to the bride's house to propose to her father. After discussing with his wife and daughter as well as checking the "pedigree" and reputation of the groom and his family with acquaintances, relatives and friends, he will make up his mind. If the answer is positive, both parties will discuss the details of the wedding. The bride and groom are, from that moment, allowed to see each other under certain conditions and supervision of the bride's family.

Thereon, the ceremony of the dowry takes place, where the future groom gives money, goods (often gold) or estate to his future bride as part of an engagement ceremony. The dowry is to be kept by the bride and spent as she pleases.

Subsequently, the religious wedding (*Malka*) can occur. This male-only ceremony involves 200 or more guests gathering at a mosque in their traditional clothes to celebrate the wedding in the main prayer room. The Imam (religious leader) officiates the wedding in the presence of the groom and a representative of the bride (her father, brother or uncle). Wedding agreements are signed and verses of the Quran (Islamic holy book) read. Afterwards, each guest congratulates the groom and his family by shaking their hands while eating traditional food.

On the female side, there are two major women-only ceremonies: The Henna takes place at the bride's home and is limited to the immediate family, close friends and relatives. Traditional music is played, the women dance and traditional food is served. Henna artists apply temporary decorations made of henna paste on the hands, fingers, arms and feet of the bride and her guests. Henna patterns symbolize enduring love, sacred beauty, increased fertility as well as removing evil spirits and bringing good luck. They are consequently crucial at a wedding.

Finally, the wedding ends with the wedding party, which takes place at night in a wedding hall. The guest list easily reaches up to 400 guests for average weddings. The bride is dressed in a modern white wedding gown and sumptuous jewelry. The ceremony starts without her, where guests are welcomed at the door by close members of the bride's family. Dancing takes places until the bride is announced.

Once the bride makes her red carpet grand entrance and takes her place on a stage by sitting on a *Kosha* (wedding sofa), the food is served and guests can eat. The bride will not eat and will stay on the *Kosha* until her husband comes to take her away; she does not participate in the festivities but only witnesses them. Guests are encouraged to dance during and after the dinner to entertain the bride. After many hours of exaltation, the groom can enter to claim his bride. This usually ends the wedding party; however, in modern families, cake cutting, a first dance and a bouquet tossing are *de rigueur*.

Omani weddings are huge, luxurious and costly functions where the bride and groom are paradoxically united together while physically being apart from each other.

CASE SUBMITTED BY KRISTEL KESSLER

Concerns about excessive wedding spending have some governments intervening. For example, in Afghanistan, a legislative bill entitled *The Law on Prevention of Extravagance in Wedding Ceremonies* was proposed to limit per guest spending, the number of outfits a bride can wear and the amount that can be spent by a groom for gifts to the bride's family; further, those who did not follow the law could face fines or prison time (Sieff 2011). While the law was recommended by government officials as a means to curb waste, critics call it unjust and argue that it will encourage corruption (Sieff 2011).

While government interference with wedding budgets is unlikely in most countries, couples across cultures often express concerns regarding straining their financial resources. Consultants act as a valuable liaison between their clients and vendors, offering sound advice during planning that should always lead to cost savings. While the occasional couple will have a no-limit budget, the vast majority of clients will truly appreciate the budget guidance that you offer. The purpose of this chapter is to outline the primary budget categories that emerge in most weddings, while offering tools to assist you in presenting organized and realistic financial information to your clients, thus empowering them to make sound expenditure decisions. The specific areas covered include wedding budget categories, budget summaries and tipping etiquette.

WEDDING BUDGET CATEGORIES

While there are many ways to organize wedding budgets, couples can more readily make rational decisions if the categories are presented in a logical manner. Use a spreadsheet and include columns for each of the following seven areas: 1) the category names and specific items in each; 2) a means of determining whether or not a given element will be included; 3) an indication of estimated cost; 4) the total final cost; 5) the down payment amount; 6) the date when the final payment is due; and 7) notes pertaining to each area. Table 7.1 offers a sample of how this information can be compiled, using reception and rentals, which is the most expensive wedding category, as an example. The online resources that accompany this text include a full wedding budget spreadsheet that you can adapt for your use.

By learning the common expenditure areas in each category, you can readily apply these same seven ideas to all budget categories and items. Table 7.2 presents the 13 common categories of spending, the average percentage of the budget allocated to each category and the common associated items.

BUDGET SUMMARIES

While you will need a detailed budget for the planning process, once a wedding is complete, it is useful to have a summary budget so that quick comparisons can be made over time. Further, when helping new clients get started, it is easier to give them a summary budget that allocates by overall category percentages rather than overwhelming them with potential costs for each and every item.

PHOTO 7.2 RECEPTION AND RENTAL COSTS COMPRISE THE MOST EXPENSIVE WEDDING BUDGET CATEGORY.

SOURCE: WWW.RODNEYBAILEY.COM

Table 7.3 uses a budget of $26,000 to highlight the amount available per category based on average expenditures. Note that the engagement ring, rehearsal dinner and the honeymoon are not included, as these are considered outside of the wedding day itself. However, these are elements of considerable expense that should not be forgotten. For example, results from studies conducted by *The Knot* indicate that the average engagement ring price tag is $5,200 in the US, while a honeymoon can range from $2,000 to $5,000 and up, depending on whether the travel is domestic or international (Patriarca 2012; XO Group 2012). The percentages offer a basic guideline, but each client will be unique in terms of the budget areas that are most important. Therefore, the percentage weights can vary considerably from wedding to wedding.

While your consultant fee is 10 per cent of the overall budget, this payment is easily recouped by your clients because of the savings that you are passing onto them through your negotiating skills and the fact that your relationship with vendors often results in discounts that are passed along to the couple. Further, not only do your professional relationships save the couple money, but you are also saving them an enormous amount of time and stress by facilitating the planning, design and implementation of the wedding. Most couples quickly realize that their consultant is worth her or his weight in gold, but some clients may be skeptical during the early planning stages. Read *Consultant in Action*, Case 7.2 and consider how you would handle this situation.

TABLE 7.1 WEDDING BUDGET CATEGORIES AND DETAILS: RECEPTION AND RENTALS SHOWN AS SAMPLE

Category Name/ Specific Items	Included?	Estimated Cost	Final Cost	Down Payment Amount	Final Payment Due Date	Notes
Reception and rentals (40%)						
Site rental fee	yes / no					
Tent rental fee and accessories	yes / no					
Food	yes / no					
Alcohol and corkage fees	yes / no					
Other beverages	yes / no					
Tables	yes / no					
Chairs	yes / no					
Dance floor	yes / no					
Lighting	yes / no					
China	yes / no					
Linens	yes / no					
Flatware	yes / no					
Glassware	yes / no					
Other decorations (e.g., ice sculpture)	yes / no					
Tips (e.g., wait staff, coat check)	yes / no					
Other	yes / no					

TABLE 7.2 BUDGET CATEGORIES AND RELATED AREAS OF EXPENDITURE

Reception and rentals (40%)

- Site rental fee
- Tent rental fee and tent accessories (e.g., decorative fabric, generators)
- Food
- Alcohol and corkage fees
- Other beverages
- Tables
- Chairs
- Dance floor
- Lighting
- China
- Linens
- Flatware
- Glassware
- Specialty rentals and decorations (e.g., ice sculpture, photo booth)
- Tips (e.g., banquet manager, wait staff, valet, coat check)

Photography and videography (10%)

- Engagement photos
- Photographer ceremony / wedding: time and album package
- Additional photos for family / friends
- Videographer ceremony / wedding: time and package
- Tips

Wedding consultant (10%)

- Consultant package
- *Ad hoc* services
- Tips

Wedding attire (8%)

- Bridal dress and alterations
- Headpiece / veil
- Shoes

TABLE 7.2 CONTINUED

- Lingerie

- Purse

- Jewelry

- Groom's formalwear

- Groom's accessories

Floral décor (7%)

- Bridal bouquet

- Bridesmaids' bouquets

- Groom's boutonniere

- Groomsmen's boutonnieres

- Parents of couple (corsages / boutonnieres)

- Grandparents of couple (corsages / boutonnieres)

- Other family members

- Flower girl (flowers and basket)

- Ring bearer (boutonniere and pillow)

- Readers, soloist, other

- Ceremony flowers, wreaths and bows
  (altar, pews / chairs, doors, petals)

- Ceremony special elements (e.g., chuppah décor)

- Reception (cake, cake table, centerpieces, serving table, other)

- Packing and delivery

- Tips

Music and other entertainment (7%)

- Ceremony musicians

- Cocktail hour musicians / band / DJ

- Reception musicians / band / DJ

- Other music / entertainment (e.g., soloist, bagpiper, drummers, master of ceremonies, dancers, dance leader)

- Tips

TABLE 7.2 CONTINUED

Wedding rings (excluding engagement ring) (4%)

- Bride's wedding ring

- Groom's wedding ring

Stationery elements (3%)

- Save-the-date notices

- Invitations (invitation card, reception card, reply card)

- Calligrapher

- Ceremony programs

- Specialized ceremony elements (e.g., ketubah, pew cards)

- Guest book

- Seating chart

- Escort, table and place cards

- Table card holders, stands or frames

- Menus

- Personalized table or cake napkins

- Personalized boxes, bags or matches to accompany favors

- Wedding announcements

- Thank-you notes

- Postage

Gifts (3%)

- Bride's attendants

- Groom's attendants

- Parents of bride

- Parents of groom

- Other bridal party members (e.g., readers)

- Wedding favors

Transportation and lodging (3%)

- Transportation for bride and groom

- Transportation for wedding party

- Transportation for guests

TABLE 7.2 CONTINUED

- Parking fees, services and valets
- Hotel room/s for couple, night prior
- Hotel room for newlyweds, wedding night
- Tips

Wedding cake and other pastries (2%)

- Wedding cake (including delivery)
- Groom's cake (including delivery)
- Cake-cutting fee
- Other pastries (e.g., cookies or biscotti)
- Tips

Ceremony and legal issues (2%)

- Ceremony site rental fee
- Officiant fee / donation / tip
- Marriage license
- Ceremony special elements (e.g., unity candle, chuppah rental, broom, crowns)

Wedding day preparation (1%)

- Bridal hair trial run
- Bridal hair day-of
- Bridal makeup trial run
- Bridal makeup day-of
- Bridal manicure / pedicure
- Groom's hair
- Groom's manicure / pedicure
- Tips

TABLE 7.3 SAMPLE SUMMARY BUDGET

Category	Budget %	Amount ($) Allocated
Reception and rentals	40	10,400
Photography and videography	10	2,600
Wedding consultant	10	2,600
Wedding attire	8	2,080
Floral décor	7	1,820
Music and other entertainment	7	1,820
Wedding rings (excluding engagement ring)	4	1,040
Stationery elements	3	780
Gifts	3	780
Transportation and lodging	3	780
Wedding cake and other pastries	2	520
Ceremony and legal issues	2	520
Wedding day preparation	1	260
Total	**100%**	**$26,000**

As discussed in Chapter 8, an open discussion of budget issues early on will help your clients complete a feasibility analysis. Couples often feel overwhelmed and experience "sticker shock" as they start to realize the number of purchases that accompany their wedding day. You can take the often emotional process of decision-making and help them approach it rationally and calmly.

Organization is absolutely critical to budgets. You can assist your clients by encouraging them to keep all of their contracts and receipts in one folder. Some consultants have personalized folders that they give to their clients for this very purpose. Encourage clients to highlight payment due dates, so that they are not charged late fees or denied service. The day of the wedding, you should have the folder close by in case any payment issues arise.

When considering total costs, it is a good idea to encourage your clients to put aside a slush fund of 5 to 10 per cent of the overall estimated costs. At times, unforeseen expenses arise and, if the extra money is in place, it can be used for emergencies. For example, suppose the bride's sister lives out-of-town. She unexpectedly loses her job and reports to the bride that she cannot travel because of her strained financial situation. The couple may use their emergency fund to pay for

PHOTO 7.3 PLANNERS HELP CLIENTS CREATIVELY STRETCH THEIR BUDGETS.

SOURCE: WWW.RODNEYBAILEY.COM

her airfare. They can do this without breaking the bank because they were prepared. If the slush fund is not needed, then the couple can spend the money as they see fit, perhaps treating themselves to new furnishings or putting it toward a house savings fund. They will feel pleased because their wise spending habits allowed for a post-wedding benefit.

CONSULTANT IN ACTION, CASE 7.2

THE GLARING GROOM

You are meeting with potential clients for the first time and agreed to have your initial interview at a reception venue they are considering. In attendance are the director of catering, the couple and the bride's parents. You listen quietly as the groom rants and raves at the catering director, aggressively questioning every listed charge on the sample menu that has been provided. At one point he states, "This is a bottom-budget wedding, and I have no idea why we would spend money on anything extraneous," and then glares at you. You agreed to an initial meeting with this couple because a close friend of yours gave them your name, but you have learned enough already to know this will be a nightmare. You begin to stand, and then notice the bride and her mom looking at you with pleading eyes.

WHAT DO YOU DO?

TIPPING ETIQUETTE

With their credit cards on fire and their savings taking a major hit, it is easy for couples to overlook the etiquette of tipping the many service providers who are involved in making their dreams a reality. Like every other aspect of weddings, tipping is not required; however, it is fair to say that, for many vendors, it is not only desired but anticipated. On the day of a wedding, it is often the consultant who hands out gratuities, so it is your job to broach the topic with the couple regarding how they would like this to be handled. Do not be surprised when they tell you that tipping has not even crossed their minds. Remember, for most couples, this is the first major event they have ever planned, so what is obvious to you is brand new to them. Many of their bills are paid in full well before the wedding, and they may not realize that the person they pay and the on-site service provider are often completely different people. For instance, the booking agent and the driver for a transportation company are rarely the same person, and the driver will definitely be expecting a tip. As another example, the owner of a rental company where your clients have reserved 200 chairs is generally not the person who is standing out in the heat setting them up, spot cleaning them and then returning after the event to pack them back up.

Once couples are comfortable with the idea of tipping, the inevitable question is: "How much?" The amount of a gratuity is either based on a percentage of the bill or is a reflection of the type and level of service. In some cases, such as catering, the gratuity for wait staff and bartenders is

Photo 7.4 Consultants can assist clients with targeting their budgets.

Source: www.RodneyBailey.com

built in and additional tips are only given for exceptional service or for those individuals, such as the banquet manager or chef, who may not automatically be included in the standard structure. It is worth your time to speak to the director of catering when you are working with a new venue to see how the gratuity is distributed. Vendors who generally receive a percentage of the bill include transportation drivers and wedding day preparation vendors such as hairstylists, makeup artists and manicurists. Percentage-based gratuities tend to start at 15 per cent of the bill and go up to 25 per cent or higher. For instance, some hairstylists and makeup artists spend the entire day with the bride to do touch-ups at a moment's notice; as such, their gratuities tend to be higher than average.

Other vendors are tipped based on the type and level of service, where the effort level should be considered. Delivery and set-up specialists for areas such as floral décor, wedding cakes, lighting, tents and other rentals may have dramatically different workloads associated with a wedding. Gratuities for service providers such as these tend to range from $10 per person to $50 or more per person. Parking valets generally are tipped on a per car basis ($2 or more per car), while powder room and coatroom attendants can be tipped based on the number of guests (50 cents to $1 per guest). Ceremony, cocktail hour and reception musicians are tipped differentially based on skill set, the amount of time devoted to the wedding and the number of musicians involved, with

$20 per musician on the low end and up to $100 for each musician. DJs usually receive $100 or more, based on their ability to mix music and/or their capacity to get the guests up and dancing. Photographers tend to receive a higher gratuity, $150 or more, due to the fact that they are with the couple for every moment throughout the wedding day. The ceremony celebrant should also receive a gratuity of at least $150, due to the fact that this person has typically spent time with the couple leading up to the wedding and is the guiding force during the ceremony.

As you become more and more familiar with the tipping amounts that are typical in your area, you can create a gratuity cheat sheet that can be shared with couples upon their request. Consultants often wonder how to handle the fact that they, too, would appreciate a gratuity. While it is never appropriate to guide your clients to tip you, chances are that your stellar service will lead this to be a given! However, you should not hold it against clients if they fail to give you a gratuity. Your pricing structure, discussed more in Section III of the text, should reflect what you feel is fair and reasonable payment for your services, irrespective of whether or not you receive a gratuity.

Please remember that some couples will be fundamentally opposed to this outlay of extra cash. It is neither your job to try to change their minds nor should you feel obliged to apologize on their behalf to the wedding vendors. Most clients, however, view this as a reasonable means of thanking

PHOTO 7.5 TIPPING ETIQUETTE APPLIES TO DELIVERY AND SET-UP PERSONNEL.

SOURCE: WWW.RODNEYBAILEY.COM

CONSULTANT IN ACTION, CASE 7.3

TIPPING SHORTFALL

You have been contracted for partial planning services for a wedding with a budget of close to $80,000. You were involved with the selection of almost all of the vendors, many of whom are good friends. When the topic of tipping came up, you gave the couple some general guidelines and offered to provide a gratuity cheat sheet, which they gratefully accepted. Several weeks before the wedding, the bride sends you a text saying that she would like you to distribute all the tips and she will bring cash in envelopes to the rehearsal. However, at the rehearsal, she tells you that she totally forgot and will stop by an ATM in the morning prior to going to the spa for her wedding day preparation. As arranged, you arrive at the spa the next morning to pick up the envelopes. The bride hands you one envelope with cash and says, "I did not have time to separate it out, so please just use your judgment. I trust you to take care of everyone!" When you get back to your car, you open the envelope and find $200, which you know will not be enough to tip the celebrant and the ceremony musicians, let alone the limousine driver or any of the vendors involved with the reception.

WHAT DO YOU DO?

the many service providers involved with the implementation of their wedding. If a client wants you to distribute the gratuities, you should ask them to provide envelopes labeled for each of the vendors who will receive a tip. These envelopes should come to you sealed with the cash amounts included. This way, the clients are ultimately responsible for determining the sum for each person, and you can avoid a situation like the one presented in *Consultant in Action*, Case 7.3.

While wedding finances and tipping etiquette can overwhelm a couple, a pragmatic, organized and sensitive approach taken by the consultant can simplify the process. Encouraging your clients to keep track of their expenditures and helping them to identify vendors who fit their stated price points will help them stay within their budgets. While some couples have the luxury to spend freely, most appreciate budget guidance that will keep them from having long-term wedding debt.

REFERENCES

CBS News (2013) '10 cheapest places to live in the US', *CBS News Money Watch*, Online. Available HTTP: <http://www.cbsnews.com/2300-505143_162-10013084.html> (accessed 2 February 2013).

Ellin, A. (2012) 'The 7 most expensive places to live in America', *ABC News*, Online. Available HTTP: <http://abcnews.go.com/Business/expensive-places-live-america/story?id=17118717#7> (accessed 2 February 2013).

Grossman, C.L. (10 August 2012) 'Average couple spends $26,989 on wedding; many break budget', *USA Today*, Online. Available HTTP: <http://usatoday30.usatoday.com/money/perfi/basics/story/2012-08-09/wedding-costs/56921020/1> (accessed 20 January 2013).

Kessler, K. (2013) 'Gender segregated weddings in the Sultanate of Oman'. E-mail (4 November 2012).

Madden, N. (11 January 2013) 'Love in China: navigating an $80 billion wedding market retailers, travel companies, household goods marketers benefit from understanding courtship and wedding trends', Online. Available HTTP: <http://adage.com/article/global-news/love-china-navigating-80-billion-wedding-market/239136/> (accessed 12 March 2013).

Patriarca, V. (2012) 'Tips to finding the perfect diamond ring', *CNBC*, Online. Available HTTP: <http://www.cnbc.com/id/48754851/Tips_to_Finding_the_Perfect_Diamond_Ring> (accessed 13 December 2012).

Sieff, K. (16 July 2011) 'In Afghanistan, an effort to expel excess', *The Washington Post*, A01, A12.

The American Wedding Study (2012) 'Brides', Online. Available HTTP: <http://candieanderson.com/2012/06/interview-2012-bridal-trends-with-brides-magazines-vice-president-and-publisher-michelle-myers.html> (accessed 8 August 2012).

The Wedding Report (2012) 'Cost of wedding', Online. Available HTTP: <http://www.costofwedding.com/> (accessed 16 February 2013).

XO Group (2012) 'The Knot: 3rd annual honeymoon study', Online. Available HTTP: <http://www.xogroupinc.com/press-releases-home/2011-press-releases/2011-05-24-2010-honeymoon-study-results.aspx> (accessed 16 February 2013).

CONSULTANT CHECKLIST AND REMINDERS FOR WEDDING BUDGETS

☐ Discuss the anticipated budget early on in the planning process.

☐ Encourage the couple to clearly delineate who will be contributing to the budget.

☐ Discuss tipping etiquette with the couple, as they may not realize that they should factor this into their budget.

☐ All down payments should be made by the couple or the party responsible for the particular budget item.

☐ Keep clients aware of final payment dates so they are not charged late fees or denied service on their wedding day.

☐ Give clients a folder to organize all of their contracts and receipts.

☐ As the consultant, you should receive your final payment at least two weeks prior to the wedding day.

☐ Remind the couple to prepare individually labeled cash envelopes for any wedding day tips that you will distribute on their behalf.

REVIEW

1. Name the seven columns that you should include on a spreadsheet to streamline the presentation of wedding budgets.

2. Name five of the thirteen common categories contained in wedding budgets.

3. What percentage of a wedding budget is generally allocated to reception costs? To photography? To wedding cakes and other pastries?

4. How is the consultant fee recouped by clients?

TERMINOLOGY

- Site fee

- Sticker shock

- Tipping etiquette

- Wedding budget categories

Photo 8.1 Timelines ensure a successful wedding.

Source: www.RodneyBailey.com

8

WEDDING TIMELINES

Timelines allow wedding consultants, vendors and their clients to stay organized, on-track and realistic. While each couple's timeline is unique to their wedding, there are certain commonalities to all weddings that will help you in assisting your clients set priorities as they plan and prepare.

The average length of engagements has stretched out over time, and now couples typically have 16 months to prepare for their weddings (US Census Bureau 2010). However, 16 months is an average, which means that some couples take longer to plan while others move more quickly. Accordingly, there is not one surefire time period from which to operate. Thus, it is appropriate to think about wedding timelines in terms of phases.

The seven phases of wedding timelines include: 1) research; 2) design; 3) coordination; 4) legal issues; 5) confirmation and details; 6) implementation; and 7) wrap-up and evaluation (Table 8.1). It is common for some of the phases to overlap, particularly if the engagement period is short. As a consultant, you may offer your clients guidance throughout the whole process or you can be brought in to assist during a single phase. Use the items in each of these phases as a checklist and reminder of what needs to be done. As each task is accomplished, indicate the associated date. Over time, you will notice consistencies in the region where you live that will help you streamline the planning process and adjust the order of the task list to fit your target market. This list can also act as a guide when considering the questions you need to ask your clients.

RESEARCH

The first phase involves research, usually starting shortly after a couple becomes engaged. One of the first things a couple needs to do is estimate the number of guests to be invited, as this influences many other decisions; in particular, the location of the ceremony and reception. For example, historic venues create a magnificent backdrop for a wedding and reception, but are often limited in their capacity. Location assessment will in turn influence the wedding date options, as popular venues are often booked a year or more in advance. A venue may take precedence over an ideal date, pushing more couples to get married on Thursdays, Fridays and Sundays in order to get their desired sites. Date selection is often informed by family commitments; however, conflicting schedules can lead to difficult decisions, as illustrated in *Consultant in Action*, Case 8.1.

The research phase is also the time to start a list of the types of vendors to be included in the wedding planning process. A list of the vendors commonly involved in weddings is provided in Table 8.2. A *vendor* is any individual or entity that is receiving payment for goods or services that pertain to the implementation of the wedding. The order of vendors is based on a typical booking necessity. This does not mean that the vendors are rank ordered in terms of importance; rather, it is reflective of the fact that some vendors, such as photographers, can only be present at one wedding per day, while vendors such as pastry chefs and florists can handle deliveries to multiple weddings on any given day. Based on the estimated budget, a realistic *feasibility analysis* can occur by having columns of "must haves" versus "include if budget permits" where, for example, a music-loving couple may state that having a 12-piece band for their reception is absolutely essential but they are fine with providing their own transportation. A different couple may indicate that having a luxury coach that fits their entire wedding party is extremely important but for reception music they will save money by having a friend set up an iPod with all their favorites. Each couple will have different priorities; as such, your job is not to dictate what those priorities should be but to help them identify the best vendors available in their budget range.

TABLE 8.1 THE SEVEN PHASES OF WEDDING TIMELINES

PHASE	TASK
Research	
	• Estimate number of guests to be invited
	• Assess potential locations for ceremony, reception and honeymoon
	• Identify wedding date options
	• Identify potential vendors
	• Determine budget
	• Conduct feasibility analysis
Design	
	• Develop theme and vision
	• Conduct site inspections
	• Select date and book venues
	• Contact and visit potential vendors
	• Determine wedding party members
	• Finalize list of guests to be invited
	• Consider desired styles of formalwear for couple and attendants
Coordination	
	• Select and book vendors, sign contracts as needed and make down payments
	• Select formalwear for couple and attendants
	• Select and book honeymoon destination
	• Mail save-the-date notices
	• Develop draft of the wedding production schedule
	• Develop draft layout of ceremony and reception sites
	• Prepare gift registry
	• Take engagement photos
	• Reserve block of hotel rooms for out-of-town guests and wedding night location
	• Mail invitations

TABLE 8.1 CONTINUED

Legal issues

- Review contract legalities for final payments and liability information
- If marrying out of resident country, determine documentation requirements (can take a year or longer)
- Obtain passports, if applicable
- Apply for and obtain marriage license
- Obtain name-change forms

Confirmation and details

- Finalize wedding production schedule
- Finalize layout of ceremony and reception sites
- Finalize confirmed guest list
- Determine security plan
- Confirm with vendors
- Prepare gifts, favors and on-site stationery elements
- Finalize seating assignments, create escort cards and place cards
- Update gift registry
- Finalize hotel block and wedding night location
- Confirm honeymoon details
- Send newspaper announcement

Implementation

- See Table 8.3 for sample wedding production schedule

Wrap-up and evaluation

- Send thank-you cards
- Solicit and compile feedback from couple
- Solicit and compile feedback from vendors
- Prepare and file wedding summary

CONSULTANT IN ACTION, CASE 8.1

FOOTBALL FEVER

Your clients, Kelly and Darren, have set the date for their fall wedding a year in advance. Darren's only brother and best man, Mike, plays college football, so they consulted with him regarding his schedule before booking the ceremony and reception venues. He was not certain about the full schedule, but shared the information that he had at the time. As the wedding date draws closer, Mike learns that his team has scheduled a game on the same day as the wedding. Kelly calls you, distraught, and relays that Darren's parents are expecting them to change the wedding date to accommodate Mike's football schedule. She asks for your advice.

WHAT DO YOU DO?

ADAPTED FROM HAX (2010)

DESIGN

The second phase of wedding planning timelines is wedding design. Discussion of design options frequently takes place during the research phase, so considerable overlap between these two stages is common. The initial design consideration is developing the theme and vision for the wedding. Vision determination is discussed thoroughly in Chapter 6. Also during the onset of the design phase, clients need to inspect possible ceremony and reception venues and book their choices, while simultaneously determining the date. Some couples put the date before the venue and will only consider venues available on their chosen date, while others feel the venue is more important than the date. Date selection may be influenced by culture. For instance, astrology is tied closely to the Hindu religion, though many astrologers have their own interpretations of reading an individual's fortune (Shah 2013). Years ago, and still today, many parents on both sides of the family request the horoscopes, time of birth and location so that their personal astrologer can do a reading to make sure the couple is truly a match and that stars align (Shah 2013). Astrological analysis applies to the couple's wedding date selection as well, to determine an auspicious date.

Chances are that your clients may only have one or two vendors in mind that they must have; you have been hired to help them identify the rest. Thus, during the design phase, you will present your clients with a list of two to four vendors in each vendor category. Part of your job is to know your area and a variety of vendors in each category so that you can match your client to the most

PHOTO 8.2 RESEARCH WILL ALLOW YOU TO SELECT THE IDEAL LOCATION FOR A
COUPLE.

SOURCE: WWW.RODNEYBAILEY.COM

suitable vendors and make the contacts that will get the wedding planned. Consultants typically offer options in the low-, medium- and high-price range for each area, allowing couples to decide where and how they want to target their budgets. During this phase, the list of guests to be invited should be finalized. Additionally, the couple should select members of the wedding party and start considering the desired formalwear that will work with their theme and vision.

TABLE 8.2 COMMON WEDDING VENDORS IN TIMELINE ORDER

| Wedding consultant |
| Ceremony and reception venues |
| Celebrant |
| Caterer |
| Photography |
| Videography |
| Musicians / Band / Disc jockey |
| Wedding attire |
| Florist |
| Honeymoon site |
| Transportation |
| Rentals |
| Invitations / Other stationery elements |
| Pastry chef / Other specialty foods (e.g., custom-made chocolate) |
| Jeweler |
| Lighting |
| Hairstylist |
| Makeup artist |
| Manicurist |
| Dentist |
| Dance instructor |
| Special effects (e.g., butterfly release, ice sculpture) |
| Favors and other gifts |
| Clerk of court's office |
| Local newspaper |

COORDINATION

Now that all of the background research has been completed and the design elements have been chosen, the third phase, coordination, moves into full swing. You will help your clients make final vendor selections and walk them through the associated contracts and down payments. Formalwear selections should be finalized. The honeymoon destination should be selected and booked, and save-the-date notices should be mailed, in particular if the couple is having a destination wedding or if the wedding date is over a holiday weekend. While couples increasingly keep family and friends notified through a wedding website or their social media accounts, some guests may not be internet savvy and will appreciate receiving a save-the-date by mail.

This is also the time for you to initiate the first draft of the *wedding production schedule*, which is a detailed timeline of specific activities and accountability that typically includes the wedding rehearsal, day-of and day-after. A detailed production schedule is provided in Table 8.3. Simultaneously you should prepare a draft site layout of the ceremony and reception, as illustrated in Chapter 16.

During the latter part of the coordination phase, the couple should prepare their gift registry, have engagement photos taken and reserve a block of hotel rooms for out-of-town guests. Many top photographers choose two weekends out of the year when they take all of their clients' engagement photos. Be certain to check with the selected photographer about these dates and then inform your clients so they can have engagement photos taken if desired. In terms of room reservations, most hotels offer a courtesy block at a discounted rate; however, the block is generally lifted several weeks to a month before the wedding date. If the block is fulfilled, it is common for the group sales manager to offer a free room that can be used by the couple. Many brides use this space as a day-of preparation location where all of the bridesmaids can meet to get ready. Benefits associated with a fulfilled block should be negotiated with the sales manager when the block is made. However, you should advise your clients to avoid signing any type of group block contract, as they can be held financially accountable for any rooms that are not reserved. Couples tend to overestimate the block size needed, so encourage your clients to be conservative when making their best guess of the number of rooms that will be needed. With the deep discounts that are often available for last-minute online hotel bookings, many web-savvy guests will forego the block rate in anticipation of a better deal. Others may earn loyalty points at a different property and therefore not stay in the accommodation recommended by the couple. As the coordination phase comes to a close, it is time to mail out invitations. Stationery elements and etiquette are discussed thoroughly in Chapter 13.

LEGAL ISSUES

With the coordination well under way, the fourth phase, legal issues, must be considered. Be certain to remind clients to review their contracts carefully for final payment and liability information. Some venues may require proof of liability insurance not only from vendors but also

PHOTO 8.3 VENDOR CONTRACTS SHOULD BE CAREFULLY REVIEWED.

SOURCE: WWW.RODNEYBAILEY.COM

from the couple in case of property damage. This is most likely to be the case for venues such as museums and historic buildings where the cost of repairing a damaged artifact or part of the building structure can run into millions of dollars. Single-day liability insurance can be purchased at a reasonable cost through select insurance agencies. You should take the time to learn the names of reputable companies in your area who provide this service.

Legal issues become more involved if the wedding is to be held outside the resident country of the couple. The Bureau of Consular Affairs (2013a) with the US Department of State outlines the requirements that must be followed when US citizens are married abroad. As the specifics vary from country to country, it is recommended that the embassy or tourist information bureau of the country where the marriage will be performed be contacted. Blood tests or travel vaccinations may be required and legal proof of identity via a passport will be mandatory. You should warn your clients that a passport card and a passport book are not the same thing. The Bureau of Consular Affairs (2013b) explains:

> The passport card is the wallet-size travel document that can only be used to re-enter the United States at land border-crossings and sea ports-of-entry from Canada, Mexico, the Caribbean and Bermuda. The card provides a less expensive, smaller, and convenient alternative to the passport book for those who travel frequently to these destinations by land or by sea.

Very importantly, a passport card is never acceptable for air travel to any destination. While individuals may be tempted to select a passport card because it is less expensive, the passport book is the safest bet unless they are certain that they fit within the noted restrictions.

The Bureau of Consular Affairs (2013a) emphasizes that the process of marrying abroad can be time-consuming, so it is essential to start early if a couple wishes to marry outside of their resident country. Locations that specialize in destination weddings are able to expedite the documentation process.

As for the marriage license itself, you need to inform your clients about the rules of their state in terms of waiting period and expiration. For over half of the US, there is no waiting period between applying for and receiving a marriage license. For those states that have a waiting period, it varies between one and five days and applies either to the period between applying for and receiving the license or how soon you can marry once you have the license in hand (Nolo 2013). Most states have an expiration provision that varies from thirty days to one year; therefore, the marriage license should not be applied for too early, as it may expire before the wedding day (Nolo 2013).

Marriage license requirements are typically dictated at the city or county level. To apply for a marriage license, generally both parties must be present and provide some form of photo identification such as a valid driver's license, passport or military identification. Often, the parties must also provide their birth certificates and social security cards. The legal age for marriage in the US is 18, but an individual who is 16 or 17 and wishes to marry can generally do so if a parent is present and provides written consent. If a person applying is under the age of 18, a parent must accompany the individual. State residency is not required, but the license must be purchased and filed in the state where the ceremony is taking place. If either individual was previously married, proof of divorce and a waiting period between the time of divorce and that of remarriage may be required. The cost of a marriage license typically ranges between $30 and $100 and cash is often the only acceptable form of payment. As the regulations vary considerably, you should be familiar with the process in the jurisdictions where the majority of your clients reside.

Finally, if one or both parties, most typically the bride, opts for a name change upon getting married, forms can be obtained in advance that will apply to documents such as the driver's license, social security card, health insurance card, workplace identification card and credit cards. While the forms should not be submitted until after the wedding date, as a copy of the marriage license is required, it will save valuable time in the long run to obtain and review these forms in advance. Importantly, the bride must know the name she intends to use once she is married when applying for the marriage license. The website *MissNowMrs.com* specializes in assisting in this often cumbersome process for a fee. Most individuals who desire a name change, however, personally review and follow the requirements as specified by their local Department of Motor Vehicles, their workplace and other applicable agencies.

CONFIRMATION AND DETAILS

The fifth phase of the wedding planning process involves confirmation and working out the final details. At this point, the production schedule and site layout should be completed and the guest list should be confirmed. A security plan should be in place; it may be as straightforward as determining who will be responsible for transporting the gifts but may include a complete security staff if the wedding is high profile.

At this point, it is essential that a final confirmation occur with each vendor. Many consultants prepare and send electronic copies of partial production schedules for each vendor. The vendors do not need the entire production schedule but can benefit from the specifics that pertain to their individual roles. The more detailed or particular the needs of the couple, the more important it becomes to provide the vendors with targeted production schedules. For example, if the couple wants their cake to come out with a formal announcement or if there is to be no father–daughter dance, the DJ should be given specific instructions on an individualized timeline so announcement errors that would be disappointing to the couple will not be made.

Other details that should be attended to at this point include the final preparation of gifts, favors and on-site stationery elements such as seating assignments and escort cards. The couple should be advised to consult their registry to determine if it needs to be updated. The hotel block should be confirmed, as should the wedding night location and honeymoon details. Finally, if the couple wishes to have their wedding details published in their local newspaper in a timely fashion, the announcement generally needs to be submitted a minimum of ten days prior to publication.

IMPLEMENTATION

The production schedule is your primary organizational tool during implementation. If done correctly, a total stranger should be able to refer to the production schedule you created and know exactly how the wedding will unfold. This is crucial because, if a crisis erupts that requires your complete attention, you can hand over the production schedule to your assistant and feel confident that the wedding will continue to proceed smoothly in your absence. Significant crisis situations may result in a last-minute overhaul to the production schedule, as seen in *Consultant in Action*, Case 8.2.

The first page of the production schedule includes day-of contact information for all key parties involved in the process. Following the contact sheet is a detailed agenda that includes each task, start time, the point of contact for the task and any details or notes. A full production schedule is detailed in Table 8.3. While you may opt to keep the production schedule on your electronic tablet, it is recommended to print out hard copies minimally for you and your assistant in case your tablet does not have an adequate battery charge for the full day. You should also bring hard copies of any partial production schedules that you have prepared for vendors. While these should be e-mailed in advance, it is best to have extra copies on hand.

Keep in mind that the day-of activities can vary significantly by culture. *Culture Corner*, Case 8.3 includes an abbreviated timeline to give you a sense of the typical order of activities for weddings in China.

PHOTO 8.4 THE PRODUCTION SCHEDULE INCLUDES ALL DETAILS OF WEDDING IMPLEMENTATION.

SOURCE: WWW.RODNEYBAILEY.COM

CONSULTANT IN ACTION, CASE 8.2

LET THE WINDS BLOW!

You were hired by the mother-of-the-bride to manage the wedding of her younger daughter as a result of a great experience in coordinating her older daughter's wedding five years earlier. The bride-to-be, early in her teaching career, lives two hours away. The groom-to-be, a member of the armed forces, is out of state preparing to graduate from dentistry school. Two weeks after the wedding date, the couple will report to Texas, where he will be stationed.

The mother and sister are very involved and supportive in the wedding planning during the bride's absence. Multiple forms of technology are used to ensure that everyone is current on the planning status. All vendors have been secured, contracts reviewed and expectations discussed. The ceremony is scheduled for 4:00 p.m. on a June afternoon at the bride's family church. A celebration for 200 will follow at the Officers' Club on a local base with a traditional cocktail reception followed by a formal three-course plated dinner, fabulous wedding cake for dessert and dancing.

The afternoon prior to the wedding day, all participants gather for a detailed rehearsal of the planned ceremonial activities. Once completed, the attendees go on their way to make final preparations before the big day. By 8:30 p.m. that evening, the events that would occur over the following hours would change the course of nine months of thorough planning! A derecho event (i.e., a windstorm that can exceed hurricane-force and is accompanied by severe thunderstorms) rolls in and devastates the area. The derecho packed wind gusts of 60–80 mph, thus producing extensive damage, downing countless trees and leaving more than one million area-residents without power. By morning, the damage forced the Officer's Club to cancel your clients' reception. The church was not affected and was prepared to go forth with the ceremony.

WHAT DO YOU DO?

CASE SUBMITTED BY MARILYN PATTERSON
JOYOUS EVENTS LLC
WEBSITE: *JOYOUSEVENTS.COM*

TABLE 8.3 SAMPLE WEDDING PRODUCTION SCHEDULE

Maryanne Cartier and Troy Morath

Wedding Date: Saturday, May 9, 2015
Ceremony Start Time: 5:00 p.m.
Reception Start Time: 6:00 p.m.
Sunset: 8:09 p.m.
Wedding Theme: Southern "Old School" Elegance
Wedding Colors: Buttercup and Ivory
Confirmed Number of Guests: 112

Wedding Implementation Points of Contact

Who / What	Specifics	Contact Information / Notes
Bride	Maryanne Cartier	Cell / E-mail
Groom	Troy Morath	Cell / E-mail
Matron of Honor	Elizabeth Boyle	Cell / E-mail (one-hour time difference)
Best Man	Al Richmond	Cell / E-mail
Consultant	Carina Webber Assistant: Kate Marish	Cell / E-mail Cell / E-mail
Parents of Bride	Dr. Mrs. Robert (Angela) Cartier, Jr.	Cell / E-mail
Parents of Groom	Mr. Mrs. Jerry Morath (Beverly) (Father & Stepmom) Ms. Barbara Sutton	Cell / E-mail (Jerry is main person to call)
Ceremony Celebrant	Father Bittman – St. Leo's Catholic Church	Cell / E-mail

TABLE 8.3 CONTINUED

Who / What	Specifics	Contact Information / Notes
Readers	Jamie Reeves: First reading Regina Cartier: Second reading Allen King: Response Jennifer Stanny: Special intentions Robert Cartier: Pre-dinner prayer	
Rehearsal Dinner Time / Location / Point of Contact	Bekkers Winery Randy Sandler	Address / Cell / E-mail
Ceremony Location / Point of Contact	St. Leo's Catholic Church / Father Bittman	Address / Cell / E-mail
Reception Location / Point of Contact	Old Town Hall Amy Miller on site	Address / Cell / E-mail
Catering	Emmarie Catering	Cell / E-mail
Cake	Zimmerman Bakery (Rafael Tighe will deliver)	Cell / E-mail
Floral Décor	Alicia Hessel (beginning florist; friend of Troy)	Cell / E-mail
Photography	Enduring Moments Photography – Calista Basch	Cell / E-mail
Ceremony Music	Gianna Campbell, Holly Abel and Vanessa Turner (harp, flute, cello)	Cell / E-mail
Cocktail Hour Music	Stephanie Blohm and Garth Felton (violin and accordion)	Cell / E-mail
Reception Music	DJ – John Norman	Cell / E-mail
Hairstylist / Makeup Artist	Julie Grover and three assistants	Cell / E-mail
On-site Stationery	Cantillon Stationery	
Lodging	Hyatt Regency	Address / Front Desk Number
Limousine Coach	Duffney Limos Inc. (Matthew Duffney – owner; Craig Kavulla – Driver)	Cell / E-mail

TABLE 8.3 CONTINUED

Monday, May 4 – Thursday, May 7, 2015
Final Preparations

Start Time	Task	Point of Contact	Details and Notes
	Maryanne will have marriage license	Maryanne	
	Final confirmation with vendors	Carina	
	Verify preparation location	Carina	
	Troy will have the rings	Troy	

Friday, May 8, 2015
Rehearsal

Start Time	Task	Point of Contact	Details and Notes
10:00 a.m.	Tux pick-up: Men's Wearhouse	Troy	
1:00 p.m.	Nails done	Maryanne	
3:00 p.m.	Carina and Maryanne meet at Old Town Hall to drop off on-site materials		
6:00 p.m. or so	Rehearsal start		Bring for Carina: anything that you want on site (e.g., guest book, pens, readings, seating stationery, other reception prep items)
6:45 p.m.	Rehearsal dinner: Bekkers Winery	Randy	39 will be in attendance

Saturday, May 9, 2015
Pre-Ceremony Preparation

Start Time	Task	Point of Contact	Details and Notes
9:30 a.m.	Maryanne prep location at suite in Hyatt Regency	Maryanne	
10:30 a.m.	Photographer arrives at prep location	Calista	
11:00 a.m.	Bridesmaids arrive		Carina will stop by around 11:00 a.m. before going to reception site

TABLE 8.3 CONTINUED

Start Time	Task	Point of Contact	Details and Notes
11:30 a.m.	Hair and makeup begins in suite	Julie and assistants	Pre-paid by Maryanne; will take at least three hours for everyone
11:45 a.m.	Brunch for bride and bridesmaids in suite		Angela will bring brunch
11:45 a.m.	Troy and groomsmen will be at Troy's house		Carina will stop by around noon to pick up boxes of photos for photo tables and custom wine bottles
12:15 p.m.	Carina and Kate arrive at Old Town Hall to begin set-up		See Cocktail Hour / Reception section for all details
2:00 p.m.	Personal flowers arrive at hotel; Troy's mom will pick up men's flowers at hotel and bring them to the house	Alicia / Barbara	
3:30 p.m.	Limo coach arrives at Hyatt Regency; will go directly to St. Leo's	Craig	Just the women prior to the ceremony; will meet the men at the church. Troy will travel with Al. Elizabeth will have after-ceremony cooler for coach (no glass, no open cups). Bring cups with lids!
4:00 p.m.	Bridal party pre-ceremony photos at church (bride and groom separate)	Calista	
4:00 p.m.	Carina arrives at church, Kate stays at reception site		Prepare two reserved rows on each side; floral décor / ribbons
4:15 p.m.	Musicians at church	Gianna, Holly and Vanessa	

TABLE 8.3 CONTINUED

Start Time	Task	Point of Contact	Details and Notes
	Order of Ceremony		
4:30 p.m.	Ushers: Matt and Justin King		
4:40 p.m.	Prelude music will begin	Gianna, Holly and Vanessa	
	Seating for reserved rows		
	Bride's side, from center: Helen Cartier Angela Cartier Robert Cartier Duncan Ferrett Leslie Ferrett		Grandmothers and mothers will process. Robert and Angela will be with Maryanne
	Groom's side, from center: Lucas Malmberg Mabel Malmberg Jeremy Morath Beverly Morath Jerry Morath Barbara Sutton		
5:00 p.m.	Processional music will begin		Ave Maria
	Groomsmen in place at front of room		
	From center: Father Bittman Troy Morath Al Richmond Joey German Eddie Herzig Nate Spain Xavier Voigt Tony Hanna		
	Procession of grandmothers and mothers		Ave Maria
	Bridesmaids, lined up in order in back of church: Melissa Brayley (will walk furthest to left)		Trumpet Voluntary

TABLE 8.3 CONTINUED

Start Time	Task	Point of Contact	Details and Notes
	Julie Wiggins Linda Caswell Tracie Dieke Courtney Lee Elizabeth Boyle		
	Ring bearer Junior will be with Grandma and then walk toward Tracie		
	Bridal entrance music will begin: Entrance of Maryanne with Robert and Angela		Canon in D
	Presentation of the bride		
	Declaration of intention		
	Words of welcome	Father Bittman	
	1st Reading: Genesis 2, 18–24	Jamie Reeves	Reading location at pulpit
	Responsorial Psalm	Allen King	Psalm 103
	2nd Reading: Corinthians 12–13	Regina Cartier	
	Gospel	Father Bittman	
	Homily	Father Bittman	
	Special intentions	Jennifer Stanny	
	Statement of intention	Father Bittman, Maryanne and Troy	
	Exchange of vows	Father Bittman, Maryanne and Troy	
	Blessing of the rings	Father Bittman	
	Exchange of rings		Elizabeth will have the rings; will hand Al Maryanne's ring, who will then give it to Troy to give to Maryanne

TABLE 8.3 CONTINUED

Start Time	Task	Point of Contact	Details and Notes
	The kiss	Maryanne and Troy	
	Blessing of the marriage	Father Bittman	
	Introduction of couple	Father Bittman	
	Recessional music (starts immediately after Father Bittman introduces Maryanne and Troy)		Mendelssohn Recess to front of church for group photo of all ceremony guests
	Order of Recessional: Father Bittman 1) Maryanne and Troy 2) Elizabeth and Al 3) Courtney and Joey 4) Tracie and Eddie 5) Linda and Nate 6) Julie and Xavier 7) Melissa and Tony		
	Reserved rows to follow Postlude music		Musicians' choice
	Maryanne and Troy will sign marriage license at the church		
5:30 p.m.	Post-ceremony group photos to start at the church; Maryanne and Troy then leave with the photographer. Full wedding party heads to reception in limo coach		
Cocktail Hour (Upstairs in Library) / Reception (Main Level): Preparation and Implementation			
12:30 p.m.	Carina and Kate will set up guest book, pen, family photos, easel with sign, photo collage, signature photo, custom wine bottles, seating stationery		3 easels will be on site. Linens will be in place prior to arrival

TABLE 8.3 CONTINUED

Start Time	Task	Point of Contact	Details and Notes
3:00 p.m.	Floral décor arrives	Alicia	Table décor, banister up to library, centerpieces, candles
3:00 p.m.	Caterer arrives		1 bar and hors d'oeuvre stations upstairs; 1 bar and dinner on main level
3:30 p.m.	Carina leaves for ceremony, Kate stays at reception site to await other vendors		
4:00 p.m.	Cakes arrive	Rafael	Wedding cake on sweetheart table, groom's cake on bar
5:00 p.m.	Final preparation walk through. Check for and pick up any packaging, boxes, etc.	Kate	
5:30 p.m.	Cocktail hour musicians arrive	Stephanie and Garth	Set up in library upstairs
6:00 p.m.	Cocktail hour music begins upstairs	Stephanie and Garth	
6:00 p.m.	DJ arrives to set up for reception on main level	John	
6:00–7:00 p.m.	Cocktail hour upstairs in library		Carina and Kate bring out seating stationery table for reception midway through
6:15 p.m.	Maryanne and Troy arrive at reception hall for photos		
6:45 p.m.	Maryanne and Troy arrive at the end of cocktail hour		No formal introduction
7:00 p.m.	Dinner bell; guests descend and pick up escort cards		Kate will assist guests with locating seating stationery

TABLE 8.3 CONTINUED

Start Time	Task	Point of Contact	Details and Notes
7:05 p.m.	Wedding party and other members to be introduced will gather in library and then line up on the stairs to head into reception area		
7:15 p.m.	Entrance of bridal party and family members via stairs		Phonetic spellings for DJ
	Order of Introduction: Bridesmaid Melissa Brayley escorted by groomsman Tony Hanna		Walking on Sunshine
	Bridesmaid Julie Wiggins escorted by groomsman Xavier Voigt		
	Bridesmaid Linda Caswell escorted by groomsman Nate Spain		
	Bridesmaid Tracie Dieke escorted by groomsman Eddie Herzig (note: ring bearer Junior with Tracie)		
	Bridesmaid Courtney Lee escorted by groomsman Joey German		
	Matron of honor Elizabeth Boyle escorted by the best man Al Richmond		
	Mr. and Mrs. Troy and Maryanne Morath		I'm a Believer
7:20 p.m.	Guests invited to be seated for dinner by DJ. Then Robert Cartier will say pre-dinner prayer	John / Robert	While guests are eating dinner, Kate will go up to library to box up cocktail hour photos and décor

Table 8.3 continued

Start Time	Task	Point of Contact	Details and Notes
7:30 p.m.	Buffet and carving station		Guests will be invited by table Dinner music: Big band
8:15 p.m.	As dinner concludes, DJ introduces first dance	John	First dance, Song: Love is Here to Stay
	Wedding party dance		Frank Sinatra song
	Dance floor opens for all guests (2nd slow song)		DJ choice
	Dance music continues		DJ choice and requests
9:30 p.m.	Carina and Kate set up custom wine bottles for guests to pick up as they leave		No more than 20 on the table at a time; Kate will stay and add more as needed
	Toasts: 1. Best man 2. Maid of honor 3. Tracie & Junior	Al Elizabeth Tracie / Junior	
10:00 p.m.	Cake cutting		Sugar, Sugar
	Bouquet toss		DJ pick
	Garter toss		DJ pick
	Cake and coffee served		
	Dance music continues		
10:45 p.m.	Last dance		Save the Last Dance for Me
10:50 p.m.	DJ announce sparklers		Carina and Kate distribute and help to light
11:00 p.m.	Maryanne and Troy depart for hotel in Troy's truck		

TABLE 8.3 CONTINUED

Start Time	Task	Point of Contact	Details and Notes
Post-Reception			
11:05 p.m.	Break down of catering, floral, etc.		Carina will return rental vases to Alicia on Sunday
11:30 p.m.	After party at hotel for wedding party		
11:45 p.m.	Final clean-up and walk through at reception site	Carina and Kate	
12:15 a.m.	Gift transportation and centerpieces	Carina	Bring back to Troy's house. Barbara is staying there
Sunday, May 10, 2015			
1:00 p.m.	Tux drop-off: Men's Wearhouse	Al will drop off Troy's tux	
2:00 p.m.	Casual lunch at Troy and Maryanne's house	Wedding party and out-of-town guests invited	Robert and Angela will pick up barbeque ordered through Red, Hot and Blue

WRAP-UP AND EVALUATION

After the implementation of the wedding, the consultant's contact with the couple will generally continue for a short time so that wrap-up and evaluation can take place. As a consultant, you should solicit feedback from the couple. Further, if any of the vendors are new to you, it would be helpful to request commentary and suggestions from them as well. The specifics of evaluation are covered in Chapters 22 and 23. This information should be compiled so that a final summary of the wedding can be filed for future reference.

Ad hoc services may also continue after the end of the wedding. For example, some couples have luncheons the day after their weddings, giving them an opportunity to unwind with their families and out-of-town guests and often acting as a forum to open wedding gifts. You may be called upon to coordinate such events and tie up other loose ends such as the preparation of thank-you notes. Therefore, your timeline should take into account all services from start to finish.

CULTURE CORNER, CASE 8.3

WEDDING TIMELINES IN CHINA

2–3 weeks prior   The couple will go to the wedding bureau, file for and receive the government's wedding certificate. Generally, no church ceremony takes place. The "ceremony" includes all of the ritual preparations on the wedding day.

WEDDING DAY

6:00 a.m.   The bride goes to the hairdresser/makeup artist in preparation for the day's events. Usually the bride's sister or closest friend will accompany her.

8:00 a.m.   The groom's family gathers at the hotel where the wedding reception will be held. They gather there for breakfast and to make sure that everything is prepared for the later reception.

9:00 a.m.   The bride arrives back home where her immediate family has started to gather for breakfast. The bride's mother, sister and friends help the bride to get dressed in her Western-influenced white wedding dress as well as pack up the other wedding dresses for the reception. The bride will have at least one traditional red Chinese wedding dress as well as many others to change into during the reception.

The hair, makeup and dressing of the bride at her home are based on family tradition and represent the ceremonial elements of the day which symbolically prepare the bride for leaving her parents' home and becoming part of the groom's home and family. In the more rural areas of China, the local brides will wear special clothes handed down from mother to daughter or made by the mother. A bride is only allowed to wear these garments upon getting married.

11:00 a.m.   The groom's family leaves for the bride's home while the groom waits at the hotel. In some cities, this is reversed and the groom goes to the bride's home while his family waits at the hotel. In either case, whoever goes travels in an entourage of cars decorated with red flowers.

11:30 a.m.	At the bride's home, the groom's family will knock on the door wanting entrance, but the bride's family will not let them in until the groom's family presents a red envelope containing 600 Renminbi (RMB, equal to about $75 US), or a multiple thereof depending upon the affluence of the groom's family. The envelope is given to the youngest male of the bride's family. Once this has been completed, the groom's family members are welcomed into the home. Pictures are taken for about ten minutes and then everyone gathers their things and departs for the wedding reception.
11:30 a.m.	The invited guests start arriving at the hotel. Only immediate family members are invited to attend the private events earlier in the day; however, other guests are invited to attend the reception and arrive early to await the bridal party.
12:00 noon	As the bride's car pulls up to the hotel, the groom comes out to greet her and hotel staff members light firecrackers to chase away any evil spirits. However, before the groom can open the car door, the bride's youngest male relative will block the groom's path until the groom gives him another red envelope, again containing 600 RMB. The groom is then allowed to open the bride's door, help her out of the car and escort her into the wedding reception.

THE RECEPTION, STAGE I:

The Announcer

12:15 p.m.	An announcer states the arrival of the bridal party to the guests by, first, introducing the groom's immediate family; second, introducing the bride's immediate family; and, finally, introducing the bride and groom. The couple may be asked to try to eat an apple together without using their hands. The announcer will then share a funny story about the couple and ask the couple to show their wedding certificate to the gathering to clearly illustrate to the crowd that they are now legally married. Then the announcer might do an exchange of rings ceremony. Under Communism, displays of wealth such as rings were historically discouraged; however, today rings and ring exchanges are very much in style. Once the rings have been exchanged, the announcer will again formally introduce the couple to the gathering. This concludes the announcer's work and he departs.

THE RECEPTION, STAGE 2:

Introductions

12:45 p.m.   The groom takes his new wife over to his immediate family and formally introduces each member of his family to his wife. Each member of the groom's family will tell the bride how she can now address him or her. Once completed, this is then repeated by the bride taking the groom over to her family and going through the same process.

THE RECEPTION, STAGE 3:

The Feast

1:15 p.m.–   The bride now changes into one of her many wedding reception
4:00 p.m.   outfits, each to be worn at some point during the rest of the day. The first outfit is usually the high-collared, red traditional Chinese wedding dress. During the wedding feast, the groom and bride do not sit down, as they must go and visit every guest at every table. After greeting each guest, a few words are exchanged and then the bride offers to light the guest's cigarette if that person smokes, feed the guest a bite of food or toast the guest with a small shot of the alcohol being served. The frequent changing of clothes gives the bride short breaks from the toasting. At the same time, guests are toasting the couple and their families. As people toast the groom, they hand him a red envelope containing money. The Western approach of giving a gift rather than cash is catching on in China, so either is acceptable. There is usually no dancing during the wedding feast. It is a sit-down affair with everyone at round tables and a "lazy-susan" in the middle. At each place setting there is a small gift basket including chocolates and sweets, as well as a pack of good cigarettes and a lighter or matches.

CASE SUBMITTED BY YAO AND DAVID WOSICKI

REFERENCES

Bureau of Consular Affairs (2013a) 'Marriage of US citizens abroad', United States Department of State, Online. Available HTTP: <http://travel.state.gov/law/family_issues/marriage/marriage_589.html> (accessed 27 January 2013).

—— (2013b) 'US passport card', United States Department of State, Online. Available HTTP: <http://travel.state.gov/passport/ppt_card/ppt_card_3926.html> (accessed 27 January 2013).

Hax, C. (30 July 2010) 'Wedding runs smack into family's football commitment', *The Washington Post*, C8.

Nolo (2013) 'State marriage license and blood test requirements', Online. Available HTTP: <http://www.nolo.com/legal-encyclopedia/chart-state-marriage-license-blood-29019.html> (accessed 28 January 2013).

Patterson, M. (2013) 'Let the winds blow'. E-mail (1 February 2013).

Shah, N. (2013) 'Astrology and Hindu weddings'. E-mail (2 January 2013).

US Census Bureau (2010) 'America's families and living arrangements: 2010', Online. Available HTTP: <http://www.census.gov/population/www/socdemo/hh-fam/cps2010.html> (accessed 7 March 2013).

—— (2011) 'Estimated median age at first marriage, by sex: 1890 to the present', Current Population Survey, March and Annual Social and Economic Supplements, Online. Available HTTP: <http://www.census.gov/population/socdemo/hh-fam/ms2.xls> (accessed 7 March 2013).

Wosicki, Y. and Wosicki, D. (2006) 'Wedding timelines in China'. E-mail (7 June 2006).

CONSULTANT CHECKLIST AND REMINDERS FOR WEDDING TIMELINES

☐ Include names and contact information for all key parties.

☐ Indicate who is responsible for each task so accountability is clear.

☐ Partial production schedules should be given to vendors who have ongoing tasks, such as transportation, catering and musicians.

☐ Include all details that might be overlooked by a vendor (e.g., no bouquet toss).

☐ Include drop-off and pick-up times for equipment and supplies.

☐ Indicate the earliest time that vendors will have access to venues.

☐ Indicate the time of sunset: refer to the website *timeanddate.com* for assistance.

☐ Indicate who is responsible for post-reception duties such as the transportation of gifts.

REVIEW

1. Name the seven phases of wedding timelines.

2. Explain two tasks that occur in each of the seven phases.

3. What is the difference between a passport card and a passport book?

4. What are two of the issues related to obtaining a marriage license that vary from state to state?

5. What are four key elements to wedding production schedules?

6. What are two unique elements associated with wedding timelines in China?

TERMINOLOGY

- Feasibility analysis

- Marriage license

- Passport book

- Passport card

- Timeline phases

- Vendor

- Wedding production schedule

PHOTO 9.1 WEDDING FOOD SHOULD BE VISUALLY APPEALING.

SOURCE: WWW.RODNEYBAILEY.COM

9

FOOD, BEVERAGE AND THE WEDDING CAKE

Food and beverage are generally the most expensive wedding elements, taking up a significant portion of the amount allocated to the budget category of reception and rentals. Most couples are not accustomed to making detailed menu decisions or serving large numbers of people; accordingly, the guidance and advice of a wedding consultant and caterer are sought. Wedding planners and caterers work as a team. While some vendors do not like working through a liaison, others often prefer working with knowledgeable consultants. This is particularly true for caterers, who often become the planner by default if a professional wedding consultant has not been hired. Many consultants have ongoing relationships with caterers, saving both the couple and the caterer valuable time. This chapter offers an overview of essential considerations pertaining to food, beverage and the wedding cake.

Food and beverage

Finding and working with a caterer is a sales process from start to finish. When helping a couple select a caterer, it is typical for a wedding consultant to first suggest a number of caterers who vary in services, style and price range. Once the group is narrowed to three or four, initial meetings take place. During the initial meeting, the caterer provides information regarding service options and packages. Some caterers focus on food and non-alcoholic beverages but most are also licensed to provide alcohol. Other services can include the cake as well as staffing and rentals. During this meeting, logistics such as time of day, number of guests and the site are provided, as well as information regarding other vendors that will influence catering, such as tent rental. One of the most important pieces of advice you can offer your clients is to be very conservative when estimating the number of guests. Clients tend to significantly overestimate their guest count. It is psychologically easier to increase the number later in the process than it is to decrease the number, as the caterer will not want to put a dent in the profit margin and the per person cost may go up when the count goes down. Be cognizant of the firm deadline for the final headcount and realistic with the initial estimates.

Dietary restrictions and other specialized needs should be introduced during this meeting, as some caterers may not be able to accommodate specific requirements. For example, it is impossible for caterers who work from set menu selections to create a menu that follows strictly kosher Jewish dietary laws. Four of the many requirements for kosher include: 1) shellfish, pork and rabbit are forbidden; 2) dairy and meat cannot be eaten together; 3) grape products, such as wine, must be produced by those who follow the Jewish faith; and 4) produce must be cleaned and examined scrupulously to ensure that no insects are present (Hendrix 2008). Couples who wish to be certain that they are getting a kosher meal must work with caterers that are fully certified kosher and they may want to verify that there is a trained kosher supervisor on staff, known as a *mashgiach* (Hendrix 2008).

Caterers may be able to address some unique dietary requests, such as vegetarian or gluten-free meals, but may charge additional fees for specialized services. The wedding planner should be aware of menu restrictions in advance and can limit the initial listing of caterers to those who can attend to the needs of the couple and their guests.

In some cases, the couple will have dietary requests that pertain to one or two guests, while, in others, the couple may impose their preferences upon all the guests. For instance, a bride who has a nut allergy may request that no nuts or nut extracts be used in any part of the meal. A lactose-intolerant groom may have a separate dairy-free cake or the entire wedding cake might be dairy-free. It is critical that the couple and the consultant clearly communicate special needs to the caterer in advance of the formal proposal. Determine if substitutions can be made for individuals with special dietary needs.

Importantly, the initial meeting is an opportunity for the caterer to get to know the couple and their food and beverage preferences. This information can be used to build a targeted proposal,

PHOTO 9.2 A TARGETED PROPOSAL CAN INCLUDE IMAGES TO "WOW" THE COUPLE.

SOURCE: WWW.RODNEYBAILEY.COM

the contents of which are well explained by event designer Rachel Gittins (2013) for Ridgewells, a prominent company that annually caters thousands of events such as weddings, corporate meetings and professional sports. The catering proposal is presented shortly after the initial meeting and generally includes the food costs, staff costs, equipment costs, taxes, gratuity and delivery. You should ask if there are set-up costs and overtime charges. In the proposal, the caterer sells to the desires outlined in the initial meeting. This document should be organized, accurate and thorough with no grammatical or spelling errors. The names of the bride and groom, their venues and other details given during the meeting must be correct. Notes regarding any specialized needs that were mentioned should be included.

Rachel explains that the proposal stage is an opportunity for the caterer to "wow" the couple by including special touches that signal to the couple that the company can and will treat each wedding as a unique event. For example, if the caterer learned during the initial meeting that the groom proposed in Australia and the wedding is going to have an outback theme, a signature drink called the koala café can be suggested by the caterer to accompany the cake. If the couple loves to garden, the proposal can be presented on elegant paper with a floral design. An outstanding proposal proves to the couple that the caterer listened during the meeting and really understood the focus of the event. Upscale caterers particularly enjoy working with what they call *foodie brides*, who are those that both understand and appreciate fine cuisine.

Even if the proposal is going to the wedding consultant instead of directly to the couple, the caterer should still include the special touches. The caterer and consultant can then create a global proposal that incorporates the catering elements. A consultant will be more eager to work with a caterer who was clearly listening during the meeting.

When meeting with potential caterers, it is critical that your clients taste the food that they are considering. Top caterers host formal tastings two or three times a year, where they invite couples

PHOTO 9.3 CUTTING-EDGE CATERERS ARE TREND SETTERS.

SOURCE: WWW.RODNEYBAILEY.COM

PHOTO 9.4 DESIGNER HORS D'OEUVRES PACK AN EXPLOSION OF TASTE.

SOURCE: WWW.RODNEYBAILEY.COM

and consultants who have expressed an interest in their services to an event in order to showcase their food, presentation and service. This savvy marketing technique exposes couples to specific hors d'oeuvres, entrées, pastries and other items that they may not have otherwise considered and also acts as a way to highlight the caterer's newest linens and tableware in a festive atmosphere.

FOOD AND BEVERAGE TRENDS

Cutting-edge caterers are trend setters. These trends are witnessed at weddings and increasingly informed by the menus showcased on television by celebrity chefs such as Bobby Flay, Guy Fieri and Giada DeLaurentiis or detailed by niche food bloggers such as Jen Cafferty and Michael Natkin (Mariani 2012; PBS 2012). Brides and grooms increasingly want their food to be innovative and memorable, with caterers and planners responding by "taking cues from food television, the farm-to-table phenomenon, the organic/seasonal/sustainable movement and every other flash in the kitchen. Even food trucks are rolling up to the fanciest receptions" (Schrambling 2012: E1).

One of the best times to showcase food trends is during cocktail hour, where designer hors d'oeuvres such as "Crostini with fig, speck ham and ash goat cheese" or "Parmesan crisps with porcini ragoût and fried tarragon" (Occasions Caterers 2013) offer a visual delight and pack an explosion of taste into a single bite. The beauty and versatility of hors d'oeuvres, sips and small plates are so inspiring that "more and more couples do not want a sit down dinner at all, which has liberated caterers" (Schrambling 2012: E5).

For clients who opt for a sit-down dinner, trends are often evidenced in the style and presentation of entrées. Specialty entrées can be designed and named to fit the theme. A growing trend, Rachel notes, is to reflect the fusion of multicultural couples with food selections. For instance, different courses may showcase the merging of couples or one element of a meal can highlight a cultural tradition. Split entrées are also stylish. This dual approach blends the diversity of the buffet with the elegance of plated service. Sushi boats and bridges have maintained popularity and allow for an Asian flair with spectacular presentation opportunities.

As suggested with the outback theme, *signature drinks* remain in demand and allow for a reflection of the theme or can imbue humor. Rachel offers an example of an outdoor wedding that coincided with an unanticipated cicada season. The bride was incredibly stressed about the large, noisy insects ruining her wedding reception. While typical measures to detract the insects would be in place (see Chapter 16 for guidance), the bride remained anxious. In order to provide some levity and relax the bride, the caterer's *mixologist* (i.e., one who studies and practices the art of

PHOTO 9.5 SPECIALTY ENTRÉES ALLOW FOR ELEGANT PLATED SERVICE.

SOURCE: WWW.RODNEYBAILEY.COM

PHOTO 9.6 SIGNATURE DRINKS REFLECT THE WEDDING THEME.

SOURCE: WWW.RODNEYBAILEY.COM

preparing cocktails) devised the "cicada-tini," a martini-like drink with a plastic bug hanging onto the side of the glass. The bride loved the idea and, once implemented, the guests thought it was hilarious. As this example suggests, signature drinks are fun and flexible, as beverages are versatile and a simple drink can have flair if given a clever name and presented in a fun glass with a unique straw or nontraditional garnish. Unique desserts offer an additional outlet for food flair, with drinkable tiramisu, edible place cards, mini pie buffets and French pastries just a few of the many replacements for traditional sweets.

Trends can also be evidenced in the equipment used by the caterer. Cutting-edge tableware can leave a lasting impression on the guests. Cocktail stations are a unique alternative to a traditional reception and present an opportunity to showcase unique and funky plates, bowls and cutlery. For instance, while guests would not normally expect soup at a cocktail station, the use of stylish shot or cordial glasses readily creates this opportunity. Trends in rentals are discussed in more detail in Chapter 16.

In general, the more upscale the caterer, the more likely that their managers can make things happen. Some caterers have set menus with little flexibility, whereas high-end businesses often operate *à la carte*. Further, if a couple wants specialty equipment that the catering company does not own, the managers may buy it if they see it as cutting-edge. They can then rent it to the couple and keep it as inventory for further use. High-end caterers are also more flexible in working with support caterers. For example, if the couple wants one specialty ethnic food item that the caterer does not carry, the primary caterer will work with the support caterer to obtain and showcase the food. By law, the primary caterer cannot pick something up from another restaurant and bring it to the reception; however, if that restaurant delivers the item to the site, the primary caterer will present it in a consistent manner. This flexibility allows the couple to know that the caterer will make the effort to ensure that their food and beverage are perfect. Rachel discusses other trends in *Vendor Spotlight*, Case 9.1.

PHOTO 9.7 MASON JARS AND COLORFUL STRAWS CREATE A UNIQUE PRESENTATION.

SOURCE: WWW.RODNEYBAILEY.COM

VENDOR SPOTLIGHT, CASE 9.1

RACHEL GITTINS

RIDGEWELLS CATERING

What are some of the latest trends in food and beverage for weddings? Anything that is miniature and with a unique presentation, such as an individual vessel or eco-friendly container makes a statement. We like to take something ordinary and make it extraordinary, for instance, truffle tater tots with caviar. This takes the element of a tater tot that is totally recognizable and puts an upscale spin on it to make it a new experience. We also have many requests for interesting, edible favors, such as a mason jar filled with a layered pie, wrapped cake pops or take-away s'mores with handcrafted marshmallows and gourmet graham crackers. Food trucks and facades are totally in, particularly if they offer something special to the bride and groom. Whether it's a pork banh mi or an Italian ice truck, it puts a unique signature on the event. Additionally, the "organic and green" movement continues to gain momentum within the wedding industry. Ridgewells continues to set the trend with our local, sustainable and organic food sourcing and environmental stewardship.

If a couple has a very tight budget, what aspects of food and beverage are the easiest to minimize or cut out? The cocktail hour is an easy place to tighten up. A delicious zucchini ribbon with Boursin mousse on an olive cracker is just as impactful as a shrimp cocktail and about half the price. We have also seen a rise in things like slider bars, southern comfort cuisine and gourmet hotdogs. The actual fare is less costly, but still allows for an elevated design and the "wow" factor of a grilling station attendant during cocktails. In terms of the main course, a piece of sliced Waygu beef or chicken tagine with potato croquettes is significantly less costly than a traditional plate of beef tenderloin or crab cakes, yet still has incredible preparation and presentation.

How have social media outlets affected your business and client base? Ridgewells keeps up on Pinterest, Twitter and Facebook daily. In addition to the obvious exposure these social media outlets provide, it's really broadened our base with other industry professionals because it allows us to promote as well as give accolades. Pinterest, in particular, has revolutionized the wedding industry. At a fundamental level, it has given brides a license to come armed with so many more definitive ideas, pictures and design schematics. All of the Ridgewells Event Designers have Pinterest accounts with food-related boards so it allows us to build bridges and conversation threads with brides.

Please share a recent, unique wedding experience. We catered a wedding where, after the meal, the guests played board games in lieu of dancing. The energy was so genuine and pure. It was simple and yet one of our most interesting stories. The pictures are so unique.

What are the most complicated requests you have had? For us there is very little that is too complicated or difficult. We look at all those scenarios as opportunities to work with our vendors and design partners to create something special for the couple. This could be something related to design and layout, logistics like turning a room over between a ceremony and dinner, producing food for 400 from a tent or coordinating an elephant entering a ceremony . . . we welcome any challenge.

Please share a crisis management story, where something went wrong and your team had to save the day. The weather is always an uncertain element that, despite all the planning in the world, creates havoc. We were fully set up for a tented reception on the grounds of a mansion when a storm rolled in and completely uprooted all the bars and the majority of the seating tables. The tent turned into a virtual swamp. It all happened in about 12 minutes. We did what we could to preserve as much of the bar and seating tables. When it was all over, we surveyed the tent and the damage was pretty severe. The guests entered the tent after the ceremony and they were all so understanding and forgiving as we passed beverages since the bars were all but incapacitated. The ladies took off their shoes and waded around in the water. It ended on a high note but not without an element of crisis and client management.

What can wedding planners do to make your life easier? For us, working with planners is always preferable. Having that team of vendors including planners makes our jobs as caterers that much easier. It allows us to wear our catering hats and put our full attention and focus on the food. Communication is key. A united force and presentation to the client adds validity and integrity to the overall product.

WEBSITE: *RIDGEWELLS.COM*

TYPES OF SERVICE

The type of service used during the main meal is dictated by the food choices, the formality of the occasion and the reception site. Three primary types of service presentation are buffet, plated and French. The necessary wait staff skills vary significantly based on the type of service. *Buffet service* is less formal and is chosen by couples who value offering a variety of foods from which their guests can choose. A buffet can follow a theme or may simply include the couple's culinary favorites. The servers are skilled in maintaining the cleanliness of the buffet and making sure that dishes coming close to empty are quickly changed. The caterer does not want guests to look at a chafing dish and be embarrassed to select what looks like the last one of any item or, if standing back a few spots, fear that a given dish will run out before they reach it. The goal for a well-presented buffet is for each guest to see it looking full and beautiful, as if it was in the original state. A buffet can be set up as a traditional layout with one long table or be broken into a variety of *food stations*, allowing for more movement and guest interaction. The buffet style is not convenient to all venues, however. For example, if the reception is held at an inn that has numerous small rooms with tables situated throughout, negotiating the guests back and forth to a buffet line or different stations would cause considerable confusion. For venues such as this, plated service would be recommended. Be certain to familiarize yourself with the venue and any restrictions or limitations pertaining to catering, so as not to be caught off-guard at the last minute, as seen in *Consultant in Action*, Case 9.2.

The majority of the work for *plated service* is done behind the scenes in the kitchen. Plated service allows for an elegant arrangement of food, where each plate is quickly but carefully prepared and then covered. At the moment the meal is ready to be served, the cover is removed, any sauce that is accompanying a dish is added and the servers proceed with their plates. Using a technique called a *sweep*, two or three waiters may work each table to get all the plates out as quickly as possible. This type of service is common to formal weddings but may be impractical for some

Photo 9.8 Catering trends include fun sips and comfort food.

Source: www.RodneyBailey.com

CONSULTANT IN ACTION, CASE 9.2

MISSING IN ACTION

Your clients are hosting both their ceremony and reception at a mansion situated in a beautiful state park. You arrive early to the venue, as the wedding is taking place on a Friday evening and traffic is certain to be horrible. Shortly before the ceremony, the off-site caterer arrives and starts unloading into the kitchen, preparing to warm the trays of pre-prepared food. She walks into the kitchen and then walks straight out, approaching you in a panic. The oven that has always been there the dozens of times she has worked at this venue is missing! You quickly call the venue supervisor, who apologizes and states that he must have forgotten to mention that they were starting renovations in the kitchen. The caterer tells you that her only option is to bring all of the food back to her place of business, heat it, load it into warmer boxes and return to serve – a process that will take several hours based on travel conditions, and significantly beyond the time the food service is slated to begin.

WHAT DO YOU DO?

CASE SUBMITTED BY BETH HENDERSON
ARIANNA'S GOURMET CAFÉ & CATERING
WEBSITE: *ARIANNASGOURMETCAFE.COM*

venues. For instance, if a site layout is such that the kitchen is on a different level from the dining area and each staff member can only carry four plates at a time due to a narrow passage, an excessive amount of back and forth movement would have to occur. If the site is not conducive to plated service, yet a formal atmosphere is still desired, then French service would be the suggested alternative.

French service is the least common of the three service styles and requires significant skill on the part of the wait staff. With French service, the entire meal for everybody at one table is brought out and served from a single large dish or platter. Each server is white gloved and has to be able to operate a fork and spoon with considerable dexterity. The server must be able to maneuver the platter, utensils and the food skillfully so that each element of the meal is presented in an attractive manner. In the US, this type of service is not very common because, even when carefully done, it is difficult to get the presentation effects that are possible with plated service. However, French service allows each guest to receive individualized attention.

PHOTO 9.9 PLATED SERVICE IS COMMON FOR FORMAL WEDDINGS.

SOURCE: WWW.RODNEYBAILEY.COM

When considering service, it is important to ask the caterer about the *staffing ratio*. At premier venues, you can expect a 1:8 or 1:10 ratio, which means there will be one server for every eight to ten guests. At venues that are less customer-oriented, you are likely to have a 1:12 ratio or higher. Buffet meals will require fewer servers than plated or French service. If there is a cocktail hour, often servers will be on hand to pass hors d'oeuvres. For this service, a 1:30 or even 1:35 ratio is acceptable. In some cultures, food service for weddings is an all-day affair. Countries such as Portugal are famous for their bountiful wedding feasts that often start at noon and last past midnight, with mouthwatering arrays of soup, fruit, salad, seafood, pork and pastries.

Irrespective of the type of service, wedding guests should be well fed in a timely fashion. This is not to say that guests should immediately sit down to the main meal as soon as they enter the reception site. However, if there is not going to be a cocktail hour, greater efficiency is necessary. The beauty of a cocktail hour is that it allows guests to mingle in a relaxed setting while enjoying hors d'oeuvres and beverages rather than rushing straight to designated tables. If the cocktail hour stretches well beyond an hour, work with your clients to ensure that the caterer will provide "heavy" hors d'oeuvres, meaning that they are filling and plentiful. The added expense is well worth it to avoid situations such as the one presented in *Consultant in Action*, Case 9.3.

CONSULTANT IN ACTION, CASE 9.3

HUNGER PANGS!

Your clients' wedding is being held at an exclusive country club that has recently hired a highly skilled, but temperamental, chef. The per person cost is just over $250, including two top-shelf open bars, designer hors d'oeuvres and a high-quality sit-down dinner. Your clients overestimated how long their evening ceremony would take, and guests began to arrive at the reception site at 6:00 p.m., 30 minutes before anticipated. The banquet manager agreed to open bar service early for a fee that was approved by the parents of the bride, who are hosting the reception. Hors d'oeuvre service is timed to begin at 6:30 p.m., yet by 6:45 p.m. there is no food to be seen. At 7:00 p.m., the first three plates of hors d'oeuvres are carried out by the servers. The hors d'oeuvres are visually exquisite, but there are only six on each plate – not enough to satisfy ten guests, let alone the 140 in attendance. As time ticks by, you can tell that the guests are getting drunker and hungrier by the minute, with literally a line of guests hovering by the kitchen door in the hopes of snagging one of the elusive hors d'oeuvres, and only one additional plate coming out every 15 minutes. At 8:00 p.m., the banquet manager approaches you, looking flustered, and states, "Chef must take a break from creating his beautiful hors d'oeuvres in order to begin preparing the meal. We are running a bit behind, and expect to serve by 9:00 p.m. or so."

WHAT DO YOU DO?

Food and beverage costs

The costs associated with food and beverage vary considerably based on the quality, quantity and variety desired and, perhaps most significantly, the geographic location of the wedding. Cost of living in the general vicinity affects food and beverage pricing, while customs within a given locale can dictate expectations of reception fare. In general, per person costs can range from $15 to $500 and up, so it is important to familiarize yourself with the range in your community.

For couples on a budget, there are some ways to cut reception costs. Some caterers allow clients to purchase the alcohol and then just charge a *corkage fee* to pour. You will need to verify this with the caterer before advising clients to consider this route. Alternatively, your clients may opt to limit the alcohol to beer and wine; however, the price of a good wine can be more expensive than liquor and has fewer servings per bottle. Some couples forego alcohol all together or just have a champagne toast; this approach is common in some regions and for afternoon receptions. A cash bar, where the guests pay for drinks containing alcohol, is another way to save on costs but this approach is likely to offend the guests and should only be considered if it is a common practice in the area.

If including a cocktail hour, the couple can save by having the most expensive hors d'oeuvres passed rather than set out on a table. For example, if shrimp are presented on a table with an elegant ice boat, guests will flock to the table and devour this pricey item. On the other hand, if a server is walking around with a tray of shrimp, most guests will not take more than one piece at a time. Less expensive items such as vegetables, cheese and crackers can be set on a table for guests to graze, and considerable savings will result.

Savings should also be realized when feeding children and vendors. When you are sitting down with the caterer, your clients need to be able to estimate how many children will be in attendance. If it is a plated meal, there should be less expensive options available to children, who often will not enjoy, let alone appreciate, the costly adult meal. Similarly, your clients should not feel compelled to feed their vendors the same $125 meal that their guests will receive. This is not to say that they can overlook the vendors, who expect and deserve to be fed. Usually the caterer can put together a tray of sandwiches, chips and cookies for the vendors. Keep in mind that all on-site vendors will want a meal, and whether the band has two people or twenty people, you have to include all of them in the budget. Also be aware that some vendors may specify a hot meal in their contract. For day-of planners, careful review of contracts will keep situations like the one in *Consultant in Action*, Case 9.4 from occurring.

Related to food and beverage are the associated rentals included in the reception budget. Rentals such as chairs, tableware and linens may come from the caterer but could be significantly less expensive with an outside vendor. You will need to know the policies of both the caterer and the venue before enlisting outside vendors for these items.

Beyond feasible ways to save, there are perceived cost-cutting measures that should be avoided. Having an unlicensed caterer or a family member acting as chef or bartender may seem like a way

CONSULTANT IN ACTION, CASE 9.4

SOME LIKE IT HOT!

You are the day-of planner for a wedding being held in the atrium of a major downtown building. Your clients did not think it was necessary for you to review the vendor contracts, as they did all of the booking themselves. When working with the couple to create the timeline, it was understood that the caterer would provide a tray of sandwich wraps, fruit and cold beverages that the wedding vendors could enjoy in a back room while the guests are eating their sit-down meal. At the appointed time, you approach the vendors and direct them to the room where the food is ready and waiting. When the photographer enters the room and sees the food, she states that her contract specifies a hot meal for both her and her assistant. The assistant states that he does not mind and goes to grab a wrap; however, the photographer loses her temper and demands two hot meals immediately. You leave the room to consult with the catering manager, who informs you that the hot meals will cost your clients $320 ($160 for each meal); or, to make an alternative, less expensive hot meal will take at least 30 minutes, overlapping with the time when the photographer and her assistant should be back on the floor documenting the toasts.

WHAT DO YOU DO?

to save money, but ultimately this is compromising the safety of the guests and putting the clients at risk for liability. You should only work with catering companies that are licensed to serve alcohol, have liability insurance and require training for all of their bartenders. Because regulations specific to the distribution of alcohol vary from state to state and country to country, it is important that you familiarize yourself with the legislative code in your area.

Having food stations with small plates or heavy hors d'oeuvres instead of a full meal may appear to be cost-effective but this is not necessarily the case. Individual hors d'oeuvres can be priced at $6 per piece or more; this quickly adds up if a couple wants five different stations and guests are estimated to consume at least three hors d'oeuvres at each station.

THE WEDDING CAKE

The cake cutting is an anticipated reception moment. Guests love to look at the wedding cake, watch the ceremonial slicing and determine if the cake tastes as good as it looks. When assisting a couple with the process of selecting a wedding cake, primary considerations are the icing, flavor, design and size.

The outside of the cake, including the icing and related decorative touches, is more likely to dictate the price per slice than the inside. There are two types of icing: butter cream and fondant. *Butter cream* is fluffy with a lightly sweet taste. *Fondant*, on the other hand, is the consistency of putty and therefore is very moldable, allowing for intricate designs. Fondant is heavier, more versatile, has a smooth sheen and is considerably more expensive because it is labor intensive. For instance, a cake with butter cream icing may run $4 a slice, while the exact same cake with fondant can cost $8 per slice. Theme-based cakes generally necessitate fondant; for example, grooms' cakes are often designed to entertain, representing anything from a largemouth bass to a sports stadium.

Some pastry chefs will only use fondant for wedding cakes because butter cream can and will melt. Other pastry chefs will consider butter cream, but only during the cooler months of the year. In particularly hot climates, any icing can become unstable. Amy Kossman (2013) of Piece of Cake Desserts in Mesa, Arizona explains that the greatest challenges she encounters pertain to the many requests she gets to display a cake outside and in the direct sun in 90-degree temperatures or higher. She strongly advises clients who are hosting outdoor receptions to keep their cakes inside until the last possible moment to keep everything intact.

Even though fondant presents greater design opportunities and is less prone to disaster, a drawback of fondant is that, in comparison to butter cream, it is very sweet and not always tasty. Tom Lally (2013) of the Alexandria Pastry Shop and Catering Company recommends a layer of butter cream covered with a thin sheet (about 1/8 of an inch) of fondant that can be molded and decorated. This allows couples to have the taste of butter cream and the elegance of fondant.

A second decision pertains to the inside flavor of the cake. The taste of the cake is a significant selection consideration and couples enjoy the process of sampling the different flavors that pastry chefs offer prior to making a final decision. The best pastry chefs bake from scratch using butter and fresh cream, often from local dairies to ensure quality, and do not use preservatives. They also use only fresh fruit and will often import fine chocolate. As explained by Tom Lally, serving a variety of flavors encourages guests to talk about the cake as they compare notes about the various flavors. He states that this also aids in presentation once the cake is cut, as guests get to visually experience the diverse textures. However, multiple flavors can prove to be challenging if one flavor is particularly popular and runs out, potentially leaving some guests disappointed. He explains that, while they have over 25 flavors for wedding cakes, the most popular are Bavarian with fresh fruit and milk chocolate mousse.

A third consideration when selecting a wedding cake is the design. Leslie Poyourow (2013) of Fancy Cakes by Leslie, who has designed cakes for celebrities and wedding couples from coast to coast, explains that about 30 per cent of her customers come in with an idea in mind but seldom leave wanting that exact design, as she likes to work with them to create their own, unique look. When setting up vendor appointments, she suggests scheduling the meeting with the pastry chef after

PHOTO 9.10 THE OUTSIDE OF A CAKE WILL DICTATE PRICE, IN PARTICULAR WITH
FONDANT ICING AND INTRICATE DESIGNS.

SOURCE: WWW.RODNEYBAILEY.COM

the couple has decided on the theme, venues, attire, invitations and floral décor since these elements can inform the shape and look of the cake. For example, one bride may want her cake to reflect aspects of her wedding dress, while another may want the flowers she selects for her bouquet to be mimicked by sugar flowers on the cake. Leslie explains that the most difficult, and therefore most expensive, designs are those with intricate "fondant on fondant" patterns, often taking several days to create. She adds that painted cakes are also very time-consuming. Leslie offers more advice about wedding cakes in *Vendor Spotlight*, Case 9.5.

A final concern, which is related to design, is the size of the cake. This is not solely determined by the number of guests. Depending on the intricacy of the design, couples can realize enormous savings by downsizing the ceremonial cake. Once it is cut and removed to the kitchen for slicing, a sheet cake with butter cream icing can be used to serve the majority of the guests, who will never know the difference. The sheet cake is the same flavor, but does not have the labor intensity of the design or the fondant icing. Accordingly, where an intricate, ceremonial cake might cost $9 a slice, the sheet cake can be $4 a slice or less. Using this scenario, if you are serving 200 guests and half of them are receiving the sheet cake, that equals a savings of $500, where the total cake cost is $1,300 rather than $1,800. Size also influences transportation and set-up costs. Most wedding cakes are delivered already built and a representative from the bakery is there to unload and troubleshoot as necessary. Because of the weight of large cakes, Styrofoam or plastic layers are sometimes used for balance and support. Tom Lally (2013) explains that, when they made a wedding cake for a reception with 500 guests, they used a 5-foot round "dummy layer" on the bottom as a support structure with four tiers of real cake separated on top. Dummy layers are decorated with the same intricate designs, so only the pastry chef is aware of the presence of a fake layer as a functional necessity. Even the most expensive of cakes are subject to disaster, and, if the delivery person has exited, the consultant must come to the rescue, as evidenced in *Consultant in Action*, Case 9.6.

PHOTO 9.11 BUTTER CREAM ICING IS FLUFFY AND LESS LABOR INTENSIVE THAN FONDANT.

SOURCE: WWW.RODNEYBAILEY.COM

PHOTO 9.12 COMPLEX DESIGNS ARE OFTEN EVIDENCED IN CLEVER GROOMS' CAKES.

SOURCE: WWW.RODNEYBAILEY.COM

Mini-cakes, upscale cupcakes and designer doughnuts, with each guest receiving an individually decorated dessert, have risen in popularity but are quite expensive because each pastry involves a significant labor investment. Specialty mini-cakes can cost $15 per person or more. It is easier for a pastry chef to design and make a four-tier cake than miniatures for each guest. Couples who love the fun and funky nature of mini-cakes will often buy them in smaller quantities for showers or rehearsal dinners.

Timing the cake cutting is very important. Most couples wait until the last hour of their reception, as the guests usually stay until the cake is served and the cutting often signals that the reception is coming to an end. After the formalities, staff members take the cake to the back and, if requested, will box up the top layer. While no longer a common occurrence, if the couple wants to save the top layer for their first anniversary, it is recommended that the cake be carefully sealed in wrap that will protect it from freezer burn. Most pastry chefs agree that the cake will not be as good as it tastes on the wedding day, but it should be safe as long as quality ingredients have been used. Instead of trying to save the cake for a year, some couples freeze it for just a month after their wedding before enjoying it or, better yet, have the top layer remade for their first anniversary.

VENDOR SPOTLIGHT, CASE 9.5

LESLIE POYOUROW

FANCY CAKES BY LESLIE

How did you get started? I have a business degree and I have always liked to bake. I worked in federal marketing for 20 years and started taking cake decorating classes for fun and got hooked. Once people began asking for my cakes all the time, I quit my job and opened my business. I have been in business for ten years and currently make over 500 specialty cakes a year. We also make cupcakes, pastries and cookies for weddings.

What trends are you seeing in cake design? Lace patterns on the outside of the cake have become popular. In terms of color, we use lots of gold and have frequent requests for a range of blues as well as teal and muted orange. Up-and-coming tastes include tea flavors and lavender flavors. Fashion affects cake design and there are also cultural influences. For instance, Asian couples prefer a cake that is not too sweet and often incorporate red into the design. Indian couples enjoy decadent flavors and the design will be intricate with gold and vibrant colors such as bright pink, orange and turquoise. Each of our cakes is unique and I sit down with my clients and we plan out the design, tier by tier.

What special services do you provide? I spend time with my clients. I am almost always the person who answers the telephone because I want people to know I am accessible. Even though I have a staff, I do the finish work on 90 per cent of the cakes. I am known for my sugar flowers, which we make by hand on the premises. While I've been very lucky to create some high-profile cakes, we create all of our cakes with the same standard. It's a policy that has worked well for me. Everyone gets our top effort!

What can wedding consultants do to make your life easier? The biggest thing would be to have the cake table set up and ready for us. I have walked into rooms where everything looks set up, but the cake table is nowhere to be found!

WEBSITE: *FANCYCAKESBYLESLIE.COM*

CONSULTANT IN ACTION, CASE 9.6

SLIP SLIDING AWAY

Cocktail hour is drawing to a close. You and your assistant are finishing up the reception décor and preparing to bring in the bride and groom before the guests enter. Your assistant notices that the wedding cake, beautifully placed in the corner of the room, is looking a little strange. After inspection, you determine that the floral arrangement installed on top of the cake by the florist is far too heavy. The front of the cake is starting to noticeably sag and it looks like the floral décor is preparing to crash to the floor. Both the pastry chef and the florist are long gone.

WHAT DO YOU DO?

CASE SUBMITTED BY JO ANN OBIE
BLESSED EVENTS AND WEDDINGS, LLC
WEBSITE: *BLESSEDEVENTS-WEDDINGS.COM*

REFERENCES

Gittins, R. (2013) 'Trends in food and beverage for weddings'. E-mail (12 March 2013).

Henderson, B. (2013) 'Missing in action'. E-mail interview conducted by Erin Anderson (23 February 2013).

Hendrix, S. (21 February 2008) 'In kosher kitchens, more than taste matters: adherence to Jewish dietary laws requires specially trained supervisors', *The Washington Post*, B1.

Kossman, A. (2013) 'Heat and cake stability'. E-mail interview conducted by Lauren Goodell (23 February 2013).

Lally, T. (2013) 'Trends in wedding cakes'. E-mail (5 March 2013).

Mariani, J. (2012) 'The worst (and best) cooking shows on television', *Esquire*, Online. Available HTTP: <http://www.esquire.com/the-side/feature/best-worst-cooking-shows#slide-1> (accessed 2 March 2013).

Obie, J.A. (2013) 'Interview regarding wedding cake disaster'. E-mail (12 November 2012).

Occasions Caterers (2013) 'Monumental market fair', Online. Available HTTP: <http://occasionscaterers.com/food/market-fair/> (accessed 11 March 2013).

PHOTO 9.13 UPSCALE CUPCAKES HAVE RISEN IN POPULARITY.

SOURCE: WWW.RODNEYBAILEY.COM

PBS (2012) 'The year in food 2012: food blogs', Online. Available HTTP: <http://www.pbs.org/food/features/best-of-2012-review-food-blogs/6/> (accessed 26 February 2013).

Poyourow, L. (2013) 'Trends in wedding cakes'. E-mail (4 March 2013).

Schrambling, R. (11 July 2012) 'Modern vows extend to the buffet', *The Washington Post*, E1, E5.

PHOTO 9.14 MINI-PIES SWEETEN THE DESSERT TABLE.

SOURCE: WWW.RODNEYBAILEY.COM

Consultant checklist and reminders for food, beverage and the wedding cake

☐ Make sure that the caterer and pastry chef are licensed and insured; permits may also be necessary when using an off-premises caterer.

☐ Bring up any dietary or menu restrictions in the first meeting with any caterer to determine if they can accommodate specialized needs.

☐ Schedule tastings with the caterer and the pastry chef.

☐ Consider a signature drink to match the wedding theme.

☐ Ask caterers to indicate the staffing ratio.

☐ Make sure that taxes, staffing, equipment, delivery, gratuity and other fees are included in the caterer's proposal estimates.

☐ Determine how long the caterer will need for set-up and tear-down.

☐ Consider both the formality of the reception as well as the restrictions of the venue when selecting a service style.

☐ Have the most expensive hors d'oeuvres passed rather than set out on a table.

☐ Consider downsizing the ceremonial cake and supplementing with a sheet cake for cost-cutting.

☐ Avoid butter cream icing during warm months due to its tendency to melt.

REVIEW

1. Name a minimum of four key pieces of information that a caterer must know before a formal proposal can be made.

2. What are at least three things that caterers can do to "wow" potential clients during the proposal phase?

3. Name three trends in catering.

4. Explain the difference between buffet, plated and French service.

5. What are the four primary considerations when selecting a wedding cake?

Terminology

- Buffet service
- Butter cream
- Cocktail hour
- Corkage fee
- Dummy layer
- Fondant
- Foodie bride
- French service
- Hors d'oeuvres
- Kosher food
- Mashgiach
- Mixologist
- Plated service
- Signature drinks
- Staffing ratio
- Sweep

PHOTO 10.1 WEDDING ATTIRE CAN REFLECT THE HERITAGE OF YOUR CLIENTS.

SOURCE: WWW.RODNEYBAILEY.COM

10

WEDDING ATTIRE AND THE BRIDAL PARTY

Soon after getting engaged, a bride-to-be begins the process of shopping for her wedding gown. This is one of the most important decisions a bride makes, as the design of the gown can set the tone for the entire wedding. Will the gown be ultra-formal with a cathedral length train or more casual with a simple colored sash? Will the gown be made of silk, organza, taffeta, lace or satin? As for color, will it be a classic choice such as white, ivory or champagne, or will it contain a modern flash of blue, red or black? These are just a few of the many considerations that go into this important decision.

Usually, the bride purchases her gown without the advice of a wedding consultant; instead, she visits bridal salons with her mother or a close friend. With that said, it is still important for consultants to be well versed in wedding attire styles and trends. Coordinating the overall look of the wedding is an important task for the planner, who will assist the bride in matching her gown to other elements, give advice regarding the selection of the menswear, offer options on the flower girl dress and perhaps even guide the mothers as they select their gowns. This chapter covers trends in bridal attire, menswear, cultural traditions, the wedding party and how to handle wardrobe malfunctions.

PHOTO 10.2 FASHION-FORWARD BRIDES LOOK TO THE RUNWAYS FOR INSPIRATION.

SOURCE: WWW.RODNEYBAILEY.COM

PHOTO 10.3 LACE HAS MADE A RETURN TO POPULARITY.

SOURCE: WWW.RODNEYBAILEY.COM

BRIDAL ATTIRE

Wedding styles come and go, so it is important for a planner to stay on top of trends through reading the latest trade magazines and attending bridal fashion shows. You do not want to recommend a dress with a ball gown silhouette to a client only to be told that it looks like her aunt's gown from the 1990s. *Fashion-forward* brides look to the runways of Paris and New York for inspiration. Fashion statements made at celebrity events such as the Academy Awards and Grammy Awards

VENDOR SPOTLIGHT, CASE 10.1

JENNIFER JOHNSTON

VERA WANG BRIDAL SALON AT SAKS JANDEL

How did you become interested in wedding gowns? While studying fashion design and merchandising, I realized that my passion was sewing and designing. After attending a couture bridal sewing seminar in Baltimore led by Susan Khalje, I became fascinated with the wedding dress. This seminar challenged me to create and complete a wedding dress in two weeks. This passion for wedding style led me to the Vera Wang Bridal Salon at Saks Jandel, where I have worked for 15 years.

Describe the Vera Wang style. The first time I saw a Vera Wang bridal gown was in the early 1990s. The model was wearing a gown with long white illusion sleeves, a high neck and full skirt. Her jet black hair was tied simply with a bow on top of her head. It was mesmerizing and made the Vera Wang style instantly recognizable. Today, Vera still uses unconventional fabrics such as horsehair trim, honeycomb tulle, tumbled tulle and eyelash organza trim. The modern swirled and draped soft fabrics offer an airy lightness with the volume of traditional ball gowns, mixed with appliquéd laces hinting of tradition.

What are the latest trends in wedding gowns? The Vera Wang bride is still a sophisticated bride. Vera's most recent collection offered her bridal gown styles in shades of red including crimson, cardinal, scarlet and dahlia, as well as the traditional ivory and white. Presenting gowns in a color garnered Vera much attention in the press and with the fashion savvy; however, it was not as popular for weddings.

What are the most popular styles for wedding gowns? The nuptials of Prince William and Kate Middleton brought a return to the traditional look of lace. Brides may not be yearning for a long lace sleeve, but the beauty and elegance of lace has struck a chord with clients. Vera's unique talent for combining lace with tulle or tissue organza offers a "veiled" effect that softens the boldness of her large lace flower patterns. A modern take on a very traditional wedding fabric.

In what ways do you assist a bride in deciding what style is appropriate for her wedding? Every bride has her own distinctive sense of style. We offer suggestions that are flattering to her figure and that take into consideration the time and location of the wedding as well as the size of the wedding. A large wedding may dictate a more elaborate gown. A church wedding with a long aisle may beg for a more traditional lace gown. A destination wedding on a beach will lend itself to a sheath of crepe back satin with more ease of movement than a ball gown.

Any humorous anecdotes where troubleshooting was necessary? After 15 years, I still believe that every young woman's dream of what her wedding day will be like is different from the next! I once worked with a bride from Saudi Arabia who purchased a beautiful lace ball gown with a long matching lace veil. Our only dilemma was how to cover her beautiful black hair. She was wearing an up do and needed to have all her hair obscured from the view of her guests. My team and I managed to create a gorgeous cap completely covered with lace flowers embroidered with pearl and crystal. Every flower petal was handmade to create each flower. I think we made hundreds of flowers to cover a fabric cap to place over her hair! It was stunning to see the veil placed over the floral cap as she walked down the aisle. I will never forget it. My alterations team wanted to kill me, and they never wanted to make another flower again!

WEBSITE: *VERAWANG.COM*

are quickly copied, becoming *knock-offs* that mainstream retailers offer as bridal attire for the general public. For example, as a result of the gown selection made by Kate Middleton, the bridal collections that followed brought long sleeves out of the shadows. Vera Wang, long considered the gold standard of bridal gown designers, often displays abrupt turns by one year having a bridal collection with bold colors and then stunning the runway press the following year with classic white and lace (Hallett 2012). Jennifer Johnston, manager of the Vera Wang Bridal Salon at Saks Jandel, discusses the latest wedding gown trends in *Vendor Spotlight*, Case 10.1.

Today's brides have a wealth of options when it comes to selecting the perfect wedding gown. There are many more fabric choices today than even 20 years ago. Materials such as polyester, nylon, rayon and silk can be woven into a range of stunning fabrics such as brocade, charmeuse, chiffon, crepe back satin, duchesse satin, dupioni, georgette, lace, organza, shantung, taffeta and velvet. Synthetic materials such as nylon and polyester are more versatile and affordable than pure silk fibers, giving designers more fabric selection than ever, translating into more choices for the bride. For a bridal shop owner who carries a variety of brands, the most difficult part of the job is predicting the styles that will sell, as illustrated in *Vendor Spotlight*, Case 10.2.

Even with a vast array of contemporary styles from which to select wedding attire, many brides look back to the fashion icons of yesterday for inspiration on their wedding gowns. Probably the most famous wedding gowns of the past century were those of Grace Kelly, Jacqueline Kennedy and Princess Diana. Grace Kelly donated her wedding gown to The Philadelphia Museum of Art shortly after her 1956 wedding to Monaco's Prince Rainer III; the carefully preserved gown is periodically brought out for enormously popular exhibits (The Philadelphia Museum of Art 2013). It is widely believed that Kate Middleton, the current Duchess of Cambridge, was inspired by Grace Kelly's gown, as evidenced by noted similarities in the bodice, sleeves, train and veil, as designed by Sarah Burton, the creative director for the late Alexander McQueen (Abraham and Rawi 2011).

VENDOR SPOTLIGHT, CASE 10.2

NGA NGUYEN

LEESBURG BRIDAL AND TUXEDO

How did you end up in the bridal industry? I have been sewing custom-made clothes for over 40 years now. As a dress-maker, there was a big interest in wedding dresses.

What is the hardest part of your career? The hardest part is inventory. I work with many designers and I have to find dresses that work in my shop and that I believe brides will pick. I have to make sure that I have enough of a selection for each bride to try multiple styles. I love when the bride really falls in love with her dress, and then I alter it and she puts it on and feels even more beautiful.

How do you select designers? You have to find out what is popular in your area and what is reasonable for your customers. Designers who appear in bridal magazines are popular because, when a woman gets engaged, buying a bridal magazine is one of the first things she does. You want to give brides different options but also have designers they recognize. When I meet with a designer's sales representative, I ask about the best sellers but I have to keep in mind what my clients like. I generally decide on 12–15 dresses from each designer.

What factors are most likely to influence a sale? You have to sell the dress to an extent, but most of the time the dress can sell itself. You need to be able to talk to the customer to answer any of her questions, but also listen to what she wants for her dress. You should also make it a unique and special experience for each bride, such as adding a beaded belt, straps or a sash.

WEBSITE: *LEESBURG-BRIDAL.COM*
INTERVIEW BY VERONICA TAYLOR

Whether a bride takes her inspiration from yesterday or today, she is not likely to consult with her wedding planner when making her dress selection. She may, however, ask for advice on the top designers or where to shop for the gown and accessories. In addition to Vera Wang, designers such as Badgley Mischka, Oscar de la Renta, Amsale, Carolina Herrera, Monique Lhuillier and Angel Sanchez are known for bridal attire. The age of the bride also influences the wedding dress style. What works for a 20-something may not appeal to a bride in her forties.

PHOTO 10.4 MANY BRIDES SELECT SEVERAL DRESSES AND CHANGE THROUGHOUT
THEIR WEDDING DAY.

SOURCE: WWW.RODNEYBAILEY.COM

In any given city, there are many options for finding the perfect wedding gown including stand-alone bridal shops, couture shops with exclusive designer labels, department stores, outlet malls, bridal chains such as David's Bridal, clothing specialists that have moved into wedding attire such as J. Crew, custom designers, consignment shops and, increasingly, online sites such as eBay, Craigslist and Tradesy. With thousands of new and used wedding gowns listed for sale, the savvy bride can get the dress of her dreams at a reasonable price. With more brides opting for attire changes during the course of the wedding day, these outlets can be used to hunt for a formal ceremony gown, stylish reception gown or a chic dress for leave-taking. Online sites such as Etsy.com are excellent resources for finding bridal accessories. Prices will vary by seller, but are usually a fraction of the retail cost.

With most brides spending $1,000 and up on the dress alone, this is probably the most expensive clothing purchase the bride will ever make. If your client seeks your advice on the dress purchase, you can offer the following three tips:

1. *Don't delay.* If a wedding gown is selected less than six months prior to the wedding date, there may be a rush charge placed on the order. This charge can be as much as 25 per cent of the cost of the gown.

2. *Alteration fees add up.* Most brides will pay $150 to $300 in alteration fees alone. Many brides do not account for this in the initial budget for attire.

3. *Size matters.* If the bride is a small size (0 to 2) or a plus size (16 or larger), there may be an extra charge of 10–20 per cent for the gown depending on the designer. Be prepared to mention this if you know that your client falls into one of these size categories.

Jennifer Johnston reinforces that time is of the essence. She states that the bride often has no sense of urgency because she may not realize what is involved when starting the planning process. However, there is a rhyme and reason to creating the perfect look and every step has to be well thought out. Brides who wait too long to start the process may be confronted with situations like the one found in *Consultant in Action*, Case 10.3

After choosing a gown, a bride must then decide on her hairstyle, hair jewelry and veil. The veil, in particular, cannot be chosen too carefully. Most favored styles are chapel length with a blusher to cover the face, and accented with lace, seed pearls or rhinestones for added sparkle. A lace veil can match a lace gown or complement a very simple, unadorned dress. Matching earrings, bracelet or necklace should also be given consideration. A wrap and gloves or a muff, either in fur, faux fur or a matching fabric, should be considered for fall or winter weddings. Before the fittings can begin, the bride must choose her shoes and necessary foundation garments, such as a Spanx tunic or body shaper, to allow for definition and a smooth line. Bridal shoes should be comfortable, first and foremost, but should also make a statement. Together, the bridal accessories complete the look.

Bridal attire and accessories vary significantly by culture. Although the white wedding gown has caught on around the globe, many cultures are still known for distinctive bridal attire. Three of these countries are India, Korea and Japan. In India, the richly woven bridal sari and ornamental maang-tikka, which is a disk set in precious stones that is worn on the forehead, are accented by dozens of gold bracelets, earrings, toe rings, necklaces and a toe gem, a testament to the fact that India is the world's largest importer of gold (Atwal *et al.* 2012). Coupled with the intricate henna designs on her palms and arms from her Mehndi ceremony (see *Culture Corner*, Case 2.6),

Consultant in Action, Case 10.3

Dress distress

Recently, you have been hired by a new client, Anne, to plan her wedding from beginning to end. She has very little free time due to her demanding job as a cardiac care nurse. For the past few weeks, she has been making the rounds at the bridal boutiques in your town but to no avail. Nothing has been quite right. With the clock ticking, Anne asks you to accompany her and her mother to look at dresses at a store not too far from where you live. You agree to meet for her appointment the following Saturday. The day arrives and Anne is excited to try on different dresses and get your advice. She falls head over heels in love with the first dress she tries on. This is *the* dress. You engage the sales associate in a conversation about the dress and discover the cost is $2,500. Knowing Anne's budget, you know this is a little out of her price range. Then the associate asks when the wedding date is and you tell her that the wedding is exactly five months from today. The associate tells you that there will be a 25 per cent "rush" fee added to the cost of the dress because the wedding is less than six months away. The dress now costs $3,125. Next, the associate says that, because your client is a size 16, there will also be a 20 per cent additional fee to the base price for the non-standard size. The dress now costs $3,625. Finally, the sales associate tells Anne that she should allow $300 for hemming and alterations. With sales tax the dress is now over $4,000, way over her budget. Anne looks at you with tears in her eyes and says, "But I love it!"

What do you do?

as well as stunning makeup, the bride is gorgeously adorned. The specifics of traditional Korean and Japanese bridal attire are detailed in *Culture Corner*, Cases 10.4 and 10.5.

Most brides do not have specific cultural traditions that influence their wedding attire; however, many wish to incorporate four elements in keeping with the sentimental phrase, "Something old, something new, something borrowed, something blue." Your clients will ask you for suggestions in each of these categories, so you can start with the ideas summarized in Table 10.1. An example of the family history attached with a vintage dress is given in *Culture Corner*, Case 10.6.

PHOTO 10.5 BRIDAL SHOES MAKE A STATEMENT.

SOURCE: WWW.RODNEYBAILEY.COM

CULTURE CORNER, CASE 10.4

TRADITIONAL WEDDING ATTIRE IN KOREA

The earliest records of Korean wedding attire date from the Chosun dynasty, which spanned from 1392 until 1910, as summarized by Hong (2003). Traditional Korean bridal attire included "Several kinds of underwear, a petticoat, a red skirt decorated with gold-leaf imprints, three kinds of jackets (*jeoghori*), and a ceremonial green robe (*wonsam*) or embroidered red robe (*whalot*). She wore a head crown with ornaments (*jokduri* or *whakwan*)" (ibid.: 54). Before the ceremony, the bride's hair was elaborately arranged in two chignons, "the symbol of an unmarried woman" (ibid.: 59). She also wore a headdress covered with jewelry. After the wedding, "the women arranged her hair in a chignon at the nape of her neck and maintained that hairdo

PHOTO 10.6 BRIDAL ATTIRE VARIES SIGNIFICANTLY BY CULTURE.

SOURCE: WWW.RODNEYBAILEY.COM

for the rest of her life" (ibid.). The bride's hair was adorned with a special pin and hair ribbon. The groom wore an official's robe known as a *samokwandae*, which was blue or dark purple with a round neckline and wide sleeves. "Tacked to the robe, both in the front and the back, was a large square embroidered with a pair of cranes. A groom wore trousers, a jacket and a coat under his wedding wardrobe" (ibid.: 58). Hong explains that, while Western-style dress has influenced many Korean weddings, "with a recent renewed awareness of traditional Korean culture, upper class grooms and brides are increasingly returning to the more traditional Chosun dynasty wedding dress" (ibid.: 64–65).

SOURCE: HONG (2003)

CULTURE CORNER, CASE 10.5

JAPANESE WEDDING KIMONO

A Japanese bride is an ethereal vision in her beautiful white silk *wedding kimono*. This stunning garment is often handed down from generation to generation, which makes sense as a new wedding kimono costs between $10,000 and $100,000 US. In addition to the kimono, the bride will wear an elaborate hood over her head to cover up *bridal horns*, which are part of a headpiece worn prior to the ceremony signifying the horns of jealousy. After the wedding ceremony, the horns are removed as the new bride is freed from the jealousy. The Japanese bride's relatives will also dress in their most formal black or dark kimono for the wedding ceremony. Encircling each waist is an *obi*, which is a very long piece of fabric usually made of silk and highly embroidered that functions as a cummerbund or large sash to keep the kimono closed. The obi is intricately wrapped around the wearer and tied elaborately in the back. An obi can cost between $500 and $10,000 US. It is not unusual for all members of a Japanese wedding party to go to professional kimono dressers in preparation for the wedding. In Japan, men and women study for years to earn a certificate to become a professional kimono dresser. As each kimono has 12 layers, it is imperative that each layer goes on as smoothly and neatly as possible. This is best accomplished with the help of a professional dresser.

MENSWEAR

What should the groom wear? Do the tuxes all have to match? Can the guys wear their own tuxes? Are khakis appropriate with a navy-blue blazer? Can the men wear their own suits? Should the men's ties match the bridesmaids' gowns? Should groomsmen rent the tux in their hometown or at the wedding destination? Should the men wear white shirts if the bride is wearing an off-white gown? These are just a few of the questions you may get when the couple begins to consider menswear.

When it comes to wedding attire, the bride almost always has a clear idea of what she wants to wear, but, when it comes to the men, your advice will be sought. Educate yourself on men's wedding attire by making an appointment to speak with the manager of your local formalwear shop. Ask how the process works from measuring to ordering to picking up and what the store's policies are. You should have a good working knowledge of the details so you can guide your clients.

Table 10.1 Sentimental "something" selections

Something old:
Items in this category usually originate from the bride's mother, grandmother or the mother of the groom. For example, the bride might wear a piece of antique jewelry that has passed down through her family or the groom's family. Alternatively, the bride might wear a vintage dress that belonged to her mother or grandmother, or she might have lace from a vintage dress incorporated into her own dress, veil or handkerchief.

Something new:
This decision is the easiest, as the bride usually makes a number of attire purchases. However, many wish to select one of these that "counts" as filling the category. If the dress is new, this is typically the chosen representation. Otherwise, her veil, shoes, purse, lingerie or a decorative hairpin can fit the bill for something new to be worn.

Something borrowed:
A bride will often turn to a very dear friend such as the maid of honor or a close family member to borrow something for her wedding day. A bride might borrow the dress worn by a friend or use the purse that a cousin carried on her wedding day. Many brides do not own expensive jewelry, so often a close aunt or family friend will insist that the bride wear her best necklace or bracelet.

Something blue:
For brides who plan to wear a garter, it is very common to have a piece of blue silk sewn in the garter, as this is a simple way to incorporate blue. If not wearing a garter, a linen handkerchief with blue embroidery is often chosen. While a handkerchief may seem like an old-fashioned idea, it is actually quite practical. Many brides cry during their weddings, and it is nice to have something more attractive than a paper tissue close by. An embroidered handkerchief can also be a lovely keepsake. If blue is the color scheme, a blue ribbon can be used for a hand-tied bouquet. Alternatively, the bride can wear a sapphire or blue topaz bracelet or hairpin on her wedding day.

Also, when you attend a bridal show, pay attention to the men's fashions so you can advise your grooms on whether a vest is currently in or out and whether or not a cummerbund is passé.

Similar to bridal attire, another good place for discovering what is going on with men's formalwear are the Academy Awards or Grammy Awards telecasts. Watching what the men wear on the red carpet can give you an excellent idea of what is fashionable. Rest assured, if the stars are wearing it today, your clients will be requesting it tomorrow. In some cases, it is the groom's attire that is easily recognizable based on specific cultural traditions, as evidenced in *Culture Corner*, Case 10.7.

CULTURE CORNER, CASE 10.6

EMMA'S GOWN

In the summer of 1905 in a small town in central California, Emma Sophronia Clapp was planning her upcoming wedding to Temple Beatty "Bate" Cochran. An experienced seamstress, she had decided to stitch her own gown for the upcoming January 3, 1906 wedding. The future Mrs. Cochran designed her wedding gown in two pieces with a lacy bodice and separate full-length skirt personifying the femininity of the style at the time. Very typical of gowns in 1905, Emma chose ivory dotted net, taffeta that she hand pin tucked, and lace panel inserts. The completed bodice showed off her fine handwork of embellished lace and ribbon ties, including a detachable bertha round collar made of net and trimmed in lace. The skirt had an attached train of taffeta, lace panels, flat ribbon with a silky under layer and at the bottom of the net-layered puffed sleeves were two inches of lace, providing a soft look.

Following their wedding, Emma carefully packed acid-free tissue paper around her wedding gown, placed it in an acid-free box and tucked it away in a trunk. The lasting impression of Emma's skillfully crafted gown with its range of textures and lace embellishment was something to remember. Among Emma and Bate's six children, two daughters wore their mother's wedding gown. The other daughters who married chose not to wear the gown due to the Great Depression, as it was "not a time to don fancy dresses or plan elaborate ceremonies when the country was suffering." For the two who did wear the gown, Lorraine married Max on August 4, 1941 and Emma Jane married Jack on January 5, 1945.

The tradition of wearing the wedding dress continued into the next generation as the Cochrans' second-born, Helen, watched her daughter Harriet Ann, who added an ivory ribbon sash, walk down the aisle to marry Jim on July 28, 1956. Then, 27 years after Lorraine wore her mother's dress, her daughter, Nancy, followed the tradition on August 31, 1968. She added a full-length blusher veil of tulle tinted with coffee to match the now half-a-century-old dress. When two more of Emma's granddaughters wanted to wear her wedding gown, their mother Harriet was not surprised. Brenda married Dave on January 29, 1972 and Lucinda married Scott on January 8, 1977. Both also wore Nancy's veil and Harriet Ann's sash.

The fourth-generation bride to wear Emma's wedding dress was great-granddaughter Jeni, who married Gary on July 25, 1987 with her grandfather Bud in attendance.

Jeni was the only bride to wear her great-grandmother's bertha detachable collar and the only relative to change for her reception into another dress "to make sure nothing happened to THE gown." The clever use of a two-piece wedding dress has made it a sustainable garment since each bride could adjust the waist or hem the full skirt.

The Cochran women value tradition and it has certainly been exemplified by their planning, from childhood, to wear the now 108-year-old handmade ivory wedding gown stitched in a small central California town by 23-year-old Emma Sophronia (Clapp) Cochran in 1905. Lying in her granddaughter's trunk, it is ready for the next bride.

CASE SUBMITTED BY HARRIET ANN HARRIS, NANCY HOYT,
BRENDA WIGGINS, LUCINDA BAUCHER AND JENI MATTESON

PHOTO 10.7 SUITS ARE BECOMING THE NORM FOR MEN'S WEDDING ATTIRE.

SOURCE: WWW.RODNEYBAILEY.COM

PHOTO 10.8 GROOMS CAN HAVE FUN WITH THEIR FOOTWEAR.

SOURCE: WWW.RODNEYBAILEY.COM

THE WEDDING PARTY

The basic rule of thumb is that groomsmen and bridesmaids should look like they belong together. If bridesmaids are in summery Lilly Pulitzer shifts, the groomsmen should be in casual summer attire like khakis and navy-blue blazers. If the groomsmen are in formal black tuxedos, the bridesmaids should be in formal attire as well. If the groomsmen are wearing ties, then by all means they should complement the bridesmaids' dresses. They need not match exactly, but they should

CULTURE CORNER, CASE 10.7

THE GROOM'S ATTIRE IN SCOTLAND

In Scotland, it is the groom's attire that is particularly noteworthy, including the tartan *kilt*, the *sporran* and the *dirk*. The tartan kilt is an easily recognized Celtic garment, with colors and plaid patterns that represent the wearer's clan. A groom in Highland attire also wears a fur pouch known as a sporran and a small dirk, which is a traditional Scottish knife. The bride may wear a clan tartan shawl with her contemporary dress. Traditional Scottish dress and the romantic mood that accompanies this culture's traditions are so appealing that many couples who are not of Scottish descent have Celtic-themed weddings in order to momentarily step into the past.

SOURCE: SPANGENBERG (2001); WINGE AND EICHER (2003)

work nicely together. Typically, the groom will look slightly different than his groomsmen; for example, the groom might wear a black vest while the groomsmen have burgundy to match the bridesmaids' dresses.

In terms of bridesmaids' dresses, knee-length and below-knee styles are currently the most popular. Jennifer Johnston states that, when designed with such fabrics as crepe back satin and chiffon, these shorter styles can be worn for both late-afternoon and evening weddings. Bridesmaids' dresses generally match but need not be identical. A current trend involves selecting bridesmaids' dresses that are made of the same fabric and color, but that come in a variety of styles to suit different body types.

The bride usually selects the attire for her bridesmaids, sometimes with their help and sometimes without any input at all. A planner is rarely consulted about this decision. However, you will probably be asked where to purchase accessories for the bridesmaids such as shoes, wraps, jewelry, hair accessories, purses, gloves and foundation garments. Be prepared with a list of stores and online retailers that you know and trust in all price ranges.

The groomsmen's tuxedos or suits are usually acquired from the same location as the groom's. It is typical for the groom's tuxedo to be rented without charge if there are enough groomsmen (usually at least four) who are renting formalwear from the same store. Determine if your local tuxedo shop rents tuxedoes for infants and toddlers, as parents of the youngest family members

PHOTO 10.9 WEDDING PARTY ATTIRE SHOULD COORDINATE.

SOURCE: WWW.RODNEYBAILEY.COM

may want to dress their children to the nines for a formal wedding. The ring bearer in particular needs to be outfitted in a tuxedo. Similarly, the bride may wish to have a small replica of her gown made for the flower girl. Knowing a designer who specializes in this area will come in handy.

Pets are being incorporated more frequently into wedding celebrations. Just like the other members of the wedding party, they need special attire for the wedding day. You should arm yourself with information on where to order special dog tuxes and other formalwear because, sooner or later, you will be asked for a recommendation. Do not get caught off-guard like the planner in *Consultant in Action*, Case 10.8.

If your local pet shop does not stock such items, there are terrific online resources such as *trixieandpeanut.com* that cater to chic dogs and cats alike. No detail is too small when considering wedding attire. The best wedding consultants can assist with finding appropriate wedding attire for the entire wedding party, pets included!

PHOTO 10.10 BRIDESMAIDS' DRESSES DO NOT HAVE TO BE AN EXACT MATCH.

SOURCE: WWW.RODNEYBAILEY.COM

WARDROBE MALFUNCTIONS

Probably even more important than knowing where to buy or rent wedding attire is the wedding consultant's ability to fix a wardrobe malfunction on the day of the wedding. Count on something becoming undone, unfastened, unsightly or unhinged at some point during the wedding day. It will be up to you to work your magic with the tools in your well-stocked emergency kit, the contents of which are discussed in Chapter 19. A needle and thread, a large safety pin and baby wipes have come to the rescue at many weddings. When it comes to clothing, be prepared for a multitude of disasters from straps breaking to heels snapping off. With so many people involved in the wedding party, a wardrobe malfunction is guaranteed to happen. Some malfunctions are easily remedied, while others are extreme, as seen in *Consultant in Action*, Case 10.9.

In addition to fixing clothing problems, the most important clothing-related skills for a wedding planner to master are: 1) how to bustle a bride's train; and 2) how to knot a tie or bow tie. Bustling the bride's train is an important precaution to keep the gown from getting soiled and to keep the bride from tripping during the reception. Reviewing the bustling procedure with the bridal shop prior to the wedding day is an excellent idea because each gown is bustled slightly differently. Many bustles, if not designed correctly, will come undone during the reception. Be prepared to

CONSULTANT IN ACTION, CASE 10.8

THE CONNOR CONUNDRUM

You have been hired to plan a very expensive and elaborate wedding. In fact, the wedding has morphed into three days of celebration that you are tasked with planning. There is the rehearsal followed by a large party in the backyard of the groom's house. Saturday, of course, is the formal wedding and Sunday there will be a brunch at the bride's home. The week of the wedding, you are at the bride's home discussing the layout for the Sunday brunch with the bride and her mother. The family dog, Connor, an adorable soft-coated wheaten terrier, comes over to say hello and to get in on the action. All of a sudden, the mother-of-the bride shrieks, and says, "Did you order a tux for Connor? And what is he going to wear to the rehearsal dinner party? He needs a casual outfit for that as well. Have you thought of that?"

WHAT DO YOU DO?

CONSULTANT IN ACTION, CASE 10.9

WINE WHINE

The traditional ceremony went off without a hitch and, now at the reception site, the bride and groom are outside taking photos while the guests enjoy cocktail hour. The couple did not want a formal entrance into the reception, but when they walk through the door there is a spontaneous round of applause. One of the guests swiftly turns around to see what the commotion is all about and crashes straight into the bride, which would have not been a huge deal, except for the fact that the guest is holding a glass of red wine that explodes down the front of the bride's dress. The guest begins to cry hysterically while the bride stands, frozen in shock.

WHAT DO YOU DO?

remedy this situation with items from your emergency kit such as a needle and thread or oversized safety pins.

Also, knowing how to knot a man's tie is a skill every wedding consultant must have. On the day of the wedding, the groom wearing a tuxedo may be too nervous to knot his own bow tie and it could be the first time wearing a bow tie for many of the groomsmen. Make sure you can knot the tie quickly and fashionably. Similarly, the skill of being able to tie eight bridesmaids' sashes into perfect bows before they walk down the aisle will carry you far in your career as a wedding consultant.

REFERENCES

Abraham, T. and Rawi, M. (2011) 'Kate's wedding gown tribute to another princess bride: how Alexander McQueen creation took style lead from Grace Kelly', *Daily Mail*, Online. Available HTTP: <http://www.dailymail.co.uk/femail/article-1381989/Royal-Wedding-Kate-Middletons-wedding-dress-tribute-Grace-Kelly.html> (accessed 21 March 2013).

Atwal, G., Khan, S. and Bryson, D. (2012) 'The communication dilemma', in G. Atwal and S. Jain (eds) *The Luxury Market in India: maharajas to masses*, Basingstoke, UK: Palgrave MacMillan.

Hallett, S. (2012) 'Vera Wang Fall 2013 bridal collection features classic ivory, lace gowns', Online. Available HTTP: <http://www.huffingtonpost.com/2012/10/14/vera-wang-fall-2013_n_1962567.html> (accessed 25 March 2013).

Harris, H.A, Hoyt, N., Wiggins, B., Baucher, L. and Matteson, J. (2013) 'Emma's gown'. E-mail (19 February 2013).

Hong, N.Y. (2003) 'Korean wedding dress from the Chosun Dynasty (1392–1910) to the present', in H.B. Foster and D.C. Johnson (eds) *Wedding Dress across Cultures*, New York: Berg.

Johnston, J. (2013) 'Vera Wang wedding gowns'. Personal interview (20 March 2013).

Nguyen, N. (2013) 'Bridal attire'. E-mail interview conducted by Veronica Taylor (23 February 2013).

Spangenberg, L.M. (2001) *Timeless Traditions: a couple's guide to wedding customs around the world*, New York: Universe Publishing.

The Philadelphia Museum of Art (2013) 'Grace Kelly's wedding dress and accessories', Online. Available HTTP: <http://www.philamuseum.org/collections/permanent/56621.html> (accessed 21 March 2013).

Winge, T.M. and Eicher, J.B. (2003) 'The American groom wore a Celtic kilt: theme weddings as carnivalesque events', in H.B. Foster and D.C. Johnson (eds) *Wedding Dress across Cultures*, New York: Berg.

CONSULTANT CHECKLIST AND REMINDERS FOR WEDDING ATTIRE AND THE BRIDAL PARTY

☐ The wedding gown sets the tone for the wedding.

☐ Become familiar with wedding gown shops in your area.

☐ Make sure you are up-to-speed on current fashion trends.

☐ Educate yourself on menswear styles.

☐ The attire for groomsmen should complement that of the bridesmaids.

☐ Make sure your client knows about rush charges, alteration fees and additional charges for gowns that are smaller or larger than average.

☐ Give the bride plenty of options regarding where to purchase accessories.

☐ Do not be surprised if you are asked to order formalwear for a dog or cat.

☐ Be prepared for wardrobe malfunctions.

☐ Know how to bustle a train and knot a bow tie.

Review

1. Name three wedding gown designers.

2. Name five different types of fabric used for wedding gowns.

3. Name two style icons from the past half-century.

4. Name five places to buy a wedding gown.

TERMINOLOGY

- Alteration fees
- Bustle
- Cummerbund
- Dirk
- Fashion forward
- Fashion icons
- Kilt
- Kimono
- Knock-offs
- Maang-tikka
- Samokwandae
- Sari
- Silhouette
- Sporran
- Strapless gown
- Wardrobe malfunctions
- Whalot
- Wonsam

11

THE CEREMONY

THE MEANING OF MARRIAGE ULTIMATELY COMES BACK TO THE MOMENT WHEN TWO INDIVIDUALS PUBLICLY PLEDGE THEIR COMMITMENT TO ONE ANOTHER. THEREFORE, PLANNING THE CEREMONY SHOULD BE OF UTMOST IMPORTANCE, AS THE WORDS AND SYMBOLS THEREIN REPRESENT WHAT IS INTERNATIONALLY APPRECIATED AS A SACRED UNION. THE PURPOSE OF THIS CHAPTER IS TO OFFER AN OVERVIEW OF THE CEREMONY AND HOW ITS INHERENT PARTS ARE UNIQUELY REPRESENTED IN WEDDINGS AROUND THE WORLD. FURTHER, EXAMPLES OF HOW DIFFERENT TRADITIONS CAN BE BLENDED FOR INTERCULTURAL AND INTERFAITH CEREMONIES WILL BE OFFERED. THE SPECIFIC AREAS TO BE DETAILED INCLUDE: 1) THE CELEBRANT; 2) READINGS AND VOWS; 3) THE INCORPORATION OF ARTIFACTS; 4) THE ORDER OF CEREMONY; AND 5) GUIDELINES AND POLICIES.

THE CELEBRANT

The celebrant or officiant of a wedding is seen as the guiding force behind the ceremony. The necessary training needed to wed two individuals differs from culture to culture and religion to religion. You must always respect and defer to the celebrant's wishes. In places of worship, celebrants are known as being very territorial, and rightly so. Some ceremony venues do not even permit a wedding consultant to be present, as they handle all ceremony planning internally. It is not your place to tell a celebrant how the wedding ceremony should run. Instead, listen very carefully and become familiar with the rules and policies of each ceremony site. Over time, you will gain the trust and respect of these valuable leaders. While celebrants have characteristically earned their venerable positions through years of service to others, remember that they are human, too, and can make errors as evidenced in *Culture Corner*, Case 11.1.

One way you can gain the admiration of celebrants of different cultures is to learn and remember their titles. Table 11.1 offers an alphabetical listing of various religions, the common place of worship, the associated leader and the sacred text. As noted in Chapter 2, while much discussion has been given to the decreasing number of individuals worldwide who directly identify with a specific religious group (e.g., Boorstein 2012; Diener *et al.* 2011), the fact remains that religion maintains a dominant force in many people's lives.

The three dominant world religions are Christianity, Islam and Hinduism, and significant variation can be found within each of these; for example, the Center for the Study of Global Christianity collects data on over 9,000 denominations of Christians (World Christian Database 2013). To lump all these various groups together and suggest they all follow the same guidelines for weddings would be inappropriate. Give yourself time. After a few years of working with a variety of clients, you will become familiar with the primary places of worship and the associated leaders in your area. Beyond the three dominant world religions, other religions of significance, in alphabetical order, include Baha'i Faith, Buddhism, Chinese Folk Religions, Confucianism, Judaism, Sikhism and Taoism.

While not always the case, many religious leaders are open to learning about other religions and will even join in a *co-celebration*, also sometimes referred to as a *concelebration*, which means that the religious service has two leaders, as illustrated in *Culture Corner*, Case 11.2. For some cross-cultural weddings, having co-celebrants may not be desirable or feasible, but it may still be the case that a couple with different religious backgrounds wishes to have both faiths represented. Couples facing this situation might consider having two separate ceremonies or marrying outside of a place of worship. The fact that more and more couples are electing to marry in non-traditional settings has resulted in an increased demand for celebrants who can address a diversity of spiritual needs. Full-time wedding officiant Reverend Bill Cochran of *Say I Do Your Way* addresses trends in wedding ceremonies in *Vendor Spotlight*, Case 11.3.

CULTURE CORNER, CASE 11.1

DO YOU TAKE THIS WOMAN TO BE YOUR HUSBAND?

Vermont is known for its progressive social values, being the first state to allow same-sex civil unions (in 2000), and the first state to permit by legislation same-sex marriages (in 2009). Vermont is also a well-known destination for weddings for both heterosexual and homosexual couples because of its abundance of picturesque barns, covered bridges and natural areas. As a heterosexual couple, we wanted a ceremony that included spirituality, but was not strongly tied to any denomination. We identified a marriage officiant who would conduct such a ceremony and met with her on several occasions prior to the ceremony for pre-marital counseling and planning. She had years of experience conducting wedding ceremonies for both opposite and same-sex couples.

During the ceremony, the officiant, who was just getting back from a long European trip, asked the groom if he would "Take this woman to be your husband?" The tired officiant didn't notice her mistake. The groom wanted his loving bride to be his wife, but he was surprised by the wording of the ceremony and uncertain of how to handle the situation. The bride and others in the wedding party also quickly noticed the wording error. This was the chance for the groom's best man to save the day . . . but he didn't. Most guests did not seem to hear or notice the issue. The ceremony dialog was at a conversational level and the groom likely could have accepted his bride as a husband without the audience noticing.

It was a small, understandable error in wording but one that the groom, and likely the couple's parents, felt was important. He wanted a wife, not a husband. So the groom quietly corrected the officiant, who became flustered by her mistake. Mistakes, small or large, often are unnoticed or forgotten later when people focus on the importance of a major event and the positive aspects of their experience. However, when the officiant repeated that part of the ceremony, she reiterated the wording mistake too! Both the groom and the bride smiled and laughed, but did not become concerned. The groom corrected the wording again more empathically, and with a bit of humor to lessen the impacts of an error that was now noticed by the audience. On the third try, the officiant asked the groom if he would accept his bride as his wife, and he happily agreed! This ceremony crisis, as many do, became a nostalgic story that made a very special day even more memorable to the new couple.

CASE SUBMITTED BY JEFFREY AND LISA HALLO

TABLE II.I RELIGIONS AROUND THE WORLD

Religion	Place of Worship	Title of Leader	Sacred Text
Baha'i Faith	House of Worship	Lay Leader	Most Holy Book
Buddhism	Temple	Priest	The Tripitaka
Christianity	Church, Cathedral, Temple or Mission	Pastor, Priest, Minister, Reverend	The Bible
Confucianism	Temple, Shrine, Seowan	N/A	Lun Yu
Hinduism	Temple	Priest	The Vedas
Islam	Mosque	Imam	Quran and Hadith
Jainism	Temple	Priest, Pandit	Siddhanta, Pakrit
Judaism	Synagogue	Rabbi	Torah, Talmud, Likrat Shabbat
Shamanism and Tribal Religions	In Nature	Shaman	Oral Tradition
Sikhism	Gurdwara	Granthi	Guru Granth Sahib
Taoism	Temple	N/A	Tao-te-Ching

SOURCE: ADAPTED FROM ROBINSON (2011)

READINGS AND VOWS

Most weddings include readings and a formal exchange of vows. Readings are generally selected by the couple or the celebrant and, for religious ceremonies, are typically taken from the sacred text of the faith. These sacred texts are summarized in Table 11.1. Many of these texts have readings that are commonly chosen for weddings. For example, in the Christian faith, the Old Testament reading Genesis 2:18–24, which speaks of the creation of woman from Adam's rib so that he would not be alone, is a classic wedding reading. Also frequently selected is the New Testament reading 1 Corinthians 12:31–13:8a, which details the importance of love. Other common Bible readings are John 15:1–17 and Matthew 22:35–40, both of which speak of love.

Many couples select readings that are not found in religious texts, but are spiritual and meaningful to them nonetheless. Prose and poetry about love or nature written by famous authors such as Maya Angelou, Charlotte Brontë, Emily Brontë, Elizabeth Barrett Browning, E.E. Cummings, Robert Frost, Langston Hughes, William Shakespeare, Walt Whitman and William Butler Yeats provide endless options for wedding readings.

PHOTO 11.2 AS A WEDDING CONSULTANT, YOU MUST DEFER TO THE CELEBRANT.

SOURCE: WWW.RODNEYBAILEY.COM

Readings offer couples the opportunity to include more individuals in the wedding party. While the couple may want to limit the number of attendants, they can readily involve two to four more friends or family members by having them read during the ceremony. Advise your clients to select readers carefully, as many people are not comfortable speaking publicly. Readings should be selected and distributed to the appropriate individuals at least one month in advance of the wedding so there will be plenty of time for review. Further, each reader should practice out loud at least once, preferably twice, during the wedding rehearsal to become familiar with the acoustics of the venue and so they will be comfortable with being "on stage."

Readings are also an excellent way to blend diverse cultures. For example, at one wedding where the bride's family was from Japan and the groom's family was American, the same readings were delivered first in Japanese and then in English. This approach allowed for a common experience for all the guests; a courtesy that was particularly appreciated by close to 30 non-English-speaking guests who flew in from Japan to attend the wedding. The dual reading format also broadened this couple's ability to involve many friends from both countries.

The exchange of wedding vows is the most important part of the ceremony, as this is the point when two individuals publicly declare their commitment to one another. Standard wedding vows are led by the celebrant, who asks the bride and the groom independently if each wishes to take the other as a spouse and will vow to love, cherish, honor, comfort and be true in times of good and bad, sickness and health, and forsaking all others for as long as each shall live. The terminology differs slightly based on religious denomination, and the traditional term "obey" has been removed from most versions. For non-denominational vows and civil ceremonies, similar phrasing is used, but the vows are read by the couple rather than recited by the celebrant.

Photo II.3 The celebrant guides the ceremony.

Source: www.RodneyBailey.com

CULTURE CORNER, CASE 11.2

THE WEDDING OF MARIA AND SAMIR: CHRISTIAN AND HINDU CONCELEBRATION

Wedding ceremonies often symbolize the commitment of two individuals to each other in the eyes of both their Creator and those closest to them, and in this integrated ceremony elements of both faiths, Christianity and Hinduism, signify various aspects of the couple's future relationship in a very tangible form.

Maria and Samir decided to live their lives together as husband and wife; however, because both sets of parents committed to assist with the cost of the wedding, the stakeholders' requirements often took precedence over what the couple wanted. The parents are active participants in their individual religions and each wanted their religious beliefs and traditions incorporated into the ceremony. The problem was that neither the bride nor groom is an active participant in the religions embraced by their respective families; however, they agreed to incorporate aspects of each faith in the ceremony. Another concern shared by the couple was the comfort of their guests. The June wedding was held mid-day, outside, in the full sun and a traditional Hindu ceremony can last for hours! One step taken to mitigate the impact of the warm weather was availability of plenty of iced water and wet, cold cloths for the guests.

The groom embraced the Indian Hindu practice of *Baraat*, arriving at the venue surrounded by family and friends atop an antique fire-engine rather than on horseback . . . it resembled a parade! The bride and groom wore traditional Western wedding attire, including a smart tan suit with white shirt and periwinkle necktie for the groom, while the bride wore a strapless white gown with a birdcage veil adorning her hair.

A Hindu Priest and I, representing the United Methodist Church, concelebrated the ceremony. We had a very tight timeline and, for the most part, adhered to it. I provided the narrative describing the Hindu practices as the Priest celebrated ten distinct rituals. From both religious perspectives, the Priest and I emphasized unity, honor, love, acceptance and respect.

During the Christian component of the ceremony, Maria and Samir promised to honor, respect and cherish each other. The Hindu ritual that speaks to acceptance and respect is the exchange of garland; and so, with the exchange of floral garlands, the couple committed to accept and respect each other's individuality. The Hindu Priest then prayed seven blessings as the couple circled the fire with seven steps ratifying their bond. And the ceremony concluded as it was meant to be, Samir and Maria were pronounced husband and wife and they sealed their bond with a kiss!

Couples who bring different experiences, beliefs, cultures and ethnicities to their relationship should be encouraged to bridge their worlds as together they create and celebrate their marriage.

CASE SUBMITTED BY LEORA MICHELLE MOTLEY, WEDDING CELEBRANT
WITH THIS RING I THEE WEDD!
WEBSITE: *WITHTHISRINGITHEEWEDD.COM*

VENDOR SPOTLIGHT, CASE 11.3

REVEREND BILL COCHRAN

SAY I DO YOUR WAY

How did you become interested in becoming a full-time wedding officiant? I pastored for 35 years and, when I was ready for a career shift, I looked around to see where I could still use my pastoral skills and passions outside the parish setting. Becoming a full-time wedding officiant was the best decision I've ever made as it fits my passions and skills perfectly. I love storytelling and every couple has their unique story. As the business grew, I found myself turning down too many brides who were looking for the unique ceremonies I provide. My wife Joyce obtained her ordination, followed by our daughter Tracy, and now both are having as much fun as I am. We had no idea it would become a family business – it just grew into that. As a family, we officiate close to 200 weddings a year.

What sets you and your business apart from other wedding officiants? We ask the couple to separately answer questions about their relationship. That gives us the perspective of each, which is usually quite different. Then we write up that information into the story of their relationship, which we feature in our remarks. We also provide the couple with many ideas on ceremony content such as readings and vows.

What changes have you observed in terms of wedding ceremonies over the past 20 years? Couples are looking for themed weddings, including the ceremony. They are also feeling much more comfortable in having their ceremony outside the church setting. Additionally, about 40 per cent of our clients write their own vows. I provide a worksheet (see Table 11.2) that leads them through the process of writing their vows.

What are some of the unique cultural traditions that you have helped couples to incorporate into their wedding ceremonies? The Philippine traditions bring a very interesting and unique Christian perspective to weddings, in particular their Senior and Junior Sponsors who participate in placing of the veil and cord as well as the presentation of the coins. I have done many ceremonies that mix traditions, and probably the most unique ceremony I officiated was a Jewish/Muslim ceremony. I love working in all of the traditions but another great favorite of mine is the Persian Sofreh Aghd which is a table spread with all kinds of symbolic things, such as food and candles.

You are also a marriage coach. What are three key pieces of advice that all engaged couples should take to heart that will help them have a long marriage? Communication is much more than saying something. It's also about letting your spouse know you genuinely heard what they were saying and feeling as well. If a couple can get their communication skills fine-tuned, they can get through anything. Being committed to the marriage, no matter what, helps a couple get through all kinds of tough situations. It's easy to say "I Do" but much tougher to "Do" it! The romance dims over time but that doesn't mean a couple should give up on romance. They need to work on keeping the dating going throughout their life. It's amazing how easy dating is when first meeting but after marriage it is so easy to neglect. Every woman wants to know that she was, is and always will be the one he chose above all others. Keep reminding her by continuing the dating!

Have you ever conducted a wedding where the couple had more than one officiant (concelebration)? If so, please explain how the duties were shared. A couple of years ago my wife and I co-officiated a double wedding in which the brides were twin sisters. Joyce represented one sister and her groom and I represented the other couple. We did a kind of tag-team deal in which we decided who would say what and when we got to the telling of the story of the couples, we went back and forth. It was a very unique and memorable ceremony! I also work with officiants who represent another religion. The most common would be working together with a Rabbi, but I have also worked with a Muslim Imam, a Hindu Priest, a Buddhist priest and others.

What can consultants do to make your job easier? Just having a wedding consultant to work with makes my job so much easier! When working with a wedding consultant, they almost always reach out to me first, as they are the more organized ones! I like to discuss with them the role they plan to play in the rehearsal and ceremony, for example, will they line everyone up and get them to the front or do they expect me to do that? I love those consultants who make it feel like a team approach. We need to trust each other.

WEBSITE: *SAYIDOYOURWAY.COM*

PHOTO II.4 READINGS ARE INTERSPERSED THROUGHOUT THE CEREMONY.

SOURCE: WWW.RODNEYBAILEY.COM

As weddings become more individualized, couples are increasingly opting to write their own vows. If your clients elect this route, encourage them to start the process early so it can be a fun and creative endeavor rather than fraught with stress. The vows should not go on forever, so encourage your clients to limit them to a maximum of six lines. Table 11.2 includes steps for writing vows that you can share with your clients.

THE INCORPORATION OF ARTIFACTS

The exchange of rings is one of many symbolic acts that occur during weddings where specific artifacts are needed. The movement to a double ring ceremony was discussed in Chapter 3. The exchange of rings is just one of many artifact-based ceremony rituals. Cultures and faiths around the globe have beautiful and unique ceremonial artifacts that are the subjects of research and analysis. For instance, Kochuyt (2012) found that the traditional Moroccan wedding caftan is not just a garment, as it also serves as a symbol that unifies generations that are increasingly challenged by acculturation and individualization.

Five groups that use particularly unique representations during the ceremony are those celebrating Jewish, Hindu, Greek Orthodox, Korean and Mexican weddings. Well-known Jewish wedding

PHOTO 11.5 READINGS AND ARTIFACTS ARE EXCELLENT WAYS TO BLEND DIVERSE CULTURES.

SOURCE: WWW.RODNEYBAILEY.COM

artifacts, such as the *chuppah* (wedding canopy), *ketubah* (wedding contract), *breaking the glass* and others are detailed in *Culture Corner*, Case 11.4.

Beyond the Mehndi ceremony and elaborate wedding attire, discussed in Chapter 2 and Chapter 10 respectively, the Hindu *mandap* (i.e., wedding canopy), floral garlands and the pouring of rice are three additional artifacts that are incorporated into most Indian weddings. A Hindu wedding can last for several days and often includes ceremonial rides on a horse or elephant.

During Greek Orthodox ceremonies, the couple has special sponsors, known as the *koumbaro* and the *koumbara* who assist with three primary artifacts of religious significance. First, the sponsors assist in the exchange of rings, which takes place three times as a symbol of strength. Further, the sponsors are involved with the interchange of wedding crowns known as *stephana*, which are held together with a white ribbon to symbolize the unity of the couple. Finally, the sponsors accompany the couple as they walk around a table or altar three times, representing their journey.

In addition to Korean wedding attire, discussed in Chapter 10, two particularly important ceremonial traditions with associated artifacts are the sharing of drink and the presentation of wild geese.

TABLE II.2 STEPS FOR WRITING VOWS

1. *Talk to your celebrant.* Before you get started, make sure that there are no restrictions as to what the vows can include. Some places of worship will not allow couples to write their own vows, so you do not want to start the process until you have approval. Your officiant can also give you some samples so you can see the various approaches that other couples have taken.

2. *Begin separately.* You should each set some time aside to write down ideas. Begin with the phrase: "I love (insert name) because . . ." or "I want to marry (insert name) because . . ." Do not over-analyze or edit at this point. Just create a list of words and phrases. You can also gather ideas based on photos as well as favorite songs, books and movies.

3. *Have a "vow-writing date."* Pick a time where you can get together in a setting that is comfortable, relaxing and private. Perhaps bring a picnic to a local park or plan a romantic meal at your favorite restaurant. If you are working from home, turn off the television and your cellphones. Each of you should take turns reading your initial ideas. This should be a fun and spontaneous time, so encourage each other. Then, with pen and paper in hand, discuss the important events and turning points in your relationship. Areas you might talk about include:

   a) when and how you met;
   b) when and how you knew you were in love;
   c) what hardships you have endured together;
   d) the qualities you most admire in each other;
   e) the characteristics that you bring out in each other;
   f) the goals you would like to reach together during the next one, five and ten years of marriage.

4. *Do not force the same wording.* Many couples want to recite the same exact vows, but this is not essential. There may be a distinctive or important characteristic that you love about your spouse-to-be that you really want to include in the vows (e.g., eye color, career type), but this same characteristic does not apply to you. Allow the uniqueness of each individual to be expressed in the vows if you so choose.

5. *Create a draft.* Work together to create a draft. Tag team with the writing so this is a truly shared effort. Aspects of your vows can be funny, but should never be cryptic or embarrassing. Vows should reflect the magnitude of the commitment you are about to make. Think about how you want to address your partner (full name versus nickname), the promises you wish to make, and get to the core of what marrying this person means to you. Be concise, and eliminate any extra words or redundancies so that the vows do not go on and on. As a general rule, six sentences or less should be sufficient.

TABLE 11.2 CONTINUED

6.   *Practice out loud.* Set the project aside for a few days and then pick it back up.
     At this point, begin to practice out loud so you can make sure there are no tongue
     twisters, awkward phrases or overly long sentences that will make you flustered. This
     is a perfect time for fine tuning. If you still love what you wrote and you are
     comfortable reading the vows out loud, you are ready to go. Share the final draft with
     your celebrant for approval.

7.   *Finalize and beautify.* Your vows are a keepsake, so prepare at least two copies.
     The copy used for the ceremony should be beautiful but also functional. Use a large
     font size (at least 16-point) for readability. Consider laminating this copy so that the
     guests hear your voices rather than the rustle of paper. You should be able to fit this
     copy of the vows on a half sheet of paper, so that they are not overwhelming in size
     and are easy to hold. Give a copy to the officiant in advance, so that you do not have to
     worry about forgetting them on the wedding day. The officiant can then hand them to
     you at the appropriate time in the ceremony. Even if you decide to memorize your
     vows, give a copy to the officiant to hold, just in case. For the second copy, you may
     want to enlist a calligrapher or have your stationery specialist use a beautiful font on
     elegant paper that can be framed and kept as a constant reminder of your pledge to
     one another.

SOURCE: ADAPTED FROM COCHRAN AND COCHRAN (2013); WEBSITE: SAYIDOYOURWAY.COM

The sharing of rice wine and exchanges of *kowtow*, which include bowing, kneeling and touching foreheads to the ground, suggest commitment, harmony and respect. The presentation of either live or wooden wild geese symbolizes fertility and fidelity, as wild geese have many goslings and mate for life.

Two important Mexican traditions include the *arras* and the *lazo*. A set of wedding arras is comprised of 13 gold or silver coins presented to the couple in a small chest that represent Jesus Christ and his 12 apostles and symbolize wealth and strength. The lazo (lasso) is a cord, rope or oversized string of rosary beads placed around the shoulders of the couple and symbolizing the love that binds the couple together. The Filipino veil and cord ceremony invokes a similar sentiment, as summarized in *Culture Corner*, Case 11.5.

Ceremony programs are an excellent way to educate guests about the various artifacts that will be incorporated during a wedding, in particular when traditions are being blended and the assumption cannot be made that all guests are familiar with the cultural customs. Specifics regarding ceremony programs are covered in Chapter 13.

Chapter 11

Photo 11.6 The ring exchange is symbolic.

Source: www.RodneyBailey.com

The order of ceremony

While there is no one-size-fits-all for the progression of a wedding ceremony, it is helpful to have some general guidelines as a starting point. The ceremony celebrant for each wedding assists with the details but relies on the consultant to get everyone lined up and ensure that readers, musicians, soloists and other wedding party members are prepared. The wedding rehearsal is a valuable opportunity to run through the specifics; however, it is not uncommon for wedding party members

CULTURE CORNER, CASE 11.4

ELLEN AND PIERRE'S INTERFAITH AND INTERCULTURAL WEDDING

The couple: Ellen is Caucasian and practices Conservative Judaism, while Pierre is affiliated with the African American-based National Baptist Convention. The couple met in graduate school and dated for nine years before becoming engaged. Prior to proposing, Pierre spoke with both sets of parents to affirm their support of the union and to ask for their blessings.

Co-celebrants: A Reform Jewish Rabbi and a Christian Methodist Episcopal (CME) Minister joined in the co-celebration. The two officiants entered together and alternated in delivering readings, priestly blessings, and the *drashah* (charge to the couple) in Hebrew and English. The Rabbi wore a traditional Jewish prayer shawl known as a *tallit*, while the Minister wore a clergy collar and a shawl of African *kente cloth*.

Jewish elements: As is required for *kidushin* (Jewish marriage ceremonies), Ellen and Pierre did not wed on the Sabbath, waiting until after sundown on Saturday. Regardless of religious affiliation, each male guest was requested to wear a *kippah* or *yarmulke*, a skullcap worn in a Jewish house of worship or consecrated area to show respect for the Lord. The ceremony and reception were held in a hotel, which is common in interfaith marriages, and also facilitated the logistics for many out-of-town guests. While a secular setting, a sacred area was established by installing a four-poled floral *chuppah*, a canopy representing the Jewish home. As marriage is the union of communities, the bride and groom were individually escorted down the aisle by their parents, and joined standing under the chuppah by the officiants, wedding party and families. During the ceremony, the *ketubah* was read – a marriage proclamation signed in a private ceremony by Ellen and Pierre prior to the service – as well as verses from the Jewish Prayer Book, *Likrat Shabbat*, and *Song of Songs*. Following recitation of the *Seven Wedding Blessings*, the couple drank from a *kiddush cup* during the wine ceremony. At the conclusion of the service, Pierre participated in *breaking the glass*. This custom originally symbolized the destruction of the temple and the fragility of life; however, in contemporary times, it has come to represent that no vessel can contain the amount of joy experienced in the coming together of two to make one. At the reception, following a heartfelt toast by Pierre's best man, Ellen's uncle recited traditional Hebrew blessings over the wine and bread. Following the meal, all joined in dancing to the *hora*, an Israeli circular folk dance.

African American elements: Several African American elements were present in Ellen and Pierre's ceremony. The groom's brother read the poem "We Unaccustomed to Courage" by Maya Angelou, which reflects upon how love leads to freedom and life. Additionally, a passage from "The Prophet" by Kahil Gibran was delivered by the officiants, as was a discussion of the tradition of the broom. Historically, African American slaves were forbidden to marry; *jumping the broom* became the ritual by which marriage was pursued. The broom was used as a symbol of family, creation of a new home, removal of evil from a joyous event and acceptance of new obligations. Entering the reception, Ellen and Pierre jumped the broom to remember the struggles of their shared past and to pay homage to their ancestors for their legacy.

The ceremony program: Ellen and Pierre designed a ceremony program that presented not only the chronology of the event, but also a detailed explanation of the many religious and cultural elements interwoven throughout the service. In this way, family and friends were better able to appreciate the festivities, and to share a more thorough understanding of Ellen and Pierre's respective and cherished traditions.

CASE SUBMITTED BY ELLEN AND PIERRE RODGERS

to have to miss the rehearsal due to travel or work schedules. Table 11.3 offers an overview to give you a sense of the process, while the full production schedule in Chapter 8 is a comprehensive example.

GUIDELINES AND POLICIES

Religious and cultural traditions, as well as ceremony venues, include guidelines and policies that can influence the experience of all involved. For example, when you work with your first Catholic or Greek Orthodox couple, you may be surprised at the length of the ceremonies common to these faiths. If standing is required throughout, lightheadedness abounds and cases of brides, grooms or other wedding party members fainting increase in frequency. Encourage the bridal party in any wedding to stand with one foot slightly in front of the other. This helps prevent the knees from locking and decreases the swoon-factor significantly. Every wedding consultant has a fainting story, but you want to do what you can to minimize these occurrences.

CULTURE CORNER, CASE II.5

FILIPINO VEIL AND CORD CEREMONY

A Filipino tradition, the veil and cord ceremony is usually performed toward the very end of the marriage ceremony. The veil is usually about a 4-ft by 2-ft rectangular piece of sheer fabric, sometimes embellished with lace or other embroidery. The cord, or lasso, as it is often called, is usually made of white rope with tassels on the ends.

Two sponsors, one male and one female, are chosen in advance to place the cord and veil over the couple. The sponsors are usually relatives of the couple, most often aunts or uncles; however, if no relatives are available, close friends are chosen instead. The sponsors are seated within the first few rows of seats so that they can quickly come up to the altar with the veil and cord when the officiant announces the ceremony. The male sponsor will stand by the groom's side, and the female sponsor will stand by the bride's side.

Once the sponsors come forward, the bride and groom kneel on the altar. The female sponsor will place the veil over the shoulders of the couple, and the male sponsor will help pin it into place, usually with clothes pins that can be painted white if preferred by the couple.

The officiant will then say a few words regarding the significance and symbolism of the veil and cord. While there are several variations, most commonly the names of the bride and groom are given followed by a statement that is specific to being covered in Christ's love, and that they will live under his mantel.

After the initial statement regarding the symbolism of the veil, the male sponsor creates an infinity symbol over the heads of the couple with the lasso, and the female sponsor will assist as needed. The officiant will then make another statement, explaining how the lasso symbolizes the Blessed Trinity and the infinite nature of marriage.

A nice way to complete this portion of the ceremony is to play a musical selection and, halfway through the song, have the sponsors remove the lasso first, veil second and then be seated. At the end of the song, the couple rises and the officiant gives the final benediction of the marriage ceremony.

CASE SUBMITTED BY TYLER FITZHUGH, RBC, CWS, CWP
VOILÀ! EVENT STUDIO
WEBSITE: *VOILAEVENTSTUDIO.COM*

TABLE II.3 ORDER OF CEREMONY: GENERAL GUIDELINES

- Prelude music will begin
- Seating of guests: groomsmen in place to act as ushers
- Processional music will begin
- Groomsmen and groom in place at front of room. They will usually walk in from side entrance. Order from center: celebrant, groom, best man, groomsmen. If groomsmen are lined up by height, generally it will be tallest to shortest, starting from center.
- Entrance of bridesmaids. If bridesmaids are lining up by height, the entrance order is shortest to tallest, so, when the shortest walks in to the far left, the order from center once all have walked in is tallest to shortest.
- Entrance of maid (or matron) of honor
- Entrance of flower girl and ring bearer
- Bridal entrance music will begin
- Entrance of bride and father (or both parents, or some other relative of importance)
- Presentation of the bride
- Declaration of intention
- Words of welcome
- 1st Reading
- Reflection on couple by the celebrant
- Musical interlude or solo
- 2nd Reading
- Exchange of vows
- Presentation of the rings
- Exchange of rings
- Blessing of the marriage
- Declaration of marriage
- The kiss
- Introduction of couple
- Recessional music. Newlyweds recess first, then maid of honor/best man, then pairings of bridesmaids and groomsmen. The flower girl and ring bearer will recess after the bride and groom if they have been standing for the whole ceremony; however, frequently they sit with their parents after the processional, depending on age.
- Postlude music
- Sign marriage license

PHOTO 11.7 CEREMONY POLICIES WILL DIFFER FOR INDOOR AND OUTDOOR WEDDINGS.

SOURCE: WWW.RODNEYBAILEY.COM

Some faiths have policies regarding when couples can marry. For example, traditionally, the Jewish faith does not permit weddings on the Sabbath or holidays or during two extended periods, one following Passover and the other preceding the fast day on the ninth of Av in the summer. A local rabbi is your best guide when determining these restrictions. In some faiths, policies also exist regarding those who can be present during the ceremony. For instance, when a marriage ceremony called a sealing ordinance takes place in a temple of The Church of Jesus Christ of Latter-day Saints (LDS or Mormon), only those who hold a valid *temple recommend*, a document which certifies that the holder is in good standing with the faith, can attend the ceremony. This means that even immediate family members without this document cannot be present. This policy can cause confusion and hurt feelings for those not familiar with LDS doctrines and practices. However, many in the Mormon faith are sensitive to these feelings and go to great lengths to make non-member friends and relatives who cannot attend the ceremony feel involved, as illustrated in *Culture Corner, Case 11.6*.

CULTURE CORNER, CASE 11.6

THE WEDDING OF KATIE AND STEVE: THE TEMPLE SEALING ORDINANCE

The couple: Katie and Steve belong to The Church of Jesus Christ of Latter-day Saints (LDS or Mormon) and wanted to have a temple marriage. While the couple and Steve's parents had temple recommends, Katie's mother does not practice the LDS faith. She respects the faith and was in full support of the couple's desire for a temple sealing. In order to prepare non-member guests, the invitations announced that the marriage would be solemnized in the Mesa Arizona Temple and indicated that guests were cordially invited to attend the ring ceremony and reception. The time of the sealing ordinance is purposefully not provided on the invitation, as this information could create confusion.

The temple sealing ordinance: The marriage sealing is a very sacred and solemn experience. The temple is only used for specific ordinances and is different from the meeting houses that are used for weekly services. While any visitor can enter a meeting house, to enter the temple requires a valid temple recommend, which is the card that indicates good standing with the church. Katie was escorted to the bridal room and Steve escorted to a changing room, where each exchanged their street clothes for modest white garments, as required when receiving an ordinance. Katie was able to wear her modest white wedding gown but not a veil, while Steve changed into white clothing specifically for the sealing. They then received counsel from a representative of the temple presidency prior to being ushered into the sealing room. Only the closest of friends and immediate family were present at the ordinance, as sealing rooms generally hold less than 20 people. Many friends with valid temple recommends did not attend in respect for the sanctity of the ordinance. The LDS sealing means that the bride and groom are sealed both during mortal life and after death. In keeping with the rules of the temple, there is no exchange of rings, no wedding party is allowed and no photographs or video can be taken. Katie and Steve kneeled across from each other at an altar in the center of the room and held hands. Rather than an exchange of vows, the marriage ordinance is recited to them by an officiator who holds the proper priesthood authority. The wording is the same for every Mormon temple wedding and acts to seal the marriage for eternity.

The greeting: As is common for many Mormon weddings, close friends and family members were waiting outside of the temple to greet and congratulate the newlyweds. After exiting the sealing room and before leaving the temple, Steve changed into his tuxedo and Katie put on her bridal veil. Photographs were taken once the couple was outside of the temple.

The ring ceremony: Similar to many Mormon couples who have large groups of friends and family, Katie and Steve had a ring ceremony that all guests could attend. This was held at their reception site, and included a wedding party with bridesmaids and groomsmen. Like other Christian ceremonies, Katie's father walked her down the aisle, there were readings, music, speeches and a friend from their church led them through the exchange of rings.

Policies may also be in place regarding second marriages. For example, in the Catholic faith, if either the bride or the groom has been divorced, the previous marriage must officially be annulled by a Catholic tribunal in order for the ceremony to take place in a Catholic church. The *annulment* process is extremely involved, usually taking over a year to complete and including a written petition, witnesses and formal hearing. The outcome is that, in the eyes of the Catholic Church, the marriage is voided as if it never took place. A couple following the Mormon faith must undergo a similar process if they wish their marriage to be unsealed.

Some couples are forbidden by law to marry, or cannot marry due to extenuating circumstances. However, many couples without the ability to legally marry still desire to have their relationship publicly recognized. As discussed in Chapter 4, same-sex couples are unable to legally marry in many countries, giving rise to commitment ceremonies where they symbolically form a union. Others may want to marry but cannot form a legal union because it would cause them to lose certain benefits that they cannot do without. For example, some individuals waiting for an organ transplant require such extensive and ongoing medical intervention that they are unable to work and their treatment is covered by government programs. However, should a person in this situation marry, the medical benefits might be lost and the new spouse could quickly face financial ruin. Commitment ceremonies present an option for couples facing legal stumbling blocks to marriage.

TABLE II.4 TIPS FOR COUPLES INCLUDING PETS IN WEDDING CEREMONIES

1. *Call ahead.* Find out if the venues will accept pets. Also, if you are having a destination wedding, locate hotels that are pet-friendly.
2. *Consider your guests.* Determine if anyone who will be interacting directly with the pet has an allergy. Also, some wedding party members may get nervous around animals and should be notified in advance.
3. *Resist kitty and puppy love.* Because kittens and puppies are unpredictable, they are particularly difficult to include in ceremonies.
4. *Test the temperament.* Many pets are uncomfortable around strangers or act differently in new surroundings. Only well-behaved animals should be included in wedding ceremonies. The pet should know who is in charge and be able to respond to commands as needed. Include your pets in the wedding rehearsal to help them become familiar with their surroundings and duties.
5. *Use fashion sense.* Pick attire that your pet will tolerate and test the chosen garments on several occasions. Avoid wires and floral varieties that are toxic to animals, such as lilies, daffodils and hydrangeas.
6. *Avoid chowhounds.* Your pet can get sick if they are not trained to avoid human food and drink.
7. *Get them ready.* Your pet should be pampered and exercised before the wedding and be taken for bathroom breaks throughout the day.
8. *Employ bribery.* Bring your pets' favorite treats and spoil them with affection so that they will be content during the ceremony and while being photographed.

SOURCE: ADAPTED FROM MOORE (2013)

Many ceremony venues are also likely to have restrictions regarding the inclusion of pets in the bridal party. As this is becoming a more common practice, you will want to be familiar with the sites that do allow animals. Award-winning pet expert Arden Moore offers tips for couples who wish to include a pet in their wedding ceremony, summarized in Table 11.4.

Pets can be endearing but are subject to mishaps, as illustrated in *Consultant in Action*, Case 11.7

You must remember that there is no right or wrong way for a couple to pledge their commitment. If you strongly support one faith or approach to marriage and do not feel comfortable with other practices, simply choose your target market and specialize in that area. If, on the other hand, you wish to support a broad range of clients, then you must be open to diverse outlooks and belief systems.

CONSULTANT IN ACTION, CASE 11.7

PUPPY LOVE

Your clients are holding their wedding at a large country home. An integral part of the ceremony is the clients' two small dogs, who are to wear handmade floral collars with hand-sewn ring pouches attached to the collars. Thus, the dogs will serve as "ring bearers" and will process down the aisle with the wedding bands, where the best man will untie the pouches and present the rings at the appropriate time during the ceremony. The two dogs are carefully groomed and adorned with the collars, rings within the pouches, and held in a small outside room close to the tented ceremony. Three minutes before the dogs are due to appear, someone unwittingly opens the door to the room and the immaculately groomed dogs escape and take off at great speed across the large property. They are long gone, with the rings.

WHAT DO YOU DO?

CASE SUBMITTED BY ALISON DE WIT
DISTINCTIVE FLORAL DESIGNS
WEBSITE: *DISTINCTIVEFLORAL.COM*

REFERENCES

Boorstein, M. (9 October 2012) 'Study: 20% list religion as "none," but many still believe', *The Washington Post*, A1, A9.

Cochran, B. (2013) 'The career of a wedding officiant'. E-mail (31 January 2013).

Cochran, B. and Cochran, J. (2013) 'Steps for writing your own vows'. E-mail (5 February 2013).

de Wit, A. (2013) 'Puppy love'. E-mail (19 October 2012).

Diener, E., Tay, L. and Myers, D.G. (2011) 'The religion paradox: if religion makes people happy, why are so many dropping out?', *Journal of Personality and Social Psychology*, 101: 1278–1290.

FitzHugh, T. (2012) 'Filipino veil and cord ceremony'. E-mail (16 December 2012).

Hallo, J. and Hallo, L. (2012) 'Do you take this woman to be your husband?' E-mail (15 November 2012).

Kochuyt, T. (2012) 'Making money, marking identities: on the economic, social and cultural functions of Moroccan weddings in Brussels', *Journal of Ethnic and Migration Studies*, 38: 1625–1641.

Moore, A. (2013) 'Arden Moore's four legged life', Online. Available HTTP: <http://fourleggedlife.com/> (accessed 18 January 2013).

Motley, L. (2013) 'A wedding concelebration'. E-mail (31 January 2013).

Robinson, B.A. (2011) 'Religions of the world', *Ontario Consultants on Religious Tolerance*, Online. Available HTTP: <http://www.religioustolerance.org/worldrel.htm> (accessed 10 December 2012).

World Christian Database (2013) 'World religion at your fingertips', Online. Available HTTP: <http://www.world christiandatabase.org/wcd/> (accessed 19 January 2013).

CONSULTANT CHECKLIST AND REMINDERS FOR THE CEREMONY

☐ Always defer to the celebrant's wishes, as this leader is the guiding force behind the ceremony.

☐ Respect the fact that many celebrants are territorial.

☐ Share the seven steps to writing vows with couples who wish to take this route.

☐ Programs are an excellent means of guiding guests through ceremonial traditions with which they are unfamiliar.

☐ Become familiar with ceremony guidelines and policies associated with places of worship in your area.

REVIEW

1. Name two religions that are common in your area, as well as the associated leader's title and the name of the sacred text.

2. Name the seven steps for writing vows.

3. Name two artifacts that are commonly used in a) Jewish, b) Hindu, c) Greek Orthodox, d) Korean and e) Mexican weddings.

4. Name and explain at least four things to keep in mind when considering the inclusion of pets in a wedding ceremony.

TERMINOLOGY

- Annulment
- Arras
- Artifacts
- Baraat
- Breaking of the glass
- Celebrant
- Ceremony program
- Chuppah
- Co-celebration or concelebration
- Kente cloth
- Ketubah
- Koumbara/Koumbaro
- Kowtow
- Lazo
- Mandap
- Sacred texts
- Stephana
- Tallit
- Temple sealing ordinance
- Vows
- Yarmulke

Photo 12.1 Floral arrangements set the tone of a wedding.

12

FLORAL DÉCOR

FLOWERS AND RELATED DECORATIVE ELEMENTS UNDERSCORE THE MOOD AND TONE OF A WEDDING. THEY ALSO REPRESENT A SIGNIFICANT EXPENSE, GENERALLY TAKING UP 7 PER CENT OR MORE OF THE BUDGET. BECAUSE OF THE PROMINENT NATURE OF FLOWERS DURING THE CEREMONY AND RECEPTION, THOUGHTFUL CARE SHOULD BE TAKEN WHEN MAKING DECISIONS. FOUR CONSIDERATIONS WHEN SELECTING FLORAL DÉCOR INCLUDE: 1) THE RECIPIENTS AND LOCATIONS; 2) SELECTING FLOWERS; 3) CENTERPIECES AND OTHER DECORATIVE ELEMENTS; AND 4) INSTALLATION AND REMOVAL.

RECIPIENTS AND LOCATIONS

Floral décor experts use an organized system of defining the "who" of personal flowers. They assist clients in determining designs for all of the following recipients and the number that will be needed for each category:

- Bridal bouquet

- Toss bouquet

- Other bridal flowers (e.g., hair, dress)

- Number of bridesmaids, including maid of honor

- Number of flower girls (petals/basket)

- Number of mothers (corsages/nosegays)

- Number of grandmothers (corsages/nosegays)

- Other women needing personal flowers

- Groom's boutonniere

- Number of groomsmen, including best man

- Number of ushers

- Ring bearer (boutonniere and pillow)

- Number of fathers

- Number of grandfathers

- Other men needing personal flowers

When considering the "other" category, this may include the officiant, readers, soloists, guest book attendant and, in some cases, all of the guests if flowers are used for or within favors.

Similarly, by using a standard checklist, floral designers efficiently help couples pinpoint floral décor needs for the ceremony and reception:

CEREMONY

- Entrance flowers and greenery, decorative wreaths and bows

- Freestanding arrangements

- Altar arrangements

- Pew/chair décor

- Aisle runner

- Ceremony special elements (e.g., chuppah, arch, gazebo)

- Other ceremony flowers (e.g., unity candle décor, kneeling bench décor)

RECEPTION

- Number of centerpieces for reception tables

- Tent décor

- Sweetheart table or head table

- Buffet table arrangements

- Cake flowers, cake table, cake knife décor

- Ice sculpture décor, punch bowl décor

- Toasting glasses décor

- Escort card table

- Bar and cocktail area

- Ladies restroom

- Banisters

- Other flowers needed (e.g., pool floats, guest rooms, cars)

The entrance to the ceremony site is the first chance to make an impression and tie in the theme of the wedding. Prior to this point, most guests have only seen stationery elements such as save-the-date cards and the invitation, so the entrance sets the stage for the rest of the day. When considering the placement of flowers and greenery at the entrance location, it is important to keep in mind that garlands can gently and gracefully welcome guests without enormous expense. Doorway treatments with a hint of color, such as swags, wreaths or garlands made of leaves, berries, pine, herbs or artfully arranged twigs and ribbons, can give a big impact with minimal investment. Similarly, *topiaries* are ornamental trees trimmed in unique shapes that are fresh and have an ethereal feel with the addition of tulle or bows.

Trees and large potted plants can be rented for weddings, offering another cost-effective means to make a statement. Floral wreaths can beautifully mark the entrance as well, but can be cost-prohibitive as a single wreath can include hundreds of flowers. However, the portability of a wreath allows it to be used at the ceremony, reception, brunch the day after the wedding and then it can be dried and kept as a beautiful memento that can be used for years. If investing in floral wreaths, keep in mind that they do not have to be round, as square, heart-shaped and vertical wreaths offer distinctive options.

With an outdoor wedding, flowers can create a focal point for the ceremony if one is not apparent. Outside weddings need fewer flowers beyond the focal point and should not be fussy or overly arranged as you will want them to complement the natural outdoor elements. Outdoor ceremonies also allow for floral décor along an aisle runner and for real petals to be dropped by the flower girl. For indoor ceremonies, these items are generally prohibited because of their ability to stain carpeted or wood floors. Even for outdoor ceremonies, it is best to select pale petals for the flower girl to scatter, as dark petals can stain the bride's dress. Dark silk petals are equally problematic as the dyes used can leave marks.

PHOTO 12.2 A WREATH CAN BEAUTIFULLY MARK THE ENTRANCE.

SOURCE: WWW.RODNEYBAILEY.COM

Photo 12.3 Pomanders are used to decorate the aisle.

Source: www.RodneyBailey.com

Both indoor and outdoor weddings may have a canopy, arch or other structure that the couple stands under during the ceremony. As you learned in Chapter 11, in Jewish weddings, this is known as a *chuppah* and for Indian weddings it is called a *mandap*. Structures such as these are often beautifully accented with flowers.

Additionally, arrangements are placed close to the couple as they add elegance to the ceremony photographs. Floral accents such as *pomanders*, which are small balls of flowers, are frequently used to mark the rows or pews.

Selecting flowers

The bridal bouquet is an excellent place to start when selecting flowers, as it is the most photographed floral element and often informs the choices for the wedding party and other floral décor. When selecting flowers for a wedding, five things to keep in mind are the season, color, scent, shape and size.

First, the season will dictate what floral elements are available. For couples on a budget who have do-it-yourself (DIY) creative flair, they can purchase the majority of their floral décor at a local farmers' market. These outdoor bazaars seasonally have the best of what is blooming in the local area at that time of year. Floral designers use local materials as well, but also work closely with international distributors from locations such as Colombia, Ecuador, Holland and Thailand to ensure that they have a broad range of flowers available throughout the calendar year. DIY couples can also purchase flowers from wholesale outlets in bulk.

Some flowers that are popular for weddings have an extremely short season, with the classic example being the three- to four-week season of lily of the valley that falls in May. The small stems are priced as high as $15 each, with even very small bouquets starting at $400. Lily of the valley stems are so expensive that many florists do not carry them. Obtaining flowers with a short season or during their off-season can be cost-prohibitive, so you will want to work closely with florists in your area to gain a sense of seasonality. In cases where a desired flower is simply not available, many florists will offer silk accents or arrangements.

The Flowers and Plants Association (2013) offers an excellent overview of the seasonal availability of specific flowers, keeping in mind that this requires the ability to ship the flowers from the location where they happen to be in season. For example, many winter flowers are exotics that are only available in tropical climates. Refer to Table 12.1 for a sample of their recommendations by season. Remember that many flowers are available off-season, but the cost is significantly higher.

PHOTO 12.4 THE BRIDAL BOUQUET INFORMS OTHER FLORAL SELECTIONS.

SOURCE: WWW.RODNEYBAILEY.COM

TABLE 12.1 SEASONAL FLOWER AVAILABILITY SAMPLER

Spring:	cherry blossom, daffodil, gardenia, hyacinth, lilac, lily of the valley, tulips
Summer:	agapanthus, alliums, goldenrod, hydrangea, peony, phlox, sweet pea
Fall:	aster, celosia, dahlia, gladiolus, hypericum, sunflowers, yarrow, zinnia
Winter:	amaryllis, hellebore, hollyberry, kangaroo paw, narcissus, protea, ranunculus
All year:	alstroemeria, bird of paradise, calla, chrysanthemum, delphinium, freesia, gerbera, iris, lily, phalaenopsis orchid, rose, snapdragon, statice, stephanotis

SOURCE: FLOWERS AND PLANTS ASSOCIATION (2013)

A second consideration when selecting flowers for a wedding is color. In terms of bridal bouquets, approximately 70 per cent of brides select white or ivory for a fresh, elegant look. Traditionalists argue that guests should look at the bride first, not her flowers, and dark flowers against a white gown will dominate the view. For the 30 per cent of brides who mix color into the bouquet, the complementary colors tend to stay on the light side such as pink, pale yellow, peach and lilac. Bold and dark bouquets are becoming more popular and can make a very dramatic statement.

Alison de Wit (2013) of Distinctive Floral Designs explains that much depends on the bride's gown, her makeup and her selected hairstyle. In speaking of the gown, she indicates that scale should be taken into consideration; for instance, if a bride is wearing a form-fitting gown a large bouquet is not recommended and, conversely, she notes that a ball gown with an extended skirt is not synonymous with a posy! Maryam Saeedi (2013) of Maryam Flowers adds that, if the dress has a very intricate design, she suggests a simple bouquet with less color so that the attention is not taken away from the dress. On the other hand, if the dress is very simple, she recommends more texture and color in the bouquet.

Alison states that, while color choices are based largely on what a bride enjoys, it is still the responsibility of the floral designer to offer advice on what colors work well with the overall look of the gown, hair, makeup and jewelry. She emphasizes that cohesion is of the utmost importance in maintaining a beautiful, coordinated look and that details such as beautiful ribbon wrapping and high-quality design accoutrements offer lovely originality. Alison offers additional insight regarding floral décor for weddings in *Vendor Spotlight*, Case 12.1.

With bridesmaids' bouquets, mixing in bright colors is more common. A trend for bridesmaids is that, in lieu of a bouquet, they will carry a purse, fan or muff accented with real or silk flowers. Generally, the chosen ornament will be a gift from the bride, which the bridesmaids carry during the wedding and then have for later use.

The scent of the floral décor is a third consideration. This is most relevant when selecting centerpieces, as a heavy floral scent can interfere with the reception meal. Magnolia blossoms, gardenias and stargazer lilies are three examples of beautiful varieties that should be kept out of the immediate vicinity of food. Gardenias brown and bruise easily, so are better used in wreaths rather than in centerpieces where they will be regularly breathed upon or touched.

PHOTO 12.5 SOME BRIDES MIX COLOR IN THE BOUQUET.

SOURCE: WWW.RODNEYBAILEY.COM

VENDOR SPOTLIGHT, CASE 12.1

ALISON DE WIT

DISTINCTIVE FLORAL DESIGNS

How did you become interested in floral décor as a career? I have always loved flowers; from a small child cutting blooms from the gardens of my grandmother and mother, I gleaned a gardener's education in floral types and seasonal blooms. I started out designing décor for small, intimate gatherings and then focused on wedding blooms – the latter always being of keen interest to me. From this I developed a business model based on designing décor for weddings and the business has grown into a full-fledged wedding décor design studio. We are discerning and we enjoy creating beautiful, high-quality work.

How do floral selections differ from culture to culture? I think there is much cross over in this area, although I would say that if a client hails from a tropical region there is a propensity to enjoy vibrant colored blooms in tropical selections. European wedding décor tends to be in the white/vanilla color way, as this has been traditional for generations and it still holds true today. Often clients who emanate from Asia Pacific enjoy orchids as they are prevalent in this region of the world and often used within wedding décor. I often work with cross-cultural clients, so it is useful to become adept at skillfully combining needs that satisfy a number of cultural parameters.

What are the latest trends for bridal bouquets? I think we are returning to more traditional mediums for personal blooms; avant-garde design is lovely but I think brides nowadays do consider that they will be looking at their wedding pictures their entire lives and they do not wish to look back and realize they chose a design for a bouquet that, whilst de rigueur the year of their wedding, does not hold true through the years. As such, we design in many traditional mediums; elegant blooms in demilune configurations or modest drape lines. I have seen a trend for customized bouquet wraps often incorporating lockets or small, meaningful emotional pieces that the bride can thus carry down the aisle affixed to her bouquet. It is very special to design a bouquet wrap incorporating a cherished grandmother's wedding band or a locket with a picture of a loved one.

How have environmental concerns impacted the floral industry? I would say on the floral production side of the industry there have been changes in the way we procure blooms; there is now more production from some countries and less from others. An uplifting aspect of procuring blooms is seeing the trend towards sustainable farming practices by floral producers in certain situations. On both a domestic and international level, we support farms engaged in sustainable farming methodologies. Many years ago, this was not even a term one heard of; it is encouraging to see the floral industry respond to environmental indicators and adopt responsible farming.

Please share a humorous anecdote that you witnessed related to a client's wedding and specific to floral décor. One of my favorites is a wedding where there were five little flower girls, all beautifully attired in white silk tulle dresses, and each holding a satin basket filled with fresh rose petals. There had been much rehearsing on sprinkling the petals down the aisle prior to the bride's processional and they all seemed entirely au fait with their responsibilities. As they processed down the aisle on the actual wedding day, they were so focused on walking correctly that they quite forgot to sprinkle the petals from their baskets. Reaching the end of the aisle, and realizing their "petal error," they simply tipped the baskets upside down depositing tidy piles of petals where they stood. There was a gentle roll of laugher, and many smiles, from the congregants. It was adorable and very dear and poignant.

What can consultants do to make your job easier? A wedding consultant is a wonderful attribute for a bride and groom! I think the most useful professional aspect from a floral design angle is the consultant having interviewed their clients and gleaned a sound sense of their look, their design leanings and a budget which is realistic and comfortable. It is our job as floral designers to meet these needs thoroughly and conscientiously but guidance and honesty is, quite simply, remarkably helpful. A good wedding consultant helps all vendors including floral designers as they have a holistic view of a wedding. We all care deeply for our clients and want the best for them on their wedding day.

WEBSITE: *DISTINCTIVEFLORAL.COM*

A fourth consideration when selecting floral décor is shape. For bridal bouquets, the three primary shapes are hand-tied, round and cascade. The *hand-tied* bouquet is natural looking, as if the flowers were just picked from a garden. Hand-tied bouquets can either be tailored, such as a grouping of six calla lilies with an elegant ribbon, or a mixed arrangement, such as peonies, dendrobium orchids and freesia stems. Some hand-tied bouquets are held with a single ribbon, while others have the stems wired or taped and then tied to finish the look. A *nosegay* is a small hand-tied bouquet that is popular for flower girls, junior bridesmaids, mothers and others receiving smaller sprays. *Tussie-Mussie* is a Victorian-inspired nosegay that is small, compact and often in a cone-shaped holder.

Round and *cascade* bouquets have a more arranged appearance and are generally mounted on a bouquet holder with a handle. A classic round bouquet is made up of hundreds of delicate stephanotis blossoms with each stem hand wrapped and tied. Often a pearl pin is placed in the center of each flower for a touch of elegance and then the arrangement is brought together in what looks like a large, round ball. Roses are also commonly used to make beautiful round bouquets. Both hand-tied and round bouquets can be *collared*, which means that the arrangement literally has a collar of greenery creating a border. A cascade bouquet, also referred to as a teardrop or waterfall shape, tends to be the largest and heaviest, incorporating long stems that give the bouquet length and drape.

A final concern when selecting floral décor is size. In terms of bridal bouquets, the adage used to be the bigger, the better. However, a large bouquet can overwhelm the bride, making her look like she is all flowers, and simultaneously is too heavy to carry for extended periods. Now the tendency is to have more compact bouquets. In terms of boutonnieres, the consensus is that smaller is better. Most floral designers will encourage clients to match the boutonnieres with some aspect of the bridal bouquet. Single roses and mini calla lilies are popular options that can be easily coordinated.

CENTERPIECES AND DECORATIVE ELEMENTS

While most couples stay fairly traditional with bouquets, boutonnieres and ceremony selections, centerpieces and other decorative elements used for the reception allow contemporary statements to be made. When entering the reception site, one of the first things that guests will see is the escort card table. This table is a key focal point that can set the tone for the rest of the reception and is often lavishly decorated. A beach theme wedding, for example, can include an escort table where the cards are set in sand and surrounded by exotic flowers and conch shells.

With centerpieces, a couple's budget and their floral designer's creative capacity are the only limits. Some couples still select classic designs such as candelabras entwined with flowers, while others employ the imagination of the designer to tie elaborate floral décor into their theme. While there can be a distinction in the formality of the floral décor for the ceremony and reception, it should not be so radical that an imbalance results. Maryam Saeedi of Maryam Flowers discusses centerpiece trends and budget considerations in *Vendor Spotlight*, Case 12.2.

A current trend in centerpieces is to use large, clear glass vases in modern shapes. On the top of the design, flowers are placed in a removable plastic riser. Beneath this tray, the sky is the limit, and options such as bright fruits, vegetables or berries, colored glass or lights, buckeyes, live grasses growing in a soil base, pinecones and live fish represent just a few design ideas. Centerpiece size should be dictated by table size, and should not be so large that the centerpiece inhibits conversation. Alison de Wit adds that that many couples are using floral pieces of varying heights and textures and incorporating beautiful candlelit elements to create vignettes or the tableaux look. Once a centerpiece design is selected, most florists will schedule an appointment for a sample showing so clients can see their selections come together and make changes as necessary. Expensive or large arrangements, such as those using bamboo or rented palm trees for a tropical theme, should be prominently displayed so the couple feels they are worth the investment.

PHOTO 12.6 WITH CENTERPIECES, THE DESIGNER'S CREATIVITY IS EVIDENCED.

SOURCE: WWW.RODNEYBAILEY.COM

INSTALLATION AND REMOVAL

Prior to meeting with the floral designer, it is a good idea to inform your clients that there are charges for packing, delivery, installation and removal. Depending on the size of the order, the complexity of the designs and the distance traveled, these fees can be significant. Basic installation charges will vary by area, but anticipate a minimum charge of $150. Installation charges are based primarily on time, and many large arrangements cannot be transported and must be built on site.

Vendor Spotlight, Case 12.2

Maryam Saeedi

Maryam Flowers

What is your background and how did you get started with floral design? I was born and raised in Tehran, Iran and lived there until I was 16 when I moved to the United States. In Iran, my mother was a home economics teacher and one of the talents she had was making artificial flowers out of paper. I learned this art when I was very young and helped her for the events where she used the flowers. When I was 11, my uncle got married and they asked me to make 250 paper flowers to be attached to tree branches for the decorations. That was the very first wedding I was involved in and that got my interest. Working with fresh flowers is different, but having an eye for design and color is the same and the passion for wedding flowers is the same.

How has technology influenced centerpiece décor for weddings? With the vast number of websites, magazines and television shows about weddings and wedding flowers, the majority of my brides pretty much know what they want when they meet with me. For those brides who want me to design for them, I start with their vision for their wedding day, their likes and dislikes, and, as I get to know the bride more after the initial consultation, I tweak colors and textures based on their personality and their venue. When I have design flexibility, I experiment to get it perfect, and the centerpiece sample I present to them is usually the third or fourth revision. I think my attention to customer service stems from my passion for weddings. Brides appreciate my responsiveness, flexibility and overall care. They all become my friends, daughters and sisters because I treat them all like I was designing for my own wedding.

Tell us about floral décor for weddings in Iran. In comparison with the United States, there are definitely design differences. Iranian brides are less interested in their own bouquets or other personal flowers. There are no bridesmaids, so no personal flowers. Most of the effort and money goes toward the reception flowers. The cost of flowers is much less in Iran than in the United States, so you will see a lot of tropical flowers, birds of paradise, ginger, orchids and anthuriums. Roses are imported, too, but not from South America so the quality is not very good – the buds are very small so they are not used that often. Ceremony arrangements are normally standing sprays. Another difference is that every couple decorates their car very extensively. The bride and groom take a ride around town after the reception and the car decoration is very important.

What trends are you seeing in floral décor selection for weddings? With the economy in recovery, wedding flowers are becoming more glamorous. The "just picked from the garden" look is very popular for the bouquet. Most of my grooms are getting non-floral boutonnieres; instead, depending on their culture and personal preference, they may use a pocket square or have a boutonniere made of feathers, rhinestones, shells or paper origami. Most mothers do not want a corsage. The ceremony is becoming very important again and we are designing elaborate altar arrangements. For the reception, we are creating lush and large centerpieces in jewel tones.

How do you assist couples on a tight budget? For couples with budget concerns, I explain that, although one type of flower might be pricier than others per stem, the size (e.g., hydrangeas) or use (e.g., orchids) could surpass other flowers that are less expensive. For example, we can design a bridal bouquet or bridesmaids' bouquets with two hydrangeas, which will be much larger and much less expensive than a bouquet designed with carnations. With centerpieces, we can design a gorgeous submerged arrangement with two orchids, which will be less expensive than a vase arrangement with low-cost flowers. When considering the reception, we can always design floral arrangements for half of the tables and use candles for the other half, or we can balance tall, expensive centerpieces with shorter, less expensive ones.

Please share a story where troubleshooting was necessary. We were setting up at a mansion for an October wedding with an outdoor ceremony and indoor reception. While we had been involved with numerous weddings at that venue, this was the first that took place in October. There is a very tall apple tree on the premises, and the apples were very ripe at that time of year. My staff and I had to carry large boxes over our heads when we were setting up the ceremony because the apples kept falling. The height was such that, if the apples had hit us, they would have knocked us out! We also had to notify the planner to reroute the path to the ceremony so the guests would not be attacked by apples!

WEBSITE: *MARYAMFLOWERSBRIDAL.COM*

A floral chuppah, for example, is raised and decorated at the venue, which usually takes a minimum of an hour. Decorated tents, where each pole is intertwined with greenery and flowers, can take several hours to install.

At most venues, nails and tape are prohibited, so hanging designs must be installed with ribbons, clips, decorative ropes and ties. When the designer has finished the installation, you should walk through to make sure that all the areas are clean and neat and that no trash or extra materials were inadvertently left behind. It is your job to make sure the "curb appeal" is maintained.

PHOTO 12.7 FLORAL CAN BE INCORPORATED INTO THE FOOD PRESENTATION.

SOURCE: WWW.RODNEYBAILEY.COM

The floral designer will also handle removal and it is common for ceremony arrangements to be transported to the reception site. When bringing floral décor into a house of worship, it is important to know the policies, as some facilities require the arrangements to stay as a donation, others insist that they be removed and others do not allow floral décor at all. Because venue policies vary considerably, it is important to familiarize yourself with the regulations before your clients make their floral décor selections.

REFERENCES

de Wit, A. (2013) 'Trends in floral decor for weddings'. E-mail (11 February 2013).

Flowers and Plants Association (2013) 'What's in season?', Online. Available HTTP: <http://www.flowersandplants. org.uk/flowers/whats-in-season.html (accessed 6 February 2013).

Saeedi, M. (2013) 'Trends in floral decor for weddings'. E-mail (5 February 2013).

Consultant checklist and reminders for floral décor

☐ Assist your clients by asking them to make a list of all individuals who will be receiving personal flowers prior to meeting with the floral designer.

☐ Seasonality dictates availability and price of floral décor.

☐ Local farmers' markets or wholesale outlets can be an excellent avenue for flowers when working with clients on a budget.

☐ Flowers set the stage and create a focal point for the ceremony.

☐ Dark petals, both live and silk, can stain wood floors, carpets and clothing.

☐ Make sure that your clients budget in packing, delivery, installation and removal as part of floral décor costs.

☐ Know the floral décor rules of the ceremony and reception venues in terms of permission, installation and removal.

REVIEW

1. Name three floral varieties that are unique to each of the four seasons: spring, summer, fall and winter.

2. Name two floral varieties that are known for their heavy scents.

3. What are the three primary shapes of bridal bouquets?

4. What are three things that should be kept in mind with floral installation and removal?

TERMINOLOGY

- Cascade bouquet

- Collared bouquet

- Hand-tied bouquet

- Nosegay

- Pomander

- Round bouquet

- Topiary

- Tussie-Mussie

Photo 13.1 Stationery elements reinforce the couple's vision.

Source: www.RodneyBailey.com

STATIONERY ELEMENTS AND ETIQUETTE

Stationery elements are present throughout the wedding process and play ongoing roles in setting and carrying out the theme of a wedding. Stationery elements also bookend a wedding, as they are generally the first thing the guests see, with save-the-date cards and invitations, as well as the last, when thank-you notes are received.

It is important to remember the spelling of stationery, which ends with "ery" and not "ary," as commonly mistaken. The purpose of this chapter is to provide an overview of the different components and purposes of stationery, including common rules of etiquette. While taking up only 3 per cent of an average wedding budget, the wardrobe of stationery elements is quite broad. This chapter will cover save-the-date notices, invitations, calligraphy, ceremony programs, seating stationery, menus, personalized paper products, wedding announcements and thank-you notes.

SAVE-THE-DATE NOTICES

Save-the-date notices, which are usually sent out 6–18 months before the wedding, have become an increasingly popular trend in the past few years. As discussed in Chapter 5, they are particularly important for destination weddings or those weddings taking place over a long holiday weekend. The use of refrigerator magnets is quite popular, since they can act as a constant reminder. Save-the-date notices generally indicate the name of the bride and groom, the date and the location. The wedding start time is sometimes noted, as well as the wedding website should the couple have one. Often the phrase "Invitation to follow" is included so that the recipient knows that this is not the actual invitation. Save-the-date notices are usually informal and fun, but should still tie into the overall theme of the wedding.

Advise your clients that all potential guests should receive save-the-date notices. Some clients may want to save money by just sending them to the out-of-town guests, but the schedules of local friends and relatives are just as busy. Further, people know each other in these groups. If one friend comments on how clever the notice was on his or her Facebook page, another friend might see it and think, "I didn't get it. I must not be invited to the wedding." So it is important to be consistent.

INVITATIONS

Invitations involve a significant number of decisions. This section will cover the parts of the invitation, printing style, paper, font, wording, ordering and delivery. The decisions that are made for the invitations are commonly carried over to other stationery elements.

PARTS OF THE INVITATION

The most formal invitations include the following: outer envelope, inner envelope, invitation card, reception card and a response card. Invitations may also include additional information such as a directions card or a card with lodging options. It is thought that the dual envelopes originated from the time when mail was delivered by horse and carriage. Unpaved, muddy roads and the open elements would cause the outer envelope to become soiled. The outer envelope was discarded upon arrival and the invitation was then presented to the guest with the clean inner envelope. Now outer and inner envelopes are used for different wording purposes, as discussed in the wording section of this chapter. The outer envelope is gummed so that it can be sealed. The inner envelope is never sealed.

The invitation card gives the specifics of the event, as conferred in the wording section of this chapter. A reception card is needed primarily when the ceremony and reception are held at different venues; if they are at the same location, the words "Reception to follow" are often included on the invitation itself.

The response card, also called the reply card, has an interesting background in that traditionally this was never included; instead, the recipient of the invitation would write a formal letter of acceptance to the event. The response card emerged as a time-saving device in response to a more hurried pace of life. Further, some response cards will include a listing of entrée options so each guest can select his or her reception meal. Importantly, the response card must include a pre-addressed, stamped envelope for return purposes.

Some clients will ask if it is appropriate to include a gift registry card in with the invitation. This card offers the details regarding the stores where the couple has registered for gifts. While becoming more commonplace, etiquette suggests that it is inappropriate for couples to include this information in a wedding invitation, as it implies to the invited guests that they are required to purchase a gift and, moreover, that the gift must come from a certain place. Guests who wish to honor the couple with a gift should not feel constrained to a predetermined listing. For those who prefer to select something from the couple's registry, the store information can be readily requested and obtained through word-of-mouth, e-mail or the couple's wedding website.

PRINTING STYLE

For wedding invitations, four primary printing styles are used: engraving, letterpress, thermography and flat. *Engraving* is a traditional printing style that is very formal and expensive. Typically, brides that request engraved invitations are encouraged to do so by their mothers, who recall this classic style. With an engraved invitation, when you run your hand over the wording, you will feel a texture that is slightly raised and, when you turn the invitation over, there is an impression. A metal plate with the wording etched in is made specifically for the invitation. The paper, which is usually all cotton and watermarked, is pressed into the inked plate, and the impression is made.

A second style, which was also historically common, is letterpress. *Letterpress* is a process that is essentially the opposite of engraving, where the letters are raised and then pressed into a soft paper, leaving an indent on the front of the invitation. When you run your hand over it, you can feel the ridges. Letterpress is a classy and very expensive style of printing, in part because there are so few companies that offer this technique.

Thermography, in contrast to the first two styles, is inexpensive and accordingly is also the most commonly chosen printing style. Similar to engraving, *thermography* is raised printing that can be felt, but if you turn the invitation over there is no impression. The invitation is printed through a regular printing press, allowing for a very fast process. While the ink is still wet, it is sprayed with a powder and then it moves to another phase that has heat. The heat allows the powder and ink to chemically react, resulting in the raised ink. Some companies do not thoroughly brush off the remaining powder, and a gritty residue may remain.

Flat printing is also inexpensive and is chosen when the couple wants to include design elements that do not lend themselves to a raised style. Contemporary invitations with photographs, graphic designs or large images are not well suited for raised printing.

Invitations may also include an embossed image, which is a raised effect that does not include ink and is used for monograms or thematic images such as cultural symbols, flowers, shells, stars, leaves or snowflakes. Additional printing and artwork trends are discussed by Isabella Espella of Kate's Paperie in *Vendor Spotlight*, Case 13.1.

PHOTO 13.2 BOXED INVITATIONS ARE EXPENSIVE, BUT MAKE A UNIQUE PRESENTATION.

SOURCE: WWW.RODNEYBAILEY.COM

VENDOR SPOTLIGHT, CASE 13.1

ISABELLA ESPELLA

KATE'S PAPERIE

What are your brides asking for right now? The DIY trend is huge right now thanks to Pinterest and wedding shows on television. Brides are bringing in their own artwork and design motifs. So, instead of simply selecting a standard shell to symbolize a beach-themed wedding, brides are coming to me with their own artwork they have created. Foil stamping is a popular design motif right now. Foil stamping is a specialty printing process that uses heat, pressure, metal dies and foil film. The foil comes in rolls in a wide assortment of colors, finishes and optical effects. Foil stamping is somewhat similar to letterpress and engraving, in that the color is applied to paper with pressure. As a result, the foil process leaves a slightly raised impression on the paper. Foil stamping can be done in a rainbow of colors but brides most often request gold and silver.

How has technology helped or hurt your business? Technology has helped my business because of search engines. If you search "stationery" and "New York City," Kate's will come up so that is a big plus. It is fun and exciting to work with brides over the phone and through e-mail. The ability to scan samples is a huge plus as is the ability to easily and quickly send out a proof of the invitation to our clients. There are so many solutions now with technology. Online ordering, however, is our one enemy.

Can you describe your favorite wedding invitation of all time? I love everything from Hannah Handmade Couture Stationery. I love the way her stationery is made using traditional methods crafted by hand. Each invitation is presented in a box so it is utterly unique and interesting. These invitations can cost as much as $100 or more per invitation so they are exquisite and expensive. Brides should order these only if the sky is the limit. Oblation invitations are modern and clean cut with really thick cardstock too. I love everything Oblation does and highly recommend them to my brides.

What do you think we are going to be seeing in the future? Paper invitations and electronic R.S.V.P.s – a mixture of printing and digital reply. Also packaging everything into one "stationery ensemble" that consists of invitations, reply cards, wedding websites, stamps, etc. Digital calligraphy, it is cheaper and quicker than hand calligraphy. Trends that I think are definitely out are bows and vellum. These are so five years ago.

How did you get started? My aunt, Angelica Berrie, former CEO of Russ Berrie, the plush bear company, bought the company a few years ago. I have always been interested in design so this was a natural fit for me. I am the youngest in my family. I love coming to work every day and I am excited by what we are doing at Kate's.

If there was one thing that you could change about the stationery business, what would it be and why? I would change the fact that some brides are ordering stationery online and going directly to the vendor. This cuts out the personalized customer service that we offer our clients at our Custom Printing Bridal Salon and deprives the bride of one of the most special parts of the wedding planning process.

WEBSITE: *KATESPAPERIE.COM*

INVITATION PAPER

The paper selected is determined in part by the printing style, but is largely a matter of personal choice and budget. The cost of invitations is determined not only by the printing style, but also by the quality of the paper. Paper that is 100 per cent cotton or linen rag is significantly more expensive than a synthetic blend of paper. *Bond weight* of paper is another indication of quality; 65 pound cardstock is a good starting point for wedding invitations. The number increases along with the thickness of the paper, often coinciding with quality and price. As a point of comparison, typical computer paper is 20 pound stock. Handmade paper and/or features such as foils, gold-leaf edging, overlays, dried flowers and envelope liners also add significantly to the cost.

When selecting paper, color is another consideration. In the US, *ecru*-colored stock, which is a soft ivory shade, is the traditional choice, while in Europe white is more frequently chosen. For contemporary invitations, a full spectrum of colors is available and a couple can readily find invitations to match the theme and tone of their wedding.

FONT

The range of fonts has grown significantly, and whether a classic or contemporary font is chosen will be based on the style of the invitation itself. Options to consider include: 1) cursive or printed style; 2) all uppercase letters versus a mixture of uppercase and lower case; 3) the inclusion of monograms or other large specialty fonts; and 4) ink color. The traditional ink color for the font is black, but colored inks have become very common. For example, a fall wedding might include a rust or olive green ink on an invitation with a leaf motif. Nancy Smith discusses ink and other stationery trends in *Vendor Spotlight*, Case 13.2.

VENDOR SPOTLIGHT, CASE 13.2

NANCY SMITH

WALTON STREET STATIONERS

How did you become interested in starting a stationery business? I have always loved stationery. I can vividly remember my first note cards. They were ladybugs and rickrack. They were adorable and cheery. I worked in retail for many years but I have always loved stationery because it is a feast for the senses. My business name, Walton Street Stationers, is named after my very favorite street in London. Lined with unique storefronts and adorable shops, Walton Street became the inspiration behind my stationery business.

What unique styles are brides requesting? Individual expressions of who they are. They are ordering less ecru invitations with black ink. Styles are a little less formal. Brides are asking for unusual-colored ink, think classic with a twist. Having said that, 50 per cent of my brides are ordering engraved invitations or letterpress. Weddings are the one time to splurge on these made-by-hand printing techniques.

What are the biggest changes in your business model? Technology is the biggest influence. With so many couples having a wedding website, there is no need to clutter the invitation with lots of inserts. Also, I love getting my brides' e-mailed proofs. It is nice to be able to show them something so quickly.

What components make an invitation fabulous? I love any wedding invitation on exquisite paper with fabulous ink. I also love when the guests get the chance and have the space to write a personal message on the response card. One of my favorite invitations of all time was one that I received that was entirely hand calligraphed. It had a silver bell at the top and the wording was written as a personal letter and the font was created by a woman who had created formal invitations for the White House. It was elegant, lovely and memorable.

Will electronic invitations be taking over in the future? On the contrary, I think there is going to be a backlash against electronic mail and more brides are going to be interested in appreciating the art of the note. Writing a note is a sensory experience. Life slows down and you can relish it and not rush through it. With a handwritten note you know that someone cared enough to write the note on good paper. It is slow and it is elegant and it is the way it should be done. I am not a fan of websites such as paperlesspost.com and Evite.com. I would love all brides to work face-to-face with a retailer instead of online.

I just think that you cannot underestimate the value of a personal relationship. There is a person who is putting his or her heart and soul into your order, looking out for you and focusing on just your order. What is not to love about that?

WEBSITE: *WALTONSTREETSTATIONERS.NET*

WORDING

Wording begins with the envelopes. The outer envelope is the most formal, with full names and titles used. For the addresses, there should be no street or state abbreviations. For example, use Road rather than Rd. and Colorado rather than CO. The outer envelope should be addressed to the primary recipient or recipients, while the inner envelope can include additional invitees using formal or informal names. For instance, the outer envelope might be addressed to Mr. Aiden Aabas, while the inner envelope states Aiden and Guest. Similarly, an outer envelope might state Commander Jackson Johnson and Doctor Grace Tighe-Johnson, while the inner states Jackson, Grace, Madison and Mason, which includes the names of the guests' children. However, the most formal invitations would use the full titles on both the inner and outer envelopes.

The wording of the invitation itself can get quite complicated when considering changing family dynamics. For example, some brides have two sets of parents or even three, so it is not feasible to list all of their names on the invitation. In general, there are six parts to the invitation wording with associated lines: host; request; bride and groom; date and time; location; and special instructions.

The wording of the response card should mimic the formality of the invitation. Three elements found in most response cards include a space for guest name(s); an indication of attendance; and the date by which a response is desired. If the guests are able to choose an entrée or if other decisions are to be made, information regarding their options is also included.

Following are three examples of how the invitation might be worded, each accompanied by a response card that reflects the invitation's tone. Figure 13.1 is the most traditional and formal, with the parents of the bride acting as hosts. Furthermore, the R.S.V.P. in the request line means that the guests are to send a personal reply; therefore, no response card will be included. A formal invitation without the R.S.V.P. line would include a response card with wording such as found in Figure 13.2, where the guests would write a formal reply and the assumption is that they will know the information to be included. The open response card can also be used for less formal weddings, as it allows guests to write creative notes that are often saved by the couple in an album.

DOCTOR AND MRS. PETER OLMSTED	Host Line
REQUEST THE HONOR OF YOUR PRESENCE	Request Line
AT THE MARRIAGE OF THEIR DAUGHTER	
SOPHIA MARIE	Bride and Groom
TO	
MR. ELIJAH MICHAEL WOOD	
SATURDAY, THE FIFTEENTH OF OCTOBER	Date and Time
TWO THOUSAND AND SIXTEEN	
AT TWO O'CLOCK	
INTERNATIONAL CATHEDRAL	Location
LA JOLLA, CALIFORNIA	
R.S.V.P. BLACK TIE	Special Instructions

Figure 13.1 Invitation wording for traditional, black tie wedding

THE FAVOR OF A REPLY IS REQUESTED BY

THE FIFTH OF SEPTEMBER

TWO THOUSAND AND SIXTEEN

Figure 13.2 Formal response card

TOGETHER WITH THEIR FAMILIES	Host Line
AVA CYNTHIA KOVACS	Bride and Groom
AND	
CARTER ANTHONY GAMBERALE	
INVITE YOU TO CELEBRATE THEIR MARRIAGE	Request Line
FRIDAY, THE THIRD OF FEBRUARY	Date and Time
TWO THOUSAND AND SEVENTEEN	
AT HALF PAST SEVEN O'CLOCK	
SAINT DOMINIC'S CHURCH	Location
DALLAS, TEXAS	
ADULT CEREMONY	Special Instructions

FIGURE 13.3 INVITATION WORDING FOR BLENDED FAMILY WITH ADULT-ONLY CEREMONY

KINDLY RESPOND BY THE FOURTH OF JANUARY

M _____

___ ACCEPTS   ___ REGRETS

___ NUMBER OF CHILDREN UNDER AGE TEN TO ATTEND

(CHILD CARE TO BE PROVIDED ON SITE)

ADULT MEAL SELECTIONS

___ CHICKEN   ___ BEEF   ___ FISH

FIGURE 13.4 DIRECTED RESPONSE CARD

Figure 13.3 offers an option of wording for a couple with blended families and therefore too many hosts to list on the invitation. The wording also gives one example of how couples can inform their guests that children are not invited to the wedding. The associated response card, seen in Figure 13.4, has directed wording, offering a line for the names, where the uppercase "M" can be used to indicate Mr., Mrs. or Ms. Guests are to check whether or not they will attend in the space provided, indicate the number of children they will bring, and select the desired meal for each guest. The fact that childcare will be provided on site reinforces the adult nature of this wedding.

Figure 13.5 illustrates how a casual invitation can be worded, where the bride and groom are acting as hosts and the reception is held in the same location as the wedding, so no reception card would be included. Notice that, in this example, the numbers are not spelled out and the lettering includes lower case. The response card, seen in Figure 13.6, is similarly casual and consistent with the beach theme. Note that, as seen in this example, most invitation specialists are now suggesting that couples use "Name(s)" rather than the uppercase "M" because it avoids the problem of what to do for doctors, attorneys, religious leaders, those with military ranks and others with titles that do not begin with an "M."

The wording of the reception card is the most straightforward and includes the location and time of the reception. If there are going to be a significant number of out-of-town guests, it is also advisable to include a directions card. Also, if it is an adult ceremony and/or reception, this is generally repeated on the reception card. Couples who feel very strongly about not having children at their wedding should indicate this in two or three different places. Ambiguity may arise as to what age represents the cut-off, as some couples do not want young children, such as those under the age of five, whereas others do not want guests under the age of eighteen. Often word of mouth and e-mail communication are used to clarify any questions that arise.

ORDERING INVITATIONS

Suggest to your clients that they start working with a stationery specialist four to six months before their wedding. Most stationery vendors can work within a shorter time frame, but the creative options get limited the closer couples get to their wedding date. It is also important to allow plenty of time to go through the proofing process. Some invitations take multiple proofs before the desired look is achieved. Remind your clients that, once they have approved the proof, they accept full responsibility for the information, spelling, print style, font, punctuation, layout and color separation.

When ordering invitations, the couple should count the number needed based on households rather than individual guests. A common mistake is to order the number of invitations based on the number of guests, but, if they are inviting 100 people, they typically do not need 100 invitations. They probably need between 50 and 75 depending on how many singles, couples and children will be invited. At the same time, encourage your clients to make sure they do not under-order, as it is much more expensive to reorder invitations than it is to have ten or so extra invitations printed. Once a company has the initial order off the press, the order is done and, if it comes back,

Chloe and Jack	Bride and Groom
Would Love to Sea You	Request Line
At Their Casual, Beach Front Wedding	
Saturday, August 20, 2016	Date and Time
12:00 Noon	
Wild Dunes Resort	Location
Isle of Palms, South Carolina	
Lunch and an Afternoon at the Beach to Follow	Special Instructions

FIGURE 13.5 INVITATION FOR A CASUAL WEDDING WITH RECEPTION AT SAME LOCATION

Please sand your reply by July 11

_____

Name(s)

____ We shell sea you there!

____ Sorry, we are all tide up.

FIGURE 13.6 INFORMAL RESPONSE CARD THAT TIES INTO WEDDING THEME

it is a brand-new job. Remind your clients that the first 25 of any stationery item will be the most expensive and the price drops significantly after that. Further, most high-end companies do not accept invitation orders of less than 50. For example, 50 high-quality invitations can cost $12 or more per invitation but, when ordering 100 of the same design, the price may drop to $10 apiece. Less expensive invitations follow the same pattern and can drop from $6 each for orders of 25 to $2 each for orders of 100 or more.

DELIVERY

Encourage your clients to have the invitations weighed for postage purposes, as many invitations weigh more than one ounce with all of the inserts, and the last thing a couple wants is for their invitation to arrive with postage due. Even if the mailing weighs less than one ounce, additional postage will still be necessary if the envelope is bulky or the invitation is oddly shaped; for example, square invitations require additional postage. You should also advise your clients to have the invitations hand cancelled, again because the number of inserts can cause bulk and can be mangled going through the postage meter. For etiquette purposes, the hand cancellation is also a more elegant look. Suggest to your clients that, before sending out the full mailing, they mail one invitation to themselves as a test run. They should include all parts of the invitation. This test allows them to see how long the invitation takes to reach them and determine if it arrives in good shape.

The post office carries an array of floral and "Love" stamps that are popular for mailing wedding invitations. Alternatively, your clients can order custom designed postage stamps through websites such as *Photo.Stamps.com*. The stamp might be the couple's engagement photo or an image that ties into the theme of the wedding. For example, if the couple is having the wedding in a vineyard, the stamp might include a photo of grapes on the vine, a wine barrel or a bottle of wine from the vineyard. Couples should also consider to whom they want the response card to be returned. Traditionally, it was returned to the parents of the bride, but today it is just as likely to be returned to the bride.

Invitations should be mailed anywhere from six to ten weeks before the wedding. Some couples will mail to their "A" list ten weeks out, then their "B" list and sometimes even a "C" list, based on rejections from the earlier groups. A *tiered guest list* has significant etiquette implications, as peer groups talk and people can quickly become aware that they are not in the top group, leading to hurt feelings.

As an eco-friendly alternative to paper invitations, some couples are going paperless. Peggy Post (2011), who is a director of the Emily Post Institute and the great-granddaughter-in-law of its namesake, states that, because electronic invitations to non-wedding and pre-wedding events, like showers, are already fairly commonplace, "It is no surprise that the online wedding invitation, complete with bells and whistles, is being hyped as a busy bride's best friend. It's fast, it's easy, it's cheap, it's green, and it's fun."

However, she encourages couples to think through this decision carefully, as an invitation sets the overall tone for the forthcoming event, and online invitations are a casual precursor for one of the most important days of your clients' lives. She explains that the time and thought that is put into an invitation with elegant paper, a handwritten address and a beautiful stamp sends a message to the recipients that they are important. With the dramatic decrease in communication by postal delivery, the wedding invitation often becomes a keepsake.

CALLIGRAPHY

A calligrapher's hand printing is a very elegant and personal way to create stationery elements. Guests have been known to talk for years about invitations they received that were hand lettered by a calligrapher. A calligrapher can be hired to letter any stationery element, but is most commonly brought on to address the envelopes. If a calligraphy specialist is hired for the invitation, menu or other item that can be used for all guests, this person will hand design a template that is then typeset and printed. Because envelopes are unique to each guest, the time investment and cost are significant, with the charge for each set of inner and outer envelopes ranging from $5 to $7. This beautiful touch is therefore usually reserved for weddings with above-average budgets.

Because hiring a calligrapher can be cost-prohibitive, couples generally explore other options for addressing their envelopes. Handwriting is considered to be more personal and some couples even have gatherings where friends or family members with elegant handwriting will help them with this task. Etiquette dictates that black ink should be used when addressing envelopes by hand. Be certain to have your clients order plenty of extra envelopes if they plan to use hand addressing, as this process is subject to error.

Because of the wasted envelopes and time associated with handwriting, couples are increasingly turning to computerized addressing. Most stationery vendors can assist with this task and calligraphy fonts now exist that are nearly as beautiful as hand calligraphy. The address should be printed directly on the envelope; be certain to advise your clients against using mailing labels, as they undermine the elegance of the invitation.

CEREMONY PROGRAMS

Approximately 70 per cent of couples use programs to guide guests through their ceremony. Programs come in all different shapes and sizes and are often designed and printed by the couple to save on costs. The purpose of the program is to introduce the guests to the bridal party and set forth the organization of the ceremony. If held in a house of worship, it is important to determine if there are any restrictions regarding program wording.

PHOTO 13.3 CROSS-CULTURAL PROGRAMS APPEAL TO ALL GUESTS.

SOURCE: WWW.RODNEYBAILEY.COM

Generally, all members of the wedding party are listed, and information regarding readings, prayers, responses, music and vows will be included. Some programs give details regarding special ceremony elements. For example, if the couple will be jumping the broom, an African American tradition, a paragraph regarding the history of this tradition might be included. Many couples also include a dedication or message of thanks in their program.

For the most part, guests do not want to read *War and Peace* during the wedding ceremony, so advise your clients that they do not have to go overboard, because too much reading will draw guests' attention away from the ceremony itself. If the couple is cross-cultural and there are guests present who speak different languages, it is a very welcoming touch to have the program printed in both languages, side by side. Some couples create a newspaper account for their program or favors, employing companies such as *newsfavor.com*.

Program design is frequently initiated late in the planning process, as the ceremony is often finalized only a few weeks before the wedding. However, advise your clients not to wait until the last minute, as they do not want to be tying ribbons on programs the night before the wedding.

Beyond the program, other specialized ceremony elements require stationery. For example, pew cards can be used when reserving special seats for honored guests or if the immediate family needs more than the first two rows. Many stationery professionals also can design a personalized ketubah, which is the Jewish marriage contract introduced in Chapter 11. Further, couples who write their own vows often like to have them printed and framed. Finally, guest books are often specially designed and can be used for the ceremony and/or the reception.

PHOTO 13.4 STATIONERY ELEMENTS CAN BE USED AS FAVORS.

SOURCE: WWW.RODNEYBAILEY.COM

PHOTO 13.5 CEREMONY ARTIFACTS CAN BE BEAUTIFULLY DETAILED.

SOURCE: WWW.RODNEYBAILEY.COM

SEATING STATIONERY

If a couple wishes to designate where guests will sit at the wedding reception, seating stationery should be used. For example, if cocktails are over at 6:45 p.m. and dinner is going to be served at 7:00 p.m., then that leaves only 15 minutes to navigate what might be several hundred people into the dining area. Seating stationery can include a seating chart, escort cards, place cards and table numbers.

A seating chart gives an alphabetized listing of guests. Next to each name, the table where each is seated is indicated. Seating charts are large and can be mounted on foam board or placed in a rented frame; however, congestion may result if the number of guests is more than 100. Alternatively, individual escort cards can be creatively presented and quickly retrieved when well organized.

Table numbers allow guests to know when they have reached the right place. If using numbers, options such as #1, ONE or Table 1 can be selected. Advise your clients to avoid using Roman numerals because, in a muted ballroom, numbers such as XI, XII and XIII look too similar and cause confusion for both guests and staff. Keep table numbers simple and make the font big and bold

PHOTO 13.6 ESCORT CARDS CAN BE IMAGINATIVE.

SOURCE: WWW.RODNEYBAILEY.COM

for easy location. Table numbers are often placed in stands or frames that can be rented from your stationery specialist, catering company or floral designer if incorporated into the centerpiece.

A place card is used if the guests have not only a specific table, but also a designated seat. When reaching that level of detail, remind your clients that they will need to allow plenty of time to work on the site layout, as discussed in Chapter 16.

PHOTO 13.7 PLACES THAT HAVE SPECIAL MEANING TO THE COUPLE CAN BE DISPLAYED
AS TABLE MARKERS.

SOURCE: WWW.RODNEYBAILEY.COM

Seating stationery allows for design touches that tie into the theme of the wedding. For example, a winter theme might have escort cards embossed with a snowflake, while a Parisian theme might use tourist sites such as the Eiffel Tower and the Louvre to designate tables. A couple that loves to hike may use the names of rivers, mountains or trees to differentiate the tables. Encourage your clients to be creative while staying organized. Avoid confusing approaches such as the seating method used in *Consultant in Action*, Case 13.3.

CONSULTANT IN ACTION, CASE 13.3

WHERE DO I SIT?

You are a relatively new wedding planner, working with a young and energetic client, Sako. All the details for Sako's wedding day are coming together smoothly. As you begin discussing the final seating arrangements for the 150 guests, Sako tells you not to worry about the table numbers because she has it covered. You have so many other tasks to think about that you assume Sako will create the table numbers herself and bring them to the reception. The day of the wedding comes and you are finalizing all details and making sure everything is set to go. One thing you forget to check on, though, is the table numbers because it was not on your to-do list. Twenty minutes before the reception doors are due to open, you make the final check of the ballroom and discover that the tables have been designated by activities such as Skiing, Bicycling, Running, etc., all activities enjoyed by the bride and groom. You look around for a seating chart to make sure that each guest has been assigned a table. Unfortunately, you cannot find the seating chart, so you step into the cocktail hour area to ask Sako where it is. Sako smiles and says, "I took care of it. We don't need a seating chart. I thought it would be fun to have the guests go from table to table looking for their seat like a scavenger hunt. They will know they have found the right table because we have enjoyed that activity together in the past and because there is a pile of photos at each table of whom I want to sit there. Isn't that the most clever and unique way to seat guests that you've ever heard of?" The ballroom doors open and the guests begin to aimlessly look for their seats with puzzled expressions on their faces.

WHAT DO YOU DO?

MENUS

Formal receptions often include menu cards that indicate the names of the dishes to be served and may also designate the primary ingredients. Menus heighten guests' expectations, create a sense of culinary anticipation and can aid in the understanding of cultural traditions.

PHOTO 13.8 MENUS CREATE CULINARY ANTICIPATION.

SOURCE: WWW.RODNEYBAILEY.COM

In terms of design, menus often include the monogram of the newlywed couple and can also include creative terminology. For example, instead of using the expression "First Course," this meal stage can be called "Romance" or another term that reflects the couple's theme. Similar to signature drinks, caterers work with couples to create specialty entrées with clever, enticing names. Menu cards can be printed on cardstock or, alternatively, a fine parchment paper that is rolled and then tied. They are often tucked inside each guest's napkin, placed on a charger plate or leaned up against the water glass.

PHOTO 13.9 MENUS AND SEATING STATIONERY ENHANCE THE DINING EXPERIENCE.

SOURCE: WWW.RODNEYBAILEY.COM

PERSONALIZED PAPER PRODUCTS

Personalized paper products such as cocktail napkins, boxes, bags or matches can further develop a wedding theme. Napkins are the most commonly chosen and come in a multitude of colors and styles. They are generally placed on the cake table and in the bar area. Often the napkins just include a monogram or the newlyweds' names and the wedding date, but they can also include a touch of humor. For example, one couple had the phrase "Eat, drink and remarry" printed on the napkins, as it was the second marriage for both bride and groom.

Personalized boxes and bags are often purchased for use with favors, and are typically filled with mints, chocolates or some other treat. Matches have become less common, in particular because most reception venues now prohibit smoking; however, when the favor is a candle, personalized match books can add a nice touch. Chapter 18 includes a detailed discussion of favors and gifts.

PHOTO 13.10 CASUAL PAPER PRODUCTS INCLUDE A TOUCH OF HUMOR.

SOURCE: WWW.RODNEYBAILEY.COM

WEDDING ANNOUNCEMENTS

If the couple has a small wedding due to budget constraints or because they held a destination wedding where many friends and family members were not invited or could not attend, then a wedding *announcement* is a courtesy notice that the wedding took place. The announcement simply states the names of the bride and groom, the date of the wedding and the location where it was held.

Announcements are only sent to those who were not in attendance at the wedding, as it would be redundant to send these notices to those who were present. They are usually mailed within a week after the wedding. Announcements should never go out until after the wedding, just in case it does not take place.

THANK-YOU NOTES

Thank-you notes, also known as *informals*, are a type of social stationery. Informals can match the invitation or they can be generic, allowing them to be used for other purposes. As stated earlier, small stationery orders cost significantly more than larger orders. For instance, 50 informals might cost $100 while 100 are priced at $130.

Informals commonly include the monogram of the newlyweds. If the bride is taking the last name of the groom, her first initial would be on the left, the initial of the shared last name is in a larger font in the middle and the groom's first initial is on the right. If she is not taking his name, it is common to have her initials or full name printed on the left followed by a large ampersand and then the groom's initials or full name.

Thank-you messages should never be pre-printed or generic, as each note should be specific to both the guest and the gift. For large weddings, consultants often assist with gift documentation and thank-you note writing so that the information is correct and the notes go out in a timely fashion. Advise your clients to keep each card with the associated gift, so as to avoid the sticky situation of not knowing whom to thank for what gift. In terms of etiquette, informals should be sent out within one month after the wedding. However, a late thank-you note is better than no thank-you note, so inform your clients that they should not use tardiness as an excuse for bypassing this important task. Separate shower and wedding gifts from the same person should be acknowledged in different notes; further, monogrammed informals indicating a changed last name should never be sent out until after the wedding has taken place.

REFERENCES

Espella, I. (2013) 'Kate's Paperie'. Personal interview, Kate's Paperie SoHo Location (7 February 2013).

Post, P. (2011) 'Wedding etiquette', Online. Available HTTP: <http://www.nytimes.com/2011/12/25/fashion/weddings/wedding-etiquette.html?_r=0> (accessed 10 March 2013).

Smith, N. (2013) 'Walton Street Stationers'. Personal interview (19 February 2013).

CONSULTANT CHECKLIST AND REMINDERS FOR STATIONERY ELEMENTS AND ETIQUETTE

☐ Remember that stationery ends with "ery."

☐ Printing style and paper quality will dictate the cost of stationery.

☐ While the wording of stationery elements is etiquette driven, reassure your clients that they should select wording that fits their personalities.

☐ A couple that does not wish to have children at their ceremony or reception should make this clear in their invitations.

☐ When ordering invitations, base it on the number of households rather than the number of individuals.

☐ Order enough invitations to prevent the need for a reorder.

☐ When mailing invitations, be aware of increased postage for bulky or square-shaped envelopes and have them hand cancelled.

REVIEW

1. Name the five parts of most formal invitations.

2. Name and explain the distinctions between the four styles of printing.

3. What are the six lines typical to invitation wording?

4. Name one rule of etiquette for each of the following stationery elements: save-the-date notices, envelopes, response cards, announcements and thank-you notes.

TERMINOLOGY

- Bond weight

- Calligraphy

- Ecru

- Embossed

- Engraving

- Foil stamping

- Informals

- Letterpress

- Save-the-date notices

- Thermography

- Tiered guest list

- Vellum

Photo 14.1 Photography takes a moment in time and elevates it to art.

Source: www.RodneyBailey.com

14

PHOTOGRAPHY AND VIDEOGRAPHY

ALL THE GUESTS HAVE RETURNED HOME, THE CAKE IS EATEN, THE FLOWERS HAVE DIED AND THE DRESS HAS AGED TO YELLOW. WHAT REMAINS ARE THE MEMORIES, MANY OF WHICH HAVE BEEN CAPTURED DIGITALLY OR ON FILM. PHOTOGRAPHY AND VIDEOGRAPHY COMPRISE 10 PER CENT OF THE AVERAGE WEDDING BUDGET; HOWEVER, THEIR ENDURING RESULTS JUSTIFY WHY MANY COUPLES INVEST 15 PER CENT OR MORE. CONSULTANTS TYPICALLY ADVISE CLIENTS TO GET THE BEST PHOTOGRAPHER AND VIDEOGRAPHER THAT THEY CAN AFFORD BECAUSE THE MOMENTS THEY CAPTURE CAN CONTINUALLY BRING THE COUPLE BACK TO THEIR WEDDING DAY.

Changes in technology have revolutionized wedding photography and videography. This chapter will highlight: 1) the movement from film to digital photography; 2) the two primary styles of photography; 3) album design; 4) other wedding-related trends in photography; and 5) advances in videography.

MOVEMENT FROM FILM TO DIGITAL PHOTOGRAPHY

While a few, specialized wedding photographers still use film, the vast majority have moved to digital because of the benefits it offers their clients. First, digital improvements over the past several years allow color, saturation and sharpness to be superior to what film can achieve. Second, digital allows for online proofing, meaning the couple and their friends and family can look through the proofs regardless of where they reside. Third, digital allows for almost instantaneous feedback. Rodney Bailey, who is the exclusive photographer for this book and is featured in *Vendor Spotlight*, Case 14.1, explains that, when he is hired for two-day coverage such as the wedding day and a brunch the following day, he can pull together a set of images from the wedding and set them to music for a slide show to be presented during the brunch. This same slide show can be made available online so the couple can share images with anyone in the world. Finally, digital images can be safely stored in multiple locations so there is no fear of losing original work.

A misnomer about digital media is that it is less expensive to execute than film. Top photographers run five or more high-end computers with enormous amounts of storage to handle the flow of processing. They also constantly update their cameras to have access to the latest technology. Rodney explains that digital processing takes three times the effort of film processing due to the number of images captured as well as the creativity that goes into modern album design. When helping your clients compare prices, ensure that the photographer's packages include photo shoot time, production time, album design, reprint costs and options regarding access to digital negatives.

STYLES OF PHOTOGRAPHY

Two primary styles of photography are traditional and photojournalistic. Consider your parents' or grandparents' wedding album. You probably see a fair amount of black and white. More significantly, all the pictures are carefully posed. Using the traditional style, photographers will even stop the reception to stage a moment. For example, the bride and groom might pretend to cut the cake to get a good pose. Then they move on to the next staged moment. Wedding albums used to include nothing but groups lined up and the couple stiffly positioned for staged shots.

VENDOR SPOTLIGHT, CASE 14.1

RODNEY BAILEY

WEDDING PHOTOJOURNALISM BY RODNEY BAILEY

How did you select photography as a career? I fell in love with photography at a very young age. At the age of 12, I worked all summer mowing lawns in my neighborhood to save up enough money for a camera. I began on the path of documenting weddings at age 16 when I took pictures, just playing around, at a friend's wedding. They had hired a professional photographer but ended up liking my images much more. So, at that point, I contacted a local photographer for an apprenticeship; he saw talent in me and allowed me to do 50 weddings on my own in the first year. I developed my photojournalistic style early on and started my business from there.

What are the most unique weddings you have ever photographed? Probably the most interesting and memorable wedding that I documented took place in Rome, where the couple received a Papal blessing. After Rome, I documented their honeymoon in Paris. Another unique wedding was a 4-day Hindu wedding where we documented close to 60 hours of activities. They had 450 guests at the ceremony, 600 at the bride's reception and 900 at the groom's reception. They were able to have 12th and Constitution in Washington DC closed for several hours for their wedding parade, including the groom riding down the street on an elephant.

What do you like about the photojournalistic style? Most of my clientele and their wedding guests don't even realize I'm there taking pictures. One of the best things about this approach is that the bride and groom really get to enjoy their wedding day, and I'm there to document the story in a witness form. I love the photojournalistic style because to me the true emotion comes through when someone doesn't realize that they are being photographed. If a moment is captured and not directed, it feels and looks more natural because it is more natural.

What distinguishes you from other photographers? Weddings I document can span over days and end up with over 4,500 images. I find that most clients are just overwhelmed, even with 500 images, with the process of saying, "How are we going to select 100 images or 150 images for our wedding album?" So I take it a step further. And that's one of those things that definitely sets me apart from a lot of the other photographers. I actually design the album myself and provide my clients an album proposal that walks them through the images I think look best. I'm going for artistry and storytelling, and spend about 10 hours in the layout and design process. I spoke to three or four thousand photographers at a conference in New York and polled them by asking if they would ever consider doing a proposal for their clients. Ninety-nine per cent of them said "No," so this is absolutely what makes my services unique. I want my clients to LOVE their wedding images and have their album be reflective of their wedding day.

Beyond weddings, what are your other specialties? Probably 20 per cent of our business comes from corporate and commercial work, which brings in everything from *Vogue* and Disney calling us to working with clients like Oprah and *O Magazine*. I did a great shoot with Oprah and 5,000 women that included an online aspect where all the event participants could download the photographs from that day's seminars and activities. It was great to meet her. It was probably one of the highlights of my career because she is just an amazing woman in every aspect. I also do quite a bit of work with the Library of Congress, and enjoy the political aspect as well.

Please share a humorous situation that occurred while you were documenting a wedding. The most recent humorous situation happened when I was taking evening pictures of a bride and groom in Georgetown. We were having a great time getting some amazing shots of night scenes while the couple was walking around. All of the sudden, a man walks past us saying, "Congratulations . . . here's to the happy couple" and then proceeds to flash the poor bride and groom. We were all in shock and did the only thing we could do . . . laugh hysterically. Of course, I had to snap a few images to document this "special" moment of their wedding day!

WEBSITE: *WWW.RODNEYBAILEY.COM*
DANIELA CONYNGHAM CONDUCTED PARTS OF THIS INTERVIEW

Only within the last two decades has the *photojournalistic style* evolved within the context of weddings. This style means that the photographer is documenting real moments, almost like telling a story. It is very candid, fluid, spontaneous and versatile. Photos are taken from a variety of directions, with pictures from angled positions more likely than those taken front and center. When hiring a photojournalist for their wedding, most couples still request a few staged photographs, primarily of family members grouped together, but the vast majority of the images represent real moments. Rodney mentions that, in a typical 8-hour shoot, he spends only about 20 minutes taking formal, staged photographs and the rest of the images are photojournalistic in nature. The distinctions between traditional photography and photojournalism are highlighted in Table 14.1.

Two other styles of wedding photography that have recently emerged are *fashion* and *fine art*. Rodney explains that fashion wedding photography emphasizes the look and feel of a modern magazine, as if working with models. Fine art wedding photography is concerned with setting a scene by manipulating effects such as lighting and color composition.

Most photographers, regardless of style, work with at least one assistant, and generally have more than one if there are more than 400 guests at the wedding. With an assistant, one photographer

PHOTO 14.2 THE PHOTOJOURNALIST STYLE IS UNOBTRUSIVE.

SOURCE: WWW.RODNEYBAILEY.COM

TABLE 14.1 COMPARING TWO WEDDING PHOTOGRAPHY STYLES

Traditional Style	Photojournalistic Style
• Posed	• Candid
• Staged	• Natural
• Directed	• Spontaneous
• Front and center	• All angles
• Hands-on	• Hands-off
• Significant communication	• Little communication
• Traditional mount album	• Flush mount album

can capture images of the bride as she is getting ready, while the other can be with the groom. Further, at many ceremony sites, one can be on the floor, while the other can get the overhead perspective from the balcony. Importantly, some ceremony sites do not allow photography and even those that do generally have strict policies regarding photographer location and flash. Experienced wedding photographers use *available light* rather than flash and stay unobtrusive by using a telephoto lens and gathering images from the back of the ceremony site.

SELECTING THE RIGHT PHOTOGRAPHER

Not all couples prefer the photojournalistic style and many photographers remain partial to the traditional style. You should introduce style options to your clients and allow them to select the one that speaks to them. The number of images that a photographer takes at a wedding can vary significantly based on personal style and approach, so this is an important consideration when comparing photographers. Recommend to your clients that they meet with a minimum of two photographers to take a look at sample albums and get to know them in person. The personality of the photographer can be as important as the skill set; it is much more enjoyable for everyone if the clients get along well with the photographer. Further, each couple has a sense of what they want their wedding album to look like. There is no single correct interpretation.

It is also important that the wedding consultant and the photographer have a good working relationship, in particular for a traditional photo shoot. The consultant is the main point of contact with the photographer. You will indicate what pictures are requested and assist with gathering individuals for group shots. This allows the couple to enjoy their day without worrying about herding the bridal party, family members and others for key photos. The photographer should also understand the cultural needs of your clients. When, where and how wedding photographs are taken can vary significantly by culture, as illustrated in *Culture Corner*, Case 14.2. Individual needs can also be addressed by the photographer. For instance, Denise Chastain (2013) of Modern

PHOTO 14.3 THE RIGHT PHOTOGRAPHER WILL DOCUMENT ALL WEDDING DETAILS.

SOURCE: WWW.RODNEYBAILEY.COM

Wedding Photography relays a story where one of the groomsmen was in the military and, at the last minute, couldn't attend the wedding because he was called to duty. In his place, the wedding party created a life-size cardboard cutout of him, dressed in a military uniform. The cutout was included in every aspect of the wedding and all of the wedding party photos, creating great fun for the guests as the cutout was "escorted" to the various locations. Denise captured these genuine moments that paid tribute to the missing groomsman and brought humor to the whole wedding.

ALBUM DESIGN

The albums that result from the two styles of photography are also vastly different. With a traditional album, the photographs are bound and bordered. Clients can split the page apart and pull the photograph out of the page. The onset of digital photography and the photojournalistic style allowed for the origination of the flush mount album. *Flush mount albums* allow a picture or a group of pictures to be the page, just like photographs in a book or magazine. Top-quality flush mount album companies offer up to a 200-year guarantee and coat the pages to protect the photographic paper from liquid spills, fingerprints, fading and peeling.

CULTURE CORNER, CASE 14.2

WEDDING PHOTOGRAPHY IN CHINA

For most Chinese couples, the wedding photography is taken three to six months before the actual wedding day. The couple will visit photography studios and look through albums and costumes to decide which studio suits their needs. Once they have decided on a studio, they select a photography package that includes hair and makeup for the photo shoot, the photos, album and then separate hair and makeup for the actual wedding day. The package does not include photos taken on the wedding day, just staged photos taken well in advance. The couple returns to the studio on the appointed day for the photography session. This is an all-day wedding shoot. This session can last as long as 12 hours and can involve as many as 15 changes of clothing and backdrops. For example, a bridal couple will be photographed wearing traditional Chinese silk wedding attire, Western wedding attire, a mix of cocktail outfits and romantic costumes inspired by the media, such as Cinderella and her prince standing in front of a castle backdrop. Each change of clothing is provided by the photography studio and worn only for the day. The resulting wedding images are a stylized mix of what the couple looks like and what they fantasize they will look like as a married couple. Photography studios are generally selected for the costumes they have rather than for the skill of the photographer. For the actual wedding day, a videographer may be hired to record the day's events or the couple will just rely on the photographic skills of their guests.

CASE SUBMITTED BY YAO AND DAVID WOSICKI

Keep in mind that, with any album, your clients will get what they pay for, with the album leaders offering noticeably superior quality. For example, only the highest-quality flush mount album companies have patented binding systems that allow the center seam to be flat, offering a beautiful panoramic spread without a bulky midpoint. Rodney notes that top-of-the-line albums have leather binding, lay-flat technology and archival mat board with options for customized graphics and 3-D effects.

The flush mounted album has also increased the options for album size. Traditionally, couples would have one album made and then get a handful of individual photos reprinted for family and friends. Now, the couple's entire album can be readily duplicated in a smaller size. Rodney explains that, for the couple, 11″ x 14″ and 11″ x 11″ sizes are the most common, and some are as large as 15″ x 15″. Commonly selected scaled-down versions are 8″ x 8″, 6″ x 6″ and even a 3″ x 3″ mini-album.

Most couples request a mixture of color and black and white photos in their albums. The flush mounted style allows for a seamless integration of color and black and white. Black and white or *sepia* (i.e., brown and gray tones) photos are classic, elegant and timeless. The lack of bright colors allows the viewer to focus on specific details; for example, rather than noticing the pinks and yellows in a bouquet, the eye is drawn to the shape of the petals and the curve of a ribbon. Also, black and white is forgiving in that inconsistent makeup or an inadvertent wine stain on a white tuxedo is less likely to stand out. From an archival perspective, black and white images allow for consistent documentation.

Counsel your clients to inquire about the average processing time for wedding albums. The time needed between the wedding and delivery of the final album is influenced by factors such as: 1) the photographer's style and post-wedding process for creating and designing an album; 2) the client's turnaround time, including the review of proofs, final image selection and/or feedback regarding album layout; and 3) the album company's production time. Rodney states that his pre-design album proposal takes three to four weeks, where he hand-selects and creates a custom layout of 100 to 160 images taken from the 3,000 or more documented. He notes that 80 per cent of his clients stay with his initial layout, while the remaining clients offer input and tweak the design.

OTHER WEDDING-RELATED TRENDS IN PHOTOGRAPHY

Beyond changes in technique and album design, three additional trends in photography are engagement, boudoir and trash-the-dress photo shoots. Top photographers will schedule engagement photo shoots two or three times a year, often during the peak weeks of spring and fall seasons. For engagement shoots, the photographer can meet with a dozen or so clients over a period of a few hours rather than making individual appointments with each couple. Engagement photos can be used for newspaper announcements, save-the-date notices or holiday greeting cards. Couples frequently select and frame their favorite engagement image. The mat of this portrait can be signed by guests on the wedding day. Another use for engagement photos is a customized, flush mount guest book that includes images throughout.

One of the latest trends in photography related to weddings is the demand for boudoir photo shoots. The goal of this distinctive style of photography is to capture images of a client in lingerie or other alluring clothing. In relationship to weddings, the target audience is primarily brides who want to have their sexiest looks documented tastefully for their soon-to-be husbands. As a woman may invest a great deal of energy and finances into looking her best for her wedding day, a boudoir photo shoot timed in close proximity to her wedding allows her to immortalize the glamour in a sensual way. Photographers also market to the male audience for what has been humorously called "dudeoir" photo shoots. With engaged men becoming progressively cognizant of their weight management behaviors (Klos and Sobal 2013), it makes sense that they, too, might want their hard-won physiques photographed.

A third trend in wedding photography pertains to the trash-the-dress phenomenon. At some point after the wedding day, the newlywed woman attires herself in her wedding gown again, with the intent of destroying it in such a way that artistic photos result. She may walk into a swamp, play paint ball, roll in the mud or partake in any other number of activities to permanently sully the gown. The idea is viewed as avant-garde by some; a daring disregard of a garment that is traditionally viewed as sacred. Critics of the practice call it disrespectful and wasteful, urging women to donate these expensive garments rather than ruining them (ABC News 2013). While

PHOTO 14.4 ENGAGEMENT PHOTOS SHOULD HAVE A MEMORABLE BACKDROP.

SOURCE: WWW.RODNEYBAILEY.COM

PHOTO 14.5 COUPLES CAN USE ENGAGEMENT PHOTOS IN CUSTOMIZED GUEST BOOKS.

SOURCE: WWW.RODNEYBAILEY.COM

this trend can be viewed as innocent fun, a woman may put herself at great risk in an effort to be audacious, with media images of women posing while their dresses go up in flames as a pervasive example (ABC News 2013). When a Canadian woman drowned because the weight of her dress dragged her into the current of the river she had chosen for her trash-the-dress photo shoot, the potential dangers of this trend were documented internationally (Holden 2012). If you work with a client who is intent upon trashing her dress, advise her to play it safe.

ADVANCES IN VIDEOGRAPHY

Videography has advanced so much in recent years that top vendors now eschew the term itself, instead preferring film design, studio film, event film or media productions as part of their company names, while the videographers themselves have been renamed as documentary filmmakers, film editors or film producers. Haynal Papp (2013), owner of Dolce Studio Films, confirms the necessity of the transition. She explains that clients are no longer satisfied with a videographer who is just going to show up, plunk down a camera and then give them a video where the only enhancements are some embedded, schmaltzy effects. Instead, modern videographers use multiple cameras capturing high definition footage on site and then apply state-of-the-art editing techniques for post-production. Thus, they approach wedding documentation as a filmmaking process.

VENDOR SPOTLIGHT, CASE 14.3

HAYNAL PAPP

DOLCE STUDIO FILMS

How did your educational background lead to wedding filmmaking? My educational background is more a happy culmination that led to a successful conclusion, rather than a traditional direct path to film. I didn't attend film school or business school, and, yet, I am a filmmaker and entrepreneur! As a teen, I attended a high school that specialized in the Arts, much like the one in *Fame*, as a Visual Artist. I then earned a diploma in Interior Design and went on to university to complete a joint Honors BA in English Literature and History. During my fourth year, I won Best Essay Prize for a thesis paper I had written that was based on oral narrative. My interest in the oral tradition led to my interest in how history is presented in film. With a bag full of enthusiasm, I went on to attend graduate school abroad, at an American accredited university in Europe and earned my MA in History. Of course, living in Europe meant that, while earning my degree, I also soaked up the art, architecture and beauty of the continent. After graduating, I helped launch a city guide in a new market as the Advertising Manager for an English-language publication in Hungary. I successfully signed major advertisers, including British Airways, Hertz and the Four Seasons. While this path seems an unlikely background for a filmmaker, the truth is there was no better training. The seemingly disparate elements convened to equip me with knowledge of composition, lighting, story, narrative, customer service, promotion and marketing: all the tools needed to blend a career in documentary art with successful entrepreneurship.

What are some different cultural weddings you have filmed? We document love and marriage in all its forms. Most of the weddings we film are traditional American weddings with Protestant or non-denominational ceremonies. However, we've also filmed many High Catholic weddings, traditional Orthodox weddings (Jewish, Greek, Russian), Chinese Tea Ceremonies, African weddings, Korean weddings and even a Coptic Christian wedding. We've filmed Persian weddings, Indian weddings (Sikh, Hindu, Muslim and Christian), Pakistani weddings and events that celebrate traditions over multiple days; like Henna painting ceremonies and Sangeets. We've filmed same-sex weddings and even a New Age wedding where all the guests wore Medieval clothing and the bride and groom wore wings! We've also filmed weddings for well-known athletes, politicians and high-profile business executives; while these aren't cultural, they tend to include high-profile attendees and require especially low-profile service coupled with assurances that the clients' privacy will be maintained. You name it, we've done it!

How do you involve clients in post-production? At Dolce, all of our couples receive our Editing Input Submission Guide before post-production. This is a 10-page document that breaks down the video chapter by chapter and explains not only how we present the footage, but offers options for how the couple might customize their film, free of charge. The couple then has a month to submit their input and the guide provides clear instruction for the formats and methods of submission. An example of what a couple might personalize is their music or the way in which we present their first dance. For example, we usually show the first dance in a montage because 90 per cent of first dances show nervous couples clinging to each other alone on a dance floor while stepping left-foot, right-foot in a circle for three and a half minutes. Nobody wants to relive that in real time! So we put it into a montage where we might show the one turn, the one dip, a wide shot, a close shot, hands holding, a pan of the dress and the groom's hand on her waist, and then we move on. But if the couple practiced a whole number and they want to be the next viral video on YouTube, then obviously it is clear that we are going to put the whole dance in from start to finish! We give the client the opportunity to specify which they would prefer.

What distinguishes photography and film for weddings? Photography takes a moment in time and elevates it to the status of art, whereas film is a portal by which you can re-experience a past moment. When you are spending the most money in your life for the biggest party you are ever going to throw, to not be able to re-experience the day at a later time will make you so upset because it is impossible to retain everything that is going on.

How can consultants make your life easier? The biggest advantage of having a planner is that, on the day-of, the bride is not trying to troubleshoot. When there is a coordinator, things run smoothly and on time, and, in all of the shots of the couple, they are smiling. If there is no consultant, when you go to film the preparation, the bride is pinched, unsmiling, stressed and answering the phone every three minutes. Planners also have an internal compass that allows them to select the right vendors for a client. If a planner recommends you, it is more likely to be a done deal. Almost 50 per cent of our business comes from referrals made by photographers and consultants.

WEBSITE: *DOLCESTUDIOFILMS.COM*

Haynal explains that two products result from wedding filmmaking. The first is an edited film that is 60 to 90 minutes in length and follows the progression of the day, including full coverage of significant spoken elements such as readings, vows and toasts. The second product is a final highlight reel of five minutes or less that captures the key moments of the day and can be uploaded to the couple's favorite social media site. Haynal explains that, while all couples want a full-length wedding film, it is typically the highlight reel that sells the business. However, she advises that couples should take the time to review full-length wedding films, as they were delivered to previous clients, before selecting a filmmaker. She explains that just about anyone can put together a gorgeous three-minute highlight, but the true talent is evidenced within the full-length film. As such, the editing expertise of the filmmaker becomes paramount to the selection process, and discerning clients should view many finished samples of work to ensure the videographer does not take a one-size-fits-all approach.

Clients should be able to exercise some measure of input to the film, including the selection of music and the presentation style. If clients start to over-participate, however, remind them that they are paying filmmakers for their time and skill and should therefore trust their post-production expertise. Haynal estimates that, when two video cameras are used, the editing process takes 40 to 60 hours for the first draft of a wedding film. In her studio, this is followed by a peer review where other shooters and editors view the film and offer feedback. This process, in conjunction with intensive training and yearly workshops, keeps her team fresh and accountable. Haynal discusses other elements of wedding filmmaking in *Vendor Spotlight*, Case 14.3.

Pricing and packages for wedding films vary considerably based on the number of cameras used, whether or not each camera is independently manned, the number of hours/days filmed and the extent to which revisions are requested. Some companies sell multiple camera packages, but only one filmmaker is manning all of the cameras; an approach that is not as effective as having a filmmaker for each camera. Revisions are charged; as such, remind your clients to be clear in their contract regarding any moments that they are certain they want to be represented in the film.

REFERENCES

ABC News (2013) 'Photos: brides trash wedding dresses', Online. Available HTTP: <http://abcnews.go.com/GMA/popup?id=3283476> (accessed 21 February 2013).

Bailey, R. (2013) 'Processes and trends in wedding photography'. E-mail interview by Daniela Conyngham and personal communication (23 February 2013).

Chastain, D. (2013) 'The missing groomsman'. E-mail interview by Nicholas Rio (22 February 2013).

Holden, W.C. (28 August 2012) 'Bride drowns in wedding dress while taking photos in Canadian river', *Fox 31 Denver*, Online. Available HTTP: <http://kdvr.com/2012/08/28/bride-drowns-in-wedding-dress-taking-pictures-in-canadian-river/> (accessed 21 February 2013).

Klos, L.A. and Sobal, J. (2013) 'Weight and weddings. Engaged men's body weight ideals and wedding weight management behaviors', *Appetite*, 60: 133–139.

Papp, H. (2013) 'Processes and trends in wedding videography'. Personal interview (1 March 2013).

Wosicki, Y. and Wosicki, D. (2006) 'Wedding photography in China'. E-mail (19 May 2006).

CONSULTANT CHECKLIST AND REMINDERS FOR PHOTOGRAPHY AND VIDEOGRAPHY

☐ Introduce your clients to both traditional and photojournalistic styles of photography, including sample albums, to determine which best suits their personalities.

☐ Be aware of the dates available for engagement photographs for photographers who schedule them two or three times a year.

☐ Help your clients make a list of the "must have" photos that they wish to be taken.

☐ Be familiar with the rules for photography and videography at area places of worship.

☐ Ensure that the photographer will have an assistant for the wedding day.

☐ Ask the photographer to tell you the average number of images she/he takes at weddings.

☐ Determine if the photographer will be shooting all color or if a percentage of black and white is available.

☐ When comparing photography packages, ensure that the photographer's options include photo shoot time, design and production time, album options, reprint costs and the option to purchase the digital negatives.

☐ Modern videographers are filmmakers.

☐ When comparing videography packages, consider the number of cameras used, whether or not each camera is independently manned, the number of hours that will be filmed, post-production expertise, the inclusion of a highlight reel and the option for revisions.

☐ Couples should watch full-length wedding film samples, as delivered to previous clients, prior to selecting a filmmaker.

REVIEW

1. Explain three advantages of digital over film photography.

2. Name three distinctions between traditional photography and the photojournalistic style.

3. What are two purposes for engagement photos?

4. Explain two advances in album design.

5. Differentiate between traditional videography and modern wedding filmmaking.

6. In what ways can couples be involved with wedding film post-production?

TERMINOLOGY

- Available light

- Flush mount album

- Highlight reel

- Photojournalistic style

- Photo–video hybrid

- Post-production

- Sepia

- Traditional photographic style

- Wedding filmmaking

Photo 15.1 Music is the soundtrack to the wedding day.

Source: www.RodneyBailey.com

15

MUSIC AND ENTERTAINMENT

A WEDDING, LIKE LIFE'S OTHER SPECIAL MOMENTS, IS ENHANCED BY SPECIAL MUSIC INTERSPERSED THROUGHOUT THE CELEBRATION. FROM THE SEATING OF THE FIRST GUEST TO THE NEWLYWEDS' GET AWAY, MUSIC FILLS THE WEDDING DAY. CLIENTS WILL RELY UPON YOUR EXPERTISE TO GUIDE THEM IN SELECTING THE SOUNDTRACK TO THEIR SPECIAL DAY. MUSIC SHOULD ALWAYS ENHANCE AND NEVER OVERSHADOW THE POINT OF THE WEDDING — THE COMMITMENT OF THE COUPLE. WHEN SELECTING MUSIC AND OTHER ENTERTAINMENT, EACH STAGE OF THE WEDDING DAY SHOULD BE CONSIDERED: THE CEREMONY, THE COCKTAIL HOUR AND THE RECEPTION. THESE STAGES ARE CONSIDERED IN TURN, AND THEN OTHER FORMS OF ENTERTAINMENT AND HIRING TIPS ARE PRESENTED.

CEREMONY MUSIC

Unless the bride and groom are music aficionados, they often turn to their wedding consultant for recommendations on music to be played during the ceremony. It is your job to assist the couple in selecting music to punctuate significant moments during the ceremony, from the bride's entrance to the recessional. From a musical standpoint, most wedding ceremonies can be divided into five main parts: prelude, processional, interludes, recessional and postlude.

PRELUDE

Just like the prelude of a book foreshadows events to come in a novel, the musical *prelude* for a wedding ceremony sets the mood for the service to follow. Prelude music occurs prior to the entrance of the wedding party, acting as a form of entertainment for guests as they arrive and are seated. The type of music selected should reflect the personalities of the bride and groom, the formality of the wedding ceremony and the setting. If a wedding is to be held on the beach in Maui, the prelude music might include ukuleles, steel drums or slack-key guitars. On the other hand, if the wedding ceremony is held at a venue such as St. Patrick's Cathedral in New York, the largest gothic-style Catholic cathedral in the US (St. Patrick's Cathedral 2013), a classical string

PHOTO 15.2 A MUSICAL PRELUDE SETS THE MOOD FOR THE CEREMONY.

SOURCE: WWW.RODNEYBAILEY.COM

TABLE 15.1 OPTIONS FOR LIVE MUSIC DURING THE PRELUDE

- Chamber music ensemble (a small orchestra with strings, wind instruments and percussion)
- Children's choir
- Church choir
- Church organ
- Classical guitar
- Flute and keyboard
- Gospel choir
- Guitar, cello and flute
- Harp
- Harp and flute
- Piano
- Solo violin
- String quartet (two violins, viola and cello)
- String trio (violin, viola and cello)
- Vocalist
- Wind trio or quartet (assorted wind instruments such as clarinet, oboe, flute, trumpet, French horn or bassoon)

quartet and trumpet player would be more appropriate. You should plan for 30 to 45 minutes of prelude music before moving into the processional music. Some options for live music during the prelude, with clarification as necessary, are presented in Table 15.1.

PROCESSIONAL

The wedding *processional* occurs when the wedding party walks down the aisle. When selecting music for this period, it is wise to consider the length of the aisle and the number of members in the wedding party. You might also time the walk down the aisle if you are working at an unfamiliar venue. Sometimes the processional is simply one song; most often, it is two or more songs played to differentiate between the arrival of the wedding party members and the arrival of the bride. The processional music, if done well, builds anticipation as the wedding party enters and increases in energy for the bride's dramatic appearance.

Wagner's "Bridal Chorus" (better known as "Here Comes the Bride") from the opera *Lohengrin* is a well-known option for the processional. However, because of Wagner's anti-Semitic writings, he remains a controversial figure and his music is seldom chosen for Jewish ceremonies (Eylon 2013). Other distinguished options are Clarke's "Trumpet Voluntary," Bach's "Jesu, Joy of Man's Desiring" and Pachelbel's immensely popular "Canon in D." In addition to the classics, some couples prefer a non-traditional twist on their processional music and incorporate Broadway show tunes, classic jazz or contemporary pop songs into their wedding day. The decision rests with the bride and groom and, in non-traditional ceremony sites, anything goes. However, if the wedding is taking place in a house of worship, be sure to clear any *secular music* choices with the officiant well in advance of the wedding day, as these non-religious selections may be prohibited.

INTERLUDES

During the ceremony itself, there may be musical *interludes* for moments such as group prayers and responses, lighting a unity candle, taking communion or making special offerings. These moments should be accompanied by a special hymn or other piece of music. The ceremony also commonly includes a performance by a soloist or even a full choir. If your clients are utilizing musical interludes, be sure the music is chosen well in advance and coordinated with the needs of the officiant. Many couples choose a close friend who is musically talented to act as their soloist. It is important that this person be given an opportunity to practice during the rehearsal to become familiar with the acoustics of the facility and the style of the accompanist. In some cultures, the ceremony music is accompanied by entertainment, as illustrated in *Culture Corner*, Case 15.1.

RECESSIONAL

Once the couple has been pronounced husband and wife, the music should turn festive and celebratory. The *recessional* music occurs as the wedding party exits the ceremony venue, setting the mood for the party to follow. Popular recessional music includes Beethoven's "Ode to Joy," Handel's *Water Music* and Mendelssohn's "Wedding March." Contemporary song choices might include selections from diverse artists such as Colbie Cailat, Adele, Mumford & Sons, Sondre Lerche, Fun., Beyoncé, Omar Akram, The Black Keys or Carrie Underwood. Most importantly, the music your bride and groom select should be joyful and meaningful to them.

For the recessional, consider a creative sound to enhance the exit from the ceremony site. Perhaps your clients want to hire a bagpiper or bell choir to play at the door of the church. If the venue is a southern inn, maybe they will hire a Dixieland jazz band to set the tone or perhaps a marching band will play the fight song from the groom's alma mater. The options are vast when it comes to recessional music. The main point is to keep it celebratory, uplifting and highly personalized.

CULTURE CORNER, CASE 15.1

JAPANESE DANCE AT A SHINTO WEDDING

During a Shinto wedding ceremony, before the bride and groom exchange sips of sake, known as *San San Ku Do* or three sets of three sips, there may be a dance performed by ladies to the accompaniment of traditional Japanese wooden flutes. The ladies or shrine maidens wear a white kimono with red skirts called *hakama*. The dancing ladies are symbols of virginity. The dance will last 10–15 minutes and will have five parts: 1) acknowledging the meeting of the boy and girl; 2) honoring the love of the couple; 3) keeping the love alive; 4) the exchange or sharing of the sake; and 5) honoring the couple's ancestors. If the wedding is held at one of the most traditional Shinto shrines, such as Izumo Taisha in Japan's Shimane prefecture, the bride and groom will join the shrine maidens in dance. As the couple dances, crossing each other, the movement signifies sharing a bed with each other. They will dance forming the shape of the number eight, which is a lucky number. It is believed in Japan that the number eight means eternal prosperity of the family.

CASE SUBMITTED BY TAKEUCHI YAYOI, KUBO SANAE, IWAMURA MICHIYO, ASAI TOSHIKO, SOGA YOSHIKO AND SUZUKI FUSAKO

POSTLUDE

As they say, "It ain't over 'til it's over," and the ceremony is not over until the guests exit. This is why planning for a *postlude*, defined as the continuous music that plays as guests exit the ceremony space, is important, in particular if there is a large guest list. You should allow for about ten minutes' worth of postlude music, allowing guests to exit quickly and smartly to the sound of upbeat music rather than to the clatter of shuffling feet.

Keep in mind that, for many weddings, the ceremony and the reception are in the same venue, such as a hotel, museum or resort. For weddings where there is not an obvious change of scenery, the postlude music becomes particularly important as a means to transition between the ceremony and reception. Music encourages movement. For example, in a resort setting, the ceremony may be located in a ballroom area and then the cocktail hour is held on a patio while the ballroom is quickly turned for the reception. Lively music gets the guests up and moving so the resort staff can quickly transition the ballroom from ceremony to reception.

COCKTAIL HOUR MUSIC

With the wedding ceremony behind them, the music for a couple's cocktail hour should be light and breezy so as not to interfere with the guests' conversation. As there are limited opportunities for guests to converse during the wedding ceremony, the cocktail hour becomes the perfect setting for them to meet and mingle. Nat King Cole, Billie Holiday and Frank Sinatra are just a few icons whose pleasing sounds are represented in compiled albums such as *The Original Great American Songbook*. Whether your clients' music is live or pre-recorded, playing the classics, light jazz or big band during cocktails starts the reception on the right note. A sample of artists whose music works especially well during cocktails can be found in Table 15.2.

If there is a piano available at the reception venue, put it to good use and hire a pianist to play during cocktails. Make sure the piano is tuned and in good working order prior to the wedding day. Other live music for the cocktail hour might include a jazz trio, a violin and an accordion, or even a banjo and a flute. When hiring musical talent, be sure to check with the local music schools for up-and-coming talent at discounted prices. Also, on-site event coordinators at venues are excellent sources for recommending a specific type of musician or specialty music such as a German polka band or a salsa band.

When advising your client on musical options for cocktails and the reception, keep the space limitations in mind. You do not want a single acoustic guitar to be lost in a large space; conversely, you do not want to overwhelm your guests with too many musicians playing in a tight space. Additionally, be certain to familiarize yourself with any noise restrictions imposed by the venue. Amplified music may be forbidden if your venue is in a residential area. There may also be a limit on the number of musicians allowed or the duration of the music. If the venue is located in a quiet neighborhood, the last dance may have to conclude by 11:00 p.m. or earlier. Check with the venue

TABLE 15.2 EXAMPLES OF COCKTAIL HOUR MUSIC

• Louis Armstrong	• Norah Jones
• The Beatles	• Yo-Yo Ma
• Jim Brickman	• Michael McDonald
• Michael Bublé	• Tim McGraw
• Mariah Carey	• Sarah McLachlan
• Ray Charles	• Van Morrison
• Patsy Cline	• Rod Stewart
• Harry Connick, Jr.	• Vivaldi
• Vince Gill	• George Winston

PHOTO 15.3 IF THERE IS A PIANO AT THE RECEPTION VENUE, PUT IT TO GOOD USE.

SOURCE: WWW.RODNEYBAILEY.COM

for specifications and discuss them with your client. Make sure these restrictions are noted in the music contract. Clients should be well aware of a venue's required end time and select accordingly. In the US, midnight is generally an acceptable time to wrap up a reception, whereas, in countries such as Switzerland, guests would be surprised by this leave-taking requirement, as wedding receptions generally continue until 3:00 a.m. or 4:00 a.m.

PHOTO 15.4 A STRING QUARTET OFFERS A PERFECT BACKDROP FOR COCKTAILS.

SOURCE: WWW.RODNEYBAILEY.COM

RECEPTION MUSIC AND ENTERTAINMENT

When cocktails have ended and the guests are invited to the reception area, the music and entertainment should take a new direction. For the dinner itself, the music is often similar to the cocktail hour so as to encourage conversation. If planning cocktail stations, the music can reflect the cultural variety of the food, as highlighted in *Culture Corner*, Case 15.2.

Once dinner is complete, there are specific moments that need to be highlighted through music and dancing. These special moments include the couple's first dance; the father/bride dance, usually done in tandem with the mother/groom dance; music for the bouquet toss; music for the leave-taking of the couple, if prior to the end of the reception; and the last dance of the night. In preparation for being the center of attention while dancing, many couples take lessons prior to the wedding. Michele Kearney, owner of The Ballroom Studio, offers insight to dance styles for weddings in *Vendor Spotlight*, Case 15.3.

The pleasure of dancing is also evidenced in cultural traditions such as belly dancing (Egypt), the Chinese Wedding Dance (China), the Highland Fling (Ireland and Scotland), the Hora (Jewish), Irish Step Dancing (Ireland), Kalamantiano (Greece), the money dance (Cyprus, Philippines, United States and others), the garter toss (United States and United Kingdom) and the Polka (Czech Republic, Germany, Poland and others).

CULTURE CORNER, CASE 15.2

LET ME ENTERTAIN YOU

There are ways to introduce a variety of interesting musical experiences to pull together an event. One event planner chose to have a Chinese *erhu* (violin) next to the Chinese food station; an accordionist next to the pasta station; and a solo jazz sax next to the martini bar. This line-up not only showed thoughtful planning, but it also made it easy for guests to talk – which would not have been the case with louder, more common alternatives (such as a single sound source, band or DJ). Guests commented on what great conversations they were having without shouting and getting hoarse and how much fun it was to move from one style of cuisine (and entertainment) to the next all in the same room.

CASE SUBMITTED BY DAVID FLETCHER
WASHINGTON'S BEST MUSICIANS
WEBSITE: *WASHBEST.COM*

When considering these dances, the comfort of the couple should be kept in mind. For instance, Egyptian brides may fear being upstaged by a sensual belly dancer. Similarly, the garter toss, common in American culture, can also push the limits of decorum, and many couples forego this tradition. Other dances are controversial for completely different reasons. Whether to have a money dance, for example, can be a source of significant conflict for a couple raised with different cultural traditions. One person might see it as an anticipated and fun way to dance with an abundance of guests in a short period of time, whereas the other may view it as greedy and tacky. Decisions regarding whether to incorporate specific dances or other forms of entertainment should be made at least a month before the wedding, as differences in opinion regarding related traditions can result in stressful conversations.

Beyond dancing, creative forms of entertainment often reflect the theme of a wedding, the interests of the couple or their cultural background. While some wedding entertainment can rival the acts of *Cirque du Soleil* performers, most is more modest. Guests may participate in cornhole pitching, horseshoes, bocce, fishing, canoeing, swimming, horseback riding or any other number of activities for outdoor weddings. Darts, pool tables, poker, ping pong and board games are just a sampling of entertaining options for indoor weddings. In many countries, anticipated forms of entertainment may precede the ceremony and reception, as evidenced in *Culture Corner*, Case 15.4.

PHOTO 15.5 PAIR MUSIC WITH CUISINE TO CARRY OUT A THEME.

SOURCE: WWW.RODNEYBAILEY.COM

VENDOR SPOTLIGHT, CASE 15.3

MICHELE KEARNEY

THE BALLROOM STUDIO

What makes The Ballroom a good environment for couples who are preparing for their wedding? I would say that 50 per cent of our business is wedding couples who come in to prepare for their first dance. We have experienced instructors who know how to adapt to all different requests when it comes to "wedding songs." We try to tell them that we want them to remember and enjoy their wedding dance, not be stressed out about trying to remember a complicated routine. Learning how to "lead" and "follow" goes a long way. If we have a request for a full-blown production, we can provide that too, but it will require sufficient lead time.

How long does it usually take a couple to prepare for their wedding dance? The most popular wedding package consists of four individual lessons and four group lessons. Believe it or not, in that short amount of time, they usually get it and are feeling 100 per cent more confident than they did when they first walked in. They should sign up around three months before the wedding. That will give them enough time to cover everything and still feel like they have time to practice enough to make it feel more comfortable and natural.

What style of dance is used most often for a couple's first dance as husband and wife? I've taught almost every dance for wedding dances but I'd have to say that the most popular are "Foxtrot" and "Foxy." Foxy is just an even tempo Foxtrot. Foxtrots are typically your Frank Sinatra, Dean Martin, Harry Connick, Jr. and Michael Bublé big band sounds. Foxy uses the exact same patterns as Foxtrot but done to an even 4/4 time, whereas Foxtrot is Slow, Slow, Quick, Quick.

What is unique about teaching a wedding couple as opposed to other lessons? What makes them unique is, for starters, they are all ga ga in love and they usually have expectations of the perfect day and the perfect dance. This puts a little bit of pressure on them. Then there's the time factor in that they have a set date they want to feel ready for. People who come in to learn dance as a hobby don't usually have a time frame in which they feel that it is necessary that they accomplish their goals, so they can learn at their own pace and enjoy the journey. Wedding couples tend to be short term because once the wedding is over they are busy with everything else falling into place. Those who take lessons out of pure curiosity tend to be more long term, where they can see the benefits of learning a variety of different dances for different occasions instead of focusing on one dance, which is what wedding couples usually do.

WEBSITE: *THEBALLROOMSTUDIO.COM*
INTERVIEW CONDUCTED BY SHARON MCMAHON

For receptions where children are permitted, special entertainment may be planned. Lisa Werth (2013), founder of Nannytainment Event Childcare, states that her company provides on-site childcare at weddings and other events so adults can enjoy themselves, while children are entertained in their own, special space. Lisa advises planners to carefully research venues to make sure that they are kid-friendly and have an appropriate, separate area for childcare activities. *Consultant in Action*, Case 15.5 sets forth a situation where the clients did not practice due diligence.

Some couples have a strong opinion regarding whether they want their music to be performed live. If they are uncertain, they will ask your advice on hiring a DJ versus hiring a wedding band.

PHOTO 15.6 LIVE MUSIC CAN REFLECT THE COUPLE'S CULTURE.

SOURCE: WWW.RODNEYBAILEY.COM

CULTURE CORNER, CASE 15.4

THE SISTERS' HURDLE

In Malaysia, the Chinese make up the second largest ethnic group forming about 25 per cent of the Malaysian population. Although the Malaysian Chinese are descendants from China who migrated during the nineteenth century, their weddings do not consist of rituals as elaborate as those of their forefathers. Today, Malaysian Chinese weddings incorporate both modern and traditional Chinese customs. As such, young Malaysian Chinese couples wanting to tie the knot tend to just follow only three significant rituals: the civil marriage, the tea ceremony and the wedding reception. The civil marriage is when the young couple is registered legally as husband and wife. A few months (and sometimes years) after the registration, the

PHOTO 15.7 SPECIAL MOMENTS ARE HIGHLIGHTED WITH CULTURAL DANCES.

SOURCE: WWW.RODNEYBAILEY.COM

tea ceremony is held. The wedding reception then follows the tea ceremony, usually on the same day or a week apart.

Of the three major rituals, a much greater emphasis is placed on the tea ceremony. An old Chinese custom, it is comparable to an exchange of vows in Western culture but involves a series of sub-events prior to the serving of the tea itself. One of these sub-events is "The Sisters' Hurdle" also known as "The Door Game." Originating from ancient times, the bride's female friends and relatives (hence the sisters) will be stationed at the main entrance (the door) to try to stop the groom's party from entering by throwing them a series of physical challenges (the game). The rationale behind this was that the bride was so cherished by her family and friends that they try to delay her departure from her family home. Today, however, it is as much an anticipated event as it is an amusing way to get the groom to prove his love for the

323

bride. Some common requests of the groom and his party include belting out a love song for the bride and consuming nasty food and drinks concocted by the bride's party. Challenges may be creative, such as one that required the groom to hit the streets announcing his wedding to the world; or painful, such as demanding that the groom's men write "I love you" on their arms with candle wax. Interestingly, nobody complains and The Door Game is always loud, joyous and good-natured. In the end, the groom will be asked for a generous *hongpau* (money in a red envelope) before being allowed into the property to claim his wife.

Following this, the couple will perform ceremonial prayers before offering tea to the elders as a sign of acceptance into the family. Although the couple could have already been legally married months ago at a civil marriage, it is only at the end of this tea ceremony that they are deemed husband and wife.

CASE SUBMITTED BY CATHERYN KHOO-LATTIMORE
AND ELAINE YANG CHIAO LING

You should be able to objectively present both sides for them to consider. The pros and cons of this important decision are listed in Table 15.3. Also, it is important that you stay up on the latest artists. If your clients say that they want a band that has a sound similar to Kelly Clarkson, Coldplay, The Band Perry or Halestorm and you have never heard of these artists, it will be hard to help them find the right talent. One way to stay up-to-date is by following artists who are on the top of the charts. Billboard.com and iTunes constantly update their listings and include biographies that will help you learn about the newest and hottest talent.

TIPS FOR HIRING ENTERTAINMENT

Professional musician Patricia Ferrett (2013), who has performed at hundreds of weddings over the years, offers valuable advice when hiring a band or DJ. Regarding bands, she stresses that musicians are interesting creatures who can make or break a wedding day; therefore, to ensure that you are hiring real professionals, you must determine: 1) if they have ever played a wedding before, as the tone of a wedding is very different than other types of performances; 2) if they are willing/able to learn any specific music that you need and, if not, are they able to play specific tunes you need from a CD or MP3 player through their speaker system; 3) how much space they need; 4) the power requirements; and 5) if they will bring lights or if the clients need to provide lighting. Patricia explains that the same general principles apply to a DJ, but the logistics are easier.

CONSULTANT IN ACTION, CASE 15.5

NO VACANCY

In order to free up the many parents who would be guests at their wedding, your clients decided to hire on-site childcare. The 30 children invited to the wedding would have a separate dining area for their kid-friendly meal, after which the childcare company would supply toys, books, games and activities. Without consulting the venue manager, Camron, about the venue's policies, your client reserved the venue and the childcare. A week before the wedding, you followed up with Camron to verify the space that would be used and shared the information with the owner of the childcare company. After conducting some of her own research, the childcare specialist discovered that the space Camron suggested was not suitable for safety reasons and out of compliance with the room occupancy needs. You call Camron to inquire about a different space, and suggest another dining area that you are familiar with at the venue. Camron refuses, explaining that there are glass tables in the room you suggested. During the conversation, Camron makes it clear that the management prefers not having children on the property at all.

WHAT DO YOU DO?

CASE SUBMITTED BY LISA WERTH, FOUNDER
NANNYTAINMENT EVENT CHILDCARE
WEBSITE: *NANNYTAINMENT.COM*

For both DJs and bands, Patricia states that it is critical that you watch the person/group perform live prior to signing a contract. She warns that, if you hire sight unseen, you are asking for trouble, as any DJ or band worth hiring will let you come see them at another event so you can see their performance and crowd interaction first hand. Additionally, if your clients want a band to learn a new song, they must make the request at least a month before the wedding. Finally, Patricia emphasizes the importance of feeding musicians, and the consequences of not doing so or feeding them poorly: "If you feed the band wilted sandwiches that were made in your Aunt Betty's kitchen the night before, you will get a performance to match said sandwich. Feed the band well, and you can expect a performance with some gratitude! Beware the 'bandwich!!'"

Whether your clients ultimately hire a soloist, a pianist, a string trio, a band, a DJ or all of the above, your communication with the entertainment is essential. You should confirm, confirm,

PHOTO 15.8 MONOGRAMMED CORNHOLE BOARDS ARE CLEVER AND FUN.

SOURCE: WWW.RODNEYBAILEY.COM

Photo 15.9 Darts provide an entertainment option.

Source: www.RodneyBailey.com

PHOTO 15.10 MUSICIANS CAN READILY ADJUST THE TONE AND SPEED OF MUSIC.

SOURCE: WWW.RODNEYBAILEY.COM

PHOTO 15.11 WATER FEATURES AT A RECEPTION SITE PRESENT ENTERTAINMENT OPTIONS.

SOURCE: WWW.RODNEYBAILEY.COM

TABLE 15.3 PROS AND CONS OF LIVE VERSUS PRE-RECORDED MUSIC

Pre-recorded Music (DJ): Pros

- Typically less expensive than a band
- Immediate access to a wide variety of music
- Do not take breaks
- Can act as emcee
- If space is tight, a DJ takes up almost no room
- Can take the pulse of the room and adjust music selections to keep the party going
- Can play the latest, contemporary music that cover bands may not play
- Because a DJ is just one person, there is less that can go wrong
- Set-up time and special equipment are minimal

TABLE 15.3 CONTINUED

Pre-recorded Music (DJ): Cons

- Personality may be abrasive or inappropriate

- May try to take over the organization of the reception

- Pre-recorded music cannot be easily adjusted to fit the timing of a moment

- Typically seen as less sophisticated and innovative than a live band

Live Music (Band): Pros

- There is great variety in bands in terms of size and style

- Live performance brings energy that gets the party going

- Even if you cut corners on everything else, a live band makes a wedding appear more high-end

- Many bands have a built-in emcee

- Can readily adjust tone and speed of music

- An excellent band is a memorable part of the wedding

- Can establish a time period through dress, style and equipment (e.g., Big Band)

Live Music (Band): Cons

- Usually more expensive than a DJ

- More complex contracts and personalities

- Takes more time to plan

- Lots of mouths to feed

- More technical requirements (space, power, lights)

- Longer set-up time

- More that can go wrong with equipment

- Their repertoire will be more restricted than that of a DJ

- Will require breaks; movement to recorded music during breaks will change tone

SOURCE: FERRETT (2013); SETO (2013)

confirm and know the cellphone numbers of the entertainers themselves, not just the booking agency. You should always bring your portable MP3 player, such as an iPod, with an array of tunes and speakers just in case, as these items have been known to save the day when musicians arrive late or do not show.

PHOTO 15.12   WELL-CHOSEN MUSIC GETS THE PARTY STARTED AND KEEPS IT GOING.

SOURCE: WWW.RODNEYBAILEY.COM

Beyond coming up with creative entertainment options and making sure the entertainment actually shows, be certain to have your clients prepare a list of songs they wish to hear and, just as important, a list of songs they do not wish to hear. This is particularly important for the reception. If your bride and groom want their reception to be free of "Gangnam Style" lyrics, it must be stipulated in writing and presented to the entertainment liaison in advance. The entertainment leader should receive a list of the wedding party for introductions, including the names and the correct, phonetic pronunciations. Any additional special instructions should be spelled out in the contract and highlighted again prior to the wedding. Examples of this would be stipulations such as "No garter toss" or "No father/daughter dance" or "Announce the cutting of the cake at 10:00 p.m." With entertainment, like the other wedding elements, nothing should be left to chance.

When hiring entertainment, prices are often negotiable based on the time of year, day of the week and time of day. Five secrets to hiring entertainment are detailed in *Vendor Spotlight*, Case 15.6.

VENDOR SPOTLIGHT, CASE 15.6

DAVID FLETCHER

WASHINGTON'S BEST MUSICIANS

Five secrets to hiring entertainment

1. *Negotiate.* It is often better to state how much you can afford to pay rather than asking the entertainer how much he or she will charge. However, appreciate the fact that the person is an artist, and do not offend an entertainer with an unreasonable offer.

2. *Consider the "proximity to the event" discount.* In other words, if your clients are willing to wait until two to three weeks prior to their wedding, they might be rewarded with paying less for musical talent that is not yet booked. While this tactic is implemented frequently in the corporate planning world, it may be more difficult to convince a stressed-out couple that there are merits to waiting.

3. *See who is already at the venue.* If your event is in the evening, see if there is a band or DJ already playing earlier in the day. You can save a significant amount by hiring them through the rest of the evening.

4. *Eliminate the liaison.* Talk directly to the person who provides the service. Online searches will provide an abundance of information when trying to find the immediate point of contact for a specific talent.

5. *Personal contact makes all the difference.* Become familiar with the best DJs and bands in your area. Learn the names of key personnel and remember them.

WEBSITE: *WASHBEST.COM*

REFERENCES

Eylon, L. (2013) 'The controversy over Richard Wagner', The American-Israeli Cooperative Enterprise, Online. Available HTTP: <http://www.jewishvirtuallibrary.org/jsource/anti-semitism/Wagner.html> (accessed 18 March 2013).

Ferrett, P. (2013) 'Live bands and DJs for weddings'. E-mail (19 March 2013).

Fletcher, D. (2006) 'Five secrets to hiring entertainment'. Personal communication (19 May 2006).

Khoo-Lattimore, C. and Ling, E.Y.C. (2013) 'The Sisters' Hurdle'. E-mail (21 January 2013).

Kearney, M. (2013) 'Dance lessons for wedding couples'. E-mail interview conducted by Sharon McMahon (23 February 2013).

Seto, L. (2013) 'Wedding reception music basics: bands vs DJs', *The Knot*, Online. Available HTTP: <http://wedding.theknot.com/wedding-planning/wedding-music-ideas/articles/wedding-reception-music-bands-vs-djs.aspx> (accessed 19 March 2013).

St. Patrick's Cathedral (2013) 'Archdiocese of New York: about St. Patrick's Cathedral', Online. Available HTTP: <http://www.archny.org/about-us/st-patricks-cathedral/> (accessed 18 March 2013).

Werth, L. (2013) 'Onsite childcare for weddings'. E-mail case study submission (11 March 2013).

Yayoi, T., Sanae, K., Michiyo, I., Toshiko, A., Yoshiko, S. and Fusako, S. (2006) 'Japanese dance at a Shinto wedding'. Personal communication (30 May 2006).

CONSULTANT CHECKLIST AND REMINDERS FOR MUSIC AND ENTERTAINMENT

☐ Each stage of the wedding day will require music: ceremony, cocktail hour and reception.

☐ From a musical standpoint, there are five main parts of the wedding ceremony: prelude, processional, interludes, recessional and postlude.

☐ Make sure the music selections are consistent with the overall tone of the wedding.

☐ Plan for 30–45 minutes of prelude music.

☐ For the processional, consider the length of the aisle and the number of members in the wedding party before deciding on music.

☐ There should be a music change or dramatic pause before the bride makes her entrance.

☐ Within the ceremony, special moments may be highlighted through music or vocal performances.

☐ Get approval on all secular music choices if the ceremony is at a house of worship.

☐ Be prepared to discuss the pros and cons of pre-recorded versus live music with your clients.

☐ Familiarize yourself with all restrictions for the reception venue.

☐ Be prepared with an MP3 player and a speaker just in case the entertainment is missing in action.

REVIEW

1. What are the three stages of the wedding day that require music?

2. Name the five parts of a wedding ceremony, as pertaining to music.

3. Name four different options for live music.

4. Brainstorm three creative ways for your clients to exit the ceremony.

5. What are the pros and cons of hiring a DJ for a wedding reception?

6. What are the pros and cons of hiring a band for a wedding reception?

7. Name three things you can do to help get the best price for entertainment.

TERMINOLOGY

- Chamber music

- Postlude

- Prelude

- Processional

- Recessional

- Secular music

- String quartet

- String trio

- Wind quartet

- Wind trio

Photo 16.1 The coordination of table layout and extensive pin spotting involves many vendors.
Source: www.RodneyBailey.com

RENTALS AND SITE LAYOUT

Rentals allow couples to set the stage for their wedding in a way that would not be cost effective if they had to purchase all of the items. Tents, lighting, tables, chairs, linens, tableware, equipment and other specialty items serve dual purposes. First, each rental has a specific function. Second, rentals add to the theme and mood of the wedding, varying from vintage sophistication to trendy modernity. This chapter offers the essentials that consultants need to know about wedding rentals and layout, including: 1) tents; 2) tables, chairs, linens and tableware; 3) lighting; 4) other outdoor considerations; and 5) bringing it together with the site layout.

TENTS

For outdoor ceremonies and receptions, tents are a common rental item because the weather is seldom perfect. Rain is not the only worry, as cold, heat, humidity, wind and bugs can also lead to uncomfortable guests. This section will cover three aspects of tents: 1) styles and accessories; 2) size and set-up; and 3) cost.

TENT STYLES AND ACCESSORIES

The two primary styles of tents are pole tents and frame tents and many subcategories fall under these two broad groupings. Davis Richardson (2013) of Sugarplum Tent Company offers information that will allow you to distinguish between different styles of tents. He explains that *pole tents* are held up by exterior and interior poles and then anchored in the ground by staking. Modern pole tents are referred to as *tension tents*, since high-tension winches or ratchets are used to create the taut appearance. Pole tents are the classic choice for weddings, as they allow for dramatic, high peaks and a sweeping, billowy look. However, the interior poles can be unattractive and obtrusive, so they are often wrapped with fabric or greenery and decorated with flowers. The newest type of pole tent is called a *sailcloth tent*, so named for the use of translucent yet durable sailcloth material, natural wooden poles and the sculpted, nautical look.

Frame tents, on the other hand, eliminate the need for interior poles, as they are supported with aluminum piping that frames the top and sides of the structure. A frame tent is necessary when the installation is on concrete, asphalt or any surface where poles cannot be anchored. While the frame tent is more self-supporting, it still must be staked down. Installation of frame tents is more time-consuming, thus rentals are more expensive. Further, the mass of aluminum supporting the top of the tent can be unattractive, so fabric liners are often used to make the interior aesthetically pleasing. A clear frame tent gives an alfresco feeling that, combined with specialty lighting, creates a stunning natural setting day or night. Frame tents are limited in size, so for large gatherings are not a viable choice.

Picking the style of tent is the first of many decisions that must be made for tent rentals. Other considerations include flooring, sidewalls, entrance canopies, lighting, liners, power generators, heating, air conditioning and staging. If the ground has poor drainage, is not level or is gravelly, flooring will keep guests from stumbling or getting covered with mud. Flooring can be wood, plastic, carpeting, ceramic tiles or an all-weather artificial turf. Full tent flooring is expensive, often costing as much as the tent rental itself. If your clients are planning on having dancing, they need to select a dance floor. Sidewalls and entrance canopies offer an elegant touch and extra protection from the elements. Generators are needed for anything requiring electrical power, such as heaters, air conditioning units, catering tents, music and lighting. Finally, staging and steps are used if a head table is desired or for musicians. Taken together, it should become clear that selecting a tent is not done to save money on a ceremony or reception site, as the tent and additional rentals are often much more costly than renting a ballroom or other venue; instead, tents offer a unique opportunity to truly tailor an event space.

PHOTO 16.2 INTERIOR POLES ARE DECORATED FOR A SEAMLESS LOOK.

SOURCE: WWWT.RODNEYBAILEY.COM

TENT SIZE AND SET-UP

David Richardson notes that a conservative rule of thumb for tent size is 12 square feet per person for a seating-only event such as a ceremony, and up to 20 square feet or more per person once you add tables, a dance floor, buffet, bar and equipment. Table 16.1 includes sample guidelines for selecting a tent size, using the indicators above. Actual dimensions vary based on the tent style and manufacturer, but, in general, sizes start at 10 feet x 10 feet, with both length and width

PHOTO 16.3 TENTS OFFER AN OPPORTUNITY TO TAILOR AN EVENT SPACE.

SOURCE: WWW.RODNEYBAILEY.COM

increasing in 10-foot increments. When estimating a tent size, it is better to have too much room than not enough, as you do not want guests to feel crowded. Most companies have a tent size calculator or the manager will provide you a cheat sheet that allows you to quickly estimate the square footage needed based on seating style, number of bars, buffet or plated service, number of wait stations, dance floor, staging and other options (e.g., Party Center 2013).

When discussing price with the tent vendor, make sure the proposal includes tent rental cost as well as the amount of time needed to set it up and the number of workers who will be dedicated to the job. Advise your clients that it is a sound investment to pay for a technician who will stay for the entirety of the event to manage the tent as needed. If the sidewalls need to be raised or the heat level adjusted, a technician can efficiently and professionally handle the task. Reputable tent companies that have liability insurance may cost a bit more but they are well worth it, as the last thing your clients want is a tent that is unsafe.

TENT COSTS

As mentioned earlier, tent costs go way beyond the tent. Tent pricing varies considerably by region and based on the surface where the tent is installed. For instance, if a company installs a tent on

TABLE 16.1 SAMPLE GUIDELINES FOR SELECTING A TENT

Number of Guests	Tent Size for Ceremony Seating Only	Tent Size with Tables, Buffet and Dance Floor
50	20' x 30' 600 square feet	20' x 50' 1000 square feet
100	30' x 40' 1200 square feet	40' x 50' 2000 square feet
150	30' x 60' 1800 square feet	50' x 60' 3000 square feet
200	40' x 60' 2400 square feet	40' x 100' 4000 square feet

SOURCE: ADAPTED FROM RICHARDSON (2013)

an asphalt rooftop, it will cost much more than a tent placed in an open, grassy field. The look of the tent influences price; for example, sidewalls may cost $300 where a fabric liner will be $4,000 for white or off-white and even more if colored fabric is chosen. The time of year is a significant consideration as well, where tent heating may cost $500, while air conditioning can cost up to $10,000. Check with the rental company to ensure that the quoted price reflects the delivered product, meaning that it includes all installation and removal charges. Table 16.2 offers an example of a tent utilized for an evening wedding attended by 140 guests. The fact that the cost for this tent set-up is greater than the total budget for the average wedding in the United States offers ample evidence for why tented weddings tend to be high-budget affairs.

TABLES, CHAIRS, LINENS AND TABLEWARE

When starting with a tent, your clients will also need to rent tables, chairs, linens and tableware. At many indoor venues, some of these items need to be rented or upgrades may be available for a price. While some venues require that you use their equipment, others are flexible and allow rentals to be brought in for the wedding. It is important to know what they have available in advance so you can gauge how the couple feels about the options and alternatives. For example, when visiting a reception venue, you may notice that the chairs all have mauve cushions, yet your clients' colors are navy and gold. Knowing this information, you can discuss the possibility of renting seat covers or alternative cushions with your clients.

Tables are the most straightforward choice and are available in a multitude of sizes. Common guest tables are 5-foot rounds, which seat 8–10, and 6-foot rounds, which seat 10–12, while an 8-foot oblong table can seat 8–10. Sweetheart tables are an option for the bride and groom who want

TABLE 16.2 SAMPLE TENT PRICING: AN EVENING WEDDING WITH 140 GUESTS

Item	Price
40' x 60' tent plus entrance canopy	$4,400
Off-white liner	$4,000
Plastic subfloor with short-pile carpet	$4,250
28' x 28' dance floor	$2,350
Two heaters	$500
Power generator	$900
Catering tent	$1,500
Tent permit	$1,500
Lighting	$10,000
Maintenance technician	$420
Overtime labor for Sunday tent removal	$400
TOTAL	$30,220

SOURCE: ADAPTED FROM ELBOGHDADY (2010)

to be seated by themselves. Should they choose to sit with the wedding party, the trend is for couples to use one or several round tables rather than a series of oblong tables lined up as a head table. Square tables that seat two guests per side are an increasingly popular alternative. Tables of various sizes are also needed for items such as the escort cards, gifts, favors and the cake, as well as wait stations for the catering staff. For escort cards, gifts and favors, 6-foot or 8-foot oblong tables are commonly chosen, while the cake can be placed on a 4-foot round.

Chairs are also relatively finite in terms of variety, with folding chairs offering a budget-friendly option. These chairs come in a variety of colors, with material options of wood, metal or plastic influencing the price, as well as the presence of padding. For upscale weddings, *Chiavari chairs* are a popular selection. Chiavari chairs are formal, elegant and enhanced by accompanying cushions which can be covered in a wide array of fabrics to match the table linens. As a point of comparison, a padded wooden folding chair averages around $3 to rent, while a Chiavari chair with cushion runs about $9 per chair.

When bringing tables and chairs into a venue, it is extremely important to know the regulations. Some historic buildings do not allow tables to be rolled on the flooring, and each table and chair leg must have a rubber- or felt-tipped bottom. Policies such as these mean the room has to be laid with pads and each item must be carefully prepared and placed; accordingly, staffing costs go up significantly.

PHOTO 16.4 TABLES COME IN A VARIETY OF SHAPES AND SIZES.

SOURCE: WWW.RODNEYBAILEY.COM

Selecting linens and tableware can be a time-consuming endeavor, as seemingly endless options pertaining to color, style and material are available. Advise your clients to have their theme, color scheme and floral décor in mind when selecting items like china, glassware, flatware and linens. Of these, linens are traditionally the most overlooked, as couples often do not think past the traditional white tablecloth. On the contrary, linens offer one of the least expensive ways to make a huge impression and most reception venues allow clients to bring in rented linens. Top rental companies offer hundreds of styles and cuts from which to choose, available in fabrics such as damask, lace, organza, satin, silk, taffeta, toile, twill and velvet. Linens are available in an endless array of colors and styles such as embroidered, floral, fringed, iridescent, pin-tucked and striped. A current trend is layering linens to create a dramatic and memorable effect. If the linens are bold and patterned, it is a good idea to go with simple floral décor to create a balance so that the elements will not "fight." Keep in mind that you will need linens for areas such as the cake table and escort table. Longer linens that do not require skirts are a current trend. The linens should be long enough to cover the legs of all tables, which are often rough looking from use.

Once your clients have narrowed down their linen options, you can work with the company specialist to procure samples. You can then schedule an appointment with the reception venue to set three tables with different linens to determine the best look. This is a good time to work with the floral designer so you have a sample of the centerpiece on hand.

PHOTO 16.5 GHOST CHAIRS MATCH ANY DÉCOR.

SOURCE: WWW.RODNEYBAILEY.COM

When placing the order, have your clients order a few extra napkins and an extra tablecloth. Spills are common, so it is helpful to have spares just in case. When the linens are delivered, always double-check the order. Make sure you receive the correct pattern and correct number, as your clients will be accountable for any missing pieces. This same advice applies to any rental item. Generally, the rental or catering staff will set the tables for you, as tableware should not just be thrown on randomly. The correct placement of plates, glasses, flatware and the intricate folds that are common to napkins for formal weddings can be time-consuming endeavors. At the end of the reception, you need to re-count the rentals. If a linen order was for 12 tablecloths and 100 napkins, you are responsible for getting 12 and 100 back to the rental company. Invariably, someone throws a napkin away, and your client will be charged. If it is $3 to rent a napkin, it will be $6 or more to replace it. Specialty table linens are much more expensive, with rental fees averaging $30 and higher each and replacement fees at least double that amount.

LIGHTING

Lighting is used to establish the mood of a setting, and innovative lighting can bring a ceremony or reception venue to life. Just as a coat of paint and new carpeting can transform a house, professional lighting can take a bland venue and make it look like a glamorous Hollywood movie set. Fred Elting (2013) of Frost Lighting, who sets up lighting for approximately 100 weddings a year, states that, beyond function, the point of lighting is to make a huge impression on the guests, so that they walk in and say, "Wow! The lighting is so cool!" Fred explains that there are three areas of concern with lighting: 1) centerpiece lighting; 2) dance floor and wall lighting; and 3) tent lighting.

PHOTO 16.6 LINENS SHOULD COMPLEMENT THE COLOR AND STYLE OF THE VENUE.

SOURCE: WWW.RODNEYBAILEY.COM

CENTERPIECE LIGHTING

In a ballroom, where existing lights are in place, Fred indicates that the first lighting consideration pertains to the centerpieces. He differentiates between pin spotting and a wash of light. *Pin spotting* is a tightly focused beam of light directed on the table centerpieces, allowing the centerpieces to "pop," as the light does not spill over onto the rest of the table. Pin spots can even be placed underneath a table to shoot up through a clear glass centerpiece for a unique effect.

The *wash of light* came about as a response to the fact that centerpieces started getting larger and taller. For large arrangements, the pin spotting would allow for one hot spot on the arrangement, but could not capture the whole piece. A wash of light is a wider beam that lights up the whole table. This light is particularly effective when the linens are spectacular, as the wash picks up any shimmer or play in the tablecloth. If the linens are bland, lighting can be a game-changer used to bring color and vibrancy to the table. Fred explains that LED lights are the latest trend because they offer an even wash of vibrant light with very little electrical usage. LEDs can change hues throughout the event, creating a dramatic, exciting atmosphere.

Irrespective of the lighting style, white light should never be used as it does not look becoming on people. Lighting should make the room, the flowers and the guests look great. In order to achieve this, lighting specialists choose from a range of pinks and ambers that are subtle and flattering.

PHOTO 16.7 INNOVATIVE LIGHTING BRINGS A RECEPTION SPACE TO LIFE.

SOURCE: WWW.RODNEYBAILEY.COM

DANCE FLOOR AND WALL LIGHTING

After the centerpieces, the next consideration is the dance floor. The dance floor is a large open space that takes up a significant portion of your room. Fred details the three possible steps in lighting a dance floor. The first and most common is a wash of light onto the dance floor, typically two pink and two lavender fixtures. These colors give a warm glow and look great on people. The dance floor becomes more appealing as opposed to having a big empty space.

The next step is a breakup of light over the dance floor achieved through the use of artistic tools known as gobos. *Gobos* are thin templates often made of metal that are placed at the end of a lighting fixture, with design options that allow for the projection of an endless number of patterns. Gobos add interest, color and texture to a dance floor, walls or ceiling. Outlines of leaves, snowflakes, stars and sunbursts are common, as well as a multitude of geometric patterns.

A third option to light the dance floor is *computerized intelligent lighting.* This allows for moving patterns that are controlled by a technician who can constantly change the look to set the tone of the reception. For example, a father/daughter dance might include amber and pink with subtle gobos moving slowly over the dance floor, but, when the music gets faster and more exciting for general dancing, the colors change to contemporary, cool spectrum colors such as lavenders and blues, and the pace is kicked up with creative textures. Behind the stage might be a black backdrop with computer-generated fiber optics that are controlled on a computer and change colors and pulse. Intricate patterns such as leopards and lions looking down on the crowd can also be employed. As noted by Fred, top lighting companies work with designers and decorators; combined, the imaginative team can do just about anything with lighting.

Wall lighting is not necessary in most hotels because the chandeliers already in place can be controlled to create *ambient lighting,* or glow. However, in cases where a client wants to add color to what is in place, *up lighting* can transform a space with minimal investment. Up lighting is an excellent choice for spaces such as a community center or hall that does not have attractive ambient lighting in place. Fred notes that, if clients are on a limited budget, up lighting should be their first choice.

TENT LIGHTING

Tent lighting is more complex and significantly more expensive than ballroom lighting because the specialist is dealing with an empty structure and has to bring everything in, including power. Fred offers the comparison that ballroom lighting can be set up in seven hours for around $5,000, while it takes an average of two days and $15,000 to install tent lighting for a wedding. The cost of lighting presents another reason why clients on a budget should think twice before selecting a tent for their wedding. The first step is a wash of light onto the ceiling to create the ambient glow. This is followed by the installation of chandeliers for illumination; these are often covered with crystal beading to make them elegant or greenery and flowers for a garden effect. A sea of paper lanterns can also be used for illumination. Lighting companies also commonly work with fabric

PHOTO 16.8 GOBOS ADD TEXTURE TO A DANCE FLOOR.

SOURCE: WWW.RODNEYBAILEY.COM

and can take a structure such as a picnic pavilion and transform it into a ballroom with draping fabric and custom lighting. A tent ceiling can also be draped with swags of miniature lights for a graceful look.

Because lighting companies use a great deal of equipment, be certain to ask how they install their fixtures. The bottom line is that the lighting should blend into the architecture of the space rather than standing out as an eyesore. Fred gives an example of a particularly complicated wedding where they installed battery-operated chandeliers in trees so they would not need to run power to the trees. This example illustrates that specialty lighting can be used outside and around a tent or venue to enhance the surrounding area; for example, a "wall" of contemporary pendant lanterns hung at different heights can offer a vivid complement to the overall décor (Frost Lighting 2013). When using a clear-top tent, Fred suggests lighting up all of the trees around the site and, in particular, any branches that are up and over the tent to create a fabulous glow.

OUTDOOR CONSIDERATIONS

Beyond weather, two significant considerations when planning outdoor weddings are bathrooms and bugs. In terms of bathrooms, if the wedding is in someone's backyard rather than at a rented space that already has restroom facilities, it is in the best interest of the homeowners to rent bathrooms. Even if the house is large, having hundreds of people traipsing through to use their facilities can put an enormous amount of pressure on the sewer line. Homeowners have had their plumbing systems literally wiped out by having a tent wedding on the property and not investing in washrooms. Bathroom rental from well-known companies such as Porta-Potty can be as simple as a holding tank or as luxuriously equipped as their Executive Restroom Trailers that include lighting, music, carpeting, air conditioning, heating, flush and running water in the sinks. Make sure to get at least one rental washroom for every 100 guests and carefully position them away from the main activities.

A second outdoor consideration is bugs. In warm climates, insects can move beyond a nuisance to extreme discomfort that shortens the guests' stay. Imagine an outdoor, southern wedding in July: mosquitoes, flies, wasps, ticks, gnats, yellow jackets and no-see-ums, just to name a few. They swarm around the food and bite the guests. They smell sugar and go crazy. They are drawn

PHOTO 16.9 BEADED LAMPS ENHANCE THE SITE LAYOUT.

SOURCE: WWW.RODNEYBAILEY.COM

to the light for evening weddings. Citronella candles help, but have a pungent smell so should be kept out of the immediate vicinity of the tent so as to not interfere with the meal. Machines that zap bugs can be rented, but have an irritating sound. Tent entryways, on the other hand, are very helpful because they control the flow of people and other outside elements. You could also spray the surrounding area, but you have to be careful as children will often run in grassy areas and the chemicals present a safety issue. A final option is to have the wait staff walk around with trays of wipes or bottles of bug repellant. A supply should also be available in the restroom facilities.

SITE LAYOUT

Your site layout does not need to be a masterpiece that any architect would envy; instead, it is a straightforward drawing that offers a concise overview of placement and spacing. If there are no online site maps available of the venues, start with a blank page for both the ceremony and reception sites and fill in the applicable essentials covered in Table 16.3.

Site layout is straightforward when weddings are held in established venues that offer few options for variation. Figure 16.1 offers an example of a blank site layout of The Atrium at Meadowlark Botanical Gardens, where Events Coordinator Renee Arellano (2013) estimates that 120 weddings are hosted every year. Figure 16.2 illustrates the same venue, where the specific information for a wedding reception is detailed.

Renee advises clients and planners to carefully consider how the parameters of a venue influence site layout. For instance, while The Atrium has a stated capacity of 230 guests, clients anticipating this maximum number would face a number of restrictions to accommodate the tight space, such as: 1) the meal must be seated/plated rather than buffet; 2) the entertainment must be a DJ rather than a band; and 3) all 5-foot round tables must seat 10 guests rather than the typical 8, and all 6-foot round tables must seat 12 guests rather than 10. As noted in Chapter 9, because clients tend to overestimate their guest counts, particularly in the early planning stages when they are conducting site visits, the layout often loosens up as the wedding date approaches. Nonetheless, it is best to pick a venue that matches the maximum number of anticipated guests, with room to spare, to avoid cramped quarters.

As the planning space becomes less defined and the number of rentals increases, the site layout becomes more complex. For example, outdoor weddings and receptions held in tents require more attention to detail and increase the number of decisions that must be made. Staff expertise becomes critical, in particular if there is a changeover between the ceremony and the reception. Fred Elting offers a changeover example where his team and the tent company staff had to hang ceiling fabric, install chandeliers and aim 100 pin spot lamps throughout the décor in the one hour while guests were enjoying cocktails between the ceremony and reception. Once the tent site layout is determined, keep the clients safely away to avoid stressful situations such as the one presented in *Consultant in Action*, Case 16.1.

Table 16.3 Site layout essentials for weddings

Ceremony

- Parking
- Room dimensions
- Entrances and exits, with special marks for accessible paths and ramps and indications of controls (e.g., metal detector, security check)
- Restroom facilities
- Number of rows, with marks for reserved areas, and indications if the areas are separated for the bride's guests versus the groom's guests
- Waiting area for bride, groom and wedding party prior to ceremony
- Indicators for the location for floral décor and other special ceremony elements
- Space to be used for central focus (e.g., altar, arch, chuppah or other visually accessible area)
- Fire lanes and other emergency information

Reception

- Parking
- Room dimensions
- Entrances and exits, with special marks for accessible paths and ramps and indications of controls (e.g., metal detector, security check)
- Restroom facilities
- Cocktail hour area, if separate from reception space
- Number of guest tables with marks for reserved tables
- Head table and/or sweetheart table
- Service stations for wait staff
- Tables and areas associated with seating stationery, gifts, the cake and favors
- Kitchen and/or food-related areas
- Bar area
- Music and dance area
- Areas for the placement of specialized lighting
- Indicators for the location for specialized floral décor and other special reception elements
- Fire lanes and other emergency information

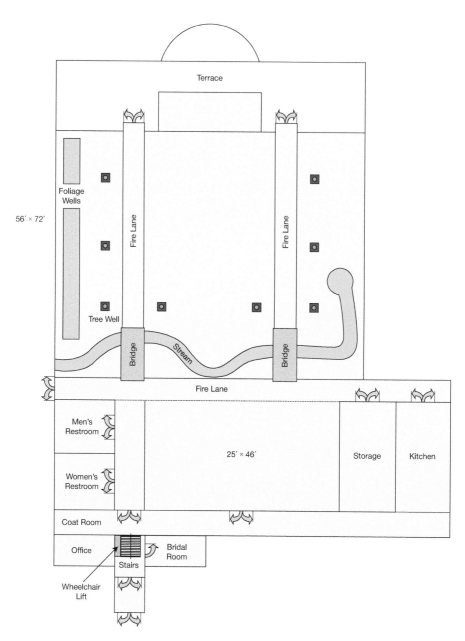

FIGURE 16.1 BLANK SITE LAYOUT OF A WEDDING RECEPTION SPACE AT THE ATRIUM AT MEADOWLARK BOTANICAL GARDENS

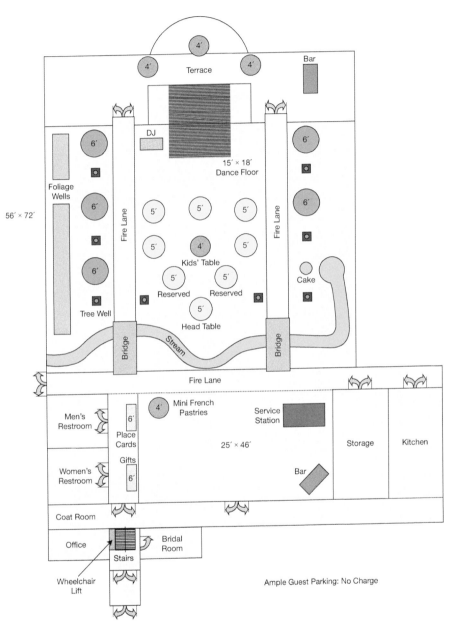

FIGURE 16.2 DETAILED SITE LAYOUT OF A WEDDING RECEPTION SPACE AT THE ATRIUM AT MEADOWLARK BOTANICAL GARDENS

As discussed earlier, tables come in different shapes and sizes, so you must understand the floor plan and the square footage of a room or tented area to determine how many tables will fit and how to space them. Be sure to leave at least 48 inches, and preferably 54, between tables so there is adequate room for guest and wait staff movement. Well-planned site layout maximizes the safety and comfort level of all participants.

CONSULTANT IN ACTION, CASE 16.1

MURPHY'S LAW

You are a senior wedding planner for an events management company. A few weeks before one of the company's biggest wedding events of the season, your boss tells you that she will not be able to be on site for this wedding and is sending you to take her place. The bride, Murphy, is upset when she is informed about the change. On the wedding day, anything that could go wrong is going wrong. It is the hottest day of the summer, over 101 degrees. The ceremony is to take place outside and the reception will be tented. A few hours before the ceremony, Murphy shows up and wants the tables rearranged, centerpieces redone and the restroom trailers moved to a more discreet location. Vendors are late, your assistants have yet to arrive and 300 chairs need to be set up for the ceremony. Time is running out and Murphy will not let go of the reins of the day.

WHAT DO YOU DO?

CASE SUBMITTED BY KELLY BOWENS AND LINDA ROBSON

REFERENCES

Arellano, R. (2013) 'Site layout considerations for weddings'. Personal communication (15 March 2013).

Bowens, K. and Robson, L. (2013) 'Murphy's law'. E-mail (24 January 2013).

ElBoghdady, D. (9 January 2010) '"I do," right here at home', *The Washington Post*, E1, E3.

Elting, F. (2013) 'Lighting for weddings'. E-mail (2 March 2013).

Frost Lighting (2013) 'Product gallery: lanterns', Online. Available HTTP: <http://www.frostdc.com/products/products/lanterns/products/index.html> (accessed 1 March 2013).

PHOTO 16.10 AN OUTDOOR FIREPLACE ADDS WARMTH AND GLOW.

SOURCE: WWW.RODNEYBAILEY.COM

Party Center (2013) 'Tent calculator', Online. Available HTTP: <http://www.apartycenter.com/tentcalc.shtml> (accessed 25 February 2013).

Richardson, D. (2013) 'What tent style?', Sugarplum Tent Company, Online. Available HTTP: <http://www.sugarplum tents.com/tentStyles.html> (accessed 1 March 2013).

The Atrium at Meadowlark Botanical Gardens (2013) 'The Atrium', Online. Available HTTP: <http://www.nvrpa.org/park/ meadowlark_botanical_gardens/content/the_atrium> (accessed 20 March 2013).

CONSULTANT CHECKLIST AND REMINDERS FOR RENTALS AND SITE LAYOUT

☐ Prior to meeting with a tent rental company, familiarize yourself with the different types of tents and accessories and prepare a draft of the desired site layout.

☐ It is better to have too much room than not enough in a tent.

☐ The cost of a tent and the necessary associated rentals is often significantly higher than renting a ballroom or other venue.

☐ Linens offer one of the least expensive ways to creatively impress guests.

☐ When placing the linen order, add a few extra napkins and an extra tablecloth in case of spills.

☐ You need to count rentals upon delivery and before pick-up to make sure there are no missing items.

☐ Lighting can transform a space from bland to glamorous.

☐ Bathrooms and bugs are two significant considerations with outdoor weddings.

☐ Site layout offers a concise overview of placement and spacing.

REVIEW

1. Distinguish between pole tents and frame tents.

2. If you have 150 guests for a buffet reception with tables and dance floor, what size tent should be selected?

3. Name at least four types of fabric that are used for linens.

4. Distinguish between pin spotting and a wash of light as related to centerpieces.

5. What are gobos and how are they used?

6. What are three ways to handle bugs for outdoor weddings?

7. What information should be included in a site layout for a ceremony?

8. What information should be included in a site layout for a reception?

TERMINOLOGY

- Ambient lighting
- Chiavari chairs
- Frame tents
- Gobos
- Pendant lanterns
- Pin spotting
- Pole tents
- Sailcloth tents
- Site layout
- Tension tents
- Up lighting
- Wash of light

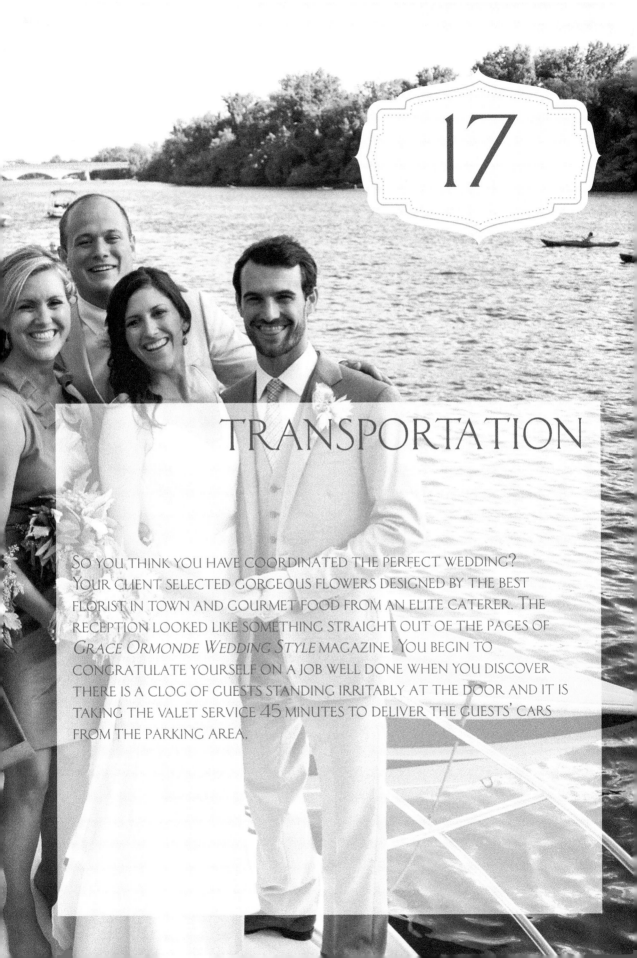

TRANSPORTATION

So you think you have coordinated the perfect wedding? Your client selected gorgeous flowers designed by the best florist in town and gourmet food from an elite caterer. The reception looked like something straight out of the pages of *Grace Ormonde Wedding Style* magazine. You begin to congratulate yourself on a job well done when you discover there is a clog of guests standing irritably at the door and it is taking the valet service 45 minutes to deliver the guests' cars from the parking area.

Coordinating transportation logistics may make you feel like a glorified dispatcher; but, at the end of the wedding, getting the guests home in a timely fashion becomes one of the most important details, especially for the guests. While they may not remember the red and green macaroons your client selected, they are sure to recall the seemingly endless wait in the cold because the transportation was disorganized. Arranging transportation for your clients' wedding involves five main areas: 1) getting started; 2) transportation to the ceremony venue; 3) transportation from the ceremony to the reception; 4) transportation from the reception to the final destination; and 5) transportation costs and final details.

GETTING STARTED

When you meet with your clients to discuss their transportation needs, a good place to start is to have them consider the number of people who will need transportation at various times throughout the wedding festivities. You need to have a clear understanding of all transportation requirements, from picking up guests at the airport to arranging a vintage Rolls-Royce that will bring the newlyweds home after their honeymoon has ended.

Prepare a list of questions to ask your clients so that you can begin to understand their unique transportation needs. These questions pertain to what, who and when. First, what style or styles of transportation do they want for their wedding day? Are they interested in a white stretch limousine, horse-drawn carriage, SUV, Lincoln Town Car or vintage automobile? The number of choices is limited only by your clients' imagination and the transportation budget.

Second, who needs to be transported? Have your clients spell out exactly who needs to be moved from point A to point B during the wedding day. It is important for you to know the exact number of people who require transportation so that you can recommend the appropriate vehicles. Have your clients prepare a list of the names of the wedding party and the guests needing transportation so that you know exactly who needs to be picked up and from where. If one of the wedding guests needs a wheelchair, this will influence the type of transportation you send to pick up the guests. All of this information is useful in shaping your vehicle recommendations.

Third, when will individuals need to be transported? For destination weddings, the transportation needs can get out of control if not coordinated. Cross-check flight schedules to determine the various arrivals and departures so the number of trips to the airport can be minimized. As introduced in Chapter 8, having a separate timeline specific to transportation can help make the wedding run smoothly.

TRANSPORTATION TO THE CEREMONY

After determining the number of people requiring transportation, the next step involves deciding how to transport the bride and her attendants to the ceremony. The bride needs wedding day transportation from the location where she is dressing to the wedding ceremony location. The bride takes this last ride as a single woman accompanied by her father, mother and/or her bridesmaids. Since it is typically the father who escorts the bride down the aisle, it is wise to keep father and daughter together prior to the wedding ceremony if at all possible.

For just the two of them, the transportation can be a classic car, a rickshaw or another intimate type of vehicle. If the wedding takes place on the family farm, the vehicle of choice might be an antique Ford truck or a hot air balloon. As long as you can match the vehicle style to the theme of the wedding, you will be well on your way to successfully conveying your bride and her father to one of the most important events of their lives.

If, however, the bride wishes to meet her father at the ceremony venue and ride with her attendants, you will need to find a comfortable vehicle to hold all of the women. A stretch limousine holds 10–12 passengers, while a regular limo can accommodate 6–10 passengers comfortably. A town car can hold 2–4 passengers. Take a headcount before selecting the vehicle.

After planning the bride's transportation, you should discuss the arrangements for getting the groom to the ceremony. Perhaps you will hire another limo to pick up the groom and his family at their home or hotel. Maybe the groom wants to ride with his groomsmen to the ceremony in a stretch

PHOTO 17.2 WHEN TRANSPORTING THE BRIDE TO THE CEREMONY, VINTAGE AUTOMOBILES MAKE A STATEMENT.

SOURCE: WWW.RODNEYBAILEY.COM

PHOTO 17.3 THE BRIDE MAKES A DRAMATIC ENTRANCE ON HER WEDDING DAY.

SOURCE: WWW.RODNEYBAILEY.COM

Hummer. Whatever the plan is for the groom, make sure that you are aware of all the arrangements and that you have a contact phone number even if the groom is simply riding with his brother in the family BMW.

Next, you may need to assist the rest of the wedding party, the families and the guests with transportation. Again, the mode of transportation selected is largely dictated by the style of the wedding and the number of people requiring assistance. Secure the transportation well in advance if your clients' wedding is during prom or graduation season, when most limos and other luxury cars are in high demand. Limousine buses with a 25-passenger capacity are a popular option for the wedding party, offering an entertainment system, multiple wet bars, champagne buckets, fiber optic light systems and luxury seating (Reston Limo 2013a). For a smaller group, a Hummer limo accommodates up to 14 passengers in plush style (Reston Limo 2013a).

It is a thoughtful gesture on the part of the bride and groom to arrange for buses to shuttle guests to the wedding and bring them back to their lodging at the end of the reception. This ensures the guests' safety and cuts down on late arrivals. Motor coaches range from 39-passenger to 55-passenger options and include entertainment systems, overhead storage areas, a restroom and wheelchair access (Virginia Coach 2013). Hiring a fleet of vehicles is another option. In addition to the standard types of vehicles, you can suggest a trolley, a double-decker bus or a boat to make

PHOTO 17.4 IMAGINE THE DASHING GROOM MAKING HIS GRAND ENTRANCE ON A HORSE.

SOURCE: WWW.RODNEYBAILEY.COM

the trip more interesting and enjoyable for all passengers. If the time spent during transport is going to be substantial, advise your clients to hire a tour guide or local expert to entertain the guests with stories and anecdotes along the way.

If your client is planning to provide transportation for the guests, this information needs to be communicated well in advance so that the guests can take full advantage of the arrangement.

Sending out a mailing with the invitations or to confirmed guests is an excellent way to coordinate this information. The information can also be posted on the couple's wedding website. Tell the guests exactly where to find the transportation and when the vehicle will depart for the ceremony. Pad this time by 15 minutes to accommodate stragglers. Make sure the transportation company is aware of any access limitations associated with the ceremony and reception sites, so as not to run into a situation similar to the one found in *Consultant in Action*, Case 17.1.

Consultant in Action, Case 17.1

A tight squeeze

Your clients are getting married at a beautiful, rented private residence in northern Michigan. Because of the long, narrow dirt driveway leading up to the house, it was decided that they would hire a shuttle to bring guests from the nearby hotel to the residence to prevent parking on the manicured lawn. You assist the couple with picking out a 35-passenger shuttle. While there are more than 35 guests who will use the shuttle service, this smaller vehicle was chosen based on the narrowness of the driveway and the limited turn area close to the house. Multiple trips will be used to get all guests to the house on time, and you plan the timeline accordingly. On the wedding day, you send your assistant, Sophia, over to the hotel to assist guests with locating and boarding the shuttle. One hour before the wedding, Sophia calls you to state that the shuttle has arrived and the guests are beginning to board. She states, "The driver mentioned that the shuttle company decided to be generous, so they sent a 55-passenger shuttle as a free upgrade." Having assisted with the booking, you know for a fact that there is no way that this larger shuttle will make it up the driveway without getting damaged, and that it will be impossible for it to turn around if it does make it up.

What do you do?

Case submitted by Alicia Caldecott
Website: *ADAYINMAYEVENTS.COM*
Interview conducted by Tori Price

TRANSPORTATION FROM THE CEREMONY TO THE RECEPTION

After your clients are pronounced husband and wife, there will be an excited press of guests anxious to proceed to the reception. To facilitate this movement of people, it again makes sense to transport guests en masse, especially if the reception venue is located in a major city. Using the same transportation that brought them to the ceremony to drive them to the reception is the most economical option.

However, if you think that the majority of the guests will drive their personal vehicles to the reception, then it might be more sensible to hire a *valet service* to assist with parking and retrieving cars. Most valet services charge $25–$35 per attendant per hour, plus gratuity. Do not estimate the number of vehicles based on the guest count, as families, couples or friends generally arrive together. A cost-conscious estimate is to base the number of cars on 40 per cent of the guest count, meaning that 100 guests would arrive in 40 vehicles. Each attendant can park or retrieve at least 8 cars in 45 minutes, assuming the parking area is in close proximity to the venue (Gold Crown Valet Parking 2013). Using the above estimates, a wedding with 100 guests would require at least

PHOTO 17.5 MAKE SURE TO HIRE ENOUGH VALETS SO GUESTS WILL NOT BE KEPT WAITING.

SOURCE: WWW.RODNEYBAILEY.COM

5 valets (40 total vehicles divided by 8 per attendant) to complete the parking or retrieval process within a 45-minute period.

If the reception is in a crowded downtown district, employ a valet service to save the guests the time and aggravation of looking for an open parking space or the expense of stashing the car in a pay lot. Be certain that your clients let their guests know well in advance that this amenity will

PHOTO 17.6 COUPLES MAY TAKE A TRANSPORTATION DETOUR BETWEEN THE
CEREMONY AND RECEPTION FOR UNIQUE PHOTO OPPORTUNITIES.

SOURCE: WWW.RODNEYBAILEY.COM

CONSULTANT IN ACTION, CASE 17.2

THE BROILING BENTLEY

The brother of the bride, Kyle, has always loved classic cars and decides to surprise his sister, Ginny, on her wedding day by renting a 1952 Bentley to bring her to the ceremony site in style. You agree to assist by making the arrangements and are just as excited as he is to see it roll up to the family home, where the bride is getting ready. The wedding is taking place on a particularly hot day in early August, and you are pleased to have worked with the transportation company to ensure that the vehicle has been retrofitted with modern air conditioning. When Ginny sees the Bentley, she hugs Kyle in delight. However, as she begins to enter the vehicle, she realizes that it is scorching hot inside and quickly steps out. You ask the flustered driver about the air conditioning and he admits that the retrofitted system does not work well. While she hates to disappoint her brother, Ginny does not want to arrive at the church looking like a melted mess, so she refuses to ride in the Bentley.

WHAT DO YOU DO?

be provided so it does not go to waste. Additionally, one of your assistants should hand out directions to the reception venue as guests exit the ceremony site. A reminder regarding the valet parking should be included on this sheet.

Another way your clients can take care of their guests is to pre-pay the parking fee if there is a charge at the venue. Have this fee built into the contract with the venue. If, for example, a hotel charges a flat fee of $15 per car and 75 cars arrive, your client will pay $1,125 to the hotel to ensure their guests park at no charge. This is a gracious gesture that, similar to valet service, should be clearly communicated to all guests so they do not end up accidentally paying for parking.

Once your clients are married, they will certainly want to depart for the reception in style. Their mode of transportation should be determined based on the distance between the ceremony and reception sites. If the reception venue is just a few steps away, then perhaps they will walk hand-in-hand to the accompaniment of a string trio. If the reception site is a few blocks away, then perhaps a ride on a Harley-Davidson will add just the right touch. However, if the reception is a good distance away, then the couple will want to be as comfortable and cozy as possible and perhaps a vintage car or stretch limousine is the way to go. When renting a classic car, part of the fun is learning about the history of the vehicle. Companies that specialize in luxury antique vehicles will often provide a detailed lineage for each car in their fleet (e.g., Regal Limousine 2013).

Whatever type of transportation your clients select, make sure that you get all the details in writing, including: arrival time (which you should pad by 15 minutes or so to be sure the transportation is on time), reception departure time, addresses of all locations, the size, color and model of the car the client is renting, the name of the driver, cost, gratuity, restrictions, special requests and the duration of time that you have contracted the vehicle. If you want the driver to take the scenic route on the way to the reception, make sure this information is included as well. Be as specific as possible and familiarize yourself with the limitations of each vehicle type. For example, if the couple yearns for a horse-drawn carriage but the wedding is held in Seattle, it will be best to ensure that it is a covered carriage, as Seattle is notorious for rain. You do not want your lack of awareness to result in a situation like the one presented in *Consultant in Action*, Case 17.2.

TRANSPORTATION FROM THE RECEPTION TO THE FINAL DESTINATION

As the reception winds down and the last dance has ended, the bride and groom, as well as their wedding party and guests, will be anxious to leave the reception and head off to their final destinations. For the newlyweds' exit, it is important that you ascertain from them exactly how they want to make their departure. Do they want to quietly steal away? Do they want to dash through an arch of sparklers into a waiting limo? Perhaps they want a candy apple red Vespa scooter ready to whisk them to their hotel. Before you book the exit vehicle, you must understand their wishes and translate them into reality. Table 17.1 includes a list of creative modes of transportation that can be used for a memorable exit or at any other point during the wedding day.

For the guests and wedding party, it is important to ferry them back to where they started that day so they can pick up their cars or fall into bed at their hotels. Leaving guests without a ride is very inconsiderate. You should encourage your clients to think about their obligations as hosts for the evening and the importance of taking care of their guests. These small considerations will be remembered for years to come. So, whether you provide a bus, a van or a line of yellow taxis, it is very important to get the guests home safely, especially those who have been drinking.

TRANSPORTATION COSTS AND FINAL DETAILS

While transportation costs vary from region to region, it is helpful to have a cost comparison. Most companies require a three- or four-hour minimum for any form of transportation, so bear that in mind when comparing costs. Check with your transportation vendor to determine if the fee structure includes the fuel charge and gratuity. Further, rental of high-maintenance vehicles usually includes a *garage time* (GT) fee for servicing after use. This fee usually pertains to large

PHOTO 17.7 A UNIQUE EXIT WILL PROVIDE MEMORIES FOR YEARS TO COME.

SOURCE: WWW.RODNEYBAILEY.COM

vehicles in which riders are eating and drinking. Table 17.2 includes a sample fee structure to give you a sense of general guidelines.

Be certain to familiarize yourself and your clients regarding policies that are outlined on the transportation contract. For instance, although it is common for the bridal party to enjoy food and beverages between the ceremony and reception while riding as a group, many coach companies do not allow breakables or open containers, so remind your clients about the restrictions before

TABLE 17.1 CREATIVE MODES OF TRANSPORTATION

- All terrain vehicle
- Antique fire engine
- Bicycle built for two
- Camel
- Canoe
- Chinese rickshaw
- Cross-country skis
- Dog sled
- Duck boat
- Elephant
- Golf cart
- Horseback
- Ice cream truck
- Mini Cooper
- Monster truck
- Moped
- Motorcycle with sidecar
- Sailboat
- Sleigh
- Snowboard
- Snowmobile
- Subway
- Surfboard
- Vintage VW Beetle

TABLE 17.2 SAMPLE FEE STRUCTURE FOR COMMON FORMS OF WEDDING
TRANSPORTATION

Vehicle Type	Minimum Charge	Additional Hour
Sedan 4 passengers	3 HR = $237	$79
SUV 5 passengers	3 HR = $267	$89
Limo 6 passengers	3 HR = $330	$110
Limo 8 passengers	3 HR = $375	$125
Limo 10 passengers	3 HR = $420	$140
Hummer 14 passengers	3 HR = $570	$190
Limo Bus 25 passengers	3 HR + GT = $700	$175
Van 14 passengers	3 HR + GT = $300	$75
Van Terra 12 passengers	3 HR + GT = $340	$85
Mini Bus 20 passengers	3 HR + GT = $380	$95
Coach 55 passengers	4 HR + GT = $700	$140
Tour Guide	4 HR = $260	$65
Greeter on site	4 HR = $168	$42

NOTES:

Above rates include Modest Driver Gratuity.

Rates do not include Parking or Fuel Surcharge.

10% Fuel Surcharge applies to Sedan, SUV, Limousine, Van and Van Terra.

15% Fuel Surcharge applies to Limobus, Minibus and Coach Bus.

Coach Buses Only – Rounded to hour after 15-minute grace period.

$15 Permit Fee (Jurisdictional Licensing Fee) applied to each bus reservation.

$12 Early / Late fee applies to trips beginning between 12 a.m. and 5 a.m.

G.T. = Garage Time: time needed to clean, refuel, and safety check each vehicle.

SOURCE: RESTON LIMOUSINE (2013B)

they pack the cooler. Strict guidelines also apply to decorating rental vehicles, so consult with the transportation operator to determine what types of vehicle décor are permissible. Well-meaning friends may get carried away in an attempt to be creative or funny, but liability for vehicle damage is anything but humorous. Cancellation policies apply to rental vehicles as well and your clients will minimally lose their deposits if they wait until the last minute to make a change.

The well-prepared wedding consultant has an eye for detail and an ear for trouble. Months prior to a wedding, you should communicate with local authorities regarding planned street closings, especially if your event is during a holiday weekend or in a large city where special events can snarl traffic for hours. For example, if your clients' wedding reception will be held at a private club close to the United Nations headquarters in New York City, call the government department that issues permits to see if there will be a high-security event taking place. You should determine potential transportation difficulties and plan alternative routes to mitigate traffic delays.

REFERENCES

Caldecott, A. (2013) 'A tight squeeze'. E-mail interview conducted by Tori Price (23 February 2013).

Gold Crown Valet Parking (2013) 'Frequently asked questions', Online. Available HTTP: <http://www.goldcrown.net/faq.asp> (accessed 14 March 2013).

Regal Limousine (2013) 'Limousine profiles', Online. Available HTTP: <http://www.regallimousine.com/reservation.htm> (accessed 8 March 2013).

Reston Limo (2013a) 'Showroom', Online. Available HTTP: <http://www.restonlimo.com/showroom/limobuses/> (accessed 10 March 2013).

—— (2013b) 'Transportation costs', Online. Available HTTP: <http://www.restonlimo.com> (accessed 10 March 2013).

Virginia Coach (2013) 'Our fleet', Online. Available HTTP: <http://www.virginiacoach.com/ourfleet.html> (accessed 10 March 2013).

CONSULTANT CHECKLIST AND REMINDERS FOR TRANSPORTATION

☐ Transportation preparation requires knowing what the couple wants, who needs transport and when transportation will be required.

☐ Be aware of how the couple, bridal party and guests will be transported to the ceremony site, from the ceremony to the reception, and to their final destinations.

☐ Prepare a timeline that is specific to transportation.

☐ Leave-taking from the ceremony and reception should be efficient.

☐ Be aware of the restrictions and limitations of each vehicle type being considered.

☐ Determine if the transportation company's pricing structure includes the fuel charge, gratuity and garage time.

☐ Confirm with transportation vendors and supply directions to each place a driver will be stopping.

☐ Get day-of phone numbers for the transportation company and drivers.

☐ Check with police and city government offices on street closing, parades, demonstrations and other special events.

☐ Encourage your clients to pay the venue parking fees for their guests.

☐ Secure transportation early if the wedding is during prom or graduation season.

☐ Familiarize your clients with policies and restrictions specific to their vehicle rentals.

REVIEW

1. What are the three main time periods during which transportation will be required on the wedding day?

2. Name five creative modes of transportation that can be used for weddings.

3. Name at least two reasons to hire transportation for wedding guests.

4. What are the key points to get in writing when hiring transportation?

5. Discuss the benefits of hiring a valet service.

6. How can you find out about known street closures and expected traffic delays that might occur on the day of a wedding?

TERMINOLOGY

- Driver gratuity

- Fuel charge

- Garage time

- Valet service

One of our most treasured discove...
as North Carolinians was the
"BEAUFORT BAR"

We'd like to now share it with yo...
as a sign of our gratitude.

Photo 18.1 Vintage suitcases purchased from a thrift store make a unique presentation for favors.

FAVORS AND GIFTS

Considerate brides and grooms recognize and appreciate all those who have helped to plan and celebrate their wedding day. From the bridesmaids to the groomsmen, from the ring bearer to the flower girl, from the parents to the guests, gift giving opportunities surrounding a wedding are truly limitless. The savvy wedding planner can helpfully make suggestions to the couple as they plan the "who, how and when" of favors and gifts. The primary focus of this chapter is on gifts from the couple, including six major types of favors, packaging options, wedding guest gift baskets and wedding party gifts. The chapter concludes by considering gifts for the couple.

SIX TYPES OF FAVORS

While favors differ from culture to culture, the hope is that the wedding guests will be delighted by the memento, and, in the spirit of health and happiness, remember the wedding day with fondness. So, even as trends and traditions change, the sentiment always remains the same. For the bride and groom, there are many different types of favors to consider giving their guests on the wedding day. These favors fall into six basic categories: edible favors, lasting favors, part-of-the-décor favors, favors inspired by nature, do-it-yourself (DIY) themed favors and charitable donations.

EDIBLE FAVORS

Everyone likes to leave the wedding with a delicious treat. Today's brides and grooms are more creative than ever in giving their guests packaged donuts, macaroons, cake pops, chocolate, candy, fortune cookies, granola, soft pretzels, cotton candy and a host of other edible and drinkable favors that might fit in with the wedding theme. For example, if the wedding is a destination wedding in Maui, the favor might be Honolulu Cookie Company's pineapple-shaped shortbread cookies hand dipped in chocolate. If the wedding takes place in Seattle, then a small box of Fran's salted dark chocolate caramels would make the perfect favor. Matching the favor to the wedding theme, location, interests, hobbies or culture of the wedding couple is always an excellent idea. Classic Jordan almonds have symbolic meanings for Italian and Greek weddings. Drinkable favors could be home-brewed beer in brown bottles with custom labels like Pale Veil Ale or miniature bottles of champagne with Happily Ever After labels affixed to the bottles. While some couples worry about the ephemeral nature of the edible favor, remind them that consumable favors are earth-friendly as there is little likelihood that they will go unused.

LASTING FAVORS

Other couples opt to give their guests a lasting favor. This type of favor is given out because the bride and groom hope that the recipient will treasure this keepsake and remember their wedding for years to come. Lasting favors often include picture frames, luggage tags, bottle openers, wine stoppers, silver napkin rings, mini photo albums, key chains, wine glasses, glass coasters, heart-shaped measuring spoons, love bird salt and pepper shakers, tea infusers, mini teapots, votive holders, wooden fans, ice cream scoops, silver bookmarks and wedding snow globes, just to name a few. Depending on the number of guests that your client is buying for, a lasting gift with true utility may be outside of the couple's budget, so it would be wise to steer your client to one of the other types of favors.

PART-OF-THE-DÉCOR FAVORS

Favors that double as wedding décor are a wonderful way to stretch your client's budget. Imagine, beautiful potted orchids gathered and arranged on the escort card table. At the end of the evening, your assistant walks around and hands out one plant per couple. The favor is part of the event's

PHOTO 18.2 HOME-BREWED BEER AS A FAVOR ALLOWS COUPLES TO SHOWCASE A HOBBY.

SOURCE: WWW.RODNEYBAILEY.COM

décor and then it does double duty as the favor. This can also be done with the centerpieces at each table. If the table seats ten for example, the favors, which are beautifully wrapped in small square boxes, can be stacked on top of a footed cake stand and placed in the middle of the table. That way, the boxes become the centerpiece for the table. If a table number is added to the stacked favors, the centerpiece does triple duty as the centerpiece, the favor and the holder for the table number. Jackpot!

Another clever way to use the favors as part of the décor is to incorporate the favor into the place card. For example, if the favor is a lovely piece of fruit such as a pomegranate, one could be arranged at each guest's place setting and the place card could be balanced on the crown of the fruit. This can be done with other types of fruit, vegetables, pinecones, twigs, seashells, driftwood, roses or other natural items. Be creative and your clients will be wowed by your ingenuity on their behalf.

FAVORS INSPIRED BY NATURE

Imagine a small bird's nest filled with two candy robin's eggs or an ivy topiary shaped in a heart placed at your seat. These are just two examples of favors inspired by nature that would make any naturalist or wedding guest happy. For many couples, having a "green" wedding is very important and this can carry over into eco-chic wedding favors as well. Seed packets, bulbs, herbs, potpourri, lavender sachets, shells, small trees and gardening tools all make for wonderful nature-inspired wedding favors. Also, birdseed hearts, bamboo coasters, hand-carved wooden bowls and anything recycled or repurposed can make for unique favors. Local farmers' markets and craft fairs are excellent sources of inspiration.

DIY FAVORS

If the wedding couple plans ahead, they can create many fabulous and creative gifts themselves. This DIY craze has been fueled by limited budgets and unlimited access to websites and wedding blogs that encourage brides to make their own favors. DIY favors work especially well if the bride is "known" for something like her famous chocolate chip cookies, homemade candles, hand-built pottery, brown sugar body scrub or hot pepper jelly. This approach also works for a motivated bride who wants to make something that fits with her wedding theme, like hot chocolate mix for a winter wonderland theme or homemade lip balm for a beach wedding. Some ideas for DIY-loving clients include: herb-infused olive oil, s'mores kit, vanilla extract, jam, homemade granola, individual cookie mix, limoncello, gourmet BBQ spice rubs, iced sugar cookies, chocolate-dipped pretzels, chocolate-

PHOTO 18.3 DIY HOT COCOA MIX IS PERFECT FOR A WINTER WONDERLAND THEME.

SOURCE: WWW.RODNEYBAILEY.COM

dipped strawberries, homemade soap, candles in a mason jar, bath bombs, salt water taffy, peppermint bark, candied nuts, honey and chocolate truffles (e.g., Willis 2011). The list can go on and on. Many DIY favors fall within the edible category, yet are distinguished by the personal effort made by the couple. Whatever your clients decide to make, encourage them to start early.

CHARITABLE DONATIONS

Some couples elect to take the money they would have spent on favors and, instead, make a charitable donation to a worthy cause or group that has meaning to the couple. This is a lovely gesture that should be communicated to the guests on the wedding day. The donation can be mentioned at the end of the wedding program or on small cards left at each place setting. The wording can be something like this:

To celebrate our marriage,
a donation to
WomenHeart
has been made in your honor.

Thank you
for sharing this special day with us.

Peejo and Campbell
September 9, 2017

PACKAGING AND PRESENTATION

Flair and creativity can be demonstrated not only in the choice of wedding favor, but also in the packaging. How the favor is packaged can reinforce the theme and the vision of the wedding day. For example, if a wedding has a carnival theme, the favor can be packaged in clear bags with labels that match the wedding colors and motifs that have been used throughout the wedding from the save-the-date to the thank-you notes. This reinforces the theme and makes for a coherent event.

A planner with clients who desire a vogue, New Year's Eve wedding in an urban setting might find that martini glasses make for a hip and unique way to present the favor. If the wedding is taking place on a farm or in a barn, a basket might make a unique presentation vehicle or perhaps even something as humble as a burlap bag. It is all about consistently carrying out the theme that your clients have selected with all the other elements of the day. Other interesting vessels include mason jars, small crates, Chinese takeout boxes, cones, mini champagne buckets, mint julep cups, tuxedo boxes, draw-string pouches, round tins, teacups, fabric, glassine bags, bottles or terra cotta pots. Let your imagination soar.

Most couples want their favors to be distributed to guests at the end of the reception, unless something goes awry like in *Consultant in Action*, Case 18.1. If you place favors directly on the

PHOTO 18.4 COLORFUL PACKAGING REINFORCES A CARNIVAL THEME.

SOURCE: WWW.RODNEYBAILEY.COM

CONSULTANT IN ACTION, CASE 18.1

THE BUNGLED BELLS

You are hired to plan and execute a late-December wedding with a silver bell theme. As their wedding favor, the couple will be giving their guests a pretty silver bell ornament tied with a satin ribbon. As a unique way to incorporate family into the wedding day, the bride tells you that she has asked her two young nieces to help at the wedding by handing out the favors as guests depart from the reception. This idea sounds lovely and you make a note in your timeline accordingly. On the day of the wedding, after the ceremony has concluded, the guests are called into dinner by the hotel staff. You are speaking with the banquet manager when you notice that the guests are walking into the dining room carrying silver bells. The meal has not even started yet and the guests have been given their favors.

WHAT DO YOU DO?

Photo 18.5 Favors may be put to use during the reception.

Source: www.RodneyBailey.com

tables, frequently they get left behind. Distributing the favors at the end of the evening, either from a table placed near the exit or from an attendant, ensures that they make it out the door. Some couples might want to surprise their guests by having valets leave a favor inside each of the cars they park; however, guests not using valet service will be missed and, in hot climates, a favor prone to melting such as chocolate can leave a mess. Remember, if favors are delivered to cars or hotel rooms, a service fee should be built into the budget, with a per person cost ranging from $2 to $10, depending on the location of the wedding.

The final consideration with favors is the messaging. Each favor, no matter the packaging, should have a small note, card or sticker attached that conveys the message of thanks and appreciation. The very best examples of this tie the gift to the message. For example, "Make, Bake, Celebrate" might be the wording on a homemade brownie mix favor, "Spread the Love" could be the message on a jar of jam, "Mint to Be" might be on the label for peppermint lip balm, "Love is Brewing" on canisters of tea or "S'more Fun for Later" could be printed on a s'mores kit. If your clients are going to have a wedding favor, make sure you help them tie it in with their theme and package and present it in a clever way.

PHOTO 18.6 CHIC BOXES WITH CUSTOMIZED MESSAGING SEND THE GUESTS OFF SWEETLY.

SOURCE: WWW.RODNEYBAILEY.COM

WEDDING GUEST GIFT BASKETS

It is always a thoughtful gesture to thank and remember those who have traveled to your client's wedding destination. These guests have gone out of their way to travel to the wedding and it is important that they are welcomed and thanked for coming. There is no better way to do this than by giving them a gift basket or bag of goodies. The gift basket does not have to be fancy and expensive; the point is that it should be thoughtful. One way to put together a basket is to think local. If your clients are tying the knot in Annapolis, Maryland, the bag might include things apropos to Annapolis like a map of the downtown area, a list of good seafood restaurants, sunscreen and a tin of Old Bay Seasoning. Tying in the basket to the wedding location is a wonderful idea and a great way to make your guests feel at home while in a new environment. Other items to include in the basket are still or sparkling water, a small bottle of champagne or wine, snacks to stave off hunger, the wedding itinerary and a welcome letter. Do not neglect the guests staying at hotels outside of the main room block or those who are staying with friends and family. If you agree to create baskets for your clients, make sure that you charge fees for design and delivery, so as to avoid situations like the one presented in *Consultant in Action*, Case 18.2.

CONSULTANT IN ACTION, CASE 18.2

BASKET CASE

You are a consultant for a wedding being held in a large metropolitan area. The groom's extended family is not from the area, so there will be a significant number of out-of-town guests. The mother of the groom, Lydia, wants to do something nice for all of these travelers, so you suggest welcome baskets for each of the hotel rooms. She thinks this is an excellent idea and says, "You are so creative! If I give you the cash to buy everything, will you put them together?" While this is not in your contract, you enjoy making gift baskets and agree to do so without stipulating any additional fee for your time and design expertise. Lydia states that she will send along some ideas by e-mail and put a check in the mail. Two days later, you receive an e-mail from Lydia. In it, she offers a variety of suggestions for the baskets and then lists the addresses of six different hotels where the guests will be staying, stating that, "You know the area so well, I am sure you won't mind dropping them off." Glancing at the hotel list and knowing the area, you realize it will take you at least five hours just to drop off the baskets, let alone the time you will spend shopping for and designing them.

WHAT DO YOU DO?

GIFTS FOR THE WEDDING PARTY

With as much lead time as possible, your clients should begin to think about meaningful gifts for the wedding party. This is not something that your client should leave for the last minute, especially if she is having silver picture frames engraved for each of the 12 bridesmaids and writing a personal note to go with each one. Who should receive a wedding gift and when should the gift be given are questions that your clients may ask you. Be ready to offer advice.

Weiss and Levine (2007) explain that wedding gifts should be presented to bridesmaids, groomsmen, the ring bearer, the flower girl and any other member of the official wedding party, such as readers, those handing out programs and favors, soloists or military personnel forming a ceremonial sword arch. Not all gifts need to be in the same price range, and can vary based on the extent of involvement in the wedding or personal sentiment. Also, it is a lovely gesture for brides and grooms to thank their parents with gifts. Weiss and Levine (2007) note that brides and grooms often give each other gifts on their wedding day. This gift should be meaningful and lasting. Encourage your clients to discuss this tradition to see if it fits in with their vision of their wedding day.

Depending on the number of bridesmaids and groomsmen, these gifts might require a great deal of forethought and the cost can be significant. The bride and groom should make sure the gifts selected match the spirit and expense of the overall wedding. For example, if the wedding budget

PHOTO 18.7 THE BRIDE RECEIVES A SPECIAL GIFT FROM THE GROOM ON THEIR WEDDING DAY.

SOURCE: WWW.RODNEYBAILEY.COM

is lavish, a bar of soap will not convey the right sentiment; instead, upscale items such as designer ties for the men and a beautiful bracelet for the women are appropriate. Frequently, the gift is something that can be worn or used on the wedding day, for instance, a pashmina wrap for the ladies and cufflinks for the men. If your clients want to go this route, make sure the information is communicated well in advance of the wedding day to avoid duplication and unnecessary expense incurred by the wedding party (Weiss and Levine 2007).

Some couples use their funds for the wedding party to pay for the bridesmaids' dresses and groomsmen's suits. This thoughtful approach takes the financial burden off the wedding party, allowing them to participate in the wedding without the added expense of purchasing or renting clothing. Instead of tangible gifts, many couples elect to treat the wedding party to a special outing, such as golfing for the men and a spa day for the women. These activities are likely to be more expensive than gifts, yet the memories tend to outlast traditional purchases.

Gifts for the ring bearer and flower girl should be age appropriate, parent approved and a lasting keepsake. For the flower girl, a silver necklace with a flower charm, a silver comb and brush set, a jewelry box and a monogrammed piggy bank are all wonderful options. For the ring bearer, an engraved silver harmonica, a silver-plated yoyo, Spiderman cuff links or a personalized engraved baseball would all make a positive impression. Similar to the adult members of the wedding party, an outing may be even more meaningful for the youngest of the group, such as a trip to a LEGO KidsFest or afternoon tea at an American Girl Café.

GIFTS FOR THE COUPLE

As introduced in Chapter 2, cultural traditions such as showers and dowry practices involve gifts for the couple. For some weddings, dowry practices can be worth tens or hundreds of millions, as is the case in the entrepreneurial city of Jinjiang, China, where billionaires compete for dowry bragging rights (Moore 2013). In other instances, couples struggle over the cultural impetus to accept a dowry, as illustrated in *Culture Corner*, Case 18.3. Gifts are sometimes integral to the ceremony itself, as showcased in *Culture Corner*, Case 18.4.

Once the ceremony has concluded, gifts of money are quite common during the reception. In many cultures, brides carry a moneybag to collect cash during special dances. Alternatively, money is sometimes pinned directly onto the bride's dress. Moneybags can be made in a variety of colors and fabrics, with embellishments used to echo the spirit of the wedding gown (Advantage Bridal 2013). As a newlywed, the bride's moneybag can be repurposed to hold the shoes, lingerie or other special items to be taken on the honeymoon (Advantage Bridal 2013).

Another option for collecting cards and envelopes during the wedding reception is the use of a wedding card holder. A wedding card holder can take many shapes and forms. Just a few examples of common holders include wire birdcages, theme-designed boxes, miniature churches, mailboxes, replicas of Cinderella's coach, vintage suitcases, wine barrels, lobster traps, rustic barrels, birdhouses and treasure chests. Remember, it should be easy to place the envelopes in

CULTURE CORNER, CASE 18.3

WHAT IS DOWRY IN A MODERN BANGLADESHI WEDDING PLAN?

Samia, a university graduate, started to speak with her husband-to-be, Ishfaq, over the telephone a couple of weeks before their official wedding. At the onset of starting their life together, they discussed personal likes and dislikes as an addition to the ins and outs of organizing a memorable wedding reception. Ishfaq was an expatriate British university graduate and had advancements in his choices. Both of them reached the decision for venue selection and attire for the day. Samia, with the consent of her parents and Ishfaq, ordered a complete suit for the groom. However, she decided to stick to the conventional Sari and moderate Bengali dresses.

They booked the Hotel Fars, a luxury five-star hotel as the wedding venue. The budget for the event crossed their prediction; however, they had to accept this due to their social status and prestige. In recalling expectations, Ishfaq tried to remember what he heard from his parents on a lazy afternoon. When Ishfaq's grandfather got married at his age of 24, 120 years ago, his grandmother was 10 years old. The husband and wife were complete strangers to each other. Their wedding was held in his maternal great-grandfather's house and in a shabby room. His grandfather was unable to bear the expenses, as he was a law student and was given cash money as dowry to complete his studies. Later on, Ishfaq's grandfather became a renowned lawyer who amassed huge wealth and property that turned him into a *Zaminder* (landlord).

Ishfaq also tried to bear in mind the events of 60 years back, when a similar situation repeated in his father's case. Ishfaq's mum was only 11 years of age at the time of her wedding, while his father was around 27. Their wedding was organized in Ishfaq's grandfather's castle-like building and the costs were borne by his father and grandfather. His father passed as a qualified physician and was earning a considerable amount of money. Ishfaq's father managed to speak for a single time to his future wife with the help of the mediator; however, his mum was completely covered with a veil. His father did not expect any dowry; however, as a token of blessings from the father-in-law, he was given a precious fountain pen, a bicycle and dresses.

Ishfaq tried to understand his case and what to expect. Educationally, he is qualified from Great Britain, which broadened his outlook and patterns of living. He met a few times with his wife-to-be with her consent, regardless of parental involvement. They openly discussed their family plans, likes and dislikes. But the big question remains: is he expecting gifts from his wife's side? Even though he is wealthy, educated and has a modernized view, he will have to accept very expensive items such as a luxury car or a flat as a token from his in-laws.

Ishfaq is a member of a family and the society; he hardly can ignore the customary patterns of weddings. Marriage is a traditional ritual of the human society and, particularly, in the typical Bangladeshi culture. For hundreds of years, people have gotten married to form a family and to offer an identity to the upcoming human beings. Ishfaq knows that so many things have revolutionized over time, including open-mindedness, social status and social values. The dowry system has evolved also, but maintains a modern form. Again, he reflected on his identity, his current position, his capacity and the actual definition of dowry as an unavoidable part of the wedding plan.

CASE SUBMITTED BY AZIZUL HASSAN

CULTURE CORNER, CASE 18.4

A TRADITIONAL MARRIAGE CEREMONY PERFORMED BY THE AKAN TRIBE OF GHANA

When Kwame met Ama and they decided to get married, representatives from Kwame's family paid a visit to Ama's father – a process referred to as *knocking*. Kwame's family came bearing a bottle of schnapps; this offering of alcohol allowed them to ask for Ama's hand in marriage. Once Ama confirmed that she wanted to marry Kwame, a list of items was given to Kwame's family. These would be the items that would be presented at the marriage ceremony, and then a date was set.

On the day of the marriage ceremony, Ama's home was decorated in festive colors, and a larger group of representatives from Kwame's family arrived early in the morning. The female spokesperson for the group then "knocked" loudly, and the door was opened only after another bottle of schnapps exchanged hands. Once everyone was seated, the spokesperson presented another bottle of schnapps to say "thank you" for being allowed in. She stated the purpose for their visit and then began to present the items on the list to a representative from Ama's family.

The first set of items was gifts for Ama's mother and father, to thank them for raising such a wonderful daughter. This was followed by the presentation of a number of items for Ama, including traditional clothes, shoes, jewelry, lingerie and a sewing machine. It did not matter that Ama has not sewn a day in her life! The items were presented amidst a lot of cheering from the crowd, made up of extended family and friends who had gathered for the festivities. The next set of items was a ring and a Bible for Ama. All the presentations also included monetary gifts, additional bottles of schnapps and other types of alcoholic and non-alcoholic beverages.

Once all of the items had been accepted by the representative of Ama's family, the representative then proceeded to present Kwame's family with gifts including some of the beverages received, as a way to show that they approved of the marriage and appreciated the honor that had been bestowed on them by Kwame and his family.

Then the time came for Ama to be brought out from where she had been waiting, as the bride and groom are usually not in the gathering room during the presentation of gifts. Since this was the one and only time Ama's family could get what they wanted from Kwame and his family, this turned into a game of "show me the money." The male relative who was tasked to bring Ama out of hiding claimed he needed money for transportation in order to be able to go and get her. The first person he brought out was a female cousin, hiding behind a veil. So were the second and third females he brought out; each after he had been given additional money for transportation. After the third "wrong" female, Kwame's family began to protest loudly, all in good fun, and insisted that since they had fulfilled their end of the agreement, they were done playing games – they demanded to see their bride.

Finally, Ama was brought into the room, as was Kwame. Then, Kwame got to put his ring on Ama's finger amidst a lot of cheering and clapping. A prayer was said by a minister present, after which words of advice were offered by elders from both families. Then it was time to party!

While a Ghanaian marriage ceremony will differ based on the tribe and individual family preferences, the experience of Ama and Kwame offers a glimpse into common customs. Even though these activities are recognized as a traditional marriage ceremony, some couples view this as an engagement ceremony and go on to have a Western-style wedding afterwards.

CASE SUBMITTED BY ABENA AIDOO

the container but difficult for someone to remove them. This layer of security gives you one less thing to worry about during the reception.

In terms of physical gifts, remind your clients to review and update their gift registries after any showers have taken place and, once again, at least a month prior to the wedding. Some guests prefer to give a tangible item rather than cash, so your clients should make it easy for them to do so by offering a range of price points in their registry selections. As noted in Chapter 13, etiquette dictates that registry information should not be included with a wedding invitation. Instead, it can be readily supplied on the wedding website. The registry should be kept active for at least a year after the wedding, as this is the common window of gift giving to newlyweds. Most retail outlets keep a wedding registry open for at least a year, and many allow up to two years. To ease the encumbrance of carrying a gift to the reception, remind your clients to update any address changes so that registry items can be mailed to the couple's home.

REFERENCES

Advantage Bridal (2013) 'Bride's money bag, wedding money bags, great gifts for the bride', Online. Available HTTP: <http://www.advantagebridal.com/money-bags-bridal-wedding-money-bag.html> (accessed 24 March 2013).

Aidoo, A. (2013) 'A traditional marriage ceremony performed by the Akan Tribe of Ghana'. E-mail (24 March 2013).

Hassan, A. (2013) 'What is dowry in a modern Bangladeshi wedding plan?' E-mail (7 January 2013).

Moore, M. (1 January 2013) 'Chinese bride marries with £100 million dowry', *Telegraph*, Online. Available HTTP: <http://www.telegraph.co.uk/news/worldnews/asia/china/9774364/Chinese-bride-marries-with-100-million-dowry.html> (accessed 24 March 2013).

Weiss, M. and Levine, L. (2007) *The Wedding Book: the big book for your big day*, New York: Workman Pub.

Willis, J. (2011) 'TLC weddings "10 DIY wedding favors your guests will love"', Online. Available HTTP: <http://tlc.howstuffworks.com/weddings/10-diy-wedding-favors10.htm> (accessed 24 March 2013).

CONSULTANT CHECKLIST AND REMINDERS FOR FAVORS AND GIFTS

- [ ] Discuss with your clients the "who, how and when" of favors and gifts.

- [ ] Help your client match the favor to the wedding theme.

- [ ] Think about packaging, presenting and messaging for the favor.

- [ ] If your clients are making the favors, encourage them to start early.

- [ ] If the couple makes a charitable donation instead of having a favor, this information should be communicated to the wedding guests.

- [ ] Encourage your clients to have wedding guest gift baskets for those coming from out-of-town, and encourage them to add a copy of the itinerary and a welcome letter.

- [ ] Determine if a moneybag or wedding card holder is needed for your client.

REVIEW

1. Name the six types of wedding favors and give an example of each.

2. What advice would you give clients who are considering DIY favors?

3. Name two gift ideas for bridesmaids, groomsmen, the flower girl and the ring bearer.

4. Name three suggestions for managing a registry.

5. What is a moneybag?

TERMINOLOGY

- DIY

- Dowry

- Favor

- Jordan almonds

- Moneybag

- Registry

- Wedding card holder

Photo 19.1 Professional hair and makeup allow the bride to look and feel like a celebrity.

Source: www.RodneyBailey.com

19

WEDDING DAY DETAILS

At last, the wedding day has arrived. Just as the bride and groom are making their final preparations, the wedding consultant should be too. While the bride is enjoying celebrity treatment and having her hair and makeup professionally done, the wedding planner is preparing for the long day ahead, reviewing last-minute details and gathering supplies. This chapter focuses on wedding day details, including bridal preparations as well as those of the consultant.

BRIDAL PREPARATIONS

While the groom's preparation for marriage is typically efficient, bridal preparation is a process that often takes several hours. As the bride awakes on the morning of her wedding, she begins what can be an exhausting day of preparation, execution and celebration. By hiring a wedding planner to manage the day for her, she can take a deep breath and focus on looking her best. It is the consultant who manages the wedding day execution, leaving the bride relaxed and excited about the upcoming ceremony and reception.

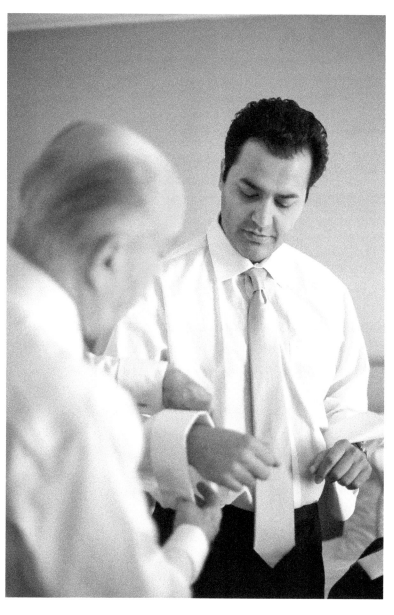

PHOTO 19.2 IN COMPARISON WITH THE BRIDE, A GROOM'S PREPARATION IS EFFICIENT.

SOURCE: WWW.RODNEYBAILEY.COM

While the groom often spends the morning of the wedding relaxing or playing golf, the bride will be with her bridesmaids having her hair styled and makeup applied. Having all of her bridesmaids with her starts the celebratory feeling of the day as the women laugh and have fun throughout the beautification process. Many hair and makeup professionals travel to the bride's dressing location to save the bride the stress of driving around town on her wedding day. Whether the bride is at her family's home, a hotel or the bridal room in a house of worship, the hair and makeup professionals will come to the bride on her wedding day. However, this service comes at a cost.

On-site fees for styling the bride's hair usually start at $100 and can go up to $400 or more depending on the city and the popularity of the stylist. If the bride travels to the salon for her hair, the fees start at about $75 and increase from there. There are fees for each additional person styled (bridesmaids, mothers, grandmothers, etc.), usually beginning at $60. Lower fees apply for flower girls and junior bridesmaids and tend to run between $35 and $55. Trial hair styling for the bride typically starts at $65. Similarly, makeup application in the salon starts at $75 and on-site fees range between $100 and $300. Each additional person receiving makeup is charged somewhat less, depending on the makeup artist. The bride should also invest in a trial run for her makeup application.

If your client is looking to cut corners on her wedding day, she might be inclined to skip professional hair styling and makeup application and simply do her own or have a close friend assist her. After

PHOTO 19.3 CONSULTANTS SHOULD REMIND ALL BRIDESMAIDS TO WEAR BUTTON-FRONTED SHIRTS FOR HAIR AND MAKEUP.

SOURCE: WWW.RODNEYBAILEY.COM

all, she has been doing her own hair and makeup for many years, why should her wedding day be any different? You would be wise to steer your client to a professional for these important services. Because the bride will be photographed constantly throughout the day, her hairstyle and makeup must stand the test of time, hugs and tears; as such, bringing in a professional hairstylist and makeup artist is well worth the investment.

WEDDING HAIRSTYLES

The hairstylist begins with the bride's hair, regardless of how many bridesmaids are waiting. It is crucial to the day's timing that the bride is coiffed and ready to go first, as she is the focus of the wedding day. Giselle Chreky (2013), owner of Hair by Giselle, details the latest trends for wedding hairstyles in *Vendor Spotlight*, Case 19.1. You can share the following advice that Giselle thinks every bride should follow: "Let your hair dictate your sense of style along with your gown before selecting your headpiece and veil. It should not work the other way around."

Prior to designing the hair on the actual wedding day, many brides have a mini trial run and then a main trial run. Giselle explains that the *mini trial run* takes place several months before the wedding, allowing the stylist to become familiar with the bride's hair, personality and special requests as well as going over some possible hairstyles. The mini trial also allows the client and the stylist to discuss if the hair should be grown out, relaxed, colored or cut before the wedding. The *main trial run* should happen one to two weeks before the wedding and should feel like the day of the wedding. At the main trial, the bride should bring her headpiece, veil and hair jewelry, and her hair should be updated in terms of color and trim. Giselle explains that hair color regrowth can start to show after two weeks, so the main trial should not take place too far in advance of the wedding. By the end of these two trials, the bride feels very comfortable with the stylist and a sense of rapport has been built. This process allows the styling on the wedding day to be stress free. Advise your clients that the day of the wedding is not the time to decide between wearing their hair up or leaving it down. Barbara Hill (2013) of Bridal Artistry states that hair accessories, floral clips, rhinestone ornaments and feather accents are in vogue. Barbara recommends Etsy.com as an online retailer that provides every type of hair accessory known to brides, whether or not they are wearing a veil.

WEDDING MAKEUP

When undergoing the transformation of hair and makeup, the preferred order is hair first followed by makeup. This order is favored because oftentimes the hair needs to be wet to begin the styling process and, in wetting the hair, there is a significant chance to ruin the makeup if it has already been applied. Further, heat is often used, which can cause the bride to sweat and the makeup to run. Additionally, after the hair is styled, hair spray is applied to keep the look in place. Some of the spray might accidentally go on the face and ruin the makeup application.

Makeup artists know the importance of applying the correct amount of foundation so that the bride's skin looks natural yet flawless. The artist also knows the tricks of the trade, including how

Photo 19.4 The bride's hairstyle should dictate the headpiece and veil.

Source: www.RodneyBailey.com

VENDOR SPOTLIGHT, CASE 19.1

GISELLE CHREKY

HAIR BY GISELLE

What are the latest trends related to hairstyles for weddings? The latest styles tend to be more natural, softer and much more comfortable. The Oscars, Emmys and other award shows seem to play a significant role in defining hair trends. Side buns and pony tails are increasingly popular. I see more silk and real flowers in the hair, accessories such as brooches and fewer tiaras. Cathedral veils are still well liked, but I see a lot of birdcage veils and fascinators too. When using a veil, I find that the brides like having it further in the back of the crown area or peaking from above, rather than forward on the head. Blushers seem to have faded a bit, but may make a comeback in years ahead.

What are currently the most popular hairstyles for weddings? I mostly do side buns and pony tails but on occasion still get the classic, Audrey Hepburn chignons that are clean and simple. Some brides prefer their hair down with large waves, but it depends on what type of wedding it is. Indoor brides typically ask for more structured, classic looks, while outdoor brides ask for softer, half-up romantic styles. At times, I get a good mix of all styles for any venue, but the weather will play a large role in how the bride wants her hair styled.

How have social media outlets affected your business and client base? Social media has had a huge impact on my business. WeddingWire shares all my reviews. WeddingWire and Facebook allow brides to view images as well. Pinterest by far is the biggest hit since it attracts people for different reasons. I myself get inspired by looking at photos on Pinterest! The more photos the better. People can download my website and images much quicker from their smartphones, thus making accessibility more quick and fun. I have found that my business continues to grow at a much faster pace now. I used to follow up with my brides via mail or e-mails, but more so now via smartphones and using social media.

How do wedding hairstyles differ from culture to culture? They differ with regard to their head dressing, depending on the culture and traditions. Some brides wear tikka pendants, bindis, mantillas, custom flower head adornments, crowns, etc. All these symbolize a specific meaning to their individual culture. Some of the headpieces are heavy with beading and sequins; some need to be propped up at a certain angle; some need extra hair underneath to support the weight, especially when the ceremonies last for a long time or if they plan on dancing for hours. Hair pin placement and comfort are key when securing headpieces. Some styles differ based on the ethnicity of the client due to their hair type.

Some brides have thick, coarse hair that requires different techniques when prepping and styling the hair. The hairstyle is meant to last so it is essential to perform these steps correctly and in accordance with the client's specifications. Some require additional hair, which I offer with hair fillers, permanent and temporary extensions, even "micro" extensions for those thinning at the crown and bang areas. All are state-of-the-art, simple and very natural!

How does the client experience differ when you go on-location versus clients coming to your studio? On-location offers more flexibility and is much more calming due to having a vendor at their site, especially if the weather is bad or if the bride is on a tight timeline. It is a higher fee, but that pays for the traveling and convenience. It makes it more manageable for them and most want the service at their venue to help make the day run smoothly. I only do one or two weddings in my studio a year and over a hundred on location.

Please share examples of challenging styles. The most challenging style was for a wedding I did last year. Not because of the styling itself, but more due to her culture in which her hair needed to change according to her attire more than once. Therefore, the hairstyle needed to be taken down and redone within a short period of time after the initial style. Usually, the change is within 15–20 minutes, which requires careful timing and knowing exactly what that next style will be in advance. Another unique occurrence was when one of my Indian brides hired me for her three days of celebration, changing her hair more than five times. It was interesting to see all the wardrobe changes and it let me be creative with introducing a new style for every outfit. It was a fun and challenging job!

WEBSITE: *WWW.HAIRBYGISELLE.COM*

to keep shine off the bride's nose and how to keep her lipstick lasting throughout the day. The bride is the center of attention all day long and she wants to look her best, kiss after kiss and hug after hug. There is no better way to make this happen than to spend the money and hire a makeup specialist. Professional hair and makeup artist Barbara Hill, introduced earlier and featured in *Vendor Spotlight*, Case 19.2, discusses some of the essentials of wedding day hair and makeup. One of the latest trends in wedding makeup is the incorporation of airbrushing techniques. Carola Myers (2013), founder of the CM Artists Group, explains that makeup techniques have evolved in response to technological advances. With the high-definition capabilities of wedding films, she felt it was essential to invest in airbrushing training and equipment that would allow even a natural look to be finished and fashionable with perfect colors. Carola uses a hybrid technique that mixes a traditional application approach with airbrushing, allowing for contouring, shading, accents and dimensions that stay perfect even in 98-degree weather. She notes that 90 per cent of her wedding clients request this combined approach.

PHOTO 19.5 THERE ARE MANY EXCELLENT ONLINE SOURCES FOR HAIR ACCESSORIES.

SOURCE: WWW.RODNEYBAILEY.COM

Carola stresses the importance of personality and the ability to customize services to the individual needs of clients. She states that, because a bride's look is closely tied to her feelings of confidence on her wedding day, the successful makeup artist is one who listens carefully, builds rapport and establishes a level of trust that allows each bride to open up so that her inner beauty shines through. Celebrity makeup artist Derrick Rutledge would agree. Having worked with Oprah Winfrey and Michelle Obama on a regular basis, as well as with a host of entertainment celebrities, Rutledge is known for his ability to transform faces as well as his gifted demeanor that "brings

PHOTO 19.6 A PROFESSIONAL MAKEUP ARTIST CAN BLEND COLORS TO HIGHLIGHT A BRIDE'S BEST FEATURES.

SOURCE: WWW.RODNEYBAILEY.COM

out beauty, confidence, the sheen of stardom" (Alexander 2011: 12). If the interaction does not go well based on mismatched personalities, a stressed bride may reject the most conscientious effort and the expensive pampering goes to waste, as illustrated in *Consultant in Action*, Case 19.3.

Carola explains that communication from the consultant makes the makeup artist's job easier. She stresses that the makeup artist needs to know the timing of the day as well as the photographer's style and schedule. The makeup will differ if the wedding is held outdoors or if it will be photographed primarily in black and white. Further, the number of guests influences makeup application. If the wedding is intimate, the bride will be seen close up; however, if it is a large wedding, the bride will be seen from a distance so her makeup needs to be more dramatic. The makeup artist needs to know this information well in advance so the makeup can be applied for maximum benefit. Carola mentions that the makeup for the ceremony may differ from that of the reception. With the ceremony, she feels that the primary commitment should be to the eyes and that the bride should look angelic. For reception makeup, she adds stronger color for a sultry look. Wedding hair and makeup application vary significantly by culture, as illustrated in *Culture Corner*, Case 19.4.

VENDOR SPOTLIGHT, CASE 19.2

BARBARA HILL

BRIDAL ARTISTRY

What is your training and background? When I left my career to be at home with my first child, I had no idea that today I would be building a multi-ethnic team of professional makeup artists and hairstylists and be a beauty industry entrepreneur. I have a BA in International Studies from Miami University and an MA in Latin American Studies from Georgetown University. I trained with two top professional makeup artists and also pursued training at a beauty institute to become a professional. Success in this business is not so much about the technical skill of hair and makeup as it is people skills, business savvy and cultural awareness. This makes my background in International Studies actually a very good fit!

What are the trends in makeup for weddings? Makeup colors run the gamut in today's weddings, although purple has been huge for several years. Unusual blends of colors make great floral bouquets and, of course, the makeup should fit and flow with the style and colors of the wedding. Red lips are trending for bolder brides who want a classic, artistic look. However, the majority of our brides are requesting defined eyes and softer glossy lips. False lashes are a desirable enhancement for nearly all but the most natural looks. To keep our brides looking fresh all day, we use a hypoallergenic oil-free foundation with excellent staying power. Each bride receives a compact of our flawless powder foundation matched to their skin tone so they can blend away any tears or sweat damage.

Tell me about your trial runs. Trial consultations are extremely important to avoid stress on the wedding day – the bride's and ours! We want to be sure we know the bride's skin and hair and exactly the look she is going for. Sometimes we need to work through some ideas to get to the look that works best for the bride. Coming to do her makeup and hair on the wedding day without a trial means that the artist/stylist will need to do what seems best to them. It is too time-consuming and stressful to figure out exactly what the bride wants when the wedding day pressure is on. We include the price of the trial in our contracts. Of course, if the bride does a trial and decides not to book us, we allow her to just pay for the trial alone.

What advice do you offer brides who are not used to wearing makeup or having their hair styled? When a bride does not wear much makeup in her daily life, she will be uncertain as to what will make her look amazing on her wedding day. A bride who never wears makeup may be hesitant to embrace even light foundation and eye liner/shadow. They look in the mirror in their t-shirt and jeans and see a different "them" than they are used to. It can take some mental adjustment. This is where the gown comes in. I hold up a photo of the bride's wedding gown and ask if she would feel comfortable wearing the gown in her grocery store. Of course not! I then tell her that, when she is wearing the gown, she might expect to need a little more polished look than her everyday look. This has always worked to give proper perspective on wedding makeup!

How much time should be scheduled for day-of hair and makeup? Since we nearly always work as a team of at least one hairstylist and one makeup artist on the wedding day, we calculate one hour for the bride and thirty minutes for each bridesmaid, mom, etc. who is receiving our services. That timing allows that, in one thirty-minute period, while one is getting makeup done, another is getting hair done. If the wedding party is larger than six, or timing needs to be condensed further, we bring on another artist or stylist from our team to double up.

What advice can you offer wedding planners when they discuss hair and makeup with their clients? Have hair and makeup stylists come to the bride wherever she is getting ready. It is a major advantage for convenience, less stress and has a cost value. Salons are packed on weekends and delays are frequent and can result in bad experiences. Also, if you have a wedding that requires major travel time, please be sure that there will be several ladies in addition to the bride getting makeup and hair done. If not, it might be best to find a vendor closer to the wedding location – especially during busy wedding months. Finally, if possible, have the same company do both hair and makeup, since there is coordination of timing and anticipation of needs among team members that can break down when stylists have not worked together before. Trust us on this!

WEBSITE: *BRIDALARTISTRYDC.COM*

For hair and makeup sessions, the bride and bridesmaids should be advised to wear button-front or zippered shirts, so they can easily change into their dresses without spoiling the look. Additional beauty treatments such as teeth whitening, waxing, spray tanning, facials, Botox injections, ear piercing, hair relaxing or highlighting should all be done in advance of the wedding day to allow any adverse reactions to fade out of sight or be modified before the big day. You do not want an orange, overly spray-tanned bride on her wedding day! The bride should check with her hairstylist as to the suggested timing of a preparation trim or processing technique. Nails are usually done before the rehearsal. Remind your clients to purchase a bottle of the chosen color in case touch-ups are needed.

PHOTO 19.7 AIRBRUSHED MAKEUP APPLICATION GIVES THE BRIDE A FINISHED LOOK.

SOURCE: WWW.RODNEYBAILEY.COM

CONSULTANT IN ACTION, CASE 19.3

DOWN THE DRAIN!

Your client, Harper, has gone to the best salon in Boston for her wedding day hairstyle and makeup application. You are to meet Harper back at her hotel to check in and supervise the delivery of a catered brunch to her suite. You arrive at her suite, only to find Harper in the bathroom rubbing off the makeup that she has just paid dearly to have applied. She thinks the makeup does not look like her, and is clearly in distress as she starts to peel off her false eyelashes and remove the color from her cheeks. You stand at the bathroom door, watching a $350 makeup application literally start to go down the drain.

WHAT DO YOU DO?

CULTURE CORNER, CASE 19.4

WEDDING HAIR AND MAKEUP IN CHINA

A bride in China goes to the same photography studio where she and the groom had their formal wedding photos taken months before to have her hair and makeup done on the actual wedding day. She will arrive early in the morning, sometimes as early as 5:00 a.m., because these services are performed on a first-come, first-served basis. At 5:00 a.m., there could already be 50 brides in line. The entire process for both hair and makeup takes 30 minutes or less per bride. There will be ten or more stylists on hand and they will give each bride the exact same look. With a population of 1.3 billion people in China, it is all about speed, not individuality. The cost for hair and makeup is 410 Renminbi (RMB) which is approximately $50 US. This may not seem very expensive, but, in a country where the average wage is 150 RMB per week, this is indeed a luxurious expenditure.

CASE SUBMITTED BY YAO AND DAVID WOSICKI

CONSULTANT PREPARATIONS

While the bride is receiving her last-minute beauty treatments and relaxing, the consultant is busy finalizing the preparations for the wedding day. These preparations include day-of details, risk assessment, security analysis and the all-important emergency kit. As the wedding day dawns, it is crucial that you review all the details that were supposed to happen the night before and early on the wedding day. For example, did the linens arrive at the reception venue by 8:00 a.m.? You need to call the venue to ensure they were delivered. If they have not been delivered, you have to call the linen company and track down the delivery. If the cake is supposed to arrive at 1:00 p.m., you should confirm that this happened at the appropriate time. Making phone calls to verify the wedding day details is a crucial component to a successful event. Nothing can be left to chance. Confirm, confirm, confirm.

Checking the weather and traffic conditions prior to the wedding is another smart use of your time on the wedding day. A quick check on your weather app and you will know if the weather forecast has been revised from the previous evening's report. If you learn that a sudden cold spell has hit the area, you can call the rental company and get more outdoor heaters delivered to the reception venue. Before you leave your house, also make sure that you have all necessary contact information, timelines and copies of all contracts and budgets. Make sure all your electronics are charged. That way, if while heading to the ceremony you learn that a major highway is backed up, you can call the transportation company and discuss an alternate route for the wedding party.

RISK ASSESSMENT

John Lennon famously said, "Life is what happens when you're busy making other plans." Before the day of the wedding, every planner should have a risk assessment plan in place for the wedding and a game plan for managing those risks should they come to fruition. A risk can take on many shapes and forms. It can be as obvious as rain at an outdoor wedding or it can be less obvious, like habitually late relatives whose tardiness causes the wedding to start late. The wise planner assesses the risks prior to the wedding and builds in a back-up plan just in case "life" happens. Table 19.1 offers a list of common wedding day risks, with examples of each.

TABLE 19.1 COMMON WEDDING DAY RISKS

- Accidents (cuts, burns, tripping, falling)
- Bugs at an outdoor event (mosquitoes, flies, gnats, bees, wasps)
- Electricity goes out (dark venue, food cannot be heated)
- Sickness (food poisoning, heatstroke, hangover, cold, flu, allergies)
- Streets around your venue are closed (water main breaks, car crash)
- Transportation (the coach or bus breaks down on the highway, the best man missed his connecting flight, airports are shut down)
- Union goes on strike (no wait staff at the hotel)
- Vendor no-show (no ceremony music, no cake)
- Wardrobe malfunction (bride's veil gets caught in a car door and tears)
- Weather (high winds, rain, heat, snow, ice, humidity, cold, lightning)

Keep in mind that every wedding is a unique entity and something may happen that you would have never anticipated, as illustrated in *Consultant in Action*, Case 19.5. Think through what the most likely risks will be for each wedding and have a plan in mind should any of the risks become a reality. Remember, "hope" is not a back-up plan.

SECURITY ANALYSIS

In a world with heightened safety concerns, it has become commonplace to see some type of security at events. From bag searches to metal detectors, security measures are the rule rather

CONSULTANT IN ACTION, CASE 19.5

BATTLE GROUND

The day was filled with love, laughter and happiness as 350 guests watched Chrissy and Sid get married on a beautiful July day. As the end of the reception approaches, you are leading guests to the bus to head back to their hotels for the night. Suddenly, you notice Chrissy and one of her bridesmaids arguing. As you walk closer, the argument turns into a shouting match and you witness punches being thrown.

WHAT DO YOU DO?

CASE SUBMITTED BY KELLY BOWENS AND LINDA ROBSON

than the exception. While it is not necessary for wedding planners to be security experts, it is important to have an understanding of security issues and how they affect your events, business and reputation. By understanding and managing security, you are protecting the assets, the venue and the people present at the wedding.

The gifts are usually the largest asset at a wedding. The gift table may be overflowing with expensive items and envelopes of cash. You need to ensure that the gifts are closely watched and monitored. There should also be a plan to deliver the gifts safely to the bride and groom after the reception has ended. Maybe the hotel valet will transport the gifts to the honeymoon suite. Perhaps the father of the groom will load the gifts into the family minivan. Whatever the plan, make sure that there is one and that you are informed of what it is so that you can assist in the execution. Do not wait until midnight when your clients are preparing to leave the reception site and surrounded by well-wishers to formulate this plan.

In addition to wedding presents, cash in an envelope is a common gift to newlyweds. As explained in Chapter 18, sometimes the envelopes are placed in a decorated box or birdcage found on the gift table, whereas at other weddings the guests hand envelopes directly to the bride for her money-bag or to the consultant's assistant for safe keeping. Regardless, each envelope should be accounted for and secured properly to ensure against theft. The last thing that you want is a phone call the day after a wedding asking you where the envelope from Uncle William was placed. If you put an assistant in charge of managing envelopes at a wedding, this person can use polite introductions to learn names and quickly jot them down, allowing for a master list in case a question arises.

PHOTO 19.8 A CONSULTANT IS ALWAYS PREPARED IN CASE OF A WARDROBE
MALFUNCTION.

SOURCE: WWW.RODNEYBAILEY.COM

The venue must also be protected from damage during the wedding. If young men at a wedding get bored and go to the restroom and place firecrackers down the toilet, there will be damage to the physical property and your clients could be held liable. If you are concerned about this type of behavior, suggest to your clients that they hire a security guard to patrol the reception looking for such incidents. If you have a large event with many people, you may need to hire several guards.

Finally, it is your responsibility to help ensure the safety of the guests at the event. If a couple's cocktail hour is to be held outdoors and you see lightning in the distance, bring the guests indoors for their protection. If you see a puddle of water on the dance floor, it is your responsibility to get venue staff to clean it up so a guest does not slip and fall. Know where the AED device is located in case someone has a heart attack. Keep an eye out for guests who appear to be intoxicated and make sure that they have a designated driver to escort them safely home. Your conscientiousness could save a life.

THE EMERGENCY KIT

A vital piece of equipment every wedding consultant should possess is the wedding day *emergency kit*. This can be a duffel bag, a canvas bag, a rolling suitcase or a large nylon zippered bag. The contents of the bag will vary based on the planner, the wedding and the region; however, Table 19.2 lists the key items that should be in every wedding day emergency kit. As discussed in Chapter 15, an iPod and a docking station with speakers are excellent additions to keep in your car just in case the musicians do not arrive.

You will be surprised by how many items you will need from this emergency kit throughout the wedding day. The father of the bride loses a button and comes to you for a needle and thread.

TABLE 19.2 WEDDING DAY EMERGENCY KIT ESSENTIALS

• Baby wipes	• Lip ointment	• Smelling salts
• Band aids	• Nail clippers and file	• Snacks (crackers, protein bars)
• Bobby pins	• Nail polish and remover	• Stapler (miniature)
• Bottled water	• Panty hose	• Static removal spray
• Breath mints	• Pepto-Bismol	• Straight and safety pins in various sizes
• Brush, comb and pick	• Powder (talc and face)	• Super glue
• Deodorant	• Q-tips and cotton balls	• Tape (duct, scotch and double sided)
• Drinking straws	• Rope (short and medium pieces)	• Tissues
• Feminine hygiene items	• Scissors	• Tylenol
• Hair spray	• Sewing kit	• Umbrella

A bridesmaid has a headache. The groom wants a breath mint. The pew arrangements come undone after the florist has departed, so you need to use a piece of rope and a safety pin to secure them back into place. A comprehensive emergency kit is worth its weight in gold. Start gathering supplies now before you really need them.

REFERENCES

Alexander, K.L. (13 November 2011) 'The makeover', *Washington Post Magazine*, 10–17.

Bowens, K. and Robson, L. (2013) 'Battle ground case study'. E-mail (24 January 2013).

Chreky, G. (2013) 'Hairstyle trends for weddings'. E-mail (19 February 2013).

Hill, B. (2013) 'Makeup trends for weddings'. Personal communication (16 January 2013).

Myers, C. (2013) 'Makeup trends for weddings'. Personal communication (12 March 2013).

Wosicki, Y. and Wosicki, D. (2006) 'Wedding hair and makeup in China'. E-mail (13 May 2006).

CONSULTANT CHECKLIST AND REMINDERS FOR WEDDING DAY DETAILS

- ☐ On the wedding day, the bride's hair should be done before starting the bridesmaids.

- ☐ Encourage the bride to have the hairstylist and makeup artist come to her.

- ☐ As a general rule, hair should be done before makeup.

- ☐ Determine if the stylist is bringing an assistant.

- ☐ Have your client meet with the hairstylist for a mini trial run prior to picking out a veil.

- ☐ Remind your bride to bring her headpiece, veil and hair jewelry to the main trial run.

- ☐ The bride and her bridesmaids should wear button-front or zippered shirts to have their hair and makeup done.

- ☐ Check weather and traffic reports on the wedding day.

- ☐ Make follow-up calls on the wedding day to ensure that items were delivered according to your instructions.

- ☐ Complete a risk assessment and security analysis for each wedding.

- ☐ Prepare and bring your well-stocked emergency kit.

REVIEW

1. Give two reasons why hair should be done before makeup.

2. Explain the difference between a mini trial run and a main trial run for wedding hairstyles.

3. Name one item that a bride must bring to her main trial run for hair styling.

4. What paperwork will a planner need on the wedding day?

5. Name five examples of wedding day risks.

6. Name ten items that should be found in a wedding day emergency kit.

TERMINOLOGY

- Back-up plan

- Emergency kit

- Main trial run

- Mini trial run

- Risk assessment

- Security analysis

- Wedding assets

Chapter 20

Writing your business plan. Business legalities. Organizing your office environment. Building a staff. References

Chapter 21

Understanding the uniqueness of the wedding market. Determining your target audience. Marketing appeals. Marketing tool development. Social media. Managing your online reputation. References

Chapter 22

Initial screening. Client interview details. Follow-up communication. Contracts. Compensation. Evaluation. References

Chapter 23

Establishing vendor relationships. Competition. Obligations. Ethics. Vendor feedback. The wedding summary. References

Chapter 24

Stress management tips. Career enrichment. References

BUILDING YOUR BUSINESS

Wedding consultants are, by and large, small business entrepreneurs. If you have decided to embark on a career in wedding planning, you need more than just a business card to get started. Before you can call yourself a wedding consultant, you must have a thorough understanding of what it takes to own and operate a sole proprietorship, partnership or corporation. Section III of this book details the key steps to follow when building your business.

You should begin with the important task of writing a business plan with a clear focus on your target audience and staffing needs, as presented in depth in Chapter 20. Once you have a business plan, you need a strategy to carry it out, so Chapter 21 explores the keys to successful marketing. When potential clients start contacting you, effective interview techniques, communication skills and knowledge of contracts become essential and are therefore highlighted in Chapter 22. Remember, you do not have a client until you have a signed contract. With contract in hand, proficiency in vendor relations, networking and negotiating becomes a must, so these areas are the focus of Chapter 23. The career of a wedding planner is time intensive, physically demanding and competitive: therefore, Chapter 24 presents tips to help you manage stress. Simultaneously, this concluding chapter offers ways to continually enrich your business and maintain your personal life.

20

BUSINESS PLAN AND OFFICE MANAGEMENT

Before opening your doors, a new business owner must have a well-thought-out business plan in order to increase the likelihood of success. Starting a business without a plan is like learning to ski from a triple black diamond run . . . maybe you can make it down the mountain, but it's not going to be pretty.

The US Small Business Administration (SBA) is one of your best resources for starting a small business. The SBA (2013a) defines a business plan as a "roadmap for business success that projects 3–5 years ahead and outlines the route a company intends to take to grow revenues." The purpose of this chapter is to outline the basics of creating your business plan, business legalities and managing your office. This chapter ends with an overview of building your staff when the time is right.

WRITING YOUR BUSINESS PLAN

Developing your plan is an important first step in showing the world you are serious about starting a business. After all, if you cannot find the time or energy to put together a plan for your business, how are you ever going to find the time or the energy to run a business? While not all entrepreneurs feel it is necessary to develop a business plan due to rapidly changing conditions, it is a core requirement if you wish to seek external financial support (Dearman 2012). In short, if you want to be taken seriously by lending institutions, vendors, colleagues and competitors, you need a business plan to achieve your goals and objectives.

Even if your dream is to eventually become an international conglomerate, you will start off as a small business. A business plan accelerates the ability of small businesses to be competitive, nimble and innovative (Ibrahim 2012). Before you begin writing your business plan, the SBA (2013b) suggests you consider core questions such as:

- Why am I starting a business?

- What products or services will my business provide?

- Who is my ideal customer?

- How will I market my business?

- How much money do I need to get started and where will I get it?

- How will I price my products and services in comparison to my competition?

- How will I set up my legal structure?

- What kind of insurance do I need?

- What taxes do I need to pay?

In short, your business plan will help you describe your business, select a target market, manage day-to-day operations and handle finances. Although there is no single formula for developing a business plan, some elements are common to most business plans. They are summarized in Table 20.1.

TABLE 20.1 ELEMENTS OF A BUSINESS PLAN

Cover Sheet

Executive Summary

Contents

Section I: Company Description

- Company name, nature of the business and organizational structure

- Mission statement, goals and objectives

- Products and services

- Summary résumé for each owner

- Environmental scan of competitive advantages

Section II: Marketing

- Target market

- Marketing strategy

- Communication strategy

- Sales strategy

- Growth strategy

- Evaluation strategy

Section III: Finance

- Personnel needs

- Historical financial information

- Capital equipment and supply list

- Funding requirements

- Forecasted income statements, balance sheets, cash flow statements and capital expenditure budgets

Section IV: Supporting Documents

- Tax returns

- Personal financial statement

- Copy of lease

- Copy of licenses, insurance and other legal documents

- Full résumé for each owner

SOURCE: ADAPTED FROM IBRAHIM (2012); SBA (2013A)

While the information in Table 20.1 may seem overwhelming, the complexity of the business dictates the complexity of the information required. Starting with Section I, you can describe your business by introducing the name, nature of the business and the organizational structure, followed by the *mission statement*, which is a clear and concise (usually one sentence) statement of being. Begin the sentence with, "The mission of (*insert your company name*) is . . ." Complete the thought by stating your focus and philosophy. A more detailed description of your business can follow, including an overview of your goals, objectives, products and services. This is also an excellent opportunity to articulate your corporate culture values. In studying business process management, Schmiedel *et al.* (2013) found that four complementary values support effective and efficient business processes: customer orientation, excellence, reliability and teamwork. As you indicate your products and services and summarize your background and expertise through a summary résumé, you should identify and embed the corporate culture values that you uphold as an entrepreneur. This section should also include an environmental scan of the outstanding features of the area where you will set up your business that emphasizes your competitive edge.

Section II of your business plan includes a thorough market analysis. In this section, you will identify your target market and indicate the marketing, communication and sales strategies that you will use to reach those who comprise the market. Additionally, in this section, you should forecast your

PHOTO 20.2 TEAMWORK IS CRUCIAL DURING WEDDING SET-UP.

SOURCE: WWW.RODNEYBAILEY.COM

potential for growth and indicate how you will foster continuous improvement through evaluation. Chapter 21 is devoted to the intricacies of marketing, while Chapters 22 and 23 offer evaluation specifics.

Section III of your business plan includes your financial information and data. Many consultants start out as sole proprietors and work from home, keeping their overheads low and alleviating the need to apply for a small business loan. Once you have built a reputation and need staff members, you will need to change your corporate structure and rent a separate space. If you have been building up steadily, your historical financial information should give you the business clout to secure a loan, so be prepared to itemize your funding requirements. Your *capital equipment and supply list* details the materials you need to run your business. Equipment is permanent or reusable over a significant period of time, such as your vehicle, office furniture and computer. Supplies, on the other hand, are consumed after one use or a short period of time; for example, printer paper and cartridges, pens, tape, staples and sticky notes. Keep an organized spreadsheet that details the equipment and supplies that you utilize in your daily operations. This information will come in handy at tax time when you are claiming your small business expenses.

If you are just getting started or in a significant growth phase that requires funding, you will want to forecast income statements, balance sheets, cash flow statements and capital expenditure budgets. Your *income statement* identifies total income, which is your revenue minus your expenses. When applied to forecasting, *pro-forma income projections* are "what-if" analyses where you estimate your expenses, revenue and income over a defined period of time. A *balance sheet* is a summary of the dollar value of everything your business owns and owes. This details the overall financial state of the business. Your *pro-forma cash flow* is a projection of cash receipts and cash payments over a specified period of time. You should also identify any capital expenditure budget needs; these apply to significant investments in property or major equipment purchases.

Section IV of your business plan includes the supporting documents that are critical to obtaining loans as your business grows. Information such as your tax returns, personal financial statements, lease (if you are renting a space), licenses, insurance and full résumé should be included in this section.

You do not have to reinvent the wheel when writing your business plan; you simply need to get it down on paper. There are many resources available to assist you in this task including websites, books, software and accountants. *Bplans.com* is an excellent resource that includes a gallery of over 500 free business plans for review.

Once you have completed the internal contents of your business plan, pick out the major highlights to include in a one-page *executive summary* to be placed at the front end of the document. The executive summary is the most important page of the document, as loan officers will go no further if you have not sold them with this abridged version. Be certain to include a professional cover page that includes your logo (see Chapter 21) and contact information. The overall plan should be organized, factual and well written. A sloppy business plan portends a sloppy business. Finally, ask another small business owner to review your business plan. Progressive small business owners have been found to be open to the scrutiny of trusted peers to foster continuous learning, accountability and problem identification (Leung and Luthans 2011).

BUSINESS LEGALITIES

Many aspiring wedding planners believe it takes little more than a business card to get started in the field. However, whether you are starting from home or leasing executive office space, you need to establish your business as a formal legal entity before attracting your first customer. This may seem like a tedious exercise but, rest assured, prospective clients will check your credentials to ensure you are a legitimate business before hiring you. If you do not have a legitimate business, the client will hire another consultant. Getting married is stressful enough. A couple does not want to hire someone to manage the most important day of their lives only to find out the person was not properly insured or legally permitted to operate a business in their home state.

WHAT'S IN A NAME?

In a word: everything. Before you fill out the first form to register your business, you must have a business name. When selecting a business name, use your imagination and conduct research. Check out the competition. Your business name should be as unique as you are. The name can be formal, contemporary, casual, funky or elegant, but ultimately your business name should reflect your style and personality, so make the decision carefully.

In creating a business name, do not make it too complicated, cutesy or confusing. "Going Places Events" might sound like an event planning business to you but it may suggest "travel agency" to someone else. An overly complicated name like "Hannah's Fabulous and Fancy Wedding Planning and Design" is too wordy for a business card and would not lend itself to a concise logo or website. Be innovative but keep it simple. Potential clients are more apt to remember your business name if it is concise, unique and interesting. In addition, many wedding planners choose to use their own first and/or last name in their business title; for example, business names such as "Ella's Events" or "Sofia's Serene Wedding Planning" allow for a personal approach. You might also consider starting your company name with the letter "A." This tactic will ensure that your company is listed at or near the top of electronic or print directories that operate alphabetically, such as those used for bridal showcases.

After you have developed three or four possible ideas for your business name, share your thoughts with family and friends. Get their feedback and support. Oftentimes, someone else will think of a good reason to use or not use a name. Once you digest their feedback, narrow your choices to two or three.

After you have narrowed down your selection, check to make sure the ideas for your name are unique and not already in use. Start by putting the name in a search engine such as Google and see what pops up. You can also review the US Patent and Trade Office website at *uspto.com* as well as vendor listings with wedding-based websites such as the Association of Bridal Consultants, the American Association of Certified Wedding Planners, The Knot and WeddingWire. Your county government should also provide access to a trade name index for your area. Remember, just because the name you select does not have a website does not mean that the name is not already taken. Do your homework and check. If the name you like best is available, register it immediately so you are not left out in the cold. If it is taken, move on to your second and third options. Do not think that just because your business called "Wedded Bliss" is located in Arkansas and another "Wedded Bliss" is located in Montana this will not cause a problem. With the internet, you will be attracting clients from all over the world to your website. If you know of another business already using the name you want to use, you could be opening yourself up to a very expensive legal battle down the road if you forge ahead and copy someone else's name.

"DOING BUSINESS AS" STATEMENT

Once you have a business name, you must register it with your local government. This is called filing your *Doing Business As* (DBA) name, also known as your *Fictitious Trade Name*. As a sole proprietor or within a partnership, you must register a DBA or else the business name defaults to your personal legal name for all government forms and applications. To learn more, go to your local city or county government's website, where you can find information regarding where to register and how much it costs and what protections a DBA affords you. A DBA filed at a local level does not have the same safeguards as one filed at the state level, let alone one that is trademarked. If you want to protect your business name, you need to consult an attorney. The DBA fee is generally between $10 and $50 and entitles you to use your business name for a set period of time, most often three years. When your DBA expires, you simply renew your statement.

THE ORGANIZATIONAL STRUCTURE OF YOUR BUSINESS

Having filed your DBA, the next step involves determining the structure of your business. The three primary types of business entities are: sole proprietorship, partnership and corporation, and many hybrids, such as limited liability companies, exist. Of these, the *sole proprietorship*, defined as one individual operating a business, is the most common for wedding consultants because it is the simplest and least expensive type of business to open. Be aware, however, that, if your business fails, your personal assets may be used to pay off your business debts because the business does not exist separately from the owner and you accept all associated financial risks. If you open a business in your own name as a sole proprietorship, you can use your social security number for filing business taxes.

A *partnership*, on the other hand, is a relationship existing between two or more persons who join together to carry on a trade or business. If you elect to form a partnership, have an attorney draw up a formal partnership agreement so that each partner is aware of her or his rights and responsibilities. Do not just assume that your best friend understands and accepts all obligations. This is a business, so get it in writing.

A *corporation* is a separate legal entity from the business owner. It requires filing of articles of incorporation, electing officers, holding an annual meeting and paying corporate taxes. It is often easier to obtain financing from banks or other sources as a corporation; thus, if you should decide to franchise your business, it makes sense to form this type of business entity.

EMPLOYER ID NUMBERS

If you form a partnership or corporation, you need an *Employer ID Number* (EIN), defined as a federal tax identification number used to recognize a business entity. The IRS uses this number to identify individuals who are required to file business tax returns. You may obtain an EIN in a variety of ways, but the IRS encourages use of the online application system available at *www.irs.gov* website (IRS 2013). To obtain an EIN, you need to complete Form SS-4m available at the same IRS website. You may also call 1-800-829-4933 during business hours to obtain an EIN immediately, or you can fax or mail in the application (IRS 2013).

THERE'S NO PLACE LIKE HOME

Many wedding planners operate out of their homes, especially when first getting started. If you decide to go this route, be sure to determine if there are any special permits or licenses required for your wedding planning business. Something as simple as a sign for your business may require a permit. Further, you need to apply for a permit from your local health department if you are planning to provide food or drink for your clients. For example, if you promise your client that you will make 100 cake pops as favors, you will need a permit from the health department. SBA offers a tool called "Permit Me" that allows you to put in your zip code to determine the permits and licenses that are required in your jurisdiction (SBA 2013c). An alternative to seeing clients in your home is to meet them at a mutually convenient location like a coffee shop, their home or a local library.

INSURANCE

Insurance is not just for homes and cars, it is important for businesses as well, especially for a small business. While you are in the process of establishing your business, an important component of getting started is making sure you are insured against potential damaging situations. For example, it is frequently your job to make sure the wedding gifts get from point A to point B. If an expensive item goes missing or the decorative box holding all the gifts of money is stolen, you might be held liable; or, if you are setting up a reception at the museum and accidentally drop a rare artifact, you will be glad you have insurance. General liability insurance is often selected:

PHOTO 20.3 YOU SHOULD RUN YOUR BUSINESS BY THE BOOK.

SOURCE: WWW.RODNEYBAILEY.COM

to cover legal hassles due to accident, injuries and claims of negligence. These policies protect against payments as the result of bodily injury, property damage, medical expenses, libel, slander, the cost of defending lawsuits, and settlement bonds or judgments required during an appeal procedure.

(SBA 2013d)

Contact a local insurance agent in your community to discuss what type of insurance is right for you. Be certain that your standard contract, discussed in Chapter 22, includes a hold harmless statement that protects you from errors, non-performance, changes or acts of negligence committed by all other vendors contracted for the wedding. For example, if the florist backs his delivery truck into the couple's limo, you will not be liable.

If you decide to establish your business outside of the home, you need commercial business insurance. Rates for this type of insurance depend on where your business is located, the type of business you own and government regulations. A knowledgeable insurance agent can help you determine if this type of coverage is right for you. Because we live in a world that is quick to litigate, it is critical that you take care of insuring yourself and your business before the first client walks through the door. This could be the most important decision you make regarding your business.

ORGANIZING YOUR OFFICE ENVIRONMENT

If you are just starting out as a wedding consultant, it is crucial that you lay a solid foundation for your business by making good business decisions from day one. Whether you work from home or lease office space, there are many facets to organizing your office environment. These office management essentials are the building blocks of a successful wedding consultancy business; after all, your office environment affects how you work, and how you feel represents who you are on a daily basis.

If you plan to work from home, get started by taking a survey of your current furniture to determine what might work in your home office. The most important item is a desk with good workspace, plenty of room for your personal electronics and an area to review spreadsheets, guest lists and sample books. Do not forget about space for an all-in-one printer, scanner and fax machine as well as your supplies.

Keeping track of all the details of a wedding is a difficult task. How you choose to manage the wealth of information is up to you, but some options include tablets such as an iPad, laptops, spreadsheets, three-ring notebooks, 3″ x 5″ cards, a day timer or a file folder system. Bookshelves, file cabinets and storage bins help tremendously by utilizing vertical space and hiding clutter.

You will get a lot of mileage from investing in a comfortable chair that offers good support and fits your body. There are many ergonomic styles to choose from, so take a trip to your local office supply store and test out a few different models. Measure the height of your desk to make sure the chair you select fits comfortably underneath your desk with you sitting in it. You do not want to hit your knees every time you sit down to work.

You know the value of good lighting for weddings and it is no different for your office. Check the lighting in your office area. If overhead lighting is not adequate, purchase a desk or floor lamp so

PHOTO 20.4 AN EXCELLENT CONSULTANT KEEPS TRACK OF ALL THE DETAILS.

SOURCE: WWW.RODNEYBAILEY.COM

you can work efficiently at all hours. If you do not have everything to outfit your home office, buying office equipment does not have to be expensive. You can scour garage sales and thrift shops or view Craigslist or other local online classified listings for affordable furniture and equipment.

In addition to deciding what your office will look like, consider setting some ground rules for yourself. For example, decide on a work schedule that fits with your body's time clock and allows you to work a reasonable number of hours each day. Are you a morning person? If so, then it makes sense for you to begin your workday at 5:00 a.m. If you operate better later in the day, then consider starting your workday later in the afternoon. Remember, you are your own boss and it is up to you to set your own hours for maximum productivity and profit.

Other ground rules to consider for your home-based business might include limiting your time spent surfing the internet and making personal phone calls, requiring yourself to take a break every hour or two, having lunch at the same time each day, not eating in your office and other no-nonsense policies. Every office has rules and your home office should be no exception.

A word of caution, working from home can be very lonely, especially when you are just starting to build your business. To avoid going stir crazy, make a point to meet with new vendors, as discussed in Chapter 23, while you are building your client base. If you are home alone without the opportunity to interact with the rest of the world, you risk boredom, isolation and depression. If you balance your outside meetings with your quiet work time at home, you will feel more productive and energized.

If you decide that working from home is not for you, leasing office space is always a viable option. From browsing real estate ads to using national websites such as *offices2share.com*, you can find a wealth of information on leasing office space month-to-month or just for special client meetings. Many of these *executive suites* are located in business parks, include furnishings, are internet ready and have optional add-ons such as mail pick-up, receptionist services and access to conference space. Whether you want day-to-day office space or just space once in a while, leasing well-equipped space is easier than you might think.

BUILDING A STAFF

Even if you are just starting out and money is tight, it is important to consider having a small staff. An assistant can easily manage the ceremony portion of the wedding so that you can be free to oversee the details at the reception. If a wedding is large, you may need two or three assistants to ensure everything runs smoothly. Assistants can complete tasks such as directing vendors for set-up, gathering the bridal party for photographs or running out to complete last-minute errands. With guidance, they can do almost anything to help you manage a wedding and can ease some of the challenges associated with being an entrepreneur. Executive burdens are particularly problematic for female business owners, who have been consistently shown to face more barriers than males to balancing work and family life (Daugherty 2012). As the vast majority of wedding consulting companies are owned and operated by women, the decision to build a staff can enhance the likelihood that a planner stays in business.

Finding a qualified assistant can be a challenge. Although there are many people who will be interested in learning the ropes as your assistant, not all of them will possess the skills necessary to succeed. Interview a few candidates to see who has the most experience and/or enthusiasm for the position. Students from a local university are often willing to volunteer for day-of implementation to gain experience. Start with universities that have programs in events management, and reach out to their program coordinators to secure the best candidates. If you have ongoing work, students may be able to assist you over an extended period of time for course credit, as associated with a *practicum* or *internship* experience. Check with the internship coordinator of the associated program to determine the restrictions and requirements of working with students for credit. At George Mason University, for example, events management students complete 120 hours for a practicum and 400 for an internship over a period of 10–15 weeks, so you want to make sure that you have enough work for the students to justify a for-credit experience. Otherwise, set the experience up as a day-of volunteer opportunity. See *Consultant in Action*, Case 20.1, for the perspective of a student assisting at a wedding. If you are reading this text for an undergraduate class, this case gives you an excellent sense of what it is like to live a day in the life of a planner.

CONSULTANT IN ACTION, CASE 20.1

A DAY IN THE LIFE

Recently, I had the pleasure of assisting with a wedding in the Washington, DC area. This long day taught me so much about the wedding planning process. The event planning team consisted of one main wedding planner, her primary assistant and three extra assistants, one of which included me. The budget for the wedding was $120,000. My assignment for the morning was to take care of the bridal party prior to the ceremony. I arrived at the hotel at 11:00 a.m. and was greeted by the wedding planner. She handed me the timeline, which had a very detailed explanation of what I was to do at each part of the day. The planner gave me a room key and told me that she had to go over to the wedding venue to set up and that I was to follow the directions on the timeline. Before I knew it, I was in planner mode! My task list prior to the ceremony included:

- 12:00 p.m.–1:00 p.m.: Steam the bridesmaids' dresses and the bride's veil, call the catering company to make sure they are on their way for the luncheon and call the jewelry store to make sure they can clean the bride's wedding rings.

- 1:00 p.m.: Organize food for luncheon and deliver to suites.

- 1:30 p.m.: Get the bride's rings cleaned.

- 2:00 p.m.: Clean the hotel room and ask the maids to come in and make the bed for photos.

- 3:00 p.m.: Lead the groom and his party downstairs to leave for the ceremony.

- 3:15 p.m.: Call the limousine company to make sure they are on their way to pick up the groom's family by 3:30 p.m. and then the bridal party at 4:00 p.m.

I called the front desk to ask them for a steamer for the bride's gown. They took about 30 minutes to deliver it. I filled up the steamer with water and plugged it in and, by the time it started steaming, I was left with about 10 minutes to finish my first assignment. I started steaming the dresses, when the steamer started squirting water all over the dress I was steaming. Luckily, the material was not silk so I used a blow dryer to dry it. This process kept happening over and over so I called the front desk and asked for a new steamer. Meanwhile, the catering arrived on time so I organized all the food for the family and bridal party. Next, I accompanied the caterers to the groom's suite and to the parents of the groom's suite, but, on our way, we had to stop at the front desk to get keys for each. The groom's suite worked out perfectly; however, the groom's parents' room turned into a huge mess. We delivered the food to the incorrect suite. When we discovered the mistake, 20 minutes had passed and I was panicked. I ran down to the room and saw ladies trying to get into the suite but unable to do so because their keys did not work. I ran over to the ladies and explained what happened. They were very nice and even offered to help me carry the food. The food was eventually delivered to the right suite. By that time, it was 1:30 p.m. and I still had not steamed the dresses. The bride then asked when I was going to get her rings cleaned. I ran over to the jewelry store, which took about an hour. I learned that "a few blocks away" actually was five blocks each way.

By the time I got back to the hotel with the clean rings, it was 2:30 p.m. and the dresses still were not steamed. I started steaming the dresses frantically and the mother of the bride even pitched in. She steamed the dresses and I began to steam the veil. This veil was enormous. It took two girls holding it up and me actually steaming it to get the job done.

Finally, with the steaming complete, I began cleaning the room and called for housekeeping to help. The room was separated into a bedroom and a sitting area. I cleaned the bedroom by picking up bottles and food and making sure it looked good for photos. I expected the bride would get dressed in the bedroom and that it would be the best place to clean since the living area was a complete mess. But when the photographer arrived he started taking pictures of the bridal party getting ready in the living area. I frantically cleaned each angle that he was using for the pictures. I then realized that we had 30 minutes to head downstairs and depart for the wedding. I announced this to the family and they all began getting dressed. The bride slipped on her dress and everyone applauded. Photos were taken and we headed downstairs. We waited for about 10 minutes when I had a feeling that there was an issue with the limousine. I called the limo company and asked them what was going on. The limo driver said that he thought he was done and he was on his way to another wedding. I told him he was wrong and we needed him to come back to the hotel. He came back and took the bridal party over to the wedding venue and I followed in my car.

When I arrived at the venue, I was instructed to stay with the bride and the bridal party and to help with the bride's dress. The ceremony began and the bride walked out. I helped her with her dress up until she hit the grassy area that was her aisle. Her veil flew off with a gust of wind and the wedding planner grabbed it and put it back in place. Everyone laughed, including the bride. It was a sweet ceremony. Afterwards, I waited for the bride and helped her with her long dress and veil. The bride and groom signed the marriage license and began to mingle with family and friends. I noticed that the catering company actually had one server follow the bride around and make sure she had food and drink at all times. I thought that was a really great idea. Then, I directed the bride and her family to get their photos taken. Afterwards, the bride was guided to a private room so she could wait to make a grand entrance. In the room I found a pair of sparkly Ugg boots waiting for her. She threw off her glamorous wedding shoes and stepped into the Uggs and sat down in a chair to wait for her entrance.

The couple made their grand entrance and then everyone sat down to dinner. I would love to tell you what they ate but, by that time, I was so hungry that I did not even notice. I had been invited to partake in the staff's buffet, and I ate with gusto.

As luck would have it, I sat next to the wedding planner's assistant who gave me insights into the wedding planning industry. The first thing she told me was that most wedding planners are independent contractors. Basically, they only make money when they have weddings to plan. I thought that if you worked for a company as a planner that you would get paid consistently throughout the year, but that is not always the case. The second thing I learned is that a $120,000 wedding is not considered to be a large budget in the DC market. Apparently, there are many weddings beyond that price point in DC each year. Another thing she told me was that wedding planners charge a flat rate for their services. I had assumed that a planner would charge more on a larger wedding and less on a smaller wedding.

While the guests danced and enjoyed themselves, the planners had work to do. I was instructed to go back to the bride and groom's suite and make it presentable for their first night as a married couple. I arranged the bride's veil on a couch and displayed her heels at the end of it. I artfully stacked all her presents on a table. The room had food and trash all over so I cleaned up. I asked the front desk to throw rose petals on the bed. I arrived back to the venue in time for the grand exit. We handed out sparklers and asked the guests to gather round. It looked really pretty. The couple took pictures in front of a vintage 1950s car and drove off into the night. After, we helped clean up and load the wedding planner's car with supplies. One of my favorite parts of cleaning up was that I got to take a few beautiful floral arrangements home.

I learned so much from this experience. First, being a wedding planner is a fast-paced job. You have to think quickly on your feet and work fast. When assisting, I learned that it is important to not ask too many questions and to try to figure things out on your own. The wedding planner is very busy and does not have much time to help you. I also learned it is all about making the bride and whoever paid for the wedding happy. Some guests complained that the room was too cold but the bride was hot so we kept the room cold to make her happy. The timeline is your best friend. The more detailed the better. It helps you to not forget things and to stay on track. Having your cellphone pre-programmed with important phone numbers is key.

I would definitely recommend assisting with a wedding if you are considering wedding planning as a career choice. I really enjoyed my experience and learned a lot. Wedding planning is definitely a lot of work, not for the faint of heart and less glamorous than I thought it would be.

CASE SUBMITTED BY ALEXIS PULLING

One point to stress to your candidates is that most weddings take place on Saturdays, so they need to be available on Fridays for the rehearsal, the wedding day itself and possibly Sunday. If weekend work is not possible for your candidate, you need to keep searching. In addition to weekend availability, a good assistant should possess the 15 skills listed in Table 20.2.

TABLE 20.2 SKILLS TO LOOK FOR WHEN INTERVIEWING ASSISTANTS

• Able to follow instructions	• Composure under stress	• Politeness
• Attention to details	• Does not gossip	• Professional demeanor
• Bright personality	• Good multi-tasker	• Organized
• Can stand on feet for many hours	• High energy level	• Self-confidence
• Common sense	• Looks comfortable even when it is hot or cold	• Quick and creative problem solver

PAY AND NON-COMPETE CLAUSES

Although some assistants work for the experience alone, you should be prepared to pay your assistants for their time and effort. An experienced assistant can earn $25 per hour or more, especially in a large city. If you do not want to pay on an hourly basis, you should negotiate a flat fee for the entire wedding, such as $200, depending on the duties that the assistant is required to perform. Consult with your tax advisor regarding how to appropriately document payment for short-term assistance. Many wedding consultants hire the same assistants over and over. This is the perfect scenario because, over time, the assistant develops a feel for what the planner expects and needs, even before the planner has to ask for it. Sometimes, two or three wedding planners share the same assistants.

When working with the same assistant over time, bringing on an intern or, most importantly, when hiring your first associate, it is in your best interest to have a non-compete clause as part of the arrangement. Most wedding consultants are hesitant to host interns because they fear that interns might work with them for 15 weeks and then turn around and open a business using all of the information and secrets they have just learned. It takes successful wedding consultants years to establish a system that works, and they are justifiably protective of their materials and methods.

A *non-compete clause* is a condition of employment statement found in an employment agreement that indicates a time frame during which the employee, upon leaving the company, cannot work for the company's competition. The purpose is to prevent former employees from taking trade secrets to start a similar type of business or to work with a competitor. For example, the clause might say that an employee is not permitted to start a wedding consulting business or work for a competing consulting firm within 18 months of leaving the position. State law governs a non-compete clause, determination and enforcement, so you are advised to consult with an attorney when drawing up this document. A refusal to sign is a justifiable means for not hiring. If the clause is violated, both the former employee and the employee's new company can be sued.

A non-compete clause may also include a *radius clause*, indicating a region of exclusivity to which the agreement applies. To extend the example above, the clause might say that an employee is not permitted to start a wedding consulting business or work for a competing consulting firm within 18 months of leaving the position if the new company is located within a 200-mile radius. This clause allows a former employee to start a business immediately if and only if the new business if located outside the specified radius.

REFERENCES

Daugherty, E.L. (2012) 'Executive women in business: exploring challenges and pathways of specialty areas', *International Journal of Business Strategy*, 12: 47–64.

Dearman, D.T. (2012) 'Factors influencing managers' decisions to prepare a business plan', *SSRN*, Online. Available HTTP: <http://ssrn.com/abstract=2133100> (accessed 12 March 2013).

Ibrahim, N.A. (2012) 'Formalized business planning decisions in small firms', *International Journal of Business Strategy*, 12: 81–86.

IRS (2013) 'Apply for an Employer Identification Number online', Online. Available HTTP: <http://www.irs.gov/Businesses/Small-Businesses-&-Self-Employed/Apply-for-an-Employer-Identification-Number-(EIN)-Online> (accessed 12 March 2013).

Leung, A. and Luthans, K. (2011) 'How do small businesses learn and process market information and their marketing implications?', *American Marketing Association*, Summer: 68–69.

Pulling, A. (2012) 'A day in the life'. E-mail (12 November 2012).

Schmiedel, T., vom Brocke, J. and Recker, J. (2013) 'Which cultural values matter to business process management?: results from a global Delphi study', *Business Process Management Journal*, 19: early cite in press.

US Small Business Administration (2013a) 'Create your business plan', Online. Available HTTP: <http://www.sba.gov/category/navigation-structure/starting-managing-business/starting-business/how-write-business-plan> (accessed 12 March 2013).

—— (2013b) '20 questions before starting', Online. Available HTTP: <http://www.sba.gov/content/20-questions-before-starting-business> (accessed 12 March 2013).

—— (2013c) 'Obtain business licenses and permits', Online. Available HTTP: <http://www.sba.gov/category/navigation-structure/starting-managing-business/starting-business/obtain-business-licenses-> (accessed 12 March 2013).

—— (2013d) 'Business insurance', Online. Available HTTP: <http://www.sba.gov/content/business-insurance> (accessed 12 March 2013).

REVIEW

1. Name at least five core questions that guide a business plan.

2. What is a DBA name?

3. Name and distinguish between the three primary types of business entities.

4. What is an EIN?

5. Differentiate between equipment and supplies.

6. Name three things you can do to organize your workspace.

7. Name five attributes you would look for in hiring an assistant.

8. Define and give an example of a non-compete clause.

9. Define and give an example of a radius clause.

TERMINOLOGY

- Balance sheet
- Corporation
- DBA name
- EIN
- Equipment
- Executive suites
- Executive summary
- General liability insurance
- Income statement
- Internship
- Limited liability company
- Mission statement
- Non-compete clause
- Partnership
- Practicum
- Pro-forma cash flow
- Pro-forma income projections
- Radius clause
- Sole proprietor
- Supplies

PHOTO 21.1 A MARKETING PLAN SHOULD SPELL OUT YOUR TARGET AUDIENCE.

SOURCE: WWW.RODNEYBAILEY.COM

DEVELOPING A
MARKETING STRATEGY

At the heart of any successful business plan is an innovative marketing strategy. Marketing is an umbrella term that pertains to the activities of a company that are associated with selling a product or service and developing a competitive advantage. Because few small businesses survive in the long-term (Ogunmokun and Tang 2012) and small business failure is frequently linked to limited marketing knowledge that leads to formulation errors and weak strategy (Cronin-Gilmore 2012), your ability to market successfully is vital to staying in business.

Traditional marketing models have been replaced with integrative strategies that focus on customer collaboration by blending online and offline initiatives that foster sustained engagement (Harris and Rae 2010). The transparency of customer involvement in modern marketing is both a blessing and a curse, as online customer feedback can make or break a small business. Perhaps in no other business context is this more applicable than in relationship to weddings. The customer base is particularly receptive to the opinions of others; this feedback chain subsequently informs their decisions. In turn, newlyweds are eager to post their own reviews on website giants such as The Knot and WeddingWire for the world to see.

If you want your wedding business to survive, you must develop a marketing plan that is creative, tactical and implementable. "The marketing plan is the central instrument for directing and coordinating the marketing effort of an organization and the content of a marketing plan includes laying out current situation, setting objectives, strategies, action program, budgets, implementation and control" (Ogunmokun and Tang 2012: 159–160). Importantly, high-performing small business ownership has been linked to going beyond thinking about the plan and putting it in writing (Ogunmokun and Tang 2012). The purpose of this chapter is to point out the key factors that will allow you to develop a successful marketing program: understanding the uniqueness of the wedding market, determining your target audience, marketing appeals, marketing tool development, utilizing social media and managing your online reputation.

UNDERSTANDING THE UNIQUENESS OF THE WEDDING MARKET

Marc McIntosh (2013) is the CEO of Showcase Events. He produces 10 bridal shows each year and, over the course of his career, Marc has interacted with thousands of wedding vendors and over 100,000 brides. When he is not producing shows, Marc spends much of his time helping vendors, including wedding consultants, discover ways to better market their businesses. Marc has won multiple awards for his efforts, including the Bridal Show Producer's International Cup Award, the highest honor of the association.

Marc explains that, while over $50 billion is spent annually on weddings in the US, ups and downs in the economy influence average spending and can, in turn, influence profits of the many small companies that depend on the business of weddings. Furthermore, he emphasizes that the wedding market has a clearly defined time period or "season" during which a bride is in need of products and services. Unlike Starbucks, where someone might go for a Frappuccino three times a week, a bride (ideally!) only needs your wedding planning services once in her lifetime. This means that you need to constantly market to brides because a bride who gets married one year will not need your services after she is married. You must continually get your name out there to each new "season" of brides that comes along. Your investment in marketing your business allows you to survive and thrive.

Another unique aspect of the wedding market, Marc explains, is that a bride is purchasing on emotion. When she buys, she is buying not goods or services, but ways to make her wedding perfect. She only cares about the end result of her wedding day. She wants everything to go smoothly so her guests will tell her that this was the best wedding they ever attended. The bride does not actually care about your wedding planning business, she only cares about what you can do to bring her vision to life. It is the savvy wedding planner who understands this and capitalizes on it through marketing. How does this information translate into a marketing strategy? Instead

Photo 21.2 Marketing to brides and grooms is seasonal.

Source: www.RodneyBailey.com

of telling a bride about the *features* of your business, you will tap into her emotions if you show her the *benefits* of hiring you. Here are some examples Marc offers:

Feature (the wrong focus): I offer personalized planning and unmatched customer service.

Benefit (the right approach): So you will be able to relax and enjoy your day.

Feature (the wrong approach): I have more than 10 years of experience planning weddings.

Benefit (the right approach): So you will have peace of mind knowing that everything will be done right.

By understanding the uniqueness of the wedding market and timing your marketing efforts to appeal to each new season of brides, you will outdistance yourself from the competition and be well on your way to establishing a successful business.

DETERMINING YOUR TARGET AUDIENCE

After you have established your business as a formal entity, it is time to get the word out that your doors are open for business. The best way to do that is through marketing. But, before you spend the first dollar on marketing or advertising, you must determine your *target audience*, defined as the group of people you wish to serve. One of the hardest things about establishing a business is finding your style and defining it. Many consultants struggle because they want to be all things to all people and are afraid to turn away business, but this generalist approach means that they cannot focus their energy on a specific target market. To help you get focused, consider the following questions:

- Who are your customers going to be?
- Is this a growing market in your area?
- How are you going to reach your customers?
- What pricing strategy will you implement?
- What is your area of expertise?
- What differentiates you from your competitors?

When selecting a target market, you have to make sure there is a substantial customer base to justify the choice. For example, if you decide that you want to focus your wedding business on same-sex weddings, you should know the facts: Are same-sex marriages or civil unions legal in your state? How many same-sex marriages or civil unions have there been in your state since it became legal? Are there enough couples to support a wedding consultant who focuses on same-sex weddings? The same series of questions pertains to any niche group, such as the brides over-40, military weddings, the second-marriage market or weddings that cater to a specific cultural or religious affiliation. Once you have drilled down and answered the questions about your potential clients, you are ready to develop a marketing plan to reach them.

MARKETING APPEALS

As you begin to think about developing specific marketing materials, you should appeal to potential clients through logic, emotion and credibility. *Logical appeals* answer all of the nuts and bolts questions that arise: who, what, where, when, why, cost and contact information. Specifically, there should be a person attached to the company (who), a description of the services you provide (what), your location and/or the areas you serve (where), how long you have been planning weddings (when) and a mission statement (why). When you are brand new to the business, you probably do not want to directly state the when (e.g., "We've been in business for three months!"); however, over time this can add significantly to your credibility (e.g., "During the past five years we have planned over 100 weddings."). If you do not want to put your price structure on the internet, the cost information can be alluded to by detailing the various packages you offer. The contact information will then be used by clients who want to follow up and get more specific details.

Emotional appeals draw your clients more closely to your services. Specifically, many consultants include pictures from weddings they have planned as a means to personalize their websites. Potential clients can get a better sense of your style and specialty areas through the visual representation of past work. If your business caters to ski resort weddings, make sure that it is made obvious with a number of associated photographs. Brides love looking at pictures from other weddings as this creates a sense of anticipation for their own day. When utilizing pictures, make sure that you get copyright permission from the photographer. Many consultants have excellent professional relationships with area photographers who allow them to post pictures from weddings that showcase their work.

Appeals to credibility can come from quotes taken from letters or feedback from satisfied clients. Further, if you receive any awards or outside recognition related to wedding planning, that should be prominently displayed on your website. Credibility can also be obtained through related courses, seminars or conferences that you have either attended or participated in as a guest speaker. Any involvement with event or wedding associations such as International Special Events Society or the Association of Bridal Consultants should also be evidenced on your website to boost your credibility.

MARKETING TOOL DEVELOPMENT

Today, more than ever before, there are so many ways to market your new business, but where do you start and how do you decide where to focus your efforts? For a new business, the two best marketing tools you can create almost immediately are your business card and your website.

However, before you develop either of these tools, it is important to consider developing a logo for your business.

What would McDonald's be without the golden arches? Or Nike without the famous swoosh? Or Apple without a bite missing? Each of these businesses is known by the company's graphic representation, known as a *logo*, as much as by the business name. When forming your company, you spent a significant amount of time selecting a business name, now it is time to design a logo that captures your essence graphically. Once you have a logo, you can move forward with developing your marketing strategy.

For such an important task, seek professional help from a graphic designer or artist. If you have minimal start-up funds, there are internet-based logo design firms that are reasonably priced. Alternatively, secure the assistance of friends who have artistic talent or consider hiring an art or graphic design student to generate ideas for you. Meet with the designer in person to describe your business, style, the type of client you hope to attract, your mission statement, philosophy and other relevant details from your business plan.

Give the artist some ideas to get the ball rolling and then allow the artist free rein to come up with designs for you to review. When the artist presents the options to you, take time to think about them. Ask yourself some questions: Which idea will carry you through many years? Which idea has the most flexibility? Which idea really personifies what you are all about? Remember, this logo will be seen on letterhead, signage, work shirts, brochures, website and social media pages. Make sure the logo you select looks like a wedding planning business rather than a florist, caterer or other wedding-related specialist. Now that you have a logo, you are ready to develop your other key marketing tools.

BUSINESS CARD BASICS

While it may seem old school, the business card is in fact one of the best marketing tools at your disposal and also one of the least expensive. Plain or fancy, self-made or professionally designed, the business card is indispensable for marketing your business.

Your business card is a tangible personification of your business so the style of your card should echo the style of your business. For example, if your business plan is to cater to those with small budgets, your business card should be casual and friendly. Conversely, if you hope to capture high-end weddings, your card should be printed on expensive paper with an elegant font. If you hope to target recent college graduates, your card should be modern and fresh so that it will appeal to a young audience.

Your business card should include the following information: your logo, business name, your name and title, contact information including mailing address, mobile telephone number, e-mail address, fax number and website address. Further, if you are going after a certain market, reflect that with

PHOTO 21.3 CULTURAL EXPERTISE SHOULD BE INDICATED ON YOUR BUSINESS CARD.

SOURCE: WWW.RODNEYBAILEY.COM

your business card. For example, if you wish to target Japanese brides, you should consider having your information printed in Japanese on one side of the card. This way, when you meet with a Japanese client, you can present your card in both languages. Small efforts like this distance you from your competition. Additionally, if your business has a specialty, you might list that on the card. Statements like: "Specializing in multicultural celebrations" or "Fluent in English, Spanish and French" provide valuable information to potential clients.

Have 500 cards printed and always keep a stack with you. Invest in a nice leather or metal cardholder so, when someone asks for your card, they are not tumbling out of your purse or briefcase. You always want to present a new card, not something that has been kicking around at the bottom of your bag or briefcase. Remember, your card is a representation of your business. If you want to present a neat and organized image, make sure your card is in pristine condition.

WEBSITE UNDER CONSTRUCTION

While your business card is a mini-billboard for your business, a professional website is an electronic billboard capable of reaching millions of potential clients. Ed Chung is the Creative Director of Ditherdog, a marketing and design firm specializing in website development. Ed offers the following reasons why wedding consultants should have a web presence:

- The web is an inexpensive, proven, mass-market vehicle to communicate corporate objectives and description of products and services.

- Unlike print marketing, a website is easy to regularly update and keep fresh.

- A website is a great vehicle for creating a stimulating, 24-hour multimedia portfolio (pictures, sound, video) to sell your company.

- Using tools like a web e-mail form allow for a passive (hands-off) way to accumulate new leads and garner customer interest.

- You can cross-market with print campaigns (direct mail or advertising) while at the same time track effectiveness of a campaign or publication by analyzing user traffic.

- Newsletters created in e-mail or web form are an inexpensive means of sending promotional updates.

(Chung 2013)

Importantly, your e-mail address should be linked to your website address. For example, if a wedding planning team's website is *weddinggurus.com*, an associate's e-mail might be *rachel@weddinggurus.net*. This is much more memorable, professional and marketable than something like *rachwedplnr1894@email.com*.

Beyond your own website, advertising on wedding sites such as The Knot, WeddingWire, Brides and the WeddingChannel can be an effective form of promotion for you. You will be charged based on the type of listing, with premium positioning coming with an extra charge. Fees that run $150 or more per month may be cost-prohibitive at first; but, if you receive one or two clients from this listing, before you know it, you have covered the fee for the entire year.

While you absolutely need a website, it only works if it contains a message that is compelling and if the bride is able to find it. Two common ways that search engines rank websites are through crosslinks with related websites and through zip code distribution, so it is worth your time to cross-promote with other vendors and to include a section listing the zip codes in the areas you serve. You should be careful, however, that you do not give away your trade secrets on your website. Instead, only give enough information to entice the bride to contact you for the complete details.

PRINT ADVERTISING

The internet has made marketing to brides easier and less expensive, so business owners may question the utility of print advertising. With so many marketing options to explore, how do you decide where to put your limited print advertising resources? You will want to put your energy into what works and what you can afford. What is the first thing that a bride will buy once she is engaged? Bridal magazines! An advertisement in a bridal magazine, even a small one, can pay off handsomely. While national magazines may be cost-prohibitive, most cities have local or regional bridal guides. Direct mail is also a good tool for you to consider. With fewer and fewer businesses investing in surface mail, your message can reach your target market and make a big splash. Think of it like this. How many holiday cards did you receive last year? How did you feel when you saw that special envelope in the mail? We are so bombarded with e-mail and texts that reading a printed message sent by traditional mail is special and meaningful.

BRIDAL SHOWS

Another important way to connect with the bride is through bridal shows. Bridal shows typically include fashion shows, demonstrations and a variety of wedding-related businesses arranged in a trade show format. Shows give the vendor the opportunity to reach many prospective customers in just a few hours and allow the bride to visit one location to see all of the options that are available for her wedding. Wedding shows are the single most effective way to meet with potential brides face-to-face and to have instant interaction. Remember, a bride is buying you. If she likes you, she will do business with you. A face-to-face informal meeting at a bridal show is an excellent way to make this connection and potentially gain new clients.

WORD-OF-MOUTH

One of the most significant forms of advertising for those involved in the business of weddings is word-of-mouth. When you have one satisfied client, she will tell her bridesmaids about you and your name will be passed along. Never underestimate the value of a heartfelt referral. Brides listen to and trust the recommendations of friends, family members and trusted vendors. You want to be the planner who is being recommended and discussed. Wedding vendors have reported to us that up to 50 per cent of their business comes from word-of-mouth referrals, frequently from other vendors. As discussed in more depth in Chapter 23, it is well worth your while to network continuously, interact professionally and extend the utmost courtesy, as others' positive experiences with you will readily lead to more business.

SOCIAL MEDIA

The concept of social media "combines two distinct terms, the first encompassing people and human relations, the second connoting modern forms of communication. Marrying the two gives a basic definition: the building of human relationships via any number of far reaching communication mediums" (Bakeman and Hanson 2012: 106–107). Leung and Luthans summarize how social media outlets can be used to identify potential customers:

> The important implication for marketing is the shift from segmenting the market based on company size and product line to identifying target customers using the social network dimension, especially in industries which are populated by small businesses. As small business owners do not have time and lax resources to conduct broad based environmental scanning, they rely on their social networks heavily to focus their efforts to adapt to specific industry trends they perceive to be most relevant to their businesses.
>
> (2011: 69)

Beyond target audience determination, firms use social media tools to market goods and services, while consumers use them to share and evaluate experiences. While the ubiquitous nature of social media has resulted in the feeling that getting on board is imperative, business owners often question the return on investment for the time and money spent on social media implementation and upkeep (Weinberg and Pehlivan 2011). Social media forms magnify consumer-to-consumer and seller-to-buyer conversations in ways that often influence behavior (Mangold and Faulds 2009) and expand reach through social contagion (De Vries *et al.* 2012; Kirtiş and Karahan 2011); however, the effect will vary based on the source, as

> social media encompasses a wide range of online, word-of-mouth forums including blogs, company sponsored discussion boards and chat rooms, consumer-to-consumer e-mail, consumer product or service ratings websites and forums, Internet discussion boards and forums, moblogs (sites containing digital audio, images, movies, or photographs), and social networking websites, to name a few.
>
> (Mangold and Faulds 2009: 358)

Weinberg and Pehlivan (2011) differentiate social media based on information depth and the half-life of the information, where depth pertains to the complexity of the content and the ability to offer multiple perspectives, while the half-life is based on how long the information is available as well as how long the topic remains of interest. Even a shallow form of social media with a short half-life can garner tremendous loyalty, as evidenced by mass followings of popular Twitter feeds.

As emergent forms of social media are popularized quickly, you will need to carefully consider the social media eggs to put into your marketing mix basket. In general, small business owners have been slower to adopt social media practices than their larger counterparts, based on limited time to learn and employ the strategies and limited funds to hire someone else to do so (Bakeman and

Photo 21.4 Brides and grooms use social media to discuss their vendor experiences.

Source: www.RodneyBailey.com

Hanson 2012; Michaelidou *et al.* 2011). One of the best and least expensive ways to improve your social media capabilities is to hire an undergraduate student as an intern to assist you (Bakeman and Hanson 2012). Undergraduate students are incredibly savvy when it comes to managing social media sites; moreover, they are early adopters of technology and can keep you abreast of the latest trends. Some of the major players to consider in your social media mix are listed below. Importantly, prior to sharing any information about your clients on a social media site, you must secure their permission in writing.

Blogs

As web publishing tools grow in terms of sophistication and ease of use, non-technical users gain access and capacity to start a blog, adopted from web log, in order to share their opinions and expertise in a journal-like fashion. By writing a blog and sharing planning tips and trends, a wedding planner will soon develop a following of regular readers and prospective clients. Some of the most popular wedding planning blogs are Style Me Pretty, the Wedding Channel, Aisle Say, Delightfully Engaged, One Lovely Day, Weddingbee, One Wed's Savvy Scoop, Wedding Chicks, Green Wedding Shoes and Beau-Coup Wedding (Bride Tide 2013).

FACEBOOK

There are now more than 1 billion monthly active Facebook users and over 42 million pages residing on Facebook (Wise Geek 2013). Facebook, founded in 2004 by Harvard student Mark Zuckerberg, is the largest social networking website intended to connect friends, family and business associates (Wise Geek 2013). Creating a Facebook page for your wedding planning business is free, easy and will allow you to connect to brides all over the world. Before you open your doors for business, you must have a presence on Facebook.

PINTEREST

Pinterest has 25 million members, many of whom are young, female, well educated and have disposable income (Pinsker and Lipka 2013). Pinterest is an electronic bulletin where brides can go to "pin" or save their wedding inspiration to "boards." A bride can organize her inspiration by categories such as wedding dresses, themes, cakes, etc. and is only limited by the amount of time she is willing to spend pinning images. You should enthusiastically view your clients' boards and assist them with understanding the budget implications of their selections. With the vast majority of today's brides seeking inspiration through Pinterest, it is imperative that you familiarize yourself with the process of sharing and commenting on ideas. If you and your client do not live in the same town, Pinterest is an excellent way to share ideas and keep in touch.

TWITTER

Who would have thought that 140 characters could be so informative? Founded in 2006, Twitter is a public forum where anyone can read, write and share brief messages known as Tweets (Twitter 2013). Tweets can include text, videos, photos or links. Twitter is a great way to instantly share information on the go or to provide exclusive content. Imagine sharing a gorgeous photo of a first kiss from one of your weddings with all of your followers. On Twitter, information is shared immediately as users employ their desktops, tablets and mobile devices to share or follow events, news and real-time conversations. People also turn to Twitter to talk about your business and your industry, and you should as well. Twitter gives you powerful context to connect directly with present and future customers in real time.

LINKEDIN

In order to present a professional image to your prospective clients, LinkedIn is the ultimate in social networking sites. On LinkedIn you have the opportunity to list all of your professional experience in a resume format. Also, you can showcase endorsements from those who know of your work. This is similar to having testimonials on your website from past clients.

YouTube

YouTube offers a forum to showcase your skills. With a client's permission, you may upload a short video that guides the viewer through the process of set-up and implementation of the ceremony and reception. Or, if you are skilled with stationery DIY techniques, you can create a tutorial illustrating how to make elegant invitations. The links to such visual content should be listed on your website.

MANAGING YOUR ONLINE REPUTATION

Social media tools provide an incomparable platform for consumers to publicize their experiences, opinions and evaluations regarding goods or services in a way that both mimics and facilitates face-to-face, word-of-mouth communication (Chen *et al.* 2011). As such, you need to carefully monitor and manage your online reputation. First, consider your own outlets. Before starting your business, clean up your Facebook page by removing any content or images that are unprofessional or reflect on you poorly. Once you start your business, never post anything about a client or vendor that is inappropriate or unprincipled, as negative commentary that you post can come back to haunt you.

While you are self-monitoring your own online activities, you must simultaneously keep a close eye on what others are saying about you. The transparency of online feedback has both benefits and drawbacks, as both kudos and criticism are available for all potential customers to review.

You need to inspect content regularly to ensure that everything being said about you is accurate and, ideally, positive. It is difficult to overcome the adverse effects of negative word-of-mouth postings, in particular when they outnumber positive reviews (Chen *et al.* 2011).

Haynal Papp (2013) of Dolce Studio Films explains that, if a client writes a brutal review of you, it is there forever; as such, it is your responsibility to minimize the damage if the review is factual or have it removed if it is not. She notes that particularly hazardous are the manipulative clients who, after all contracted services have been rendered, threaten you with a bad online review if you are not willing to give them a partial refund or additional products or services for free. While such threats of extortion are rare, they do occur and have legal implications that are often difficult or cost-prohibitive to address.

Receiving a negative online review is stressful, as it deleteriously influences your personal credibility and the bottom line of your business. Haynal offers valuable advice regarding the management of negative online reviews. First, formulate a paper trail so you can establish your side of the case, if necessary. Be certain to fulfill your contract obligations and save all of your files and every e-mail from each client. You should maintain physical and electronic file folders for each client to make this process as simple as possible. Second, when a bad review is posted, seek input from colleagues before you act. Chances are that someone in your peer network has dealt with a similar situation and can offer valuable advice. Third, if the review is erroneous, send your documentation and a copy of your contract to the online source (e.g., The Knot, WeddingWire, Yelp, Angie's List). Generally, with evidence in hand, a false review can be removed within 24 hours.

Finally, if the review represents at least a version of reality, do not just let it go, as the facts may be embedded in venomous attacks that make the situation seem much worse than it was. If you cannot get the review taken down, you have the opportunity to respond. Haynal advises that you should respond briefly, concisely, diplomatically, kindly and with no spelling or grammatical errors. Respond to the community of readers, not the client. You have to protect yourself and the income of your team. For instance, if your wedding consulting company receives a negative online review on WeddingWire regarding your day-of services, you might respond:

> Dear WeddingWire Community,
>
> It saddens me when our company receives a review that is anything less than excellent. We at (*insert your company name*) strive to exceed expectations with our consulting services. Even with our day-of clients, we meet a minimum of three times prior to the wedding, complete a comprehensive timeline and site layout, confirm with all vendors, attend the rehearsal and have a minimum of two staff members from our team on during the ceremony and reception. Our goal is to sweat the details so your wedding will run smoothly and you can relax and enjoy your incredible day!

By taking the high road, you can project an air of assurance and professionalism that will offer a stark contrast to the review. Do not state anything that is not 100 per cent true about your services. With a mindful approach, you can mitigate the damage and move on confidently to your next client.

REFERENCES

Bakeman, M.M. and Hanson, L. (2012) 'Bringing social media to small business: a role for employees and students in technology diffusion', *Business Education Innovation Journal*, 4: 106–111.

Bride Tide (2013) 'Top 100 wedding blogs', Online. Available HTTP: <http://www.weddingblogs100.com/> (accessed 8 March 2013).

Chen, Y., Fay, S. and Wang, Q. (2011) 'The role of marketing in social media: how online consumer reviews evolve', *Journal of Interactive Marketing*, 25: 85–94.

Chung, E. (2013) 'Salient reasons to have a web presence for a wedding planning business (personal communication)', *Ditherdog*, Online. Available HTTP: <http://www.ditherdog.com> (accessed 26 February 2013).

Cronin-Gilmore, J. (2012) 'Exploring marketing strategies in small businesses', *Journal of Marketing Development and Competitiveness*, 6: 96–107.

De Vries, L., Gensler, S. and Leeflang, P.S.H. (2012) 'Popularity of brand posts on brand fan pages: an investigation of the effects of social media marketing', *Journal of Interactive Marketing*, 26: 83–91.

Harris, L. and Rae, A. (2010) 'The online connection: transforming marketing strategy for small businesses', *Journal of Business Strategy*, 31: 4–12.

Kirtiş, A.K. and Karahan, F. (2011) 'To be or not to be in social media arena as the most cost-efficient marketing strategy after the global recession', *Procedia – Social and Behavioral Sciences*, 24: 260–268.

Leung, A. and Luthans, K. (2011) 'How do small businesses learn and process market information and their marketing implications?', *American Marketing Association*, Summer: 68–69.

McIntosh, M. (2013) 'Marketing to brides'. Personal interview (25 March 2013).

Mangold, W.G. and Faulds, D.J. (2009) 'Social media: the new hybrid element of the promotion mix', *Business Horizons*, 52: 357–365.

Michaelidou, N., Siamagka, N.T. and Christodoulides, G. (2011) 'Usage, barriers and measurement of social media marketing: an exploratory investigation of small and medium B2B brands', *Industrial Marketing Management*, 40: 1153–1159.

Ogunmokun, G.O. and Tang, E.C.H. (2012) 'The effect of strategic marketing planning behavior on the performance of small-to medium-sized firms', *International Journal of Management V*, 159–170.

Papp, H. (2013) 'Managing online reviews'. Personal interview (1 March 2013).

Pinsker, B. and Lipka, M. (2013) 'Why retailers are pinning hopes on Pinterest', Online. Available HTTP: <http://www.reuters.com/article/2013/02/27/net-us-consumer-retail-pinterest-idUSBRE91Q19920130227> (accessed 4 March 2013).

Twitter (2013) 'Twitter 101: an essential intro into our powerful platform', Online. Available HTTP: <https://business.twitter.com/twitter-101> (accessed 4 March 2013).

Weinberg, B.D. and Pehlivan, E. (2011) 'Social spending: managing the social media mix', *Business Horizons*, 54: 275–282.

Wise Geek (2013) 'What is Facebook?', Online. Available HTTP: <http://www.wisegeek.com/what-is-facebook.htm> (accessed 5 March 2013).

REVIEW

1. What are two characteristics about the wedding market that make it unique?

2. Name a minimum of three questions to consider when determining your target market.

3. What information should be included on your business card?

4. What are four benefits of websites?

5. Name and explain the three types of appeals that should be represented in your marketing materials.

6. Define social media and discuss two ways in which it has transformed marketing.

7. Name three things you should do to manage your online reputation.

TERMINOLOGY

- Appeals to credibility

- Blog

- Emotional appeals

- Features versus benefits

- Logical appeals

- Logo

- Marketing

- Social media

- Target audience

- Tweet

- Website

CLIENT RELATIONS

ONE OF THE MOST DIFFICULT ASPECTS OF STARTING YOUR BUSINESS IS
ATTRACTING YOUR FIRST CLIENT. GETTING THAT INITIAL BRIDE TO ASK
FOR A MEETING WILL SEEM AS EASY AS DOING *THE NEW YORK TIMES*
CROSSWORD IN PEN, BUT WITH GOOD PLANNING, MARKETING AND
CREATIVE THINKING, IT WILL HAPPEN. THE PURPOSE OF THIS CHAPTER IS TO
DISCUSS THE ELEMENTS OF SECURING A CLIENT, INITIAL SCREENING, CLIENT
INTERVIEWS, FOLLOW-UP COMMUNICATION, CONTRACT, COMPENSATION
AND EVALUATION.

INITIAL SCREENING

Through your marketing efforts, you will eventually receive a cellphone call, text, e-mail or web inquiry requesting a meeting with a potential client. By and large, the primary point of contact is the bride. Before you grab your iPad and rush out the door, it is wise to have a brief conversation over the telephone with your potential client. During the conversation, you can screen the potential client by asking a few preliminary questions such as: "What is your wedding date?" and "Where will your wedding ceremony and reception take place?" The first question allows you to quickly check your calendar to make sure that you do not have a conflict, while the second gives you a sense of the budget, as the venue often dictates overall cost, allowing you to judge whether or not this wedding will be worth your time. The second question also allows you to verify that the wedding and reception are taking place in an area where your profits won't be eaten up at the gas pump. If the venues are significantly far away, make sure you build the additional travel time and transportation costs into your fee.

During this initial screening, you can begin to determine whether or not you and this potential client are a good fit in terms of personality and approach to planning. Remember, this is your time to screen this potential client just as much as it is the bride's time to screen you. Some consultants inquire about the budget amount during the screening interview. Because this may result in a defensive reaction so early in the process, this question is only recommended if your fee structure is such that you only work with above-average budgets.

After the initial screening, arrange to meet with your prospective client face-to-face. This meeting can take place at any number of locations such as your home office, the bride's reception venue or the bride's home. Try to make the appointment as convenient as possible. If you elect to meet with your prospective client at a public place, make sure the environment is conducive for a conversation. You do not want to compete with the sounds of baristas making lattés in the background or, worse, be asked to leave if you are taking up space for too long at a popular restaurant.

During the screening, determine who the bride will be bringing to the client interview. The groom is a good addition to the meeting, but both mothers, both fathers and five members of the bridal party are way too much. A bridal entourage participating in the meeting will hamper the process. Remember, this is your opportunity to discover what a potential client wants and it is your chance to really sell yourself and your planning business. If there are competing messages and agendas at the meeting, you will not get the information you really need. However, you do not want to begin the process by coming across as overly dictatorial. Some consultants have a "the more, the merrier" attitude, while others prefer one-on-one conversations. Checking with the bride in advance allows you to make sure that the meeting place is appropriate and gives you time to get psychologically prepared if it will be a large gathering.

CLIENT INTERVIEW DETAILS

Think of the client interview as a "first date" or a "get to know you" meeting. If you have decided to specialize in outdoor country weddings, a bride who has visualized her wedding in a chic hotel ballroom will not be a good fit for your business. If this information comes out during the course of your interview, it will save everyone time and money if you gently steer the bride toward another planner. The client interview is a golden opportunity to find out what the bride wants and expects for her wedding day. Chances are she has been dreaming of this special day all her life and now it is your responsibility to translate those dreams into reality.

TABLE 22.1 CLIENT INTERVIEW QUESTIONS

- How did you and your fiancé meet?
- Where are you going on your honeymoon?
- What are your hobbies and interests?
- What type of music do you like?
- What colors are appealing to you?
- Where are your favorite places to travel?
- Where did you grow up?
- What is your cultural background and would you like to incorporate special traditions or customs into the wedding day?
- What tasks have you completed for the wedding?
- How many guests are you expecting?
- What are your "must haves" for your wedding day?
- How would you describe your style?
- Where do you like to shop?
- What is your approximate budget?
- What are your expectations of your wedding planner?
- What are your greatest fears for your wedding day?
- Do you have any special needs or requests?
- Is there anything that I have not asked that I should?

When you meet with your prospective client, remember to dress appropriately. You should look neat and professional while conveying a sense of good organization. No bride is going to hire a rag-tag planner who forgot business cards or shows up late to the initial meeting. Further, when you sit down, allow the bride to do 75 per cent of the talking. Listen carefully to your potential client, maintain eye contact and ask questions that encourage her to offer details. In order to start the conversation flowing, Table 22.1 includes a list of open-ended questions you can ask. When considering the list, the most sensitive question pertains to budget amount. As noted earlier, you should not start with this question; instead, as you learn of her tastes and vision of her wedding, you will begin to get a sense of the overall budget. As the conversation begins to flow, she will most likely share the budget amount without any prompting. The objective during this conversation is to find out as much as possible about your potential client and her vision for her wedding day. Ask your potential client to show you her wedding boards on Pinterest or to bring along all the pages she has been tearing out from bridal magazines. Understanding the bride's vision for her wedding day is crucial in determining whether or not you can deliver that vision.

Once she has sketched out the details, you can pick up the conversation by telling her about your background and experience, especially as it relates to her wedding. If you do not have any wedding-

PHOTO 22.2 THE INTERVIEW IS AN OPPORTUNITY TO LEARN ABOUT YOUR CLIENTS' INTERESTS.

SOURCE: WWW.RODNEYBAILEY.COM

specific experience, tell her about other events you have assisted with, the classes you have taken or the ideas you have for her wedding day. This is your chance to make the sale and convince her that she needs to hire you to plan her wedding.

FOLLOW-UP COMMUNICATION

Immediately after the meeting, send additional communication that reinforces what you learned at the meeting and highlighting why the bride should hire you. Oftentimes, a bride interviews several potential planners. Your follow-up communication may be just what it takes to set you apart from the other planners. You can send an immediate e-mail followed up by a short written thank-you note, or you can write a more thorough recap of the meeting with a wedding planning contract attached. Whichever path you select, your communication must be flawless. When sending a thank-you note by mail, it is wise to invest in some elegant personal stationery or letterhead. Any communication that leaves your office is a reflection of you. Take time to review for typos, spelling mistakes, misused words and factual errors. A sample thank-you note is found in Figure 22.1.

Chloe's Creative Events
Business Address, Telephone and E-mail

November 1, 2015

Dear Amelia and Aiden,

I'm so glad we met yesterday at the Ritz Carlton to discuss your December 3, 2016 wedding. I enjoyed hearing your ideas for your special day and I especially liked your color scheme of platinum, gold and black. How elegant!

As I mentioned during our meeting, I have worked with the Ritz Carlton staff on many occasions and feel that my knowledge of the venue and my considerable background in the floral industry are key elements that set me apart from other planners in the area.

I enjoyed meeting with you both and look forward to the possibility of working with you in the days ahead.

Sincerely,

Chloe Ashcraft, Owner
Chloe's Creative Events

FIGURE 22.1 SAMPLE THANK-YOU NOTE AFTER INITIAL CLIENT MEETING

CONTRACTS

Either during the initial meeting or shortly thereafter, a potential client may tell you that she is ready to commit to hiring you as a wedding planner. This is excellent news and should be followed up immediately by sending out a contract. A wedding *contract* is a written set of obligations that clearly spells out the responsibilities of the consultant and the client.

Whether you send the contract via e-mail or surface mail, it is important that you already have a standard version on hand that can be quickly customized and sent out without delay. If you wait a week or two to mail the contract, your potential client may have already secured another planner.

Send your contract out with a cover letter thanking the couple for selecting you to plan their wedding and reassuring them that you are excited about working with them on this event. While there is no standard contract for all planners to use, there are some key elements that should be included in all contracts:

- Today's date

- Wedding date and time

- Rehearsal date and time

- Name of the bride and groom

- Contact information for both including address, all phone numbers and e-mail address

- Conditions, including roles and restrictions

- Your compensation including total fees, initial deposit and payment schedule

- Terms, including liability and other legal issues

- A listing of your duties

- A *force majeure* clause, which protects you from natural disasters or other "Acts of God" beyond your control

- Signatures of all parties and the associated dates.

Important! You do not have a client unless you have a signed contract. Until you have the executed contract in your hands, you should not begin working for that bride. Without a contract, a bride is only a potential client. No contract, no client, no work!

A sample contract is included in Figure 22.2 and can be used as a guide. In preparing your own contract, it is recommended that you show your contract to a lawyer, mentor or small business advisor. Laws vary by state and what is appropriate for a planner in Jackson Hole, Wyoming may not work for a planner in Lincoln, Nebraska.

PHOTO 22.3 REMEMBER, YOU DO NOT HAVE A CLIENT UNTIL YOU HAVE A SIGNED
CONTRACT.

SOURCE: WWW.RODNEYBAILEY.COM

Today's Date:
Wedding Date/Time:
Rehearsal Date/Time:
Name of Bride:
Name of Groom:
Name of Client (if different from above):
Primary Contact Address:
Primary Contact Cellphone Number:
Primary Contact E-mail Address:

Conditions:

- The role of the wedding consultant is initially that of an advisor. The client will make the actual selection of service providers, and the consultant will implement those selections.
- The client makes payments directly to the service providers and not to the consultant, unless otherwise agreed upon.
- The consultant does not accept any commissions from the recommended vendors.
- The consultant must be notified of any necessary changes made between the client and the selected service providers.

Fees:

The agreed-upon fee for this wedding is $_____

Payment Schedule:

A non-refundable deposit in the amount of $_____ is due with the signed contract to hold the wedding date. The remaining balance should be paid in accordance with the following schedule:

Partial payment of $_____due on _____ (Date)

Final payment of $_____due on _____ (Date)

Terms:

- Service providers accepted by the client shall be liable for their own business practices. XXX wedding consultant does not assume responsibility for the negligent acts nor omission of such professionals.
- The client agrees to hold harmless the consultant for any error, non-performance or change made by any vendor.
- This contract shall be construed according to the laws of the XXX (state/district).
- The parties agree that exclusive jurisdiction and venue for all claims of breach of this agreement shall be in XXX.
- Liability is limited to the fee paid. The client understands that XXX wedding consultant will not enter into this agreement without this clause.
- Force Majeure clause: The client agrees to hold harmless XXX consultant for an Act of God, weather conditions that may affect the event, acts of war, etc.

Duties:

XXX wedding consultant agrees to provide the following services to client XXX:

(Note: These duties will vary from contract to contract. Below are sample duties.)

- Assist with the selection of suitable vendors in the following categories: caterer, pastry chef, floral décor, photographer, stationery specialist and transportation company. All other categories will be selected by the clients.

FIGURE 22.2 SAMPLE WEDDING CONSULTANT CONTRACT

- Maintain ongoing communication with all selected vendors.
- Perform a pre-wedding venue site visit.
- Meet with clients a minimum of three times before the rehearsal, with additional meetings planned as needed.
- Provide ongoing consulting during the time period leading up to the wedding.
- Complete agreed-upon tasks leading up to the wedding.
- Create a detailed timeline for the organization and implementation of the ceremony and reception.
- Confirm with all selected ceremony and reception vendors.
- Attend and oversee the rehearsal.
- Manage, with an assistant, day-of duties at the ceremony and reception sites.

The client by signing this contract agrees to the terms and conditions of this contract.

_____   _____
Client's signature   Date

_____   _____
Consultant's signature   Date

FIGURE 22.2 SAMPLE WEDDING CONSULTANT CONTRACT *CONTINUED*

The best contract is the one that is signed, filed and does not have to be pulled out again, because, when that happens, it means there are problems. Should the need arise, the contract is there to protect you. When you deviate from the contract provisions, you are taking a financial and emotional risk, as illustrated in *Consultant in Action*, Case 22.1.

Finally, although the contract specifies the duties you will perform, your obligations do not necessarily stop there. For instance, if you are hired for day-of duties only, this does not absolve you from the responsibility of producing a trouble-free wedding. "I didn't hire the DJ" is no excuse when a consultant is faced with a microphone-hogging bore dressed in a tux and insulting the guests with off-color jokes. You still must intervene when necessary to pull off a lovely wedding even if you didn't plan it from start to finish. Be careful to invest the time up front getting to know as much as possible about the venues, vendors and VIPs for each day-of wedding. Whether you are hired to plan the entire wedding or just manage the day-of duties, it is your responsibility to meet your client's expectations. After all, a wedding full of impressed guests will lead to more work for you down the road.

CONSULTANT IN ACTION, CASE 22.1

SHORT SHIFT

Your client, Georgia, is tall and graceful. She has hired you for day-of services only, meaning that no vendor recommendations are included in the contract. When Georgia goes for her final dress fitting, she realizes that the flat shoes she recently switched to due to an ankle injury cause the dress to drag considerably. She cannot switch to high heels and the on-site seamstress is not available for a rush job, so Georgia calls you for a recommendation. You do not hesitate to suggest your favorite seamstress, a woman with whom you have worked on many occasions for alterations. Two weeks before the wedding, you receive a call from Georgia, who is livid. She tells you that the seamstress botched the job completely, and that her lace overlay is now bunched up around her waist and six inches above the rest of the dress. She texts you a photo and you see immediately that Georgia is not exaggerating – the dress is ruined.

WHAT DO YOU DO?

CASE ADAPTED FROM CASWELL (2013)

COMPENSATION

When you were writing your business plan, you probably thought about setting the fees for your business. Start off by determining what other consultants in your area are charging. Planners in Manhattan can charge more than planners in Minneapolis. Further, if you are a new planner with little or no experience, you cannot expect to charge as much as a seasoned wedding consultant. You must start out small and gradually increase your fees over time as your reputation grows.

There are various ways to charge for your planning services, including a flat fee, package deals, an hourly rate or a percentage of the wedding budget. Each of these options has pros and cons so you must decide which type of fee structure will work best for you. Regardless of the approach you take, do not expect to be able to fully support yourself full-time from the onset. Most consultants start out part-time and gradually build their businesses or work with other consultants to maximize talent and resources.

A *flat fee* works well when you have a client who wants you to manage the wedding from start to finish. With a flat fee, you do not have to keep track of billable hours and you know exactly how much you will earn based on the set price. Some consultants only accept clients that desire full service planning, allowing the flat fee to be an appropriate pricing strategy.

For consultants who address a variety of planning needs, the use of *package deals* is appropriate. Many wedding planners come up with clever names for various types of services using names like gold, silver and bronze, or diamond, emerald and sapphire. No matter what titles you apply, include a defined list of services for each option, where the fee increases along with the number of duties. Common services associated with various wedding packages were introduced in Chapter 1.

An *hourly rate* works well when your client only wants a few things from a planner, for example, you may be asked to provide a list of venues that already have a piano or recommend three florists who carry both fresh and silk flowers. Sometimes, a client hires a consultant on an hourly fee basis and ends up needing the planner for many more tasks than initially thought. When you meet with your client, try to determine what the exact needs are and suggest the compensation package accordingly.

Some planners charge a *percentage fee* of the overall wedding budget, generally in the vicinity of 10 per cent. This can be an efficient way to charge for your services. However, if you do not have a fair amount of experience, this method should be avoided. As a new planner, you will probably start out with weddings with modest budgets and, if you charge a percentage of a modest budget, your compensation is likely to be very small. Further, wedding budgets tend to be moving targets, so confusion can result if the overall budget amount changes significantly.

EVALUATION

Another successful wedding to your credit! The vendors came through, everyone had a fabulous time and the newlyweds are off to Fiji for their honeymoon. You are ready for a well-earned vacation, but don't close the book on this wedding just yet. As you learned in Chapter 8, the final phase of wedding timelines includes wrap-up and evaluation, and there are some essential tasks that still need to be completed, including satisfaction assessment and the completion of a final wedding summary. You may also be involved in some *ad hoc* services that take place after the wedding day. This section introduces the basics of conducting a post-wedding evaluation.

A *post-wedding evaluation* is defined as a process of collecting information from clients in order to make conclusions about the consultant's services. Successful wedding consultants are always looking for ways to improve their services, and obtaining feedback from clients can be constructive and enlightening. When conducting an evaluation, there are eight things to keep in mind: 1) why evaluation is necessary; 2) when to evaluate; 3) what to evaluate; 4) quantitative and qualitative evaluation; 5) types of questionnaire items; 6) writing questionnaire items; 7) questionnaire format; and 8) the cover letter.

WHY EVALUATE?

Evaluation in the context of weddings should be conducted for four interrelated reasons. First, feedback allows you to pinpoint areas of success and areas that need improvement. Second, the information provided allows you to prioritize. For example, if your full service packages include the provision that you will accompany the client on each vendor visit, but your clients consistently give you feedback that they did not feel this service was necessary, you can re-prioritize the options for this package. Third, constructive criticism encourages you to make changes and stay fresh. Finally, change can lead to increased client satisfaction over time. Do not be afraid to get feedback, both positive and negative. No business is perfect, but your openness to the ideas of others will get you one step closer to perfection than your competition. Over time, the evaluation process will result in saving you both time and money, as you hone in to the needs of your customer base.

WHEN TO EVALUATE

The timing of an event evaluation can be either formative or summative (DeGraaf *et al.* 2010). The evaluation of weddings is generally *summative* in nature, meaning that it takes place after service delivery is complete. For other types of events, *formative* evaluation also occurs, meaning that information is collected during the actual implementation of the event. In the world of weddings, it would be absurd to ask clients to fill out a brief questionnaire on their wedding day! However, you are encouraged to conduct an informal formative evaluation at every wedding by jotting down notes of things that go awry as well as those that run particularly well.

WHAT TO EVALUATE

A wedding evaluation should include items that assess three primary areas: product, process and psycho-social elements. The *product* pertains to the tangible goods and services, while the *process* is specific to how the work was done (DeGraaf *et al.* 2010). For example, a "product" questionnaire item might pertain to satisfaction with options of vendors provided to the client, whereas a "process" item would relate to whether the consultant was consistently organized. Finally, the *psycho-social* relates to the human element and all of the emotions that are tied into weddings; for instance, you might ask whether your services allowed the couple to be less stressed on their wedding day.

QUANTITATIVE AND QUALITATIVE EVALUATION

Quantitative evaluation is concerned with numbers that can have real or implied meanings. For example, if you ask a client to give a budget breakdown, this will be based on actual expenditures. On the other hand, if you ask a client to rate how well you communicated during the wedding planning on a scale from 1 to 5, the numbers have an implied meaning, with 5 indicating the most positive rating. Quantitative evaluation offers a quick way for you to obtain feedback within an understood and set range, and facilitates easy comparison over time. For example, if you ask every client to rate his or her overall satisfaction with your day-of services, you can use a scale from 1 to 5 or from 1 to 10 to gather this information. Over time, you may see that this number starts to get higher as you become more confident and more familiar with all of the venues in your area. Quantitative information can also be readily compiled. For example, if in a given year you have 15 wedding clients, you can collect data from each using the same questionnaire and then at the end of a year calculate the average of the compiled responses.

Qualitative evaluation, on the other hand, deals with words rather than numbers and generally is less structured. Every questionnaire should include at least two items that allow clients to openly express their thoughts and opinions. While you cannot formulate averages on qualitative data, over time you may start to see that themes emerge that offer valuable guidance. For instance, if you include an item that asks your clients to comment on the quality of the reception venue and you find that, at one particular venue, comments such as "It was too hot," "The ladies bathroom was cramped" and "The chairs felt unstable" crop up again and again, you may seriously want to reconsider whether you recommend that particular venue.

THREE TYPES OF QUESTIONNAIRE ITEMS

Questionnaires typically include three types of items: fixed-alternative, scale and open-ended. *Fixed-alternative* items generally assess knowledge, meaning that there is technically a response that "is the case." Fixed-alternative items that you are familiar with are true/false and multiple choice items that you have answered when taking exams. For wedding evaluation, common fixed-alternative items include yes/no items, items where clients check off specific services used and items requesting demographic information. Figure 22.3 includes a sample questionnaire. In this questionnaire, numbers 1, 2 and 7a are fixed-alternative items. Note that fixed-alternative items are usually written as questions.

Scale items are used to assess feelings and therefore allow for a range of responses. Many questions that you have for your clients deal with their emotions rather than fact, so there is not a right or wrong answer. Such a question should allow for more "gray area"; thus, it is more appropriate to use a scale item rather than a fixed-alternative. For example, assume that you wanted to determine if the client found that you were easy to contact when needed. This would be difficult to put into a yes/no format, because it forces the client to make a choice when it could have been the case that sometimes you were accessible and at other times you were not. By allowing the client to answer on a scale that ranges from strongly agree to strongly disagree, there is more response latitude. In Figure 22.3, the items contained in numbers 3 and 4 are examples of scale items. Note that scale items are usually written as statements.

Open-ended items are used to assess behaviors and impressions and must be presented in such a way to encourage written feedback. Because open-ended questions take much longer to answer than fixed-alternative and scale items, you should limit the number to no more than four. If there

Weddings by Pippa
Post-wedding Client Questionnaire

By completing this questionnaire, you are helping the consultants at Weddings by Pippa
to consistently improve their services

Your answers will remain confidential

Client's Name:
The Couple:
Wedding Date:
Consultant's Name:

1. How did you learn about Weddings by Pippa? *(please check all that apply)*

[ ] Word of Mouth   [ ] Bridal Showcase   [ ] Weddings by Pippa Website   [ ] WeddingWire
[ ] Other *(please explain)*:

2. What service package did you select?

[ ] Full package   [ ] Partial package   [ ] Day-of package
[ ] *Ad hoc* services *(please explain)*:

Please rate the quality of the services provided,
where 5 = Strongly Agree and 1 = Strongly Disagree

3. My wedding consultant was …	Strongly Agree	Agree	No Opinion	Disagree	Strongly Disagree
helpful	5	4	3	2	1
punctual	5	4	3	2	1
organized	5	4	3	2	1
professional	5	4	3	2	1
knowledgeable	5	4	3	2	1
conscious of my budget	5	4	3	2	1
easy to contact when needed	5	4	3	2	1

FIGURE 22.3 SAMPLE POST-WEDDING QUESTIONNAIRE FOR CLIENTS

4. Having a wedding consultant …	Strongly Agree	Agree	No Opinion	Disagree	Strongly Disagree
saved me time	5	4	3	2	1
saved me money	5	4	3	2	1
made selecting vendors easier	5	4	3	2	1
made my planning less stressful	5	4	3	2	1
allowed me to fully enjoy my wedding	5	4	3	2	1

5. What services did your consultant provide that were most helpful?

_____

_____

6. What services, if any, did your consultant provide that you felt were unnecessary?

_____

_____

7a. Based on your experience, would you recommend your consultant to a friend or family member?
   [ ] Yes   [ ] No

7b. If no, please explain: _____

_____

Comments and suggestions:

_____

_____

_____

THANK YOU FOR YOUR FEEDBACK!

Please return this questionnaire in the postage-paid envelope that has been provided.

FIGURE 22.3 SAMPLE POST-WEDDING QUESTIONNAIRE FOR CLIENTS *CONTINUED*

are too many open-ended items, your clients will suffer from what is known as *response fatigue*. You have taken essay exams in the past and know how tiring that can be. Don't put your clients through that sort of experience, as they may get frustrated and not finish the questionnaire. Also, while not as structured as fixed-alternative and scale items, you want open-ended questions to be directed so that the answers will be useful. You should also always leave an area that requests comments and additional suggestions so that your clients can provide you with information that you may have not considered requesting. Numbers 5, 6, 7b and the "Comments and suggestions" area are examples of open-ended items in Figure 22.3. Open-ended items can be written as questions or statements.

WRITING QUESTIONNAIRE ITEMS

When writing questionnaire items, there are some common wording problems that you should avoid. In this section, five types of poorly written items and their more appropriate counterparts are presented.

First, avoid double-barreled questions. Babbie (2012) explains that double-barreled questions are those where you ask the respondent to give a single answer to a combination of questions. This problem frequently emerges in scale items. For example, consider the two options below for a scale item where you are assessing the respondent's level of agreement:

Poorly written item: "My wedding consultant was punctual and organized."

Better: "My wedding consultant was punctual."

"My wedding consultant was organized."

In the poorly written example, two questions are presented in one statement, and it could be the case that the consultant was punctual but not organized, or vice versa. Make sure that each question can stand alone.

Second, avoid writing questions that have confusing language such as double negatives. Consider the scale items below:

Poorly written item: "I was never not satisfied with the communication skills of my wedding consultant."

Better: "I was satisfied with the communication skills of my wedding consultant."

The poorly written item is incredibly difficult to interpret and sure to lead to confusion.

Third, avoid writing items that are overly vague. Consider the open-ended items below:

> *Poorly written item:* "Please talk about your vendors."
>
> *Better:* "Please list the three vendors that you enjoyed working with the most."

The poorly written item creates more questions than answers. The respondent is left to think: "Which vendors? What do you want to know about them?" On the other hand, the item that is clearly written will help you hone your list of vendors to recommend to future clients.

Fourth, items should be written as concisely as possible. Babbie (2012) explains that a respondent should be able to read an item quickly, understand the intent and provide an answer quickly. Consider the following open-ended items:

> *Poorly written item:* Wedding planning can be stressful with various influences and thoughts that you are dealing with, not to mention the pressure of family and financial burdens that you have to worry about all the time; nonetheless, your wedding consultant probably helped you deal with this stress so please explain how.
>
> *Better:* Please list three ways in which your wedding consultant made your wedding day less stressful.

The poorly written item is so long and complicated that it is almost impossible to discover the point.

Finally, avoid items that are leading or biased. Questions that exclude respondents or encourage respondents to answer in a particular way are problematic for two reasons. First, leading or biased items remove the neutrality of the evaluation process by excluding certain groups or thoughts from consideration. Second, leading or biased items often are embedded with *social desirability cues*, meaning that the respondent will be pushed to answer in a certain way because it appears that there is a "correct" answer that the researcher wants to get. Consider the following scale (strongly agree to strongly disagree) item:

> *Poorly written item:* To what extent do you agree that all intelligent brides will hire a wedding consultant to help make wedding planning less stressful?
>
> *Better:* My wedding consultant helped make the wedding planning less stressful.

The poorly written item assumes that only brides hire wedding consultants, which is biased in that it excludes grooms, couples or parents from being the point of contact. Further, it has a social desirability cue of intelligence; that is, if the respondent wants to be perceived as intelligent, she or he will feel forced to agree to the statement.

FORMATTING THE QUESTIONNAIRE

When formatting the questionnaire, keep the usability in mind, as you want it to be as easy as possible for respondents to efficiently answer all items. Below are 15 formatting rules that you should take into consideration:

- Start with a clear heading that has your business name and sets forth the fact that this is a client questionnaire.

- A brief statement that gives the purpose of the evaluation should follow the heading.

- Below the purpose statement you should include an assurance of confidentiality. If there is a particularly fabulous statement that the client writes that you would like to include on your website, you should follow up and ask permission to do so.

- Include a space where you fill in the name of the client, the couple's names, the wedding date and the name of the consultant. The client may or may not be the same as the couple. In some cases, the client may be the parent of the bride or groom, for instance, if the couple is out-of-town and a parent is planning on their behalf. Mail the evaluation to your primary point of contact to avoid confusion.

- Similar item types (fixed-alternative, scale, open-ended) should be clustered together so the respondent can easily flow from one item to the next.

- As necessary, include instructions to facilitate the completion process. This is usually needed prior to the presentation of scale items. Do not take anything for granted or assume that the respondent will understand what to do.

- The items themselves should be easy to read, so make sure the font is big enough so the respondent does not have to squint. Avoid unusual font styles that are difficult to read.

- The layout should be organized and straightforward. Items should neatly line up and all of the open-ended lines should be the same length.

- There should be adequate room for the respondent to write, in particular for open-ended items. If the lines are squished together, it will discourage feedback.

- Do not try to crowd too much on a given page, as this will create confusion.

- If the questionnaire is more than one page, consistently direct the respondent to the next page. For instance, something such as "Please continue on the opposite side" can be used on a two-sided questionnaire.

- Do not expect your clients to write a dissertation. Usually 10 items, and certainly no more than 20, will be sufficient.

- At the end of the document, you should include a message of thanks and a request for the return of the questionnaire.

Weddings by Pippa
Business Address, Telephone and E-mail

August 8, 2015

Client Name
Client Address

Dear Sophia,

I hope that you and Ethan had a fabulous honeymoon in New Zealand. It was such a pleasure working with you and watching your elegant planetarium theme come to life at your wedding.

I am writing to ask you to fill out a brief questionnaire. The Weddings by Pippa team is always looking for ways to improve our services, and your feedback is very valuable to us.

Please complete the enclosed form and return it in the postage paid envelope by September 1st. If you have any questions, do not hesitate to call or e-mail me.

Sincerely,

Pippa Smith
Owner, Weddings by Pippa

FIGURE 22.4 SAMPLE POST-WEDDING QUESTIONNAIRE COVER LETTER

- Always include a self-addressed, stamped envelope to facilitate the return process. Alternatively, you can send it via e-mail and ask that it be returned the same way.

- Grammatical, typographical and printing errors will harm your credibility. You are better off having no evaluation than having a sloppy evaluation.

THE COVER LETTER

Once you have carefully crafted your questionnaire, you will be anxious to send it off to a client. But not so fast. If you just toss it into an envelope without an appropriate cover letter, all of your efforts may have been in vain. When writing a cover letter for a post-wedding evaluation, be certain to include the following elements: 1) date sent; 2) greeting; 3) naming of the couple and reminder of the wedding; 4) purpose of the questionnaire; 5) desired return date and indication of an included return envelope; 6) contact information; and 7) final words of thanks. The cover letter should be short and to the point. Invest in letterhead stationery for the professional touch. Figure 22.4 offers an example of a cover letter. Give the couple a few weeks to enjoy their honeymoon and get settled in before mailing out the questionnaire.

References

Babbie, E. (2012) *The Practice of Social Research*, Belmont, CA: Wadsworth Publishing.

Caswell, A. (2013) 'Short shift'. Personal communication (21 March 2013).

DeGraaf, D.G., Jordan, D.J. and DeGraaf, K.H. (2010) *Programming for Parks, Recreation and Leisure Services: a servant leadership approach*, State College, PA: Venture Publishing, Inc.

Review

1. Why is it difficult to get your first client?

2. What screening questions should you ask a potential client over the telephone?

3. Name and explain three different types of compensation methods?

4. Name three crucial elements that should be found in every wedding contract.

5. Name three reasons why evaluation is important.

6. Distinguish between formative and summative evaluation and explain why one of these is inappropriate for wedding evaluation.

7. Distinguish between quantitative and qualitative evaluation.

8. Name the three types of questionnaire items and explain how they differ.

9. Give three examples of common wording problems that you want to avoid when writing questionnaire items.

10. Name a minimum of five rules for formatting a questionnaire.

TERMINOLOGY

- Client interview
- Client screening
- Compensation
- Constructive criticism
- Contract
- Day-of fee
- Double-barreled items
- Fixed-alternative items
- Flat fee
- Follow-up communication
- Force Majeure clause
- Formative evaluation
- Hourly rate
- Leading items
- Open-ended items
- Package deal
- Percentage fee
- Process evaluation
- Product evaluation

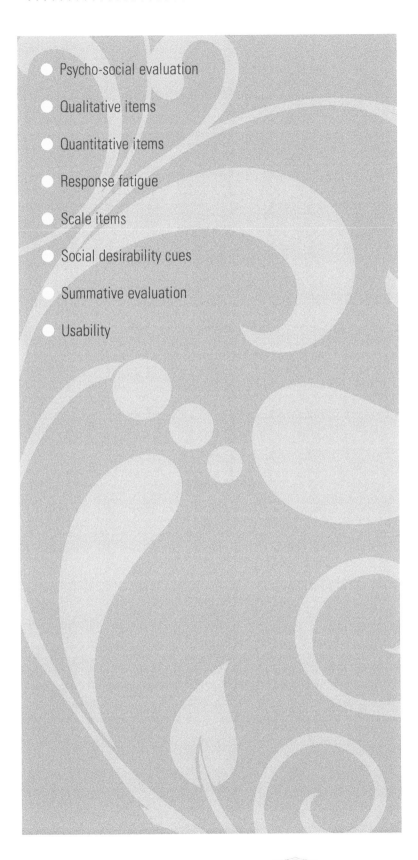

- Psycho-social evaluation

- Qualitative items

- Quantitative items

- Response fatigue

- Scale items

- Social desirability cues

- Summative evaluation

- Usability

PHOTO 23.1 WEDDING VENDORS FORM A TIGHT-KNIT COMMUNITY.

SOURCE: WWW.RODNEYBAILEY.COM

VENDOR RELATIONS

While waiting to land your first client, one of the least expensive and most effective marketing strategies you can employ is to systematically get out there and meet your fellow wedding vendors. Meeting vendors is a valuable exercise that will pay dividends for years to come. As you will learn, wedding professionals form a tight-knit community. The stationers know the calligraphers, the caterers know the rental companies and the photographers know the videographers. Ideally, all of these vendors will come to know you.

The first part of this chapter highlights the importance of establishing vendor relationships, networking and negotiating. The second section is focused on competition, as brought on by an increasing number of wedding consulting businesses. Third, the obligations that emerge as you develop your business are summarized. Fourth, ethical business practices are delineated. Finally, as an extension of Chapter 22, post-wedding evaluation for vendors and the compilation of the wedding summary are detailed.

Establishing vendor relationships

Introducing yourself to other wedding vendors is critical because they will become an endless source of referrals for you. For example, Ashley Davis has just become engaged. She and her mother rush out to find the perfect wedding gown. They make an appointment and begin their search at an exclusive boutique. During the process of trying on gowns, Ashley becomes overwhelmed and says, "If picking out a wedding gown is this tough, I don't know how I will handle the rest!" The boutique owner might casually ask Ashley if she has thought about hiring a wedding planner to help ensure a beautiful and stress-free wedding day. Ashley's mother might say that they hadn't thought about this option, as Ashley has only been engaged for a week. If her interest is piqued, however, Ashley's mother might ask the owner if she has any recommendations for a wedding planner. This is the point where cultivating a sterling reputation with other vendors will pay off, as the owner might mention your name.

Wedding vendors get to know each other by working for the same clients and at the same events, during which they develop a sense of camaraderie. They quickly discover who is reliable and who is not. They grow to trust each other and develop an *esprit de corps*, meaning a sense of enthusiasm and morale-building for the entire team that puts on a wedding.

Oftentimes, couples begin the wedding planning process by securing one or two key elements for their wedding, for example, a couple may select a place of worship for the ceremony and then find a reception venue that is close by. Somewhere along the way, they might decide to hire a planner to help them with the numerous decisions that have to be made. So, if the local country club's banquet manager thinks highly of you and your work, he might refer you to a potential client. Or, if you have successfully guided many brides down the aisle of a specific church, the altar guild of that church is usually more than willing to recommend your services.

You never know where your next referral might come from, which is why it is so important to meet everyone in the business. Think beyond the usual vendors by touching base with local makeup artists, travel agents and ballroom dance instructors. Additionally, make sure you introduce yourself to all the local wedding consultants in your market. Other planners are not your competition; instead, they can be a tremendous source of leads. Four hypothetical planners: Sophia, Liam, Emma and Mason, will be used to illustrate the benefits of working with other consultants in your area. Imagine that Sophia is a long-established planner in your market. When she gets a call from a bride who has a small budget and Sophia does not want to take the job, she might

PHOTO 23.2 WHEN VENDORS WORK IN HARMONY, THE RESULT IS HAPPY CLIENTS.

SOURCE: WWW.RODNEYBAILEY.COM

gladly give the bride your name and number. That way she has helped the bride and you at the same time. Another planner, Liam, might get a call for day-of help and, if he does not offer this service, he might pass along your name and number if he knows that you offer day-of assistance. If another consultant, Emma, is already committed on a certain date, she might refer the bride to you if your calendar is free. Last but not least, if a bride is looking for a certain style or specialty such as knowledge of military protocol, another planner, Mason, might give the bride your contact information if he knows that this is your area of expertise. Cultivating professional relationships with other wedding planners is an excellent way to grow your business.

MAKING A LIST

As you begin the process of identifying and meeting other wedding vendors in your area, the first thing you should do is develop a list of individuals you would like to meet. You can develop this list from a variety of sources, such as:

- The Knot and WeddingWire
- A "best" list, often compiled in regional magazines

- By category; for example, you may want to meet all floral décor specialists and photographers

- Vendors who specialize in what you specialize in (e.g., eco-friendly weddings)

- A listing of vendor names gleaned from a bridal show program or local wedding publication.

After you have compiled a list of names, set a goal to meet a certain number of vendors each week. Depending on your time commitments, you might meet two or even five new vendors each week. By systematically meeting all the wedding vendors in your area, you will begin to get your name out and establish yourself.

After you have your list, call each vendor to arrange a brief (e.g., 15-minute) appointment to introduce yourself. By taking the time to make the call, you are showing respect for the vendor's time and you are conveying a professional image. You don't want to just drop in unannounced on a vendor. Make the appointments for early in the week, as most vendors get busier as the week unfolds. Also, keep in mind that the busiest wedding months are May, June, September and October. With that in mind, try to schedule your appointments during the quieter months of January, February and August.

After you have secured the appointment, you should sketch out what you are going to say in advance. Learn about vendors by familiarizing yourself with their websites, blogs and Facebook pages. Reading about their products and services will help you during these meetings. If you are going to meet with a local florist, you might make a note of any recent awards or recognition the owner has received. In addition to doing your research, you might practice what you want to convey about your business. If you have completed your business plan, as discussed in Chapter 20, you will be prepared to answer any questions about your business with confidence.

The last point you should consider is what you can do for the vendor. Vendors are going to remember you if you have a unique specialty, shared interest, helpful skill or can cross-market their goods and services with a posted link to their business on your website. Anytime you go out of your way for another vendor, you increase the chance of that vendor going out of his or her way for you.

NETWORKING

Networking, it is often said, is small talk with a purpose. Put more precisely, "Networking is the art of building and maintaining connections for shared positive outcomes" (Zack 2010: 4). An important aspect of this definition is the mutual perspective, where the focus goes beyond positioning your own product and service to truly considering how knowing you can help others leverage their business as well. Other terms closely related to networking are social assets, social capital and community capacity. Irrespective of the term you use, the point is that relationships influence business development. Cultivating networking skills allows you to work successfully with wedding vendors and, as a result, assists in building your business.

The best way to start your networking program is by joining the organizations where people involved in the business of weddings gather. One of the most popular networking groups for wedding planners is ISES, the International Special Events Society. ISES has chapters in most major cities and they offer a wide variety of services such as educational and professional development, professional resources, subscription to *Special Events* magazine, discounted business services and listings for all members on their website. ISES holds monthly meetings at different venues, and vendors associated with the society supply the linens, floral, catering, entertainment, invitations and other elements as a way to showcase their businesses. Attending these gatherings is an excellent way to meet wedding vendors and consultants. If you are still a student, the time to join ISES is now, because annual student membership dues are much less expensive than professional membership dues. Once you start your business, the professional membership fee is a tax-deductible expense, so joining is a win-win proposition.

Other groups to consider joining are the National Association for Catering and Events (NACE), the Association of Bridal Consultants (ABC), the American Association of Certified Professional Wedding Consultants (AACPW) and the International Festival and Events Association (IFEA). Similar to ISES, these groups encourage ongoing training, education and professional development and host meetings and conferences that allow you to associate with people who have similar goals and interests. You should also familiarize yourself with business-related groups in your area such as the Chamber of Commerce, the Young Democrats/Republicans, the Junior League, Toastmasters, the "Friends of" or event planning arm of any major museum or art gallery, college or university alumni associations, the Rotary Club, etc. These are all excellent resources for face-to-face networking.

While all of this may sound good on paper, it does not change the fact that many people dread networking. If the thought of meeting new people puts you in a state of panic, know that you are not alone. Most people do not have personality types that are predisposed to comfortably interact with strangers (Zack 2010). The fastest way to overcome your fear is to volunteer for a committee where you can put your skills to use. All associations clamor for volunteers to assist with generating new topics for meetings, planning the meetings, marketing them, identifying vendors and assisting with registration and check-in. Once you pitch in a few times, the leaders will recognize you and make a point of introducing you to others. Remember that networking takes time and you will get out of it what you put into it. Many people join associations and get frustrated or give up after one or two meetings because they feel like they are not meeting anyone or feel left out. Keep in mind that many of those relationships took years to cultivate, and you will break in over time.

As discussed in Chapter 21, just as important as face-to-face networking is social networking. With Facebook, Twitter, LinkedIn, Pinterest, blogs and YouTube, there is no shortage of ways to go about announcing your wedding planning business and letting the world know about you. In a review of research pertaining to social networking sites Hanafizadeh *et al.* (2012) identified six business impacts, including marketing/advertising, knowledge management, social capital, relationship management, e-commerce and the creation of business/economic models.

NEGOTIATING

"Conflicts of interest that materialize in group processes often impede potential opportunities for collaboration and collective decision-making, while the process for their resolution could in turn help to build trust and solidarity among the parties concerned" (Maemura and Horita 2012: 821). From a business perspective, refining your negotiation skills will enable you to effectively reduce the tension and defensiveness that often accompany seemingly conflicting agendas by, instead, focusing on joint gains achieved through cooperation (Tzafrir *et al.* 2012). Whether you are working with a bride who wants a discount on your fees or a vendor who wants to charge your client a premium for delivering ice cream in August, you will be faced with many situations that call for thinking on your feet and negotiating the best deal for yourself or on behalf of your client, while not alienating the other party.

Much of your time will be spent honing your skills in the art of negotiating. For example, suppose your clients ordered and paid for a chartreuse-colored liner for their tent. The rental company arrives with a white liner, which you know is nearly $1,000 less expensive and clearly will not make the bold statement that your clients wanted. It is your job to negotiate with the rental vendor in order to secure the correct liner for your clients in time for their wedding. Even when well intended, incorrect goods and services can cause difficulties that the planner must mitigate, as illustrated in *Consultant in Action*, Case 23.1.

While cultivating your skill set takes time, academic researchers and industry pundits have identified some general guidelines for effective negotiating (e.g., Abrahams *et al.* 2012; Maemura and Horita 2012; Mims 2012; Sebenius 2013; Tzafrir *et al.* 2012). Below, five rules for negotiating set forth by these authorities on the subject are adapted and applied to the business of wedding consulting.

1. Know your best alternative to a negotiated agreement (BATNA)

The universal requirement for successful negotiation is confidence in your alternatives (Mims 2012). Before entering into the negotiations, think through your options and prepare a back-up plan. If your clients want a specific ballroom for their reception but fear that the rental costs will be too expensive, present some other options that they might not have considered prior to meeting the ballroom manager. By having other venue ideas in mind, there will be less of a sense of desperation for the space and you can leverage the other options, possibly giving you more bargaining power.

2. Employ integrative bargaining

Integrative bargaining involves a win-win outlook that operates with the understanding that pro-social, cooperative negotiators achieve better joint outcomes than pro-self, egoistic negotiators (Tzafrir *et al.* 2012). This does not mean you have to be a pushover, but it does mean that you should avoid a combative, winner-take-all approach. If you cultivate a reputation for being demanding and unreasonable, word will travel quickly. You may also need to rein in the occasional

CONSULTANT IN ACTION, CASE 23.1

UPDO DECEPTION

Kaitlin and her bridesmaids have gathered at an upscale salon to have their hair and nails done. With nine women in her bridal party, all with long hair, Kaitlin decided that the photos would look better if they all had updos, and she communicated this desire to the salon manager. As Kaitlin was paying for the salon services, the bridesmaids were all on board with this plan, except for Pandora. You stop by the salon to bring Kaitlin a special note from the groom, and decide to walk around to greet all of the bridesmaids. As you pop into the various spaces, you comment on all of the gorgeous styles that have already been completed. Pandora has moved to a section of the salon away from the rest of the bridal party, and as you walk her way you notice that her hairstyle is just about done, and it is down. The stylist, one of three hired for the bridal party, gushes, "Isn't this look perfect for her? How wonderful that Kaitlin changed her mind and said the girls can pick any style they want!" You ask Pandora if this is true, to which she replies, "I will pay my own way if I have to, but I think Kaitlin is being ridiculous and I am not wearing my hair up!"

WHAT DO YOU DO?

CASE ADAPTED FROM SHANNON HARPER
A TOTAL DIFFERENCE HAIR SALON
INTERVIEW BY KAYLIN ZIEMBA

client, as illustrated in *Consultant in Action*, Case 23.2. Integrative bargaining involves empathy; this does not mean that you agree with the other side; however, it implies that you are willing to listen carefully and consider alternative perspectives. Empathy leads to fairness, which is of critical importance if disputants will be maintaining some level of a relationship after the issue is resolved (Abrahams *et al.* 2012), which is certainly the case with planners and vendors.

3. Be willing to wait

The more anxious you or your clients are to make a purchase or sign a contract, the more likely that the other side will get whatever they want. Patience is a virtue when it comes to negotiating. As long as you have your BATNA in hand, you will not be afraid to walk away if the negotiation fails, and perhaps a month later the discussion can reopen. You should time negotiations with the business cycle of the vendor. For instance, is the dress shop ready to get in next season's gowns

CONSULTANT IN ACTION, CASE 23.2

AFTER-WEDDING ANTAGONISM

The wedding of your clients, Brooklyn and Henry, went off beautifully and the newlyweds are honeymooning in Greece. You are working on the timeline for an upcoming event when your cellphone rings. It is your friend, Aubrey, who is a pastry chef at a shop where you regularly send clients for wedding cakes. She tells you that Brooklyn's mother, Ellie, has just threatened the shop owner with a bad online review unless she gets half of the money back that they spent on the wedding cake because Ellie felt there was not enough fruit filling in the cake. Aubrey said that Ellie was screaming at the manager and had just stomped out of the shop. You thank Aubrey and quickly call Ellie to discuss her concerns. Ellie states, "I am getting money back from them and I am going to the florist next, because the hydrangea on the wedding day were not the same shade of blue as the sample."

WHAT DO YOU DO?

but has not yet discounted the one your bride loves? Suggest a reasonable discount and negotiate the price. The dresses are getting ready to be outdated. Use this knowledge to your advantage.

4. Use humor to ease tension

If the discussion becomes contentious, take the high road. Stifle your negative emotions, stay on the issue and leave personalities out of the discussion. Remember, you do not want to burn any bridges with vendors or clients. Rather than becoming antagonistic, looking for the humor in the situation can salvage a negotiation:

> By changing the structure of arguments, humor can be used to alter the content and process of negotiations. This leads to suggest that a conscious grasp and efficient use of humor can be used to encourage better negotiation practices by helping negotiations explore new issues, break out of deadlocks and prevent circular argumentation.
>
> (Maemura and Horita 2012: 837–838)

5. Assist the other side with managing their conflicts

Creative negotiation involves empathy, fairness and understanding the conflicts faced by the other side. When considering negotiation:

Often implicit in much of this work is the view that each side's leadership is best positioned to manage its *own* internal conflicts. Traditionally, a negotiator does this by pressing for deal terms that will overcome internal objections and by effectively "selling" the agreement to key constituencies. The ways that one side can help the *other* side with the other's "behind-the-table" barriers (and vice versa) has been territory much less traveled by negotiation analysts.

(Sebenius 2013: 8)

For example, a rental company sales agent may want to give your client a price break, but states that his boss will give him a hard time about it and he does not want to face her wrath. By assisting the agent in devising a valid argument for why the discount makes sound business sense, you allow the agent to save face, while ultimately brokering the deal for your client.

COMPETITION

With almost 2.1 million couples marrying each year in the United States (National Vital Statistics Systems 2012) and tens of millions more around the globe, there is tremendous opportunity to start and grow a wedding consultancy business. As discussed in Chapter 3, Hollywood movies and reality television have thrust the wedding planning profession into the spotlight. Ever since the hit movie *The Wedding Planner* starring Jennifer Lopez got the ball rolling over a decade ago, the field of wedding planning has been glamorized, sensationalized and legitimized. Hiring a wedding planner is no longer a luxury reserved for the rich and famous, as couples with all types of budgets are hiring consultants.

Just as couples have learned from film and television, aspiring wedding consultants have also watched as wedding planning is increasingly portrayed as a legitimate profession. Thanks to this unprecedented publicity, more women and men than ever are entering the field of wedding planning and enrolling in events management and wedding planning classes at colleges and universities.

Even when the economy falters, most engaged couples feel they can afford a wedding planner. Your last name does not have to be Gates, Buffett or Winfrey to be able to hire a consultant for your wedding. However, it is not just the demand for consultants that is growing, but also the supply. With the pool of certified consultants getting bigger, competition is keen. Today more than ever, consultants are more assertively marketing their businesses and hashing it out for brides' attention and business.

Thankfully, even with the uptick of those entering the wedding planning field, there is enough business to go around. Brides continue to far outnumber planners. The Association of Bridal Consultants (2013) is a professional organization with over 4,000 members from 27 countries; this same organization estimates that, in the US alone, there are approximately 10,000 consultants. This means that, for every US planner, there are approximately 210 potential couples, certainly more work than most wedding planners could handle in one year. Industry estimates vary regarding the percentage of couples that are using planners, but they tend to range between 19 per cent and 50 per cent, depending in large part whether the wedding is local to the couple or a destination wedding, where the usage increases dramatically (e.g., Medina 2012; XO Group 2011). Using a conservative lens of 20 per cent, that still equates to over 40 weddings per planner per year. Because there is so much work available, there exists a strong sense of cooperation rather than competition among wedding consultants.

Despite a spirit of cooperation, it is still the case that the consultants in a given market are forced to compete for the best weddings. It is common practice for a bride to interview three to five planners before deciding on the right consultant for her wedding day. This process of elimination causes some new consultants to get discouraged. They may quickly become jaded, seeing the business as cut-throat or down and dirty.

Also, there is significant competition between consultants who specialize in the same type of weddings. For example, if a bride is looking for a planner who specializes in Jewish weddings, then she will interview all the planners in the area who have that focus. The bride you meet today may very well be interviewing your competition tomorrow. When a high-profile or high-budget wedding is at stake, planners will put forth their best efforts in order to land the prominent client.

This sense of competition can actually benefit the wedding profession as a whole, as it encourages consultants to constantly raise the bar in terms of standards and practices. Competition keeps planners sharp and up-to-date, urges them to be constantly on the lookout for new trends and ideas, and inspires them to create something unique for each client. Competition also leads to continuing education through classes, workshops and seminars. Wedding consulting is a business and, like any business, those involved must consistently study their market and hone their skills to stay on top.

Competition can take an ugly turn, and it would be false to say that it never results in questionable actions. Throughout this text, we have emphasized the necessity of ethical, trustworthy and respectful interactions with clients, vendors and other consultants. While antagonistic and dishonest practices may help a consultant in the short run, once the word gets out, vendors and clients will shy away from working with such a planner.

OBLIGATIONS

As a wedding planning professional, you have many important obligations, including those to clients, vendors, the wedding profession as a whole, your own business and, of course, to yourself and those in your social network. The challenge is to manage all of these responsibilities that vie for your time with grace and finesse.

Your primary business obligation is to your client, typically the bride. If the bride's parents have hired you, then your obligation is to them as well. As a rule of thumb, if the bride is happy, then everyone around her will be happy. It is your job to make the bride happy, even if that means negotiating with your vendors to ensure the bride's satisfaction. For example, suppose a bride has selected an historic Federal-style hotel for her late-November wedding reception. The hotel has a lovely staircase leading to the front door. It has long been the dream of the bride to be photographed outdoors on the staircase on her wedding day. The wedding day arrives and the photographer tells you that he would prefer not to take the outdoor photographs, as it is too cold. This is where your obligation to your client comes into play. You must diplomatically tell the photographer that the bride still wishes to be photographed outside even though it is colder than anticipated because the photo on the staircase has long been the dream of the bride and is therefore non-negotiable. You then tell the photographer that you will have hot coffee sent out to keep everyone warm.

Wedding planners also have obligations to their vendors. So, in the example above, the planner should try to accommodate both the bride's wishes and the desires of the photographer. Sometimes this is a balancing act, and, if the planner must choose, the bride's needs almost always come first. However, be careful. If you anger your vendors and treat them poorly, soon they will refuse to work with you. Treat your vendors with respect and courtesy and they will recommend you time and time again.

As discussed in Chapter 9, you have an obligation to feed your vendors. No one works well on an empty stomach. When determining the final headcount for the caterer, remind your clients to include the total number of vendor meals. It is your responsibility to make sure that your clients understand the importance of feeding the vendors, including you and any assistants you have. It is also your duty to tell the vendors when their meals are ready and where they can take a break to eat. A well-fed team is a highly productive team.

In addition to obligations to the client and vendors, wedding consultants have an obligation to the wedding profession. Since wedding planning is a relatively new career path, it is important for consultants to give back to the profession in order for all facets to move ahead.

Most important are the obligations you have to your business, yourself and those with whom you are closest. When you are in business for yourself, it is entirely up to you to ensure that your company succeeds. Part of that success is driven by the decisions you make on a daily basis. One of the most important business policies you should have is to always collect your final payment at least two weeks prior to the wedding day. There are countless hair-raising stories of planners not collecting their final payment until the last minute or even after the wedding, leading to situations like the one found in *Consultant in Action*, Case 23.3.

Once a wedding has ended and your services have been provided, it is often impossible to collect the money without the assistance of a legal professional. Rather than learning a lesson the hard way, always collect the final payment well in advance of a wedding to give the check enough time to clear the bank. If there is a problem such as insufficient funds, you will still have the leverage of not managing the wedding day. The vast majority of couples do not set out to intentionally defraud their wedding consultants. However, as the wedding approaches, couples are met with many financial pressures and may look for ways out of making final payments. Ultimately, it is up to you to ensure that you are paid for your wedding consulting services.

You also have obligations to yourself in terms of balancing your career and your personal life. Chapter 24 gives numerous ways to manage the stress that is associated with wedding consulting as a career. Top planners emphasize that you have to remember that the more clients spend for your services, the more they expect from you. This adage includes the fact that your personal crises are not your clients' crises and it is the case that your clients will expect to come first. *Consultant in Action*, Case 23.4 highlights one such scenario.

PHOTO 23.3 WELL-FED VENDORS ARE HIGHLY PRODUCTIVE.

SOURCE: WWW.RODNEYBAILEY.COM

CONSULTANT IN ACTION, CASE 23.3

PAYMENT POSTPONEMENT

You have been working on a 250-guest, lavish outdoor garden wedding to take place in Santa Monica, California for your clients, Brett and Elisa. As stipulated in the contract signed prior to engaging your services, they paid you the initial $5,000 deposit and made an on-time second payment of $5,000 six months prior to the wedding date. Two weeks before the wedding, you remind Brett and Elisa that their final payment of $5,000 is due. One week prior to the wedding, the check still has not arrived. Five days prior to the wedding, you tell the couple that you will not be on hand to manage their wedding day unless they pay you before the rehearsal on Friday. Elisa knows that they are not remotely prepared to coordinate the extensive wedding activities themselves, and encourages Brett to write the check. On Thursday evening, you finally receive a check for the final payment of $5,000. You are so busy with the rehearsal on Friday and the wedding on Saturday that you do not deposit the check into your account until Monday morning, at which point you learn that Brett has issued a stop payment order on the check.

WHAT DO YOU DO?

CONSULTANT IN ACTION, CASE 23.4

HEART-TO-HEART

Your consultancy business is located in St. Louis, Missouri, and you eagerly agreed to manage a destination wedding in Belize, which is just south of Mexico. On the second day in Belize, which is the day before the wedding, you receive an urgent call from your sister, who tells you that your dad had a heart attack and has been admitted to the hospital for emergency coronary artery bypass surgery.

WHAT DO YOU DO?

ETHICS

In the wake of such high-profile business scandals as Lehman Brothers, Bernie Madoff and Solyndra, it becomes easy to believe that the business world rewards bad behavior. However, the fact remains that there is a documented connection between personal integrity and business success (Tullberg 2012); therefore, it is imperative for you to be a business owner with clear ethical principles right from the start. From your first day in business, you must lead by example and show others that you are honest, fair, responsible, compassionate and just.

For example, assume you have back-to-back appointments with two different brides who are considering your services. The first bride, Isabella, asks what the fee would be for your comprehensive planning services and you tell her $3,500. Later in the day, the second bride, Mia, asks you the same question. You notice that Mia is wearing an expensive designer outfit and showing off her 5-carat diamond engagement ring. For her, you quote your comprehensive planning fee as $6,000. Both weddings require the same amount of work on your part, yet you have quoted two different fees based on what you believe each bride can afford. Imagine the consequences if these women are friends and compare notes of their meetings with you. Your inconsistent pricing structure will be exposed, your credibility will become suspect and neither bride will hire you to plan her wedding.

If you want a flexible price structure, set forth your fees as a firm percentage of the overall budget, allowing for a consistent application and addressing the fact that a $100,000 wedding may be more labor intensive than a $20,000 wedding. But do not just randomly throw out fees based on appearances, as you will come across as disorganized, in particular if you are unable to remember the amount that was quoted at a later date. Your fee structure should have no ambiguity whatsoever. The bottom line is that it is much tougher to keep a series of lies straight than it is to be honest in your practices.

Ethics also pertain to private information that your clients share with you. As you begin working with a couple on their upcoming wedding, you will become privy to all kinds of secrets about the bride, the groom and the families. It is your responsibility to treat this information with the utmost discretion. What is told to you in confidence must remain between you and your client. Imagine the consequences if comments such as "I'm not crazy about my new father-in-law," "Please keep Aunt Camilla away from the booze," or "I'll just die if my boss speaks to the other guests during the wedding" were made public. As the wedding pressure begins to build, the bride, the groom and other family members will let off steam by telling you how they feel. Exceptional wedding consultants listen intently and empathically, and then keep their clients' secrets forever.

Sometimes during a reception, guests may come over to you and strike up a conversation, usually beginning with an innocent compliment about the wedding. After you acknowledge their comments, they might ask you how much your clients have spent on a certain item. A conversation might go like this:

> *Guest:* What a great idea for dessert. I don't think I've ever seen a s'mores station before. And the flowers are magnificent. My, the Smith family has certainly outdone themselves with the reception tonight. How much do you think an event like this would cost?

> *Wedding consultant:* I couldn't agree with you more. The décor and special touches are fabulous. In fact, this is one of the most spectacular weddings I've ever managed. As for the cost, I never disclose my clients' financial information.

The ability to safeguard your clients' privacy is a quality every planner should possess. If you have this skill, it will serve you well.

A final ethical issue that consultants must consider pertains to kickbacks. Some vendors and consultants believe that an effective networking tool is to promote *kickbacks*, where you receive a percentage of the price your clients pay to given vendors. Here is how this works. A hypothetical transportation specialist, Joe Limo, might tell you that, for every client you send his way, he will give you 10 per cent of the client bill as a kickback. In other words, you are getting paid to recommend this vendor. While the practice of kickbacks is not illegal, the ethics of it are shaky, and many consultants and vendors are offended by the proposition of kickbacks. If you have a clear policy against kickbacks, it is best to put this in your contract (see sample contract in Chapter 22 for wording). For those consultants who use kickback strategies on a regular basis, they should let their clients know. If you accept a kickback behind your clients' backs and they find out, they may feel betrayed.

Instead of kickbacks, we suggest the process of giving back, a practice that is more lucrative in the long run. This can work in a couple of ways. If vendors offer you kickbacks, tell them that you would rather pass that saving along to your clients. When your clients discover that you were able to secure a discount on a good or service on their behalf, they are likely to talk about your excellent negotiation skills with their friends. Giving back also applies to not-for-profit associations and your local community. Many vendors offer free goods and services to groups or organizations in need. These generous donations have a payback that cannot be measured in dollars.

VENDOR FEEDBACK

Chapter 22 covered the intricacies of questionnaire design for clients in detail. While the same approach applies to vendor questionnaires, the same necessity does not. Vendor questionnaires should be used with extreme discretion; do not send a questionnaire to the same vendors each time you work with them, as they will get annoyed. The best time to request feedback is the first time you work with a vendor. Once they get to know you personally over time, you can send an e-mail or make a quick call if you have anything you would like to discuss about a particular wedding. A sample vendor questionnaire can be found in Figure 23.1.

Similar to the client questionnaire, you need to fill in the top part of the form. If you do not remind the vendor of the clients' names, your name and the wedding date, the vendor will have no idea which wedding is of interest. Do not get distressed if vendors do not return the form or if their feedback is not stellar. During the busy wedding season, there simply may not be time. Further, some vendors do not fully appreciate the services that consultants provide. Do not try to force the issue and be appreciative of any feedback you do receive. Sample question number 5 is included as a cross-check to make sure you have not requested feedback from this particular vendor in the past. If you have several associates, you need to be very careful so as not to bombard your vendors

PHOTO 23.4 VENDOR FEEDBACK ALLOWS YOU TO CONTINUOUSLY IMPROVE YOUR SERVICES.

SOURCE: WWW.RODNEYBAILEY.COM

Weddings by Pippa
Post-wedding Vendor Questionnaire

By completing this questionnaire, you are helping the consultants at Weddings by Pippa
to consistently improve their services

Your answers will remain confidential

Vendor's Name:
The Couple:
Wedding Date:
Consultant's Name:

Please rate the quality of the services provided,
where 5 = Strongly Agree and 1 = Strongly Disagree

1. The wedding consultant was …	Strongly Agree	Agree	No Opinion	Disagree	Strongly Disagree
helpful	5	4	3	2	1
organized	5	4	3	2	1
professional	5	4	3	2	1
knowledgeable	5	4	3	2	1
easy to contact when needed	5	4	3	2	1

2. Working with a wedding consultant …	Strongly Agree	Agree	No Opinion	Disagree	Strongly Disagree
saved me time	5	4	3	2	1
saved me money	5	4	3	2	1
made my job less stressful	5	4	3	2	1
made working with the couple easier	5	4	3	2	1

3. What services did the consultant provide that helped you perform your job more effectively?

_____

_____

FIGURE 23.1 SAMPLE POST-WEDDING QUESTIONNAIRE FOR VENDORS

4. What other services would you like to see our consultants provide that would help your company?

_____

_____

5. Was this the first time that you worked with a consultant from Weddings by Pippa?
   [ ] Yes   [ ] No

6. Based on your experience, would you recommend the consultant to your clients?
   [ ] Yes   [ ] No
   If no, please explain: _____

   _____

Comments and suggestions:

_____

_____

_____

THANK YOU FOR YOUR FEEDBACK!

Please return this questionnaire in the postage-paid envelope that has been provided.

FIGURE 23.1 SAMPLE POST-WEDDING QUESTIONNAIRE FOR VENDORS *CONTINUED*

with questionnaires. Compare notes, and, once you have feedback from a particular vendor, have a master list that can be readily accessed. As you get to know your vendors well, the need for structured feedback will decrease.

THE WEDDING SUMMARY

The hardest part about evaluation is giving it meaning. When you plan your first wedding, it will seem incomprehensible that you could ever forget even a single, minute detail; however, over time, your weddings start to run together and you will not remember the specifics unless you make a point of always completing a wedding summary or after-action report.

If you have been organized all along, compiling the final wedding summary should be a fairly efficient process. Each client should have a separate file folder. In your file, order them alphabetically by last name. Further, create a cross-reference spreadsheet on your computer that includes the clients' names as well as the date of the wedding. The wedding summary should include the following six main parts: 1) an executive summary; 2) the write-up of the wedding, if announced in a local newspaper, as this generally also includes a picture of the couple; 3) the entire production schedule (see Chapter 8), including the vendor list; 4) budget notes (see Chapter 7); 5) the returned client questionnaire and any completed questionnaires from new vendors; and 6) self-evaluation.

The executive summary should be a 1–3-page overview of the wedding, including the most important and unique aspects of the wedding. If carefully written, the executive summary should immediately spark your memory and bring you back to the wedding, even if it took place ten years ago. Consider including the following aspects when writing the executive summary:

- Clients' names, both before and after the wedding
- Ceremony and reception venues
- Theme
- Final budget
- Vendors who provided service excellence
- Vendors who presented difficulties, and how the challenges were managed
- Elements and ideas that were particularly unique
- Moments that did not go well, how they were addressed and how similar problems can be avoided in the future
- Feedback from the clients that will assist with continuous improvement
- As applicable, feedback from vendors that will assist with continuous improvement.

Complete the bulk of the wedding summary as soon as possible after a wedding. While it may take several weeks to receive final feedback from a client or vendor, do not wait until this information arrives to complete the summary. First of all, the feedback may never come if a client or vendor is not inclined to return the questionnaire. Second, as days and weeks pass, you will start to forget the specifics of one wedding as you move on to the next.

The final part of the summary should be your self-evaluation. After each wedding you complete, whether you provided day-of service, full service or something in between, take the time post-event to evaluate your performance. This does not have to be formal or fancy. The point is to capture in writing what you did well during the wedding and areas where you need improvement. For example, if you have just finished planning a military wedding, one of your critiques might be "Did not learn enough about the military to differentiate the ranks. So, when the groom asked me to go find Captain Gregg, I could not tell a captain from a lieutenant."

Break your assessment down into pre-event, ceremony, reception, post-event and miscellaneous categories so that you can capture the important duties associated with each phase of the wedding day. Other comments you might find yourself noting could be things like, "Find a more comfortable pair of dress shoes," "Learn a bit of the language that your clients are speaking," "Never use Cheap Bus rentals again" and "New catering manager was fabulous!" Reviewing your self-evaluation data periodically will help you refine your business practices, reveal the areas that need improvement and reinforce all the things that you are doing right.

As a final follow-up, consider sending each of your couples a first anniversary card or holiday greeting. A simple, thoughtful gesture will keep your business on the couple's radar screen. During a casual conversation with an engaged friend, a former client may mention your act of kindness, and this just might lead to a new client!

REFERENCES

Abrahams, B., Bellucci, E. and Zeleznikow, J. (2012) 'Incorporating fairness into development of an integrated multi-agent online dispute resolution environment', *Group Decision and Negotiation*, 21: 3–28.

Association of Bridal Consultants (2013) 'President's welcome', Online. Available HTTP: <http://www.bridalassn.com/Welcome.aspx> (accessed 4 March 2013).

Hanafizadeh, P., Ravasan, A.Z., Nabavi, A. and Mehrabioun, M. (2012) 'A literature review on the business impacts of social network sites', *International Journal of Virtual Communities and Social Networking (IJVCSN)*, 4: 46–60.

Maemura, Y. and Horita, M. (2012) 'Humour in negotiations: a pragmatic analysis of humour in simulated negotiations', *Group Decision and Negotiation*, 21: 821–838.

Medina, K. (19 June 2012) 'TheKnot.com, WeddingChannel.com debut second destination weddings study', Online. Available HTTP: <http://www.travelpulse.com/theknotcom-weddingchannelcom-debut-second-destination-weddings-study.html> (accessed 1 January 2013).

Mims, C. (2012) 'How to negotiate for anything', *Quartz*, Online. Available HTTP: <http://qz.com/#39074/how-to-negotiate-for-anything/> (accessed 2 March 2013).

National Vital Statistics Systems (2012) 'National marriage and divorce rate trends', Centers for Disease Control and Prevention, Online. Available HTTP: <http://www.cdc.gov/nchs/nvss/marriage_divorce_tables.htm> (accessed 1 March 2013).

Sebenius, J.K. (2013) 'Level two negotiations: helping the other side meet its "behind-the-table" challenges', *Negotiation Journal*, 29: 7–21.

Tullberg, J. (2012) 'Integrity: clarifying and upgrading an important concept for business ethics', *Business and Society Review*, 117: 89–121.

Tzafrir, S.S., Sanchez, R.J. and Tirosh-Unger, K. (2012) 'Social motives and trust: implications for joint gains in negotiations', *Group Decision and Negotiation*, 21: 839–862.

XO Group (2011) 'The knot unveils 2010 real weddings survey results', Online. Available HTTP: <http://www.xogroupinc.com/press-releases-home/2011-press-releases/2011-03-02-2011-real-weddings-survey-results.aspx> (accessed 7 March 2013).

Zack, D. (2010) *Networking for People who Hate Networking*, San Francisco, CA: Berrett-Koehler Publishers, Inc.

REVIEW

1. Why is it important to establish vendor relationships?

2. Why is it important to have good working relationships with other wedding consultants?

3. Define networking and name a minimum of two networking organizations for wedding consultants.

4. Name and explain three of the five rules for successful negotiating.

5. Why do you think it is difficult to pinpoint the exact number of wedding consulting businesses?

6. What are the benefits and drawbacks of competition?

7. Discuss the multiple obligations of a wedding consultant.

8. Why should you always collect your final payment at least two weeks prior to the wedding?

9. List three things that you can do to help maintain the highest ethical standards as a wedding consultant.

10. What are the six parts of a wedding summary?

TERMINOLOGY

- BATNA
- Community capacity
- Competition
- *Esprit de corps*
- Ethics
- Integrative bargaining
- Kickbacks
- Negotiating
- Networking
- Referral
- Social capital
- Wedding summary

Photo 24.1 A wedding consultant should take steps to reduce stress.

Source: www.RodneyBailey.com

24

STRESS MANAGEMENT AND CAREER ENRICHMENT

While not as nerve-wracking as putting your life at risk to protect your country, wedding planning is not a profession for the faint of heart. In fact, in a study conducted by CareerCast, Event Coordinator ranked sixth in a list of the most stressful careers, behind only Enlisted Military Soldier, Firefighter, Airline Pilot, Military General and Police Officer (Brienza 2012). Just a few of the standard measures that are used to measure job stress include travel, deadlines, competitiveness, concerns for growth potential, requirements of meeting the public and physical demands (Nelson 2013), all of which apply to the wedding consultant.

Consulting is a high-pressure job with demanding clients and little margin for error. In order to succeed, a top-notch wedding planner must be part diplomat, part counselor, part cheerleader, part negotiator and part sponge. Sponge? That's right. As a consultant, you have to be part sponge because you are hired in large part to absorb the wedding stress and pressure from the couple. It is the planner's job to stress over the details so the couple can enjoy their wedding day. If the cake has not arrived, the officiant has caught a cold or the maid of honor is missing in action, it is the wedding planner who worries while the bride and groom are blissfully unaware of these potential disasters. The first purpose of this chapter is to present stress management tips that will help keep you calm and energized. Like the popular saying goes, "Keep Calm and Carry On!" The second part of the chapter will highlight career enrichment techniques to keep you feeling relevant and in touch with today's brides and grooms.

STRESS MANAGEMENT TIPS

Because wedding consultants often find themselves in pressure-packed situations, they must learn to be effective stress managers. Imagine the stress level that would occur if, during an upscale wedding reception, two tables of guests complain that the band is too loud and demand to be moved immediately. An easily flustered consultant might fly off the handle and tell the guests to sit down and deal with it. This flippant response will only anger the guests and encourage them to take matters into their own hands. The last thing you want is to have chaos among wedding guests. A composed planner will move into action to resolve the problem with the least amount of disruption possible to both the guests and the couple. Issues arise at weddings, and, if you remain calm and can think on your feet, you will be able to handle anything that might be thrown your way. Even the smallest details can be stressful, as demonstrated in *Consultant in Action*, Case 24.1.

While it is the job of the planner to deflect wedding tension from the bride and groom, who will take on the job of helping to manage the consultant's daily pressures? While having your own business is empowering, entrepreneurship can undermine personal satisfaction and social connections if not carefully nurtured (Datta and Gailey 2012; Eddleston and Powell 2012). As an independent wedding planner, it is up to you to recognize the stressful nature of the job and to take the appropriate steps to reduce the stress level in your life.

One of the best methods for reducing anxiety is to know the details of each wedding inside and out by spelling them out on a production schedule (see Chapter 8). The more familiar you are with the details, the less nervous you will be. For example, have you confirmed with all the vendors? Do you have copies of the contracts? Have you finished the seating assignments? Have you thought about event security? Do you have a Plan B in case of inclement weather? Have you checked in with the couple to see if there are any last-minute changes? If you plan your work and work your plan by organizing and confirming each element in advance of the wedding, you will lower your stress level and feel confident that everything is under control. A structured approach allows you to focus on execution rather than becoming overwhelmed due to an issue that was neglected.

CONSULTANT IN ACTION, CASE 24.1

ANT ATTACK!

As the bride, Claire, was in the final stages of preparing for the ceremony at her parents' home, the photographer borrowed her bouquet to take some shots of it in the beautifully landscaped backyard. When the limo arrives to pick up Claire, you dash outside to inform the photographer and retrieve the bouquet for Claire. As you pick up the bouquet, you notice that the photographer inadvertently placed it near an ant hill, and dozens of black ants are crawling all over the elegant white bouquet.

WHAT DO YOU DO?

CASE ADAPTED FROM MARYAM SAEEDI
MARYAM FLOWERS
WEBSITE: *MARYAMFLOWERSBRIDAL.COM*

This is not to say that unexpected emergencies will never crop up. However, knowing that you have all the essentials covered will give you the flexibility to pass responsibility on to an assistant if you need to troubleshoot.

Another great way to reduce stress is to recommend vendors you trust based on successful past experiences. These go-to vendors should have a stellar reputation for superior service, professionalism and punctuality. Each vendor recommendation is a reflection of you and your business. You will be calm when you are absolutely certain that a recommended vendor is an excellent fit for the couple and will come through on their wedding day. Will the florist drive through a snowstorm to deliver flowers to the wedding? Will your caterer find authentic sake cups for your Japanese clients? Will your tent company search high and low to find Pantone Emerald 17-5641, the exact shade that you require for your tent liner? After you have planned many weddings, you will have a list of go-to vendors who are dependable and trustworthy. Surrounding yourself with a team of dedicated, reliable and knowledgeable professionals will greatly reduce your stress and make your job more enjoyable.

Even with months of dedicated planning and the profession's top vendors working by your side, there is no escaping day-of wedding stress. Regardless of how long you have been in business or how many weddings you have planned, most wedding consultants admit to feeling some degree of stress on the day of each client's wedding. This is only natural. You just have to know

PHOTO 24.2 KNOWING THE DETAILS INSIDE AND OUT WILL ALLEVIATE STRESS.

SOURCE: WWW.RODNEYBAILEY.COM

in your heart that you have done everything possible to prepare for the wedding and that it will run smoothly. Simultaneously, make a point of learning and applying stress management skills. Three wedding planners at various stages of their consulting careers share their thoughts on ways to reduce stress while planning and managing a wedding, as summarized in *Vendor Spotlight*, Case 24.2.

Stressful situations come in all shapes and sizes, and how you handle them will determine how much of a production they become. For example, assume you are checking on the preparations for a 6:30 p.m. reception. You enter the ballroom of a downtown hotel only to find a DJ's equipment set up where the couple's dinner buffet table is intended to be. By thinking on your feet and catching the mistake early, you can remedy the situation quickly and use your sense of humor. Instead of making a negative statement such as, "Move this equipment now or I'll scream!" you can joke with the DJ that he is supposed to enhance the meal, not *be* the meal.

By working in a few stress management techniques each day, you will greatly reduce your desire to snap at clients and chew out vendors. Remember, brides and grooms will take their cue from you. If you are stressed, they will be stressed. Conversely, if you exude a sense of quiet calm, the couple will pick up on this vibe, take it as a cue that all is well, and they will relax and enjoy their wedding day.

VENDOR SPOTLIGHT, CASE 24.2

"KEEP CALM AND CARRY ON!"

Wedding planners give advice on stress management

1. "When I first got started, I booked every bride that wanted to work with me, BIG mistake. Before you take on a client, get to know as much as possible about them. At the initial consultation, the clients are interviewing you. Be sure to interview them as well. You want to make sure you are a good fit for them and able to provide the level of service that they require. I now make it a point to get to know our potential clients before committing to their most important day. As the planner, you are the captain of the ship. You will spend a lot of time working with and for the bride. As long as you communicate with the client and understand their vision, goals, etc., stress can be greatly eliminated or managed." Geomyra Lewis, Website: *geomyralewis.com.*

2. "Working out is a huge stress reliever for me, even if it's only going out for a quick run to get my mind off something that is causing lots of stress or frustration in my job." Anne Kelley, Website: *atrendywedding.com.*

3. "All I can say about stress management is that you have to be so organized and confirm all vendors two weeks before the wedding and really get all the details down. I take deep breaths and realize when I feel stressed that it will all work out." Wendy Joblon, Website: *wendyjoblon.com.*

4. "Setting boundaries is a must. Brides will abuse your time and will call, e-mail and text throughout the day (and night). Be clear with your clients regarding your office hours and availability. As planners, we want to be readily available, but even Tiffany, Nordstrom and Bloomingdale's have set hours. Setting boundaries will allow you to focus on the client's needs at designated times, which will help you manage their wedding even better." Geomyra Lewis, Website: *geomyralewis.com.*

5. "I think having a good support system of friends/colleagues that understand your job is super important to help alleviate stress. Creating relationships with others in the event industry who understand the pressure you often face, the kind of work that you do and the passion behind it (even when you are feeling overwhelmed or stressed by it) helps you know that you are not the only one facing these kinds of problems." Anne Kelley, Website: *atrendywedding.com.*

6. "Make yourself a priority. Schedule a day where you are out of the office and not focusing on work. We all need time to refresh and regroup. Get out and do something fun and that makes your heart sing." Geomyra Lewis, Website: *geomyralewis.com.*

If you ask ten wedding consultants what they do to relax, you will get ten different answers. There is no one-size-fits-all relaxation strategy. One consultant, a dedicated exerciser, gets up at 5:30 a.m. and goes for a power walk regardless of the weather. Another takes time out of her busy schedule each week to have a pedicure. She gets a kick out of having her toes painted in funky colors and styles and uses this as a conversation starter during her events. A third loves to refinish furniture purchased from thrift stores and garage sales. Whatever hobby or interest you enjoy, continue to pursue it. You will be a much happier person and a better wedding planner.

Career enrichment

In addition to monitoring your stress level, it is also important for wedding planners to seek out opportunities to enrich their careers. Instead of waiting until you are bored with managing the same type of wedding over and over, sign up for a floral design class to learn about different styles of floral arranging. Maybe branch out by learning calligraphy. Perhaps take a seminar taught by a leading caterer in your area. By attending workshops and classes, consultants from all over the world learn about new ideas and products and can begin incorporating them into the weddings they plan.

The last thing that you want to hear a guest say at one of your weddings is: "This must be an event planned by (*insert your company name*), they always use sparklers." You do not want your clients to think that their wedding will look exactly like the last five weddings that you planned. Clients want something new and different. It is the ability to present the unexpected that keeps a consultant in high demand.

Travel is another excellent way to enrich your wedding planning career. With the explosion of multicultural brides and grooms, it is particularly helpful to your clients if you have traveled and experienced different cultures. If you have toured Asia extensively, you will be better informed to plan the wedding of a Japanese bride and a Vietnamese groom. While you can always read about Asian customs and solicit advice, nothing takes the place of travel for opening your eyes and giving you cultural insight. With the uptick in destination weddings, you will stand out from the competition if you can say, "Which island in Hawaii do you want to get married on? I've been to Maui, Oahu, Lanai and the Big Island. I especially love the Lodge at Koele on Lanai for a destination wedding."

After you have built a successful career as an independent wedding consultant, you might find yourself growing tired of the business. You may wistfully dream of the day when you will not have to leave your house at the crack of dawn on a lovely Saturday morning in June to head off to work. The important thing to remember about a career as an independent wedding planner is that you can accept as many or as few jobs as your time and budget will allow. If you want to take the month of August off, then do it. Your schedule is entirely up to you.

Planning flawless weddings week after week can become tiring. Seasoned planners frequently move their businesses in a different direction, with perhaps less stress and more manageable hours.

This is called a *career shift*. As you break into wedding planning, you might think that there is nothing you would rather do than plan weddings for the rest of your life. The good news is that you can, or, alternatively, you can take your business down a different path.

Many consultants keep a hand in planning while exploring other opportunities, usually still related to the business of weddings. Perhaps the easiest way to transition is to go to work for someone else. Oftentimes, wedding planners will shift to working for a country club, a hotel or even another wedding planner or group of planners. The hours are usually better when there are more planners to share in the work. Another way to shift your career is to focus on one aspect of the planning process. Do you love all things pertaining to wedding flowers? Then maybe opening up a florist shop is the next logical step for you. Wendy Joblon, a sought-after planner in the Southeastern Massachusetts area who is featured in *Vendor Spotlight*, Case 24.1, recently opened Folia, her own invitation and stationery boutique, much to the delight of her clients. Joyce Scardina Becker, a popular Northern California wedding planner, teaches a wedding consultant certificate program at California State University Hayward. Celebrity wedding consultants are no different, with planners such as Colin Cowie, Mindy Weiss and David Tutera involved in television, retail, training and book projects.

PHOTO 24.3 WITH AN OPEN MIND, YOU CAN TAKE YOUR BUSINESS DOWN A NEW PATH.

SOURCE: WWW.RODNEYBAILEY.COM

Whether you plan two weddings a year or have a team that plans two hundred, a career as an independent wedding consultant is rewarding, challenging and meaningful. You will have the privilege of working with clients as they prepare for one of the most important events of their lives. Because of your hard work, their wedding day memories will be of their commitment and carefree enjoyment rather than the nuts and bolts of planning.

Whether you long for a career in wedding planning or you simply long for your own perfect wedding day, it is our sincere hope that *Wedding Planning and Management: consultancy for diverse clients* has inspired you to think about the cultural significance of weddings and the intricacies of the wedding profession. These are exciting times for wedding consultants, with trends such as the growth of destination weddings, the changing family, an increase of multicultural traditions and the legalization of same-sex marriage broadening the scope and visibility of this career. Now, perhaps more than ever, the wedding profession needs entrepreneurs who understand and respect today's diverse clients and can translate their needs into extraordinary weddings.

REFERENCES

Brienza, V. (2012) 'The 10 most stressful jobs of 2012', Online. Available HTTP: <http://www.careercast.com/jobs-rated/10-most-stressful-jobs-2012> (accessed 15 February 2013).

Datta, P.B. and Gailey, R. (2012) 'Empowering women through social entrepreneurship: case study of a women's cooperative in India', *Entrepreneurship Theory and Practice*, 36: 567–587.

Eddleston, K.A. and Powell G.N. (2012) 'Nurturing entrepreneurs' work–family balance: a gendered perspective', *Entrepreneurship Theory and Practice*, 36: 513–541.

Joblon, W. (2012) 'Stress management tips for wedding consultants'. E-mail (9 August 2012).

Kelley, A. (2013) 'Stress management tips for wedding consultants'. E-mail (12 August 2012).

Lewis, G. (2013) 'Stress management tips for wedding consultants'. E-mail (13 August 2012).

Nelson, S. (2013) 'Study lists 10 most and least stressful jobs of 2013', Online. Available HTTP: <http://wqad.com/2013/01/07/study-lists-10-most-and-least-stressful-jobs-of-2013/> (accessed 27 February 2013).

Photo 24.4 Consultants translate a couple's vision into happily ever
after.

Source: www.RodneyBailey.com

REVIEW

1. Why is the job of wedding consultant so stressful?

2. Name two things you can do as the planner to help each wedding go smoothly.

3. What are four simple things you can do to reduce your personal stress?

4. What are three steps you can take to enrich your career?

5. If you ever grow tired of wedding planning, what are some new directions you can explore for your business that relate to the profession?

TERMINOLOGY

- Career enrichment

- Career shift

- Day-of stress

- Stress management techniques

INDEX